CANADA AND IMPERIALISM

Canada and Imperialism

1896-1899

NORMAN
PENLINGTON

University of Toronto Press

Copyright, Canada, 1965, by
University of Toronto Press
Printed in Canada

TO MY WIFE

without whose assistance and forbearance
this work would never have been completed

This work received the

DISTINGUISHED MANUSCRIPT AWARD OF 1959

from the University College of

Michigan State University

Preface

WHEN THIS STUDY was first undertaken it was concerned to explain participation in a war fought 7,000 miles away for a cause of no direct concern to Canada. Manipulations from Downing Street and British propaganda then seemed the answer, and the research was concentrated on Anglo-Canadian relations and in particular the role in events of the Colonial Secretary, the Governor General, and the General Officer Commanding. Gradually as the study was periodically pursued the salient fact emerged that English Canada had been eager, if not anxious, to fight and had forced the Canadian Government to send troops.

At the outset Canadian-American relations had been excluded from the study, but it soon became clear that matters in question between the two countries in the years immediately preceding 1899 could not be ignored in an attempt to explain Canadian participation in South Africa. The Venezuela affair, the Dingley Tariff Bill, United States enforcement of the "open door" in the Yukon, and the disputed Alaskan boundary all seemed to contribute to a current of resentment against the United States which was in marked contrast to the pro-British enthusiasm with which English Canada launched into the South African affair.

The ensuing analysis has tended to push Anglo-Canadian relations into the background. Indeed it is the major thesis of this study that the importance of Anglo-Canadian relations, which in that day sailed under the euphemistic phrase of "Imperial unity," was largely that of a counterpoise of Canadian-American relations; that imperial unity contained much anti-Americanism; and that the latter constituted the significant underlying reason for Canada's participation in the South African War.

ACKNOWLEDGEMENTS

I owe a particular debt of gratitude to the Public Archives of Canada, that admirable institution, which permits research at all hours of the day and night. I am appreciative of the photostats, microfilm loans, and replies to many inquiries in the course of this study. I wish to thank Dr. W. Kaye Lamb, Dominion Archivist, M. Pierre Brunet, Assistant Dominion Archivist, Mr. Norman Fee, former Assistant Archivist, and Mlle Juliette Bourque, Librarian, for many courtesies; and especially Mr. W. G. Ormsby and Mr. Wilfred Smith, Heads of the Manuscript Division, and Miss Nora Story, former Head, and their assistants for aid and suggestions.

I am grateful to the following for the use of manuscript collections: The Public Archives of Ontario; Professor J. J. Talman, Librarian of the University of Western Ontario, for the Mills Papers; Mr. H. Pearson Gundy, Librarian of Douglas Library, Queen's University, for the Walter Dymond Gregory Papers; Mr. Justice S. H. S. Hughes, Toronto, for the papers of Sir Sam Hughes, and Professor E. G. R. Ardagh, Toronto, for the Gowan Papers.

I am much indebted to Professor C. P. Stacey, former Director, Historical Section, Canadian General Staff, for his own personal notes, information on many points of Canadian military history, and the use of the MS history, "The Organization and Development of the Canadian Militia," by Lieutenant-Colonel J. F. Cummins, and to Colonel G. M. C. Sprung, present Director, and the staff of the Historical Section; to Professor D. Schurman, Royal Military College, for the use of his doctoral dissertation, "Imperial Defence 1868–1887" (Cambridge, 1955); to Professor Lovell C. Clark, University of New Brunswick, for the use of notes; to Miss Ida E. Leeson, former Mitchell Librarian, Sydney, Australia, for information on the history of New South Wales in 1894; to Mr. W. Stewart Wallace, former Librarian of the University of Toronto, and Dr. Fred Landon, former Vice-President of the University of Western Ontario, for valuable suggestions; and to my former professors at the University of Toronto for ideas and sources.

I wish to thank Michigan State University Library for extensive purchases of books on subjects related to this work and for assistance of the staff, especially Mrs. H. Alubowicz, Reference Librarian. I also acknowledge the assistance of the staff of the University of Toronto Library, Toronto Reference Library, and the Parliamentary Library, Ottawa; Mr. C. H. Stewart, National Defence Library, Ottawa; Mr. H. Pearson Gundy, Queen's University Library, Kingston; the staff of the Royal Military College Library, Kingston; Mr. W. A. Stewart, Royal Canadian Military Institute, Toronto; and the staff of the University of Michigan Library and the Library of the State of Michigan, Lansing.

I am indebted too to Miss M. Jean Houston, Associate Editor of the University of Toronto Press, for the careful editing brought to the preparation of this work for publication. The assistance of the Publications Fund of the University of Toronto Press is gratefully acknowledged.

In addition to my thanks to University College, Michigan State University, for making possible a publication prize, I am grateful to the All-University Committee on Research for grants-in-aid and to the Committee on Western History for a Rockefeller grant. I appreciate the stimulus of my colleagues whose discussion on all sorts of subjects have assisted me more than they knew and the constant confrontation of meaning and interpretation which the teaching of the Humanities course requires. For all mere opinions I alone am responsible.

Contents

Abbreviations

UNLESS OTHERWISE STATED in the footnotes all manuscript sources will be found in the Public Archives of Canada.

A.B.T., III, IV	*Proceedings of the Alaskan Boundary Tribunal*, III, IV (Washington, 1903–4), Senate Doc. no. 162, 58th Congress, 2nd Session (ser. nos. 4601, 4602)
A.G. (followed by number)	Correspondence of Adjutant General
Can. Sess. Pap. (by number and year)	*Canada, Sessional Papers*
Campbell	Charles S. Campbell, Jr., *Anglo-American Understanding, 1898–1903* (Baltimore, 1957)
Cd. 1789	*Report of the Royal Commission on the War in South Africa* (London, 1903), Cd. 1789
Cd. 1790, Cd. 1791	*Minutes of Evidence* to the foregoing report (London, 1903), I, Cd. 1790; II, Cd. 1791
Conf. 7161	Part X, *Further Correspondence Respecting the Boundary between the British Possessions in North America and the Territory of Alaska, February to September, 1898,* Confidential 7161, printed for the use of the Foreign Office, July 1899 (this document is bound in *Alaska Boundary, Foreign Office Confidential Series, Correspondence 1886–1901,* copy in the University of Toronto Library)
Conf. 7340	Part XI, *Further Correspondence Respecting the Boundary between the British Possessions in North America and the Territory of Alaska, February to December 1899,* Confidential 7340, printed for the use of the Foreign Office, June 1900
Conf. 7135	Part I, *Correspondence Respecting the Proceedings of the Joint Commission for the Settlement of Questions Pending between the United States and Canada, March 1898*

	to *March 1899*, Confidential 7135, printed for the use of the Foreign Office, June 1899 (copy in Pope Papers, vol. 23)
Conf. 7309	Part II, *Further Correspondence Respecting the Proceedings of the Joint Commission for the Settlement of Questions Pending between the United States and Canada, April 1899 to December 1899*, Confidential 7309, printed for the use of the Foreign Office, April 1900 (copy in Pope Papers, vol. 24)
Debates	*Debates of the House of Commons*, Canada
D.M. (followed by number)	Correspondence of the Deputy Minister of Militia and Defence
Foreign Relations, 1895–99	*Papers Relating to the Foreign Relations of the United States*, vols. 1895–99 (Washington, 1896–1901)
G 1, G 3, G 9, G 10, G 17C, G 20, G 21 (Governor General's numbered file)	Correspondence of the Governor General's Office
G.O.	General Orders (orders issued for the Canadian militia)
P.C. (followed by a number)	Orders in council, minutes of council, dispatches, and dormants of the Canadian Privy Council (Cabinet)
Report No. I, "Secret"; *Report No. II*, "Secret"	*Report No. I* and *Report No. II of the Committee on Canadian Defence 1898*, "Secret" (London, 1899) (copy in P.C. Despatches 295L, May 29, 1900)
Tansill	Charles Callan Tansill, *Canadian-American Relations, 1875–1911* (New Haven, 1943)

CANADA AND IMPERIALISM

1. The Effects of American Pressure, 1867-1895

THE FEDERATION of the British North American colonies in 1867 was essentially the product of American pressure, British support, and Canadian need. Without American pressure, British North Americans would not have willed to solve their problems together; without British support they would have despaired of doing so.

As a colony the new Dominion of Canada derived its strength not from its own power but from membership in the British Empire and from institutions and loyalties largely inherited from Britain. But many Canadians scarcely treasured that heritage, which was the condition of the country's existence and one of the characteristics that most distinguished it from the United States. On the contrary, they hoped that Canada would imitate and surpass its neighbour. The pessimism engendered by unfavourable comparisons between the two countries, a long-continued depression, and the failure to realize personal ambition drove hundreds of thousands of Canadians to emigrate to the nearby pastures of prosperity. No state can suffer such a haemorrhage of energy without putting its life in doubt. Under such circumstances the continued existence of Canada was a considerable achievement. Those Canadians who feared for the future of their country cherished British institutions and traditions and sought British political and economic aid. At the end of the nineteenth century Britain, feeling itself under pressure, responded to Canadian overtures for help, but did so in the expectation of Canadian military aid.

I

In the first four years of the Dominion's history, American imperial ambitions, responsible for the new nation's birth, hovered over its existence. In 1866 the United States denounced the Reciprocity Treaty of 1854 and raised a tariff against the natural products of the British North American colonies; in the same year and again in 1870 Fenians raided and threatened them from bases in the United States; and in

1869 the Chairman of the Senate Committee on Foreign Affairs implied that Canada might be accepted as settlement for British conduct in the Civil War. These threats were climaxed by the Riel Rebellion of 1869–1870, which menaced Canada with the loss of the West, for the United States coveted the territory. A "visible symbol"[1] of British support was essential for its maintenance, and a combined British-Canadian expedition under Colonel Garnet (later Field-Marshal Viscount) Wolseley assured British sovereignty in that area.

But British support of Canada was reluctant and half-hearted. A widespread Little-England attitude would have welcomed Canada's separation from the British Empire, an attitude fortified in the sixties and seventies by Britain's need to confront strategic perils closer to home: the rise of Prussia and the unilateral denunciation by Russia of the Black Sea clauses of the Treaty of Paris 1856.[2] Hence Britain completed the withdrawal of British troops from central Canada and made a general settlement with the United States in the Treaty of Washington in 1871.

By that treaty, the United States in effect grudgingly recognized Canada's existence, and Great Britain, by the inclusion of the Canadian Premier among the British plenipotentiaries, its status. Macdonald regarded the treaty as a sacrifice of Canadian interests, but Canada's existence really depended on that sacrifice. In contrast to the British Government's appeasing attitude towards the United States, the Colonial Office, in Britain's day-to-day relations with Canada, sympathized with Canadian ambitions and smoothed Canada's transition from an awkward colonialism to an adolescent autonomy.[3] The growth of autonomy, which largely resulted from Canada's exercise of external powers, became a considerable source of national inspiration—often a kind of compensation for frustrated material ambition.

In 1867 Canada had embarked on its career in high hope of securing a continental domain. Within four years a truncated North Atlantic state expanded to the Pacific. Canada purchased the Hudson's Bay Company lands in the West, and shortly afterwards induced the colony of British Columbia to enter the Dominion on the promise of a railroad to the East. The acquisition of this vast territory and Canada's consolidation

[1]Cited in J. R. M. Butler, "Imperial Questions in British Politics, 1868–1880," chap. ɪɪ in E. A. Benians, Sir James Butler, and C. E. Carrington, eds., *The Cambridge History of the British Empire* (Cambridge, 1959), III, p. 21.

[2]C. P. Stacey, "Britain's Withdrawal from North America, 1864–1871," *Can. Hist. Rev.*, XXXVI (Sept. 1955), pp. 185–98.

[3]David M. L. Farr, *The Colonial Office and Canada, 1867–1887* (Toronto, 1955).

into a national unit thus demanded the construction of expensive railways to the West and to the eastern Canadian provinces, which by 1873
included Prince Edward Island.

In prosperity, this work of nation-building went confidently forward;
in depression, Canada's economic vulnerability undermined the national
faith. Macdonald's solution to depression and to the growth of the
Dominion was western settlement, eastern manufacturing, and a Pacific
railway. Only Britain could readily supply the necessary settlers and
finances. But why should Britain, the home of laissez-faire, help Canada
in this national work? To overcome British objections, the Canadian
Government continually proclaimed the essential identity of Canadian
and British interests, that is, that the building of Canada was an imperial
work. Thus Canada justified the appointment of a Canadian High Commissioner to London in 1879 by maintaining that the Dominion was
looking after British imperial interests in North America and that the
country's material growth reinforced the British Empire. The construction of the Canadian Pacific Railway was especially justified as a British
military route to the East.

By the mid-eighties Canada found an increasingly favourable response
to its requests. One result was the summoning of the first Colonial Conference of 1887, which, however, accomplished little, for Britain was as
reluctant to enter into closer trade relations with the colonies as they
were to enter into closer defence relations with Britain. Nevertheless
the more sympathetic atmosphere for colonial interests raised the price
of Canadian Pacific Railway bonds in London and enabled the Canadian
Government to obtain a mail subsidy for the company's steamship line
across the Pacific linking Canada to Japan and Hong Kong. It is indicative of the strength of Canada's contentions that George (later Viscount) Goschen, the Chancellor of the Exchequer, complained to Sir
Charles Tupper, the Canadian High Commissioner, that he had made
all the concessions in the negotiations for the subsidy.[4] In 1887 also,
the Salisbury Government supported Canada diplomatically in the
fishery negotiations at Washington; in 1890 it gave what amounted to
naval protection of Canadian sealing rights in the Bering Sea against
the United States; and in the same year it disallowed a reciprocity treaty
between Newfoundland and the United States inimical to Canadian
interests.

Canada needed this support, for the late eighties and early nineties
saw the deepening of the depression. National policies could not counter

[4]July 25, 1888; E. M. Saunders, ed., *The Life and Letters of the Rt. Hon. Sir
Charles Tupper, Bart., K.C.M.G.* (London, 1916), II, p. 123.

the emigration of Canadians to the more prosperous United States; the census of 1890 estimated that one and a half million Canadians dwelt in the United States—nearly one-third of Canada's existing population. Many of the provinces were in effect trying to revert to an earlier colonial status in which they had enjoyed greater powers and relatively greater resources. In 1887 five provincial premiers in a conference at Quebec City demanded larger subsidies and the abolition of the power of disallowance of provincial legislation. The general pessimism was made worse by the split between English and French Canadians and between Protestants and Roman Catholics over the execution of Louis Riel and over the Jesuits' Estates Act of 1889. In addition to these already perilous divisions, Canada was confronted with a graver one—the commercial union movement and its vague alternative, unrestricted reciprocity. Reciprocity recalled the economically nostalgic era of the 1850's and 1860's. In those days, perhaps, reciprocity had helped save Canada from the United States; in the 1880's it was regarded by many Canadians as a threat because of its coincidence with a strong, or at least noisy, agitation to annex Canada, and the movement provoked appeals of loyalty to Britain based on the feared political consequences of closer commercial relations.

II

While the new Dominion pictured itself as an important state needing assistance, Britain was responding more favourably to colonial economic importunities because of the relative weakening of its own position diplomatically, economically, and defensively. In the 1860's and 1870's, for example, Britain suffered diplomatic checks; the shock of the quick German victory over France in 1870 speeded up British army reform, and the naval scares of the 1880's and 1890's led to increases in the navy; foreign tariff walls were being raised against British goods; and the United States and Germany having settled their own internal problems by the 1870's began to compete successfully with British goods in the world market.

Britain's response to this relative decline of strength was the maintenance, consolidation, and expansion of imperial power. Exponents of imperialism looking to power as the solution of Britain's problems opposed the Gladstonian solution of freedom. They preferred, for example, the maintenance of the Transvaal, not in its state of qualified freedom, but as a dependency, and they opposed Home Rule for Ireland. But to Britain's rivals, the most spectacular aspect of British imperialism was not the consolidation, but the expansion of the Empire in Africa,

Asia, and the South Seas. In the 1880's, political, strategic, and economic interests largely explain particular annexations. In the 1890's, democratic imperialism played a large part, for that decade saw the British masses, made politically conscious by the vote, mass education, and an interest in their own economic and social welfare, exercising an increasing political influence. The power of democratic imperialism was further intensified by jingoism—mass xenophobia—in the late nineties by, for example, the demonstration of naval might at the Diamond Jubilee, the victory of Kitchener at Omdurman over the dervishes, and the humiliation of France at Fashoda.

British imperialism came to a focus in Joseph Chamberlain, the mouthpiece of British democracy, who assumed office as Colonial Secretary in the Salisbury Government in 1895. His choice of that office, which surprised his countrymen but delighted colonials, was implicit in his philosophy and career. His Unitarianism, Benthamism, and radicalism all enjoined help for the less fortunate; and his bitter and vehement manner of advocacy constituted a considerable political asset. His skill in organization found scope in business, municipal reform in Birmingham, and the foundation of the Liberal Caucus. The latter organization, which played a large part in the Liberal victory of 1880, helped him force his way into the second Gladstone administration and gave him the support to introduce advanced social legislation. As President of the Board of Trade he became apprehensive about strategic, commercial, and colonial pressures on Britain. Thus Irish Home Rule appeared to threaten British power. On the other hand, his personal observations on the contributions of British imperialism to Egypt convinced him of the value of imperial expansion. Finally the racial and mystical tinge of his imperial ideas turned him to advocacy of Anglo-Saxondom, consolidation of the British Empire, and closer Anglo-American relations.

The man and the time arrived in 1895. As the leading British democrat and imperialist and an able public orator, parliamentary debater, and committee man, Chamberlain was one of the most influential figures in Britain. Apprehensive of Britain's position he sought as Colonial Secretary to augment British power, not by laissez-faire drift, but by government action. He offered economic assistance to the colonies, encouraged welfare in neglected colonial areas, and sought to transform "into practical results" the sentiment of imperial unity which the Venezuela affair and the Kaiser's telegram to Kruger had evoked within the colonies.[5] Threats to the British Empire were threats to Canada's

[5] J. L. Garvin, *The Life of Joseph Chamberlain* (London, 1934), III, p. 179.

existence. Canada therefore responded loyally and enthusiastically to Chamberlain's and the Salisbury Government's interest in and support of Canada. But Canada could not expect favours without having its own professions of loyalty and support for the Empire taken at their face value.

III

Britain's reaction to its relative decline does not fully explain public support for imperial programmes. This was largely the work of publicists and pressure groups. Among the chief examples of each were John R. Seeley's *The Expansion of England* (1883) and the Imperial Federation League. The league was founded in 1884 to consolidate the self-governing colonies with Britain into a federation. For a few years it exercised considerable influence in Britain: for example, in the summoning of the Colonial Conference of 1887. But proposals for a political or a defence federation had little appeal to Canadians proud of responsible government and weighed down by the debt of public works. In 1889, Sir Charles Tupper, active in league affairs from the beginning, called for the abandonment of the platform of parliamentary federation and the summoning of another colonial conference to consider imperial preference. This speech, together with Lord Salisbury's challenge in 1891 to produce a practical constitutional scheme, led to the league's virtual collapse in Britain.

By contrast the league in Canada, after an uncertain beginning, suddenly sprang to life in 1887, provoked by the political implications of the commercial union movement which coincided with widespread anti-Canadian propaganda in the United States from 1887 to 1892. Its members described commercial union as "vassalage to the United States" and "political suicide."[6] In speeches, pamphlets, articles, and meetings they strove to combat commercial union by reawakening stirring historical memories and a sense of loyalty to British institutions and imbuing Canadians with the idea of imperial unity. More concretely the league advocated imperial preference with Britain. But this was impossible so long as the Belgian and German trade treaties of 1862 and 1865 respectively stood in the way. These treaties forbade a British colony granting a preference to Britain without extending it to Belgium and Germany. As a result of the league's agitation the Canadian House

---

[6]Speech of Archbishop C. O'Brien in 1888 at Halifax, and William Mulock in the House of Commons moving resolution of loyalty, Jan. 29, 1890, cited respectively in Col. George T. Denison, *The Struggle for Imperial Unity: Recollections and Experiences* (London, 1909), pp. 119, 133.

of Commons unanimously passed a resoluton in 1891 requesting Britain to denounce the treaties. The British Government refused to do so; and the British free-trade members of the league, apparently alarmed at this ambition of imperial preference and disappointed at the failure to obtain direct defence contributions from Canada, secretly dissolved the league in 1893. This action dispirited its Canadian members, for without league support in Britain their own agitation was vulnerable. They therefore used their influence to help establish in Britain a successor organization, the British Empire League, with a programme more in harmony with Canadian interests.[7]

Because an increase in inter-imperial trade was a national necessity against the pull of the north-south routes, the Canadian Government had long sought to reinforce the east-west route, which formed the essential link in a national economy, by extending it to the Australasian colonies. In 1889 Canada took the lead by authorizing an annual subsidy of £25,000 for a steamship line to Australasia. New South Wales contributed an additional £10,000 when the line was established in 1893. To enlist Australasian trade support further and to promote the laying of a trans-Pacific cable to Australasia, Mackenzie (later Sir Mackenzie) Bowell, the Canadian Minister of Trade and Commerce, visited Australia late in 1893. Out of this visit came a proposal for a trade conference, for all the colonies testified to the same deficiencies of men, money, and markets, which Britain alone could easily supply. All the Australasian states except Western Australia sent delegates to the Colonial Conference held in 1894 at Ottawa, as did Cape Colony. The British Government, though professing an interest, was not pleased at this exhibition of colonial initiative. It could not object, having set the precedent of a conference primarily for defence, but it sent not an accredited delegate but only an observer; and Lord Aberdeen, the Governor General, in opening the conference cautioned the delegates to confine themselves to the agenda—the Pacific cable and commercial subjects.[8]

Interest centred on the Pacific cable and inter-imperial trade. The conference unanimously passed a resolution approving the cable on grounds of trade and the need to provide an alternative and safer, "all-red" route between Great Britain and Australia via Canada. It was suggested that Britain might contribute to such a cable because of its essentially imperial nature. The conference resolved that an immediate

[7]*Ibid.*, chaps. XVIII and XIX.

[8]John T. Saywell, ed., *The Canadian Journal of Lady Aberdeen 1893–1898* (Toronto, Champlain Society, 1960), p. 100, n. 1.

ocean survey test the feasibility of the proposed route, and charged the Admiralty with the undertaking, the costs to be shared equally by the Australasian colonies, Canada, and Great Britain. Canada was authorized to take all necessary steps to prevent the Pacific cable project from officially stagnating, as it had done since the Colonial Conference of 1887. On inter-imperial trade, Canada received more qualified support. In the early stages the conference passed a general resolution requesting Imperial legislation to permit inter-imperial reciprocity and preference and to terminate any treaties standing in the way. Later Canada moved resolutions asking, in effect, for an imperial *Zollverein*, or failing that, for inter-imperial preferences; these passed only after much discussion and opposition.

Of the minor resolutions, the conference approved the Canada–New South Wales steamship route and Canada's intention to provide trans-Atlantic and trans-Pacific first class mail and passenger service. In view of Imperial subsidies on British mails on or over foreign countries— £104,231 on Liverpool–New York mail, for example—the conference asked for British aid on the proposed Atlantic and Pacific lines.

Thus Canada received colonial sanction to advocate in Britain policies primarily of benefit to the colonies, an outcome which appears to have been Canada's main expectation from the conference.[9] And although the Colonial Office rejected the conference demand to terminate the commercial treaties,[10] the demonstration of the Dominion's status *vis-à-vis* the other colonies represented a relative success for Canada.

IV

The status of Canada was for a long time to remain a major preoccupation of many Canadians. Canadian leadership at the conference of 1894 demonstrated that Canada was more than the colony that Britain and the United States considered it to be; rather it was on the way to

[9]Cf. George E. (afterwards Sir George E.) Foster, the Canadian Minister of Finance: "We are a colonial conference; we are brought here to look after colonial interests first; we are not an Imperial conference; . . . we are here to press what we think would be for the colonial advantage, to press it upon the only one that could give it to us; that is Great Britain"; though a few moments later he qualified this by urging Britain to make concessions so far as it was in Britain's ability, interest, and generosity, and "for the sake of broader considerations." Proceedings of the Colonial Conference 1894, *Can. Sess. Pap.* (no. 5B), 1894, pp. 244–45; cf. *ibid.*, p. 208. The report is also in *Parliamentary Papers*, 1895, LVI (C. 7553).

[10]Marquis of Ripon to Gov. Gen. of Canada, June 28, 1895, in Arthur Berriedale Keith, ed., *Selected Speeches and Documents on British Colonial Policy 1763–1917* (London, 1918), II, pp. 156–64.

becoming a colonial nation, a junior partner in the British Empire. But when Canadian leaders took advantage of Canada's colonial status to obtain benefits for Canada they showed that they were not ready to accept full national status. For example, in 1892 George E. Foster opposed the acquisition of treaty-making power by Canada on the ground that under existing conditions Canada enjoyed the advantage of British prestige and diplomatic facilities. So long as the British Empire was "bound together . . . there must be . . . one seat of sovereign and absolute power, and that seat must be . . . in the Mother-land."[11] Again, by emphasizing the diplomatic unity of the British Empire at the conference of 1894, Foster tried to demonstrate that inter-imperial trade was a purely domestic matter.[12] It seems certain that his purpose was to avoid an excuse for American retaliation if preferences were introduced. Similarly, as we shall see, the Laurier Government accepted a colonial status if such appeared to be of advantage to itself or to Canada. This did not mean that either Conservative or Liberal governments envisaged permanent colonial status for the country. Rather they were aware that Canada's mere existence next to an expansionist United States depended on Britain's support. As Sir Oliver Mowat, long-time Liberal Premier of Ontario, stated in an open letter in 1891 to Alexander Mackenzie, former Premier of Canada: the British connection was the greatest single source of unity to Canada.[13]

Imperial unity, however described, was a matter of national survival for Canadians; neither Britain nor the other self-governing colonies had such a corresponding need. Canadian supporters of imperial unity were ardent Canadian nationalists, who had no intention of bartering away hard-won rights of responsible government. To them "Imperial federation," which was used indistinguishably from "Imperial unity," meant the orientation of Canadian policy towards Britain for the attainment of specific political and economic purposes. The desired end was the strengthening of Canada, not to aid Britain, but the better to defend the Dominion against the United States.

[11]April 7, 1892, cited in J. Castell Hopkins, ed., *Canada: An Encyclopaedia of the Country* (Toronto, 1900), VI, p. 172.
[12]*Can. Sess. Pap.* (no. 5B), 1894, p. 167.
[13]Dec. 12, 1891, in C. R. W. Biggar, *Sir Oliver Mowat* (Toronto, 1905), II, pp. 597–98.

2. Canada's Defences

THE MILITARY POLICY of a nation and the structure of its defensive institutions reflect a people's historical experience and ideological outlook. With Britain's military and diplomatic help, the British North American colonies had grown to maturity in spite of invasions and military threats from the United States. Britain had long borne their chief military and financial burdens in wartime and practically all the cost of preparations in peacetime. The colonies' interest in material development, their pacifist disposition, and faith in their ability to improvise quickly almost blinded them to Britain's military protection. With the gradual withdrawal of British troops, the Province of Canada reluctantly assumed responsibilities of defence in the 1850's. The perils of 1860 raised the Canadian defence system to a relatively high state of efficiency, but as military threats subsided in the 1870's and 1880's the defence system sank into a demoralized state and Canadians forgot their strategic dependence on Britain. They wanted, not strategic, but economic aid to resist American pressure. At the same time, Britain, feeling apprehensive in a changing world, sought relief from increasing defence burdens; Canada should be able to defend itself, and, if necessary, to render assistance in an imperial war.

I

Except in times of crisis, Canadians, like the British, have been indifferent to military questions. This indifference comes primarily from concern for economic interests and a desire to ignore military questions as thwarting those interests. After 1815 the absence of military danger to Britain, the demands of peacetime economy, and middle-class pacifism and anti-colonialism undermined the British army in numbers and efficiency. Consequently, when military threats confronted Britain in the period 1840–71, British Regulars were withdrawn from all the self-governing colonies—even from the most exposed colony, the Province of Canada. Canadians opposed withdrawal, because of the prospect of themselves bearing defence responsibilities; the old Canadian system of a *levée en masse*, the only peacetime defence responsibility, had been virtually "annihilated" as early as Lord Durham's day. By the mid-fifties a militia force of 5,000 Canadian volunteers had been established to replace the Regulars temporarily withdrawn because of the Crimean War. An effective Canadian force, however, came into existence as a result of the Civil War and its aftermath. The force comprised an increased number of volunteers, and was strengthened by the careful enrolment of the old sedentary militia and by the training of a large number of officers at schools of military instruction.

Meanwhile Little Englandism and pessimism at Britain's exposed military position in North America increased the number of hints that Canada sever her connection with the British Empire. British pessimism and American threats alarmed Canadians to the extent of taking further steps in defence in order to conciliate the British and retain their alliance. The Brown-Macdonald coalition ministry, established to create Confederation, voted a $1,000,000 military supply bill in 1864 as an earnest of Canadian determination. The ministry also came to a far-reaching agreement with British leaders in 1865: Canada agreed to erect fortifications "at and west of Montreal" and to continue the high level of spending on the militia. Britain, on its part, agreed to complete the fortification of Quebec and provide its armaments, to guarantee a loan for the construction by Canada of fortifications, and "in the event of war [to] undertake the defence of every portion of Canada with all the resources of the Empire."[1]

When the Dominion came into being the defence system established by the Province of Canada was applied to the whole country. The new Canadian force consisted of about 43,000 men for which Parliament annually appropriated about $1,500,000. This amount was only about one-quarter of what Britain still spent on Canadian defence for the purpose of maintaining 16,000 Regulars, arming Canadian volunteers with new Snider breech-loading rifles, and undertaking other defence measures. But the prevailing British belief in the need for colonial self-reliance, the demand for economy, and the strategic needs of Britain made the final recall of the British Regulars inevitable. After engaging in the Riel Expedition in 1870, they were withdrawn from central Canada in the following year.

The departure of British troops, which coincided with the abatement

<hr>

[1]Hon. N. W. Rowell, "Canada and the Empire, 1884–1921," in J. Holland Rose, A. P. Newton, and E. A. Benians, eds., *The Cambridge History of the British Empire* (Cambridge, 1930), VI, p. 717.

of American threats, removed from Canada a well-trained core, excellent military instructors, and perhaps a standard of military excellence.[2] The withdrawal prompted the Canadian Government to create an artillery unit, which became the nucleus of the Permanent Force formed in 1883, and in 1876 it founded an officer-training institution, the Royal Military College. But there was a drop in efficiency, accentuated by the depression, for the militia appropriation in the late seventies fell to $550,451, less than half that of a decade earlier.

The one test the force met was the North-West Rebellion of 1885. This rebellion was essentially an attempt of the Métis (halfbreeds) and the Indians, both primitive hunting folk, to stay the onrush of Western civilization. The nearly completed Canadian Pacific Railway quickly brought to the scene a Canadian expedition under the command of a British general. The campaign's success, however, produced not efficiency but complacency; as the troops were being welcomed on their return to eastern Canada the Canadian voyageurs in the Sudan were being praised for their energy and the Canadian Pacific Railway was being completed as a strategic route to the East.

The militia was adversely affected too by the decline of the Conservative party from 1892 to 1896, when five ministers of militia succeeded Sir Adolphe Caron who had previously held office from 1880 to 1892.[3] Patronage seems also to have been more blatant in the early nineties. Finally, in the late eighties and the early nineties a kind of pacifism, probably prompted largely by a desire to enter the United States market, helped to lower militia morale still further.

II

By the early nineties all branches of the Canadian defence system were suffering decay. The University Rifles founded in 1860 at the University of Toronto disappeared in 1892; high school cadet corps languished. A public agitation arose to abolish the Royal Military College, which was regarded as a "place where a few young fellows, who have more money than brains, play soldiers for four years at the expense of the Canadian tax-payer."[4] This agitation had the support of the rural militia who thought that their own appropriation was starved to main-

2Their departure may have benefited the militia in some ways, for it was no longer awed by virtually unreachable standards.
3Mackenzie Bowell, Jan.–Dec. 1892; J. C. Patterson, Dec. 1892–March 1895; A. R. Dickey, March 1895–Jan. 15, 1896; Alphonse Desjardins, Jan. 15, 1896–April 30, 1896; David Tisdale, May 1, 1896–July 12, 1896.
4F. W. Falls, "The Royal Military College," *Can. Mag.*, IV (Jan. 1895), p. 262; the University Rifles formed "K" Company of the Queen's Own Rifles.

tain the college. Complaints were also made that it was run down and that its graduates would not enrol in the Mounted Police, the Permanent Force, or the volunteer militia. In 1895 a board of visitors, provided for under the Royal Military College Act, in effect recommended the replacement of the Commandant, Major-General D. R. Cameron—a son-in-law of Sir Charles Tupper—by a younger and more up-to-date man. The secret Committee on Canadian Defence in 1898 confirmed the low state of the institution. Of the total of 159 qualified cadets from the founding of the college in the 1870's to 1898 only 20 had entered the volunteer militia and only 10 the Permanent Force, even though granted, or perhaps because granted, the rank of captain. The committee was puzzled at their reluctance to enter the active militia or the Permanent Force.[5]

Undoubtedly, however, the low reputation of the Permanent Force was the reason for the refusal of Royal Military College cadets to join it. The Permanent Force was unpopular too with the rural militia, who complained that their needs were being neglected to maintain it.[6] Yet the force served essential functions of defence. It provided military instruction of three types: special short courses of a few days for officers, short courses of three months, and long courses of six or nine months. The instruction offered, however, was elementary, and an officer could even rise to the rank of lieutenant-colonel in the force "without further examination."[7] Not only did officers lack up-to-date training and the possibility of a professional career; they also lacked pensions. With such leadership, the rank and file could hardly be expected to show much enthusiasm or efficiency. Occasionally it suffered even humiliation and fraud.[8] In 1890 desertions, other military "crimes," and discharge by purchase amounted to nearly half the force. The Permanent Force was not unique in this respect, for as late as 1902 the British Army also suffered "enormous" wastage.[9]

[5]"Royal Military College, Kingston," chap. XI of *Report No. II*, "Secret," pp. 63–64. See also *Debates*, April 18, 1896, p. 6715.
[6]William Mulock (Liberal, North York, Ont.), *Debates*, June 6, 1895, p. 2199; see also p. 2200 and *passim*.
[7]*Report No. II*, "Secret," p. 18; three months of long-course instruction took place at the Royal Military College and the rest at the local schools.
[8]For example, having to saw wood in public (*Can. Sess. Pap.* (no. 11), 1890, p. 171); paying extra for a "serviceable article" to the same contractor who had previously supplied an "inferior" one (G.O. 49, 1892); and (a type of fraud perpetrated by officers) illegally signing men who had no intention of enlisting, or fighting for their country, on battalions' rolls to send them to military schools. Such men, having obtained a "fair smattering of military matters . . . go across the line, and are only too gladly taken by regiments in the United States" (E. G. Prior (Conservative, Victoria, B.C.), *Debates*, June 14, 1899, p. 5066).
[9]Question to, and answer of, Gen. Sir Evelyn Wood, Cd. 1790, q. 4205.

But the first reforms were at hand. The able General Officer Commanding of the early nineties, Ivor J. C. Herbert (later Lord Treowen; 1851–1933), improved the Permanent Force by building up its morale as a unit, giving it purpose, and improving its training. In 1893 the infantry received the name of the Royal Canadian Regiment; and its purpose was declared to be to provide a standard "for the guidance of the Militia" and a "supply of trained Instructors. . . ."[10] Probably General Herbert's reforms explain the force's change in emphasis from a fighting to an instructional unit.[11] Furthermore he sent officers and men to England at government expense for military courses.[12] In 1894 he concentrated the four infantry companies, together with two companies of volunteer militia, at Lévis for six weeks' intensive training. The commendation of the "general excellence" of the Permanent Force by a later General Officer Commanding, General Hutton, was a tribute to General Herbert's energy.

In contrast to the improvements in the Permanent Force, the volunteer militia, the backbone of Canada's defence system, probably reached its nadir in this period. In January 1895 the *Canadian Military Gazette* wrote, "The militia has never been in a worse condition than it is to-day. Ignorance, incapacity and systematic neglect are the prominent characteristics of the present militia system."[13] The authorized establishments totalling 35,000 were not fulfilled: the actual strength was about 18,871, the average number of militiamen trained between 1877 and 1896. Nor was the militia an organized force, but a congeries of disconnected units. In the late nineties, it was divided into 89 battalions—26 urban and 63 rural, in strength ranging from 168 to 668 or from 4 to 10 companies. This lack of uniformity in size largely reflected contrasting urban and rural conditions, a fact which produced considerable urban-rural jealousy and made brigade formation difficult. Methods of training also differed: the city corps trained weekly at their own headquarters;[14] rural, in summer camps. The Committee on Canadian Defence, reporting in 1898 when conditions had improved a little, pointed out other conditions of difference; city corps had a large number of recruits, full

---

[10]*Can. Sess. Pap.* (no. 19), 1894, p. 35.

[11]Minto Papers, letter book no. 2, pp. 146–47, Lord Minto to St. John Brodrick, "Confidential," Dec. 4, 1900.

[12]In 1893 at the age of 56, Senator C. A. Pelletier was sent for an artillery course.

[13]Cited in *Debates*, Jan. 22, 1896, p. 448. Hutton's commendation is in *Can. Sess. Pap.* (no. 19), 1899, p. 28.

[14]According to Maj.-Gen. R. H. O'Grady-Haly, G.O.C. in Canada, 1900–2, pay for 48 to 50 drills was equal to 12 days' pay at summer training camps; Cd. 1790, q. 8487.

attendance on parade, use of drill halls, and command by well-to-do officers. A rural corps, which was an "aggregate of independent companies" scattered over the countryside, suffered a great turnover in personnel, estimated at 33 per cent a year. The population was on the move, economic conditions were attractive, and men turned out as a "favour" rather than as a "duty."[15]

The consequence of the turnover of men was a large proportion of officers and non-commissioned officers to privates. The high age limits, the ability to defy those limits by political pressure, and the regulation that promotion was by seniority frustrated young energetic officers. Besides lacking adequate opportunities of promotion, and being plagued by politics, many an officer was also deficient in training. These and other militia difficulties often produced a poorly trained battalion. Drill was elementary and discipline seems to have been generally wanting.[16] Musketry practice was perfunctory owing to inadequate ranges and the worn-out single-shot Snider rifle dating from the 1860's. The rifling of this "gas-pipe," as it was familiarly known, was shot out, and the sights were worn. Artillery pieces were occasionally of even more ancient vintage, "Noah's Ark guns," as Lord Wolseley would have described them. One member of the Dominion Artillery Association in 1898 plaintively expressed the hope for "something better than smooth bores of . . . the year 1793." In 1898 also Captain W. G. White, R.N., of the Committee on Canadian Defence wrote: "At present there are no modern guns of any sort in the country."[17] Artillery training of some batteries was even more perfunctory than musketry practice: either no practice or as few as three rounds per year. Supplies for the volunteer militia, such as clothes, boots, blankets, knapsacks, and the like were either lacking or unsuitable. On the other hand cavalry uniforms were "needlessly good," and

[15]The Committee on Canadian Defence heard evidence that "fault-finding may result in a man returning his uniform . . . and going off in a huff," and that enforcing penalties against men who absented themselves would make the "service . . . unpopular, and recruits would not come in." *Report No. II*, "Secret," pp. 28–29, 67. But cf. Sam Hughes's defence of the rural corps in letter to D.O.C. Mil. Dist. No. 3 and 4, Nov. 29, 1898, Hutton Papers, pp. 1102–18.

[16]The author of a Canadian manual on militia practice actually had to justify discipline at weekly drills in the preface; Lieut.-Col. W. D. Otter, comp. *The Guide* (Toronto, 1880).

[17]*Globe*, Feb. 11, 1898. Wolseley's statement describing English militia guns is in Cd. 1790, q. 9009. For an account of musketry conditions, see Capt. Charles F. Winter, "The Re-Armament of the Militia," *Can. Mag.*, V (June 1895), pp. 107–14; for artillery in the eighties and nineties, see Lieut.-Col. C. E. Long, "Forty Years in the Canadian Artillery," *Can. Def. Quart.*, VI (Jan. 1929), pp. 228–35; the committee member's comment is in C.O. 42/859, p. 435, Report of Capt. W. G. White, R.N., to Admiralty, Nov. 29, 1898.

suffered not from wear, but from being soiled; recruits, if they had any self-respect, would object to wearing the soiled clothes worn at the preceding training period.[18]

The most serious deficiency of the Canadian defence system was the absence of headquarters plans for the defence and of administrative departments to feed, arm, and transport the men in the field. These departments were essential for the defence of Canada, which in the past had relied on the spirit of improvisation and military enthusiasm generated by the immediate prospect of war. Even though departments had long been recommended the only important step in that direction was the appointment in 1893 of a quartermaster-general, an officer who relieved the adjutant-general of many onerous duties.

The Canadian militia could thus be described as a "mere holiday force"[19] at summer training camps. But lack of comforts, inadequate food, and ill-chosen sites must have tempered a miltiaman's enjoyment. The large number of raw recruits or of those enrolled fraudulently because too young, too old, or of poor physique[20] simply magnified the inefficiency of the militia. Officially, the period of the summer camps was 12 days, but Sundays and time lost travelling to and from camp reduced the time to 9 days, provided the camp was close by and the weather was fine.[21] To improve the quality of the training, General Herbert proposed cutting the establishments to 10,000. This was a militarily sound but politically impossible proposal.[22]

If the Canadian militia in 1895 was in so demoralized a state, why did it not collapse utterly? We have examined the main influence, the national but unenthusiastic support of the Dominion Government.[23] The

[18]*Report No. II*, "Secret," p. 24.

[19]Lieut.-Col. [W.E.] O'Brien, M.P., "Our Militia," *Can. Mag.*, II (Dec. 1893), p. 103. Cf. T. S. Sproule (Conservative, East Grey, Ont.) describing the motives of the rural militiamen attending summer camp: ". . . the loyalty question does not appeal so much to their hearts as having a holiday, and having some drill, and being out with the boys" (*Debates*, July 10, 1899, p. 7066).

[20]For conditions in Quebec, see *Debates*, June 20, 1899, p. 5419, and July 11, 1899, p. 7149.

[21]An extreme example of time lost travelling to and from camp was 6 days, leaving only 6 days' training, probably including a Sunday (*ibid.*, June 20, 1899, pp. 5416–17).

[22]For a general description of conditions in the late eighties and early nineties, see "Odd File," *Militia Organization* (Toronto, 1892) and O'Brien, "Our Militia," pp. 101–6.

[23]Cf. Hutton Papers, p. 1739, where Hutton complains that only twice "at this period" did a minister or the Government show "any active interest in the efforts which were being made on behalf of the Military Forces of Canada" ("My Command in Canada: A Narrative").

second influence was the local patriotic spirit found among individual citizens, among members of the militia, and in municipalities. The "cause of Defence" was "left in the hands of a few military enthusiasts," as Hutton wrote. Many officers and men gave freely of their time and money. Possibly motivated by frustrating national weakness, in 1891 the Scots of Toronto appealed to ancestral loyalties and created a very successful battalion of Scottish Canadians, the 48th Highlanders.[24] Leading citizens often donated prizes for military efficiency; municipal governments granted sites and money for the construction of drill sheds, for which there was federal legal provision. County councils, notably Wellington and Huron in Ontario, increased the efficiency of the local corps by granting 25 cents per day extra per man in addition to the regular government grant earned during summer training camp.[25] A corollary to local support and local enthusiasm was the intense local jealousy. Promotions virtually remained within the local battalion, and a regulation even specified the desirability of this procedure. In 1895, the Adjutant-General might proudly write of the benefits of organization, training, equipment "under Dominion control," but it was largely a formal control for the spirit of the militia was intensely local.[26]

III

A third source of encouragement to the Canadian militia was Britain. British policy was to foster efficient self-defence by each part of the British Empire in order to contribute to the defence of the whole. Up to 1871 Britain played the decisive role in Canadian defence; thereafter, an important but diminishing role.

Broadly speaking this role may be described first as an over-all "imperial" authority, which, together with Britain's diplomatic control, might involve Canada in war because of membership in the British Empire. Secondly, it included British naval protection of Canada's extensive merchant marine on the seven seas and the command of the sea approaches to Canada. Perhaps this latter protection accounts for

[24]Alex Fraser, *The 48th Highlanders of Toronto* (Toronto, 1900). For the inauguration of another Scottish-Canadian battalion—the 78th Pictou Highlanders —see E. M. Macdonald, *Recollections Political and Personal* (Toronto, n.d., 1938?), pp. 521–22; the quoted words are from Minto Papers, vol. 19, p. 10, General Sir Edward Hutton, "A Narrative of Lord Minto's Career."

[25]*Debates*, July 10, 1899, pp. 7066, 7070; see also *Can. Sess. Pap.* (no. 11), 1890, app. 2, p. 12.

[26]Col. Walker Powell, *Can. Sess. Pap.* (no. 19), 1896, p. 16; see also Militia Act, 1886, s. 78.

the popular indifference to, as contrasted to the official interest in, the annexation of Newfoundland at the strategic gateway to Canada.[27] Thirdly, it included the maintenance and the manning of the Halifax naval base. In the 1890's this was still an Imperial base like Gibraltar and Malta, a strategic outpost in Britain's relations with the United States. Although war with the United States was not considered probable, it could not be ruled out; and the base was regarded as necessary in case Russian or French raiders prowled the seas.[28]

Fourthly, Britain shared with Canada the defence of Esquimalt at the south end of Vancouver Island. This base came into prominence when the Canadian Government advertised the newly completed Canadian Pacific Railway as a strategic route to the Orient. The Government tried to induce the British Government to consider Esquimalt like Halifax as an Imperial base, and thus assume the full costs of improvement, maintenance, and manning. But Canada had set the precedent of co-operating with both the British and the British Columbian governments in the construction of a dry dock at Esquimalt. Nor could it overcome the Admiralty's view that the base was relatively unimportant among the British bases of the world. In 1893 the Canadian Government agreed to make an annual payment of $76,500 and maintain a militia unit of garrison artillery, in return for War Office maintenance of defence works and armaments and provision of a regular body of troops.[29]

Although the foregoing defence controls might be described as external, they had internal significance, and this fact constituted a fifth British influence. The governor general and the general officer commanding the Imperial troops at Halifax and Esquimalt might be in receipt of secret information of importance to Canada's defences which the Canadian authorities might never see. Moreover the Militia Act of 1886 seemed to

---

[27]From 1896 to 1899 the question of Anticosti in the estuary of the St. Lawrence figured in several parliamentary questions, a debate, a sessional paper of 1899, the Laurier Papers, and in C.O. 42.

[28]For an analysis of Halifax as a naval base, see C. P. Stacey, "Halifax as an International Strategic Factor, 1749–1949," *Report of the Canadian Historical Association*, 1949, pp. 46–56.

[29]The Canadian Government did not seem to think much of the Esquimalt base practically for it had not provided the base with direct telegraph connection with the outside world, the nearest being Victoria four miles away; memorandum for Mr. Laurier reporting the complaint of Admiral H. B. Palliser of the North Pacific Station from John Sinclair, Governor General's Secretary, "Confidential," December 31, 1896, inc. in Sinclair to Laurier (no date), Laurier Papers, pp. 8413–14. See also D. M. Schurman, "Esquimalt: Defence Problem, 1865–1887," *Brit. Col. Hist. Quart.*, XIX (Jan.–April 1955), pp. 57–69. For the strategic significance of the Canadian Pacific Railway, see Gerald S. Graham, *Empire of the North Atlantic* (2nd ed., Toronto, 1958), pp. 282, 287.

allow both legislative and executive power within Canada to British authorities. Section 9 concerned War Office powers of expropriation in Canada for military purposes; section 37 provided for the appointment of a colonel of the British army to command the Canadian militia; section 79(3) gave permissive authority to the general officer commanding the Imperial troops to command all Canadian forces in wartime; section 82 enacted that Queen's Regulations and Orders, the Army Act of Great Britain, and other British military law affecting Canada, with certain Canadian modifications, had authority in Canada.[30] The enforcement of section 82, however, was fitful, for unofficially Canadian authorities seem to have assumed that any British military laws or regulations they disliked need not apply in Canada. But whatever their actual significance, all these provisions, and especially the presence of a British general officer commanding, symbolized British power in North America, warned the United States that Canada was British, and reassured Canadians of British support.

However, British military controls were generally ineffective in improving Canadian defence. Canadians were usually content with existing defence arrangements and, possessing the control of the purse, could oppose British pressure for improvement. For example, Britain failed to induce Canadians to embark on naval defence. As far back as 1865 the Colonial Naval Defence Act permitted colonies to build navies, but the act had remained inoperative in Canada. Early Canadian naval efforts—the gunboats in the Fenian raids, the marine militia at Halifax in 1868, and the Admiralty training ship of the early 1880's—had all been practically forgotten. Governor General Lansdowne's suggestion to the cabinet in 1886 concerning "the formation of a small Canadian Navy always available for the defence of our coasts but forming a part of the Royal Navy" seems to have been met by the reply that Canada's fishery patrol vessels formed the nucleus of a naval force and that Canada's seafaring population might be embodied.[31] British hints in dispatches and at the colonial conferences of 1887 and 1897 for naval defence were also lost on Canada. On the other hand a general officer commanding such as Herbert was able to effect minor improvements.

Britain was equally insistent but even less successful in trying to commit Canada to render military aid to the rest of the British Empire.

[30]For a more extended discussion of section 37 of the Militia Act, see below, p. 132, and its relation with section 82, pp. 174–79.

[31]G 21, no. 165, vol. IV, p. 7, draft memorandum to Privy Council, Nov. 20, 1886 and *ibid.*, vol. V, report of Min. of Mil., Jan. 23, 1888, inc. in P.C. Despatches, 1141G, Jan. 24, 1888. Canada appears to have taken over the fishery service about 1885.

Amid the growing international tension of the 1890's General Herbert formally embarked on policies of "association" and "assimilation." In North America Canadian forces had often been in association with British forces: in the American Revolution, the War of 1812, and the expedition to the Red River; and they annually underwent combined exercises for the defence of the naval bases of Halifax and Esquimalt. These not very efficient exercises were regarded by British authorities as important not only in the defence of Canada but also in the creation of one big imperial army. Herbert proposed an interchange of units of the two forces in which a Canadian unit would serve out of Canada in association with British forces and a British unit would replace it in Canada. Presumably in pursuit of this policy, the Thompson Government in 1894 offered Canadian troops for Imperial garrison duty in Hong Kong, but for a variety of reasons the offer was not accepted.[32] Under General (later Sir) William J. Gascoigne (1844–1926), Herbert's successor, the policy was twice modestly carried out in Canada.[33]

The policy of association was regarded as a way to assimilation, for Britain hoped to make Canadian militiamen, who in a sense were already assimilated as "Soldiers of the Queen," into British Tommies. Britain formally encouraged assimilation by offering to the best qualified Royal Military College cadets a variable number of commissions in the British and Indian armies and two cadetships in the navy. The result by January 1899 was that 82 Canadian officers—possibly not all graduates of the Royal Military College—were serving in the Imperial army, a fact of which many Canadians were proud.[34] Canadians were also encouraged to participate in British military tournaments; an artillery team representing Canada won the championship in 1893 and the 48th Highlanders won the bayonet championship in 1897. A Canadian contingent took part in the Diamond Jubilee, and a laudatory account of its performance, written by Chamberlain, was published as a General Order of the Militia, August 1897.

However beneficial the long-run effects of association and assimilation might be, Britain never ceased pressing for the goal of precise military commitment. Its purpose was not so much practical as political, for Britain desired not manpower but participating colonial units symboliz-

[32]Guy R. MacLean, "The Canadian Offer of Troops for Hong Kong, 1894," *Can. Hist. Rev.*, XXXVIII (Dec. 1957), pp. 275–83; see also Lieut.-Col. J. F. Cummins, MS hist., "The Organization and Development of the Canadian Militia" (Historical Section, Can. Gen. Staff, 1932–36), pp. 177–78, and D.M. 13610.
[33]See below, p. 187.
[34]Laurier Papers, pp. 30141–42, George Wyndham, Under-Sec. of War, to Laurier, "Private," Jan. 31, 1899; see also J. Hampden Burnham, *Canadians in the Imperial Naval and Military Service Abroad* (Toronto, 1891).

ing a united and powerful Empire. It seemed odd that Britain, after its political cold-shouldering of Canada in the 1860's and 1870's and the peremptory withdrawal of troops, should expect a military commitment. But if the Canadians viewed their country as a nation in alliance with Britain, then the British promise of 1865 implied reciprocal aid in return.

As early as the Russian war scares of 1877–78 and 1885 Britain began requesting Canada to make a commitment for imperial defence. The Canadian Government put off answering these requests as long as possible.[35] In 1887 Lord Lansdowne, the Governor General, sent "emphatic communications" to his ministers on Canada's share in the defence of the Empire, but found they had decided views on two points: (1) the Canadian people would not tolerate large defence expenditures and (2) they had already contributed much to imperial defence by raising the militia and by constructing the Intercolonial and the Canadian Pacific railways.[36] Perhaps as a result of this kind of pressure, the Government officially answered British dispatches, apparently going back nearly ten years, by refusing to accede to British requests. It reviewed the history of Canadian defence policy since 1865, and emphasized that the Dominion had spent more than $27,000,000 on defence and that "her system of Militia and Defence has been developed as thoroughly and as rapidly as the financial condition of the Dominion would admit." Moreover Canada had the legal power to use for defence the "able-bodied population" which would amount to about 1,000,000 men of the "Reserved Militia." Of these, more than 300,000 had received training in the active militia.[37] This reliance on the obsolete provision of *levée en masse* which was to provide a phantom force of 1,000,000 men demonstrates Canada's difficulties in withstanding British pressure. In 1892 the Government, in answer to dispatches going back to 1885, used much the same argument, but added that since the United States was "the only contiguous power to Canada," Canada hoped that the existing friendly relations between Britain and the United States would continue and that

[35]G 21, no. 165, vol. V, Synopsis of the salient points of the correspondence on the Defences [prepared by Lord Melgund] by Colin Campbell, Ret. Asst. Paymaster, R.N., Jan. 15, 1887, inc. in Campbell to Capt. Henry Streatfeild (Sec. and Mil. Sec. to Gov. Gen., Lord Lansdowne), "Private and Unofficial," March 27, 1888. As an example of the kind of disregarded pressure, the Colonial Office in 1885 sent dispatches to the colonies "upon the legislation (Colonial) required to make Colonial Land Forces, when employed beyond their own limits, unconditionally subject to British military law" (*ibid.*, p. 12).

[36]*Ibid.*, vol. IV, note in Lansdowne's handwriting, March 12, 1887.

[37]It added that "others have become more or less familiarized with the details of organization during recent years"; *ibid.*, vol. V, report inc. in P.C. Despatches 1141G, Jan. 24, 1888, inc. in Lansdowne to Sir Henry Holland, Jan. 30, 1888.

Canada could easily beat off coastal attacks.[38] Even after the threat to Canada in the Venezuela incident, Sir Charles Tupper, who had been indefatigable in presenting this type of argument as Canadian High Commissioner in Britain, asserted again in the Canadian House of Commons:

I hold—and I presume hon. gentlemen in this House will not differ with me—that expenditure for the defence of Canada is expenditure for the defence of the Empire, in its highest sense. And, whether it be to maintain a fast line of steamers, to act as Royal naval reserve cruisers in time of war, or whether it be to maintain a small permanent force, or a large militia or voluntary force in this country, I say that it is essentially a defence of the Empire, for I hold that Canada is as much a portion of the Empire as Yorkshire is, and I regard, therefore, that whatever expenditure is made by Canadians for the defence of Canada is made as absolutely for the defence of the Empire, as any similar expenditure that is made in the United Kingdom.[39]

Canada would not bind herself by an automatic commitment: it seemed to smack of colonial controls which Canada was just escaping, and might close the door to the autonomous freedom to which she was aspiring.

It was not that Canada would never help in a war in which Britain participated. If Britain were fighting a life-and-death struggle Canada would contribute. But she could scarcely be expected to contribute to all the small Imperial wars and punitive expeditions Britain was engaged in during the nineteenth century. The choice, the time, and the manner of contribution must be left to the free choice of Canada. In the Crimean War the British North American provinces had contributed to the assistance of the widows and orphans of Britain and France, the Province of Canada voting £20,000, New Brunswick £5000, and Nova Scotia £2000.[40] In 1858 popular interest in the Indian Mutiny led to the formation of the 100th Regiment, Canadian in officers and men, but paid for by Britain. Twenty years later in the scare of 1877–78 with Russia, Canadian colonels volunteered their regiments and tentative plans were made to raise a division of 10,000 Canadians.[41] Had Britain accepted these volunteer offers she would have been expected to bear the full costs of equipment, transport, and maintenance. In 1884 Britain employed 400 Canadian voyageurs to ferry Lord Wolseley's unsuccessful expedition up the Nile to rescue General Gordon.[42] In February 1885

---

[38]*Ibid.*, P.C. Despatches, 432H, Jan. 20, 1892.
[39]*Debates*, March 23, 1896, p. 4425.
[40]Sir Charles Lucas, ed., *The Empire at War* (Oxford, 1921), I, pp. 66–68.
[41]C. P. Stacey, *Canada and the British Army 1846–1871* (London, 1936), p. 114, n. 1.
[42]C. P. Stacey, "Canada and the Nile Expedition of 1884–85," *Can. Hist. Rev.*, XXXIII (Dec. 1952), pp. 325–28.

when the failure to rescue General Gordon became known, volunteer offers poured into Ottawa to help reconquer the Sudan. New South Wales, however, went a step further and officially offered a body of men which served for a short time at Suakin on the Red Sea.[43] The British Government, moved by this official offer and by expectations in England,[44] inquired if the Canadian Government would do likewise. The Canadian Government had no objection to the enlistment of Canadians at Britain's expense, but Sir John Macdonald emphatically objected to official aid, which in this instance Sir Charles Tupper favoured. In Macdonald's view, Canada had no national interest in the Sudan or in sacrificing men and money to get "Gladstone & Co. out of the hole— they have plunged themselves into by their own imbecillity [sic]."[45]

In spite of this absence of official Canadian co-operation, the offers of help in the Sudan crisis made by the other colonies engendered in Britain expectations of military commitments. But the Colonial Conference of 1887 signally failed to fulfil such expectations. Nor did Canada's puzzling offer of the Royal Canadian Regiment of Permanent Infantry for service in Hong Kong in 1894, at Britain's expense, imply a reversal of the Canadian attitude. General Herbert explained to the War Office that the Canadian Government did not expect the offer to be accepted and that the purpose of the offer was to " 'boom Canada.' "[46] In view of the great publicity Canada had received less than four months before from the meetings of the Colonial Conference of 1894 in Ottawa, this explanation seems likely. It may also have been intended to demonstrate that though Canada was not prepared to be automatically committed to assist in Imperial skirmishes she was capable of offering help of her own free will.

In any event by 1895 Britain had had little success in reforming the inefficient Canadian militia, and none in committing it to overseas aid. But would Canada react favourably, not to a petty "subaltern's war" nor to one threatening Britain's existence, but to one demonstrating imperial solidarity? This would require a radical change of attitude, a realization of the need of each country for the other.

[43]On Feb. 17, 1885, the Royal Colonial Institute moved a resolution calling upon the British Government to respond to the colonial offers "at their own cost"; *Proceedings of the Royal Colonial Institute*, XVI (1884–85), p. 214.
[44]Stacey, "Canada and the Nile Expedition of 1884–85," p. 336; see also strikingly similar observations of Lord Wolseley to Lady Wolseley, Feb. 22, 1885, in Sir George Arthur, ed., *The Letters of Lord and Lady Wolseley 1870–1911* (London, 1922), p. 171.
[45]Stacey, "Canada and the Nile Expedition," pp. 319–24; for a description of their operations, see C. P. Stacey and E. Pye, "Canadian Voyageurs in the Sudan, 1884–1885," *Can. Army Jour.*, V (Oct.–Dec. 1951).
[46]MacLean, "Canadian Offer of Troops," p. 281.

3. The Venezuela Incident, 1895-1896

THE REACTION of Canadians to the Venezuela incident is a curious phenomenon: at first a defensive attitude, soon giving way to a seeming indifference to any possibility that Canada might become the battleground of an Anglo-American war. This indifference may be explained partly by Canadian understanding of the nature of United States "spread-eagleism" or jingoism, the significance of which they usually discounted. Yet two and a half years later jingoism played a decisive role in engulfing the United States in the Spanish-American War, and the next year it played a similar role in bringing Britain and Canada into the South African War.

"Jingoism" took its name from a music-hall ditty sung during the Anglo-Russian crisis of 1878:

> We don't want to fight;
> But by Jingo, if we do,
> We've got the men, we've got the ships,
> We've got the money too.

The braggart nature of the ditty suggests that the jingo hoped for national victory not by negotiation but by intimidation[1] and that he concealed an underlying fear. But while fear was probably an element in much late nineteenth-century British jingoism, it was not a characteristic in the United States, where a national thrill appears to have been indulged. On the other hand, in 1899 Canada's anger against United States' policy was a primary motivation of the Canadian jingo. Although these illustrations show jingoism as an expression of hostility, it was also an element in the exaggerated loyalty for Queen Victoria in 1897.

Later students of the Imperialist era have tended to ignore the phenomenon of jingoism probably largely because of its unpleasant associations with democracy and their preference for the term "imperialism" to

[1]Cf. J. A. Hobson, *The Psychology of Jingoism* (London, 1901).

symbolize what was repulsive about the era. Contemporaries could not ignore the contribution of jingoism to participation in the Spanish-American and South African wars, nor its ugly intensity in the Fashoda crisis. But national issues such as these, which jingoism seized upon, and power ideologies such as racialism, militarism, navalism, and social Darwinism, through which jingoism could express itself, explain something of its intensity and importance in the era.

I

Writing during the heyday of Senator Joseph R. McCarthy, Professor Richard Hofstadter described the United States of the 1890's as in a "psychic crisis" of frustration and alarm. The depression with its fierce strikes, the disappearance of old competitive opportunities in business, the alleged end of free frontier land, and widespread municipal corruption intensified such tendencies of thought as Populism and the Christian social gospel, on the one hand, and the emphasis on power, on the other. The latter emphasis may be seen in the founding of more patriotic groups in the 1890's than in any other decade, the growth of the navy and navalism, racialism, and above all the rise of jingoism. Among its manifestations were the provocative United States reply to the Italian Government's protest at the lynching of eleven Italians in New Orleans in 1891, the threatened chastisement of Chile over the killing of two American sailors in a Valparaiso riot in the same year, and the Venezuela incident. In no case was an American national interest involved; in each case the United States reacted with aggressive excess, even to the contemplation of war, and even, possibly, with the intention of diverting internal class hatreds against the foreigner.[2]

Traditionally that foreigner was the Englishman, and Anglophobia was an important element in the Venezuela incident. This was a sentiment found chiefly among the American Irish, provoked by English policy in Ireland, and among American supporters of a silver standard against English supporters of the gold standard. Consequently when the United States paraded the spirit of contemporary imperialism it could easily be directed against England. The long-standing boundary dispute between Venezuela and British Guiana provided an obvious incitement.

[2]See Rep. Paschal to Sec. of State Olney, Oct. 23, 1895, in Charles Callan Tansill, *The Foreign Policy of Thomas F. Bayard 1885–1897* (New York, 1940), p. 709, n. 191. For jingoism see Richard Hofstadter, "Manifest Destiny and the Philippines," in Daniel Aaron, ed., *America in Crisis* (New York, 1952), pp. 173–82.

In the course of the dispute the British had offered to mediate all conflicting claims except those in long-settled areas, but the Venezuela Government, its interest intensified by the discovery of gold in some of those areas, demanded that all disputed territory be arbitrated, and endeavoured to involve the United States by invoking the Monroe Doctrine.[3] The United States for its part was also conscious of its own strength and desirous of exercising it, particularly against the one nation that often seemed to ignore Uncle Sam. President Cleveland had seen the power of Anglophobia in the election of 1888, and had perhaps been its electoral victim; and the appointment of the pugnacious Richard Olney as Secretary of State seemed decisive in bringing the Venezuela dispute to a head. In the truculent dispatch of July 20, 1895, only slightly blunted by President Cleveland before transmittal to London, Olney alleged that the unsettled Venezuela boundary menaced the United States. The Monroe Doctrine, the dispatch argued unhistorically, was "unquestionably due" to Britain which had never withdrawn from the doctrine's support. The distance of 3,000 miles separating Europe and America "make any permanent political union between an European and an American state unnatural and inexpedient." In addition, America believed in republicanism, that is, "the idea that every people had an inalienable right of self-government." In effect, the United States charged that Britain, by enlarging her claim against Venezuela, and then refusing to arbitrate it, was violating the Monroe Doctrine. If arbitration was not effected future relations would be greatly embarrassed.[4]

Lord Salisbury, the British Premier and Foreign Minister, having been delayed in part by a difficult international situation, finally sent his answers dated November 26, 1895. He denied that the Monroe Doctrine was relevant, for the original doctrine did not apply to frontier disputes; nor could any nation proclaim international law of its own volition. Furthermore, it was far-fetched to assume that the United States was menaced by the unsettled boundary or that it was " 'unnatural and inexpedient' " to have an American state joined to a European. "The necessary meaning of these words is that the union between Great Britain and Canada" was " 'inexpedient and unnatural.' " Finally the

---

[3]In 1894 a former United States Minister to Venezuela, then in the employ of the Venezuela Government, published a pamphlet to that effect: William L. Scruggs, *British Aggressions in Venezuela, or the Monroe Doctrine on Trial* (Oct. 1894), cited in Tansill, *Bayard,* p. 664.

[4]Olney to Bayard, July 20, 1895, *Foreign Relations,* 1895, I, pp. 545–62.

British Government denied emphatically that the United States could be concerned with every dispute in the Western hemisphere.[5]

The accuracy of Salisbury's answer provoked President Cleveland's special message to Congress of December 17, 1895. In it he reiterated the United States belief that the extension of the boundaries of a European state did constitute an extension of the European form of government and a violation of the Monroe Doctrine. Because of the threat of the unsettled Venezuela boundary and of Britain's repeated refusal to arbitrate, the President proposed to Congress to vote money for a commission to ascertain the boundary, which would be drawn if necessary by force.[6] In an epidemic of enthusiasm, Congress—especially Republican senators—voted the money. Although commanding much popular and newspaper support, however, the President's proposal aroused strong opposition among academic and ministerial circles, in many newspapers, and in Wall Street, where the prospect of war produced a stock market crash. The English response was unexpectedly mild; few Englishmen had ever heard of the dispute, and in any event the Jameson raid and the Kaiser's telegram of congratulation to Kruger turned Britain's attention to matters of greater strategic moment.[7]

The subsequent history of the negotiations was marked by a series of British diplomatic retreats. Lord Salisbury was forced by the threat of war to recede from his original contention that the Venezuela affair was no concern of the United States. He was also unable to compromise by playing for time: the United States would not budge from its stand that Britain's failure to arbitrate seemed proof that the United States was in the right. Thus by February 1896 Britain agreed to the transfer of negotiations from London to Washington and by the following November accepted the principle of negotiation virtually on United States terms: except for territory politically controlled and settled for fifty years, all other territory would be arbitrated. A boundary commission was therefore appointed, and three years later reported substantially in favour of the British contention.

Britain's growing strategic disadvantage in view of the construction of navies by the United States, Japan, and Germany, British preference for

[5]*Ibid.*, pp. 563–67, 567–76.
[6]The message drafted by Olney himself may be found *ibid.*, pp. 542–45. For a hostile Canadian comment, see David Mills, "The New Monroe Doctrine of Messrs. Cleveland and Olney," *Can. Mag.* VI (Feb. 1896), pp. 365–80.
[7]E. Alfred Heath to Bayard, Jan. 11, 1896 (Tansill, *Bayard*, p. 737). Prominent Englishmen—especially the Prince of Wales—polled by the enterprising Joseph Pulitzer all expressed abhorrence of such a war.

South African rather than British Guianan interests, and Lord Salisbury's tendency to concentrate on the European balance of power explains Britain's abject surrender. Its lack of bitterness, however, was primarily due to a sense of Anglo-Saxon kinship towards Americans. The United States was doing in the Americas, and thus justifying, what Britain was doing in the rest of the world.[8]

II

If war had come Canada would have been the chief battleground. In the recent past United States politicians and newspapers had shown truculence towards Canada. Now a President took the lead with the vehement support of the Congress. His speech and Olney's dispatch of July 20, 1895, challenging Canada's right even to remain a part of the British Empire were published in full in Canada. These documents shocked Canadians and produced a resurgence of anti-Americanism. Nor could Canadians mistake the warlike mood in press and in action: an appropriation bill of $100,000,000 to raise an army of 900,000 men was introduced into Congress and 42 out of 45 governors approved the President's message and promised to enrol troops.[9] General Nelson Miles, the American General Commanding, declared that Britain could never transport sufficient troops to defend Canada: "By the time these vessels could go back for reinforcements and return there would probably be no British troops in Canada to be reinforced. . . . Canada would fall into our hands as a matter of course."[10] In view of Canada's experiences with the United States in the American Revolution, the War of 1812, the Hunters' Lodges in 1838, the Trent affair, the Fenian raids, what guarantee was there of America's "sober second thought" becoming effective?

Canada's first reaction to the American menace was amazed disbelief. The *Manitoba Free Press* noted the general opinion of Cleveland's

[8]On the British surrender see the valuable chapter, "The Venezuela Crisis, 1895–1896" in A. E. Campbell, *Great Britain and the United States, 1895–1903* (London, 1960), pp. 11–47; see also Geo. T. Blackstock, "Canada and the Venezuela Settlement," *Can. Mag.*, VIII (Dec. 1896), pp. 170–75.

[9]Lieut.-Col. J. F. Cummins, MS hist., "The Organization and Development of the Canadian Militia" (Historical Section, Can. Gen. Staff, 1932–36), pp. 224–25. Cf. Pope Papers, Diary, "Anglo-American Joint High Commission at Quebec and Washington, 1898–1899," Nov. 16, 1898: at a White House dinner, Pope sat opposite Sec. of War R. A. Alger, "who told me *inter alia*, that we were on the *very verge* of war over the Venezuela Affair."

[10]San Francisco *Examiner*, Dec. 23, 1895, cited in John Buchan, *Lord Minto: A Memoir* (London, 1924), p. 124.

speech as a "Mischievous Piece of Electioneering."[11] When the crisis did not quickly abate, Canada's second reaction was to put aside old partisan quarrels and affirm faith in the possibility of self-defence and in the power of the British Empire. The reaction of D. McGillicuddy, editor of the Huron *Signal* and vice-president of Goldwin Smith's Committee on Continental Union, was significant: "All Canadians Grit or Tory, Colonist or Continentalist, would march to the frontier to defend the sacred soil of Canada singing the Maple Leaf Forever and . . . would fight and die in the last ditch but never yield."[12]

How long Canada could have been defended in 1895–96 is difficult to say. In contrast to the situation in the War of 1812, Canadian defences were ludicrously inadequate. The protecting forest was gone, there was no force of well-trained, well-equipped, and well-led veterans, and *levée en masse* was considered a dead letter. The Canadian militia itself was in a woeful state of inefficiency. Possibly United States military incompetence later displayed in the Cuban campaign of the Spanish-American War would indicate that Canada might have hung on until British support arrived. Although the Canadian Government realized that political considerations were uppermost, for the moment it deemed Canada defensible and decided on a long-overdue rearming of the militia.

When the Canadian Parliament met in January 1896, it reflected a determination to defend both Canada and the Empire, for by that time the situation had become more dangerous as a result of the Kaiser's telegram. The speech from the throne stated that the Government would provide for the rearmament of the Canadian militia, an intention that was applauded by speakers on both sides of the House. The alternatives for Canada, as one speaker put it, were to prepare for an invasion or encourage a "holiday excursion."[13] At the end of January the Minister of Finance announced an increase in estimates to provide for annual drill and military accoutrements in view of "recent events." He did not believe that the fulfilment of these aims would provoke the United States, and he opposed those who thought peaceable annexation of Canada would not be the "worst of calamities." Opposing bloodshed and yet desiring friendship, Canada had to defend her heritage and her con-

[11]Part of newspaper heading, Dec. 19, 1895; see also statement in editorial that President Cleveland "must have taken temporary leave of his senses" (Dec. 20, 1895). Note that the Halifax *Morning Chronicle* was much more sober in the crisis.

[12]Quoted in George T. Denison to Lord Salisbury, Jan. 20, 1896, Denison Papers, p. 2984.

[13]*Debates*, Jan. 23, 1896, p. 563.

nection with Britain.[14] On February 5 the House passed a resolution not unlike one passed in 1890, expressing loyalty to British institutions, promising sacrifices, and yet asserting friendship with Americans.[15]

The resolution and the debate were directed against United States demonstrations. Was not Canada, it was argued in the debate, entitled to remain a free country and maintain its political union with Britain, if it so desired? Determined to make any necessary sacrifices, Canadians stood confident, fortified by the knowledge that the Empire's "resources . . . of fighting men . . . are practically inexhaustible." Yet no Canadian, it was also argued, relished the prospect of a fratricidal war. Canada should therefore avoid any demonstrations of enmity. After all, as another speaker hoped, the dispute was but a "lovers' quarrel," and was partly inspired by partisan motives. The best defence was the " 'good sense of the people of the United States,' " but the crisis had also disclosed the existence of a "disreputable and rowdy section" against which Canadians had to be on their guard.[16] Despite all provocations, most speakers asserted that Canada wished the United States well in solving its difficult labour and negro problems.

Only one speaker in the debate took a "realistic" attitude—Sir Richard Cartwright (1835–1912), the political mainspring of the commercial union movement. In effect he blamed Britain for Canada's involvement in the dispute and came near to implying that Canada's position was hopeless. Speaking to the resolution Cartwright argued that Canada's choice lay between "two alternatives . . . Canada will either have to be a hostage for the good behaviour of England to the United States, or Canada will have to be a bond of union between those two countries."[17] Canada, Cartwright lamented, possessed one of the most defenceless boundaries in the world. That defencelessness, which was the result of British diplomatic failures, put the mother country under obligation to help Canada, he implied. Canadians also had a "right to claim co-equal voice in all things appertaining to affairs in North America," and even in South America. If an English-speaking "alliance" of 140,000,000 people could be created it would bring

[14]George E. Foster, *ibid.*, Jan. 31, 1896, pp. 972–73.

[15]See apps. A and B. The resolution was moved by the Conservative Alexander McNeill of North Bruce, Ontario, and seconded by the Liberal, Louis H. (later Sir Louis) Davies of Queen's, Prince Edward Island; *Debates*, Feb. 5, 1896, pp. 1186–87. For the whole debate see *ibid.*, pp. 1186–1222. Similar resolutions were passed by the legislature of the province of Ontario at least, and by the Canadian Press Association; *Can. Mag.*, VI (March 1896), pp. 482–83.

[16]Quotations in *Debates*, Feb. 5, 1896, pp. 1188, 1209, 1205, 1189, respectively.

[17]*Ibid.*, p. 1196.

security for peace, welfare, and progress.[18] Towards the end of March John Charlton (1829–1910), who was also prominent in the commercial union movement, observed that Canada's contribution to Britain in such a war could be a "devastated country."[19] The expression of such ideas met opposition in the country.[20]

On April 21, 1896, two days before the expiration of Parliament, the Government asked for and received a special $3,000,000 defence appropriation, approximately $2,000,000 of which was for a rearmament contract signed with the War Office and $1,000,000 in effect for defence contingencies. This appropriation met strong political opposition on a variety of grounds: the purposes of the $1,000,000 were unspecified; there was no need to rearm (though no one had denied its necessity early in the session[21]); the letting of the contract was unconstitutional without consulting Parliament because the cabinet was but a "committee of this House."[22] On the very last day of the session a French-Canadian member of the Opposition moved a resolution condemning the making of such a contract without consultation of Parliament while in session. The resolution, which received among prominent Liberals the support only of Laurier, Cartwright, Davies, and Charlton, was defeated nearly two to one. Although there were many abstentions on both sides the names of several French-Canadian Conservatives were recorded in support of rearmament.[23] A tired and divided Tory Government was being kept on the defensive by such issues as the Manitoba school question, the exclusion of Canadian cattle from Britain, and the special defence credit.[24]

III

The Venezuela affair had important effects in the next few years. In the first place there can be no doubt that it contributed to the Liberal victory of 1896. It united Canadians in the defence of their country and exposed the falsity of the stale Conservative charges of Liberal dis-

[18]*Ibid.*, pp. 1195–1203.

[19]*Ibid.*, March 23, 1896, p. 4423; Charlton also envisaged a reunion with the United States.

[20]Cf. answer of *Man. Free Press* to this attitude, Feb. 8, 1896.

[21]George E. Foster, *Debates*, April 21, 1896, p. 6903. This was the first appropriation on the defence capital account since Confederation.

[22]Louis H. Davies, *Debates*, April 21, 1896, p. 6923. This erroneous view seems to have been not uncomon in the period. For a refutation see Eugene Forsey, *The Royal Power of Dissolution* (Toronto, 1943), and Sir Ivor Jennings, *Cabinet Government* (2nd ed., Cambridge, 1951), pp. 210–14.

[23]*Debates*, April 23, 1896, pp. 7147–48.

[24]*Ibid.*, April 21, 1896, pp. 6901–43.

loyalty warmed up from the election of 1891. Members of Parliament, including Conservatives, during the debate on the loyalty resolution deplored partisan accusations of Liberal disloyalty that encouraged the American belief that Canadians would welcome annexation.[25] Having demonstrated its loyalty during the crisis, the party now attracted to itself prominent supporters of imperial unity—notably Lieutenant-Colonel George T. Denison.[26] In the period of this study Colonel Denison was a figure of national importance through his weighty influence in Toronto and Ontario: on the one hand, because of the prominence of his position as social leader and as Toronto police magistrate, which brought him immense publicity, as a soldier and public figure, a speaker and publicist, member of patriotic societies and a prominent Anglican layman; on the other hand, because of the simplicity of his creed: (1) beware the United States and (2) call on Britain.[27] Not only did his creed receive striking confirmation during the crisis itself, but Denison had also been extraordinarily fortunate in publishing in an English magazine less than four months before the crisis a warning against trusting American friendliness. In the article he outlined British sacrifices of Canadian interests that had resulted from trust in American friendliness, refuted an "unfair" article on Canada by Goldwin Smith, and appealed to Britain to stand by Canada.[28] Thus as an ardent Canadian nationalist and original member of the Canada First party, Colonel Denison was dedicated to preserving the possibility of a Canadian nationality.

Denison made the first overtures to the Liberals, writing as a "stranger" to Wilfrid Laurier, leader of the Liberal party, to congratu-

[25]*Ibid.*, Feb. 5, 1896, pp. 1195, 1203, 1213. It is possible too, that the affair weakened Liberal rank and file opposition to the idea of a "national policy."

[26]A. H. U. Colquhoun (prominent Canadian journalist) wrote to Denison, "Private," June 16, 1896 (Denison Papers, p. 3073), that his name was "the only one prominently connected in the public mind with the Imperial movement here. The country press are apt to be lukewarm about it. Yet some of its best friends are Liberals who control newspapers."

[27]Col. Denison (1839–1925), a lawyer, served in the Fenian raid of 1866 and the North-West Rebellion of 1885; Lieutenant-Colonel of the Governor General's Body Guard; President of the Imperial Federation League and of the British Empire League; Fellow of the Royal Society of Canada. Among his more permanent writings were military works including *Modern Cavalry* (London, 1868) and *History of Cavalry* (London, 1877), which won the Tsar of Russia's prize (a second edition of this work was published by the United States Cavalry Association in 1913); *The Struggle for Imperial Unity* (London, 1909); and *Recollections of a Police Magistrate* (Toronto, 1920). He also published many political tracts.

[28]"Canada and Her Relations to the Empire," *Westminster Review*, CXLIV (Sept. 1895), pp. 248–65, and Goldwin Smith, "The Colonial Conference," *Contemporary Review*, LXVII (Jan. 1895), pp. 105–16.

late him on the "loyal tone of your remarks upon the militia."[29] Out of this letter developed a mutually influential friendship between the two men in the period 1896–99. During the election campaign of 1896, Sir Oliver Mowat tried to induce Colonel Denison to run as a Liberal in the riding of his recently deceased Conservative brother.[30] Denison refused because he did not want to sacrifice his national influence; he had already refused a title for the same reason. One of Mowat's chief lieutenants, George W. (later Sir George W.) Ross (1841–1914), Minister of Education, also asked Denison for comments on a proposed electoral speech, evidently designed to appeal to those favouring imperial unity. Consequently Denison counselled Lord Salisbury not to worry over the loyalty of a prospective Liberal Government, for he had observed their conduct during the Venezuela crisis and knew that his loyal friend Mowat was to enter the Liberal cabinet as Minister of Justice.[31]

Another prominent supporter of imperial unity who transferred his allegiance from the Conservatives to the Liberals was the Rev. G. M. Grant (1835–1902), Principal of Queen's University, prominent Presbyterian divine, speaker, and publicist.[32] As a leading divine and a kind of keeper of Protestant Canada's moral conscience, he was shocked at the corruption in the Conservative party displayed in the McGreevy scandals of the early 1890's. This led him to support the Liberals, and he too became a friend of Laurier. Grant lacked his friend Denison's dread of the United States and does not appear to have been much moved by the Venezuela affair. Under the circumstances, however, Grant's prominence in the movement for imperial unity could hardly have avoided influencing those Canadians who thought Canada threatened during the crisis.

Of great influence in the election also was the attitude of the militia, for it is certain that a considerable block of militia votes turned from the Conservative to the Liberal party because of maladministration of the militia.[33] Their anxiety reflected a second outcome of the affair—

[29]Denison Papers, draft, Feb. 1, 1896, p. 2993; reply, *ibid.*, Feb. 6, 1896, p. 3002; see also Alexander McNeill to Denison, *ibid.*, Feb. 24, 1896, p. 3013.

[30]*Ibid.*, Mowat to Denison, "Confidential," May 22, 1896, pp. 3059–62. A deputation also called upon him to ask him to run. He had been warned by his brother, Lieut.-Col. Clarence B. Denison, that the Conservative party was doomed in the coming election.

[31]*Ibid.*, p. 3042, Denison to Salisbury, May 2, 1896.

[32]William Lawson Grant and Frederick Hamilton, *Principal Grant* (Toronto, 1904).

[33]Laurier Papers, pp. 4733–34. W. J. Gascoigne, General Officer Commanding the militia, warned Laurier of the political importance of the militia in the elec-

an awakened concern for national defence. The Conservative Government had begun unobstrusive preparations, purchased up-to-date armaments and supplies, but refrained from any action provocative to the United States. Although less than six months before the crisis it had cancelled an order for 8,000 discarded Martini-Metford rifles,[34] early in January 1896 it secretly dispatched Colonel (afterwards Lieutenant-General Sir) P. H. N. Lake to take charge of the details of the purchase of 40,000 Martini-Metford or Martini-Enfield rifles, 2300 carbines (short rifles), field guns, and necessary accoutrements. As a result of discussion among the public and military men, the cabinet substituted the latest and best available—Lee-Enfield rifles and carbines. Accordingly on March 4, 1896, the contract for £399,000 was signed with the War Office, and the first rifles arrived in May and the last guns in October.[35] Meanwhile the War Office warmed up to Canada's unwonted interest in defence. It acceded to General Gascoigne's request for surplus heavy artillery at Halifax to be used in the defence of Quebec city (although the transfer was apparently never made) and for the loan of army engineers from the General Officer Commanding Imperial Troops at Halifax to select sites for the defence of Montreal owing to the supreme "importance of preserving Montreal from the enemy."[36] Later it paid the expenses of two engineers sent from England to make

---

tion: "I take this view from things said to me by Militia Officers of rank: Conservatives by tradition: who were yet so disheartened at the manner in which political influence governed the Militia that they turned against the Government"; "Private and Confidential," June 26, 1896. See also Lieut.-Col. F. R. Henshaw of the Montreal Victoria Rifles, who, when informed that economy would cut out militia training for 1889, headed a delegation to Ottawa to inform the Militia Department: "If you will not train the Militia we will soon get a government that will." This ended the no-drill idea for 1889. Typescript by A. S. McCormick, M.D., "The Victoria Rifles of Canada 1861–1914" (Akron, Ohio, 1960), p. 6.

[34]The Government had applied for them on January 26, 1894, and the proposed purchase was cancelled on May 17, 1895 (Imperial Despatches, no. 4, pp. 1488). The Minister of Militia justified the abandonment of summer training camps in 1894 because of the intention to purchase these arms, but the militia obtained neither. However, the Permanent Force, plus two volunteer companies, had been concentrated at Lévis for six weeks' training in 1894.

[35]D.M. 14417, memorandum of G.O.C. to Min. of Mil., March 11, 1896. This militia file contains the details of the purchase; others will be found in *Debates*, April 21, 1896, pp. 6901ff.; see also C.O. 42/838, pp. 26–27, 72, 73, 177; on the advice of Lord Wolseley heavy artillery was substituted for a large number of machine guns.

[36]R.G. 9, E.1, J. F. Cummins' notes, folder, Defence of Montreal and St. Lawrence Bridge, Maj.-Gen. J. C. Ardagh, Head, Intelligence Division, W.O., to Lieut.-Gen. A. G. Montgomery-Moore, G.O.C. Imp. Troops in Canada, "Secret," June 23, 1897.

a formal defence plan of Montreal in connection with the general defence of Canada.[37]

In spite of this quiet leadership, hesitation and lack of urgency marked the other Canadian military preparations in the crisis. Military intelligence apparently was not gathered, as Colonel Lake suggested, nor were the old Snider rifles collected and overhauled, as General Gascoigne proposed; and not until April 1896 was a defence scheme drafted. Appearing in a special General Order, the scheme, prepared by General Gascoigne and Captain Lee, provided that after mobilization units were to be placed in divisions, brigades, and garrisons at alloted mobilization centres. But it remained a paper plan: few preparations could be made because the composition of the proposed units remained secret until communicated to the local district officers commanding.[38] In the summer training camps of 1896 Lee lectured on the subject of mobilization —a lecture that was published as a General Order in October. These leisurely actions contrasted with the Militia Department's prompt dispatch of missing annual militia reports to complete the files of the United States War Department at the height of the crisis, a courtesy which suggests that for the Canadian administration the Venezuela affair had elements of an *opera bouffe* crisis.[39]

To the public, however, the affair did not have that appearance. On the contrary it now saw a purpose for the militia and a test for its efficiency: how well could it defend Canada? Largely because of General Herbert's scathing criticisms in the annual militia reports, the public had become more informed on militia matters and could better judge of Canada's unreadiness. Even the seconder of the address in the reply to the speech from the throne reminded the House that the "present Government, and all other Canadian Governments, have been unkind to the militia of Canada" in failing to provide for annual drill.[40] A deputation came from Toronto to press on the Government the necessity of increased defences.[41]

[37]*Ibid.*, Gascoigne to Dep. Min. of Mil., "Confidential," June 8, 1896. The two engineers, Col. E. P. Leach, R.E., and Maj. Hamilton Smythe, together with Col. Lake and Capt. A. H. Lee, R.A., Professor of Strategy at the Royal Military College (afterwards Viscount Lee of Fareham; 1868–1947), drew up a list of sites for Montreal's defence works in June 1896.

[38]Cummins, "The Organization and Development of the Canadian Militia," pp. 228–31.

[39]D.M. 14423, Brig.-Gen. A. W. Greeley, Chief Signals Officer, to Col. C. Eugene Panet, Dep. Min. of Mil., Dec. 27, 1895, and Jan. 13, 1896.

[40]*Debates*, Jan. 16, 1896, p. 159.

[41]*Ibid.*, Feb. 6, 1896, p. 1254; see also *ibid.*, Feb. 5, 1896, p. 1217, for a western Canadian interest.

In the third place, the Venezuela incident laid bare Canada's strategic dependence on Britain. National survival for Canada required not only rearmament, but also the proclamation of a national will to remain within the British Empire. Nevertheless, in spite of British cabinet ministers' grateful acknowledgement of the Canadian resolution of loyalty and A. J. Balfour's promise with "our will and power to defend" the colonies,[42] Canadians disdained the acknowledgement and the strategic fact it implied, and kept their eyes on the presumed trade opportunities of the country that had just threatened their own extinction.

IV

Canadians seem to have regarded the Venezuela incident as a public rather than a private affair, like an artillery barrage aimed at an objective beyond the soldiers in fox-holes. It was a newspaper war which did not seem to concern individual Canadians. Already by December 28, 1895, eleven days after the crisis began, the *Manitoba Free Press* could put a heading over a news story: "The War is Over." Longtime neighbours to Americans, Canadians shrewdly estimated the professions and practices of American politicians, and discounted the meaning of the spread-eagle oratory of a country one of whose national games is poker. Colonel Denison took the Americans' bluster at its face value: most Canadians did not. However much they might dislike Americanism, they did not dislike Americans, and could couple a resolution of loyalty to British institutions with one of friendship for the American people.

Canada's attempt to minimize the crisis can be explained first as prudence, to avoid provocation. Canadians were, moreover, intensely preoccupied with their own domestic affairs: the breakup of the Conservative administration and the political manoeuvrings prior to the election campaign; the Manitoba school question and the related conflicts between federal and provincial rights, Protestantism and Catholicism, and English and French Canadians; the continuing economic depression. Indeed, Canadians were not unaware that the gesture of friendship in the resolution of February 5 might open American markets to Canadian goods. Many Canadians, too, received ideological support and purpose from the economic and political ideals of Americans, and tended to ignore American affronts. They were receptive, then, to the Liberal election charge that Tory policy had produced

---

[42]G. J. Goschen and A. J. Balfour, Feb. 11, 1896, *Parliamentary Debates*, 4th series, vol. 37, pp. 75, 108, respectively; see also Denison Papers, p. 2969, Salisbury to Denison, "Private," Jan. 3, 1896.

friction with the United States, and to the programme of conciliation the Liberals advocated.

All these results and events paled before the fact that Canada's existence had been recently threatened. It was difficult now to plead that the annexation threats did not command the support of the Congress or the bulk of public opinion.[43] Canada had had to rearm; her loyalty to Britain had had to be asserted. In spite of the threat that made these actions necessary, however, Canada, and especially the new Premier, continued attempts to conciliate the United States.

[43]Donald Frederick Warner, *The Idea of Continental Union* (Lexington, Kentucky, 1960).

4. Attempts at Conciliation

BY TRADITION and ideology the Liberal party tended towards economy, conciliation, and freedom. Its older members espoused much of English mid-Victorian liberalism, believing in economy rather than expenditure, harmony rather than rivalry, and individual freedom within the state rather than assistance and direction by the state. In place of the Tory vision of a transcontinental economy, these Liberals saw a depressed economy, a country living beyond its means and hag-ridden by debt, bound by an "unnatural" railway monopoly, and supporting a ruinous national policy. Trusting in Scottish frugality rather than North American expansiveness they seemed to prefer an easier and less costly course —a satellite rather than a national economy. They professed to believe that, if Canada would but show goodwill, the United States would respond by opening American markets to Canadian goods. Demonstrations of Canadian goodwill would, of course, involve reversal of Tory high-tariff policy and the acceptance of the geographic and economic advantages of the proximity of the United States.

I

The new Premier, Wilfrid Laurier, shared many of these views. He believed that every Canadian should be permitted to exercise his individual and collective rights with due regard to those of other individuals and groups. Furthermore, his policy was an expression of the character of a kindly and courteous gentleman who would often prefer to win over a political enemy rather than to reward a friend, not because of any lack of courage, but from political wisdom. To settle the Manitoba school question, for example, Laurier proclaimed himself the apostle of a "sunny way" and of conciliation rather than coercion, policies which succeeded in gaining their objective. His attitude symbolized a new age that was tiring of extreme political partisanship,[1] and demonstrated that he was an ardent upholder of the federal nature of the Canadian

[1] Laurier Papers, p. 4385, William Mulock to Laurier, June 24, 1896.

nation. Indeed his political power depended on federalism for it was the political condition for the existence of his French-Canadian, Roman Catholic supporters. But Laurier was aware that the compromise of conflicting national and provincial interests must not be at the expense of national unity, for he was not simply a leader of French Canada but also premier of all Canada. Finally, in the years of this study, memories of the political and ideological rigidities that had destroyed the previous Liberal Government, Mackenzie's (1874–78), warned Laurier—the practical politician—not to hesitate in bending his policies to the necessities of political power.

Nor was there any essential difference between his internal and external policies of conciliation. He admired both British liberalism[2] and American democracy, and was a keen student of Abraham Lincoln, for whom there existed a considerable cult among Canadian liberals.[3] No perspicacious student of Lincoln could fail to note the enormous military, economic, and political potential of the United States. Yet the question of military power was a consideration that a nineteenth-century liberal tended to shy away from. On the contrary, he assumed that peace ought to exist between nations and that the friendly attitude of one nation would help produce the same attitude in another. Thus Laurier at an early meeting of his cabinet announced that "close and friendly relations with the United States must be a cardinal feature" of Canada's policy.[4] As early as August 1896 he proclaimed this policy when he told an American reporter of the Government's intention to renew "neighbourly relations with our friends across the border." Difficulties such as the North Atlantic fishery dispute should be settled by "an enlightened and friendly people, by the simple process of give and take." He suggested co-operation in the construction of a deep St. Lawrence waterway system, and in trade he was prepared "to make an arrangement with your country for the free exchange of such natural products and such manufactured articles as may be mutually agreed upon."[5]

Thus there soon began a series of pilgrimages—mostly to Washington

[2]H. Blair Neatby, "Laurier and Imperialism," *Report of the Canadian Historical Association*, 1955, pp. 24–32.

[3]Sir John Willison, *Reminiscences Political and Personal* (Toronto, 1919), pp. 165–66. Willison himself had a Lincoln collection, as did Isaac Campbell, prominent Winnipeg Liberal. The writer also saw a collection during the 1930's in the office of W. D. Gregory, K.C., friend of Goldwin Smith and one-time editor of the *Weekly Sun*. It is significant, however, that Colonel Denison with his aristocratic point of view favoured the South.

[4]O. D. Skelton, *Life and Letters of Sir Wilfrid Laurier* (Toronto, 1921), II, p. 123; see also Edward Farrer, "The Anglo-American Commission," *Forum*, XXV (Aug. 1898), p. 653.

[5]Chicago *Record*, reprinted *Globe*, cited *Debates*, Aug. 24, 1896, pp. 12–14.

—to settle specific disputes. Sir Richard Cartwright, low-tariff stalwart of the cabinet, was dispatched in September 1896 to sound out Joseph Chamberlain, who was in the United States to help settle the Venezuela affair, on the subject of a preference between Canada and the United States. Chamberlain, alarmed at the prospect, observed that Britain would not object to a lower tariff for all nations, but would object to one with the United States discriminating against Britain. Nor, under such circumstances, would Britain support such Canadian projects as the fast Atlantic steamship line,[6] a project whose defensive aspects were much emphasized in 1896. After the election of a high-tariff Republican President and Congress in 1896, the prominent Liberal, John Charlton, M.P., visited Washington unofficially in the hope of modifying the proposed Dingley Tariff Bill, which promised, and turned out to be, the highest American tariff up to that time. He went at Laurier's behest and almost certainly in his own private interest as an exporter of saw logs, but brought back little hope of modification.[7] In February 1897, Louis Davies, Minister of Marine and Fisheries, and Sir Richard Cartwright, Minister of Trade and Commerce, were dispatched on the same errand. They saw the principal leaders of Congress and were greeted with such affability that Davies was sanguine as to the results of their visit.[8] By March, however, few Canadians would have misunderstood the significance of the new President's summoning a special session of Congress to deal with import duties and revenue alone. Although much of the spade work on the promised tariff had been done in the previous session, the Dingley Bill was precipitately passed by the new House of Representatives within two weeks of its introduction on March 31, 1897. The response to Canada's economic overtures by this "aggressive spirit of protectionism"[9] demonstrated an indifference, if not hostility, that neither Canada nor other nations could ignore, especially as the Dingley Bill promised to aggravate Canada's already unfavourable balance of trade with the United States.

The general Canadian sense of outrage against the bill as a whole

---

[6]Chamberlain's memorandum on conversation with Cartwright, Sept. 25, 1896, in J. L. Garvin, *The Life of Joseph Chamberlain* (London, 1934), III, pp. 183–84.

[7]Skelton, *Laurier*, II, pp. 124–25, and note; New York *Tribune*, Jan. 16, 1897, cited C.O. 42/851, p. 229; Laurier Papers, pp. 9992, 11180–81, 11727.

[8]Laurier Papers, pp. 224431–38, 224443, Davies to Laurier, Feb. 7, 9, 11, 1897. Laurier apparently planned to visit McKinley before inauguration, but Charlton seems to have dissuaded him (*ibid.*, pp. 9993–94, Charlton to Laurier, "Private," Dec. 23, 1896). This probably is the explanation of the erroneous story of Laurier's visit to McKinley in Tansill, pp. 444–45.

[9]To use F. W. Taussig's phrase to describe the final bill, *The Tariff History of the United States* (7th ed., New York, 1923), p. 358.

was sharpened by specific Ontario grievances against its lumber clauses. Friction over lumber was one of the persistent causes of anti-Americanism in Ontario and harked back at least to 1866, when the free lumber clauses of the Reciprocity Treaty of 1854 were terminated and a general American tariff of 20 per cent on Canadian lumber was substituted. Canada at once retaliated by placing an export duty of $1 per thousand board feet on saw logs. In 1870 the United States exempted saw logs from the 20 per cent duty, thereby showing its dependence on the sources of supply, and in 1872 replaced the 20 per cent duty on sawn lumber by a duty of $2 per thousand board feet. This tariff remained substantially the same until the late 1880's. By that time the depletion of Michigan lumber limits induced Michigan lumbermen to take up forests estimated at two-thirds of the stands around Georgian Bay in Ontario, logs from which were towed across Lake Huron and sawn in the Michigan lumber mills. Canadians complained at the depletion of their natural resources and the continued American refusal to admit their sawn lumber free. The drastic increase of the Canadian export duty from $1 to $2 in 1886 and to $3 in 1888 on sawn logs, though angering Michigan lumbermen, eventually produced a tariff accommodation between the two countries. The Canadian duty was reduced to $2, and the McKinley Tariff of 1890 reduced the American duty on sawn lumber to $1 in response to a promise by Canada to abolish its export duty—a promise which was shortly fulfilled. From 1894 to 1897 virtual free trade in lumber flourished between the two countries except that the American tariff of 1894 contained a minatory clause threatening, if any country laid an export duty on its sawn logs, to impose in retaliation the same amount of duty in addition to the regular duty on the imported sawn lumber from the exporting country.[10]

It was the continuance of this minatory clause in the Dingley Bill, rather than the reimposition of $2 on sawn lumber, that angered Ontario lumbermen. Firm in the belief that the United States needed

[10]For the background of the lumber question see "Competition for Canadian Raw Material, 1870–1900," chap. xiii in A. R. M. Lower, *The North American Assault on the Canadian Forest: A History of the Lumber Trade between Canada and the United States* (Toronto, 1938), and Robert C. Johnson, "Logs for Saginaw: An Episode in Canadian-American Tariff Relations," *Michigan History*, XXXIV (Sept. 1950), pp. 213–23. The Ontario Conservative, T. S. Sproule, declared that many Canadians held the opinion that Charlton was "instrumental in inducing" the United States Senate to adopt the minatory clause in the Wilson-Gorman Tariff of 1894. Sproule affirmed that Charlton virtually admitted his influence when he said "he was entitled to credit if he could influence them so far as to get a reduction of duties on Canadian lumber." *Debates*, June 19, 1897, pp. 4703–4.

Canadian lumber, they demanded that the Government retaliate even though it would lead to "war."[11] The Government yielded by passing a retaliatory act, but, fearing for its policy of conciliation, refused to enforce it. In the period of this study non-enforcement of retaliatory laws was the Government's chief technique of emasculating legislative anti-Americanism.[12] It followed the same procedure after being compelled to impose export duties on nickel, copper, and lead.[13]

In effect the Government also made the Canadian Alien Labour Act little more than a gesture of retaliation. The Alien Labor Law of the United States had been a sore point with many Canadians since Congress had first enacted it in 1885. The law forbade contract labour, that is, forbade aliens making a contract with an American employer outside, before working inside, the United States. In origin the law seemed directed against eastern European labour, but enforcement fell heavily upon Canadians though the strictness of enforcement varied among ports of entry. In 1890 the Canadian Parliament considered retaliation. In the election campaign of 1896 the Conservatives advocated a retaliatory law, and in the short session of September 1896 such a law was discussed. One of the advocates argued its necessity because of "self-defence, in protecting our men along the boundary, and in order to maintain our dignity as a great nation."[14] Individual cases of harsh treatment of Canadian aliens by American immigration inspectors, which the press possibly exaggerated, were the chief ground for the agitation. Organized labour appears to have given the bill little backing. Perhaps that was one reason why Laurier then had the bill withdrawn, but there can be little doubt that his policy of conciliation was the main reason.[15] By the following spring the situation had changed, and the demand for retaliation proved irresistible. In spite of the shrill note in the parlia-

[11]Laurier Papers, pp. 224457–59, memorandum from four Georgian Bay lumber companies, inc. in John Bertram to Laurier, March 26, 1897, and pp. 14271–73, Clifford Sifton to Laurier, "Personal," April 29, 1897. The Canadian tariff of April 22, 1897, did not affect lumber.

[12]*Debates*, June 19, 1897, p. 4701.

[13]*Ibid.*, p. 4714. That the Government, formally at least, had not only assumed its predecessor's tariff position but surpassed it is shown by the protest of the previous Minister of Finance, George E. Foster, against the amount of protection involved in placing an embargo on lead.

[14]*Ibid.*, N. Clarke Wallace (Conservative, West York, Ont.) Sept. 9, 1896, p. 936; and see protest of Winnipeg Typographical Union against the American law to Laurier, Feb. 10, 1897 (Laurier Papers, p. 11970).

[15]This agitation, which preceded that caused by the Dingley Bill, was the first open anti-American agitation since the Venezuela affair. Was the suppressed resentment against the United States now finding expression? The writer is inclined to think it was, but until a careful study of all the issues of the election of 1896 is made the truth cannot be known.

mentary debate, however, most speakers deplored the necessity for an alien labour law, and, because of Laurier's insistence that the minimum of force should be used, the Canadian law was made weaker than the corresponding American law, and its enforcement was to be discretionary.[16] But there can be no question of the growth of anti-American feeling in Canada during the spring of 1897,[17] and that the immediate source of that feeling was the single-hearted pursuit by Americans of their own interests.

II

The contrast between Canada's rather abject reaction in the Venezuela crisis and the demand for retaliation against the Alien Labor Law and the Dingley Bill was marked. In the spring of 1897 Canadians of course no longer needed to place questions of military prudence uppermost, and their own domestic divisions and problems were on the way to being met by the vigorous leadership of the new Liberal Government. They interpreted the Dingley Bill as an attempt to prevent Canada's emulation of the United States, to reduce Canada to a state of economic tutelage, or even to force political annexation. These conclusions were not unreasonable in view of a plank of the Republican party platform of 1896 which called for the annexation of Canada if its citizens agreed. None of these implied threats was new. What was new was the intensification of anti-Americanism in Canada until by 1899 it had become virtual Americanophobia. Open expressions of anti-Americanism in 1897 imply a degree of confidence lacking in the previous year. Its sources appear to have been three: the return of prosperity, the confidence of the business community in the new Liberal Government, and the acceptance of imperial unity as a policy for Canada.

Probably the return of prosperity was most decisive. There could be no doubt of its return in 1897, for its signs abounded. From 1896 to 1899, Canada's external trade and bank deposits increased more than a third, mineral production more than doubled, and a wheat boom began in the West. Prices and external conditions were particularly favourable to Canada. In western European markets, where continued industrialization provided an expanding market for raw materials, prices

[16]*Debates*, April 7, 1897, pp. 621–60, and June 7, 1897, pp. 3545–59.

[17]The secretary of the Ontario Liberal Association with headquarters in Toronto reported to Laurier on the intensity of this feeling and of the elation at the victory of the Australian R. Fitzsimmons over the American J. J. Corbett in the world's heavyweight boxing championship in 1897; Laurier Papers, p. 13294, Alex Smith to Laurier, "Private & Confidential," March 22, 1897; and see *ibid.*, pp. 12504–56.

of raw materials rose faster than prices of imported manufactured goods. As business prospered investors put money into Canada. Immigrants from Britain, the United States, and Continental Europe poured into the "last best West." The external world was providing the men, money, and markets that Canada so desperately needed, if she were to become a viable power. To encourage expansion still further the Canadian Government bent every effort to attract settlers, stimulate the flow of capital goods, and complete the nation's transportation system.

Prosperity was a symbol of nationhood and national virtue, for to the colonial Calvinist, who saw the supreme virtue in work, prosperous nations were worthy nations—nations for whom a high destiny was waiting. The immense possibilities of Canada's future, which too often became fantasies of material impossibility, were sources of national inspiration and pride. Laurier reflected this attitude when he later proclaimed: "The Nineteenth Century belonged to the United States, the Twentieth Century belongs to Canada." This statement reflects both the Canadian faith in the future and the implied acceptance of American standards to measure that future.

To the business community especially, prosperity brought confidence, which had already risen during the election campaign when the Liberal party accepted business views on protection. During the campaign when Liberal prospects seemed bright, the Conservative Government trained its guns on Opposition pamphlets supporting free trade. An awareness that the Liberal party could not suddenly abolish Canadian tariffs crept into the speeches of party leaders and the editorials of the *Globe*, the chief party organ. Sir Oliver Mowat counselled a public statement from Laurier on behalf of a dependable tariff.[18] Laurier was beholden to Mowat, for the Ontario legislature in January 1896 had passed a resolution calling for a factual investigation of the Manitoba school question and a policy of conciliation, and Mowat himself promised to join a victorious Liberal Government. Laurier obliged with an exchange of public letters with George H. Bertram of Toronto, a Liberal manufacturer: each denounced protection, and advocated freer trade especially with Great Britain and the United States, and, if possible, a "fair . . . reciprocity treaty with the United States." Laurier asserted, however, that any tariff changes must be gradual and that a primarily revenue tariff would have the advantage of stability. With the Liberals in power he hoped that the tariff issue would be eliminated[19] because his goal was

18*Ibid.*, p. 4285, May 22, 1896, and C. R. W. Biggar, *Sir Oliver Mowat* (Toronto, 1905), II, pp. 645–52.
19J. S. Willison, *Sir Wilfrid Laurier and the Liberal Party* (London, 1903), II, pp. 282–86, and Skelton, *Laurier*, II, p. 51.

a united Canada. After the election the business community was further reassured by the appointment of the moderate W. S. Fielding, rather than Sir Richard Cartwright, as Minister of Finance. The sympathetic attitude to business of the new Government's tariff commission also provided reassurance.

One effect of this attitude towards protectionists, however, was to cast doubt on the party's professions in favour of low tariffs, and so lose the support of a powerful, or at least vocal, section of the party. How was the Government to reconcile its professions with its probable practices?

Its chief and surprising answer was a unilateral preference on British goods. A reciprocal preference had often been suggested; as we have seen, it was the subject of a resolution of the Canadian Parliament of 1891. But the suggestion of a unilateral offer was new and its source is at present unknown. By March 1897 Laurier had submitted a memorandum on the proposal to at least two Ontario businessmen who responded favourably.[20] By March 25 a correspondent was reporting to the London *Times* the existence of the proposal. But the Government budget had not only to placate the tariff wings of the party; it had also to vindicate the Canadian economy against the prospective Dingley Bill, check the prospect of a growing unfavourable balance of trade, and threaten some kind of economic retaliation that would satisfy anti-American resentments. Thus on April 22, 1897, the Minister of Finance introduced the first Liberal tariff with three notable features: (1) the adjustment of items of the tariff itself, 150 being lowered, 100 being raised, and 1200 remaining the same;[21] (2) the withdrawal of the offer, which had existed since 1879, of reciprocity to the United States; and (3) the substitution of a maximum and minimum tariff—the latter offered to any country treating Canadian trade "reciprocally." The Minister of Finance interpreted this latter feature as meaning that Britain qualified for an immediate preference of 12½ per cent on all goods and a further 12½ per cent by the middle of the next year. Any nation in the world might similarly qualify if "reciprocal treatment" for Canadian goods was forthcoming.[22]

On the surface the threat to transfer Canadian trade from the United States to Great Britain looked like retaliation. But it is doubtful whether

[20]Laurier Papers, p. 14345, Jamestun Osborne (Massey-Harris Co.) to Laurier, May 1, 1897, and pp. 13282–85, George H. Bertram to Laurier, "Confidential," March 22, 1897. Bertram informed Willison of the Toronto *Globe*, who also approved; see also *ibid.*, p. 13665, Willison to Laurier, "Private," April 2, 1897.
[21]*Ibid.*, pp. 15410–11, estimate of A. G. Jones to Laurier, May 31, 1897.
[22]James A. Colvin, "Sir Wilfrid Laurier and the British Preferential Tariff System," *Report of the Canadian Historical Association*, 1955, pp. 15–19.

Laurier himself entertained much hope that the preference would divert American senators from their protectionist course or that the circumscribed reciprocity clauses of the Dingley Bill would mean anything practical. Rather, any Canadian effort to have the Dingley Bill modified would provide an opportunity to broach his aim of a general settlement with the United States. Already in January, John Charlton had hinted to Congressman Nelson Dingley the probability of the Liberal Government's desiring to settle all outstanding questions between the two countries.[23] After the inauguration of the preference Laurier now began to press for such a settlement. At the end of April he "most particularly" desired Charlton to meet congressional leaders in order "to have a Commission" appointed to settle the many problems between the two countries and secondarily to press for tariff concessions in lumber, coal, and agricultural products, which the Canadian Government would reciprocate.[24]

Charlton failed, as he was to fail in two more lobbying trips to Washington in June and July. His outraged response at American obduracy in April and May was a measure of the general Canadian resentment in view of his own personal financial interests. Charlton reported to Laurier that Congressman Dingley was "incensed about the discrimination clause of our tariff"; Dingley granted that Canada was "entitled" to make a reciprocal preference, but maintained that the existing preference was "entirely gratuitous," for England had not made the "slightest concessions" to Canada. Charlton reminded Dingley of British subsidies to steamship lines carrying Canadian trade, of the fact that Canadian duties were heavier against Britain than against the United States, and of the hope for new preferences and for restoration of preference on live stock. But Dingley remained unconvinced, and "deprecated the inauguration of commercial war which would be likely as a first consequence, to lead to the abrogation of the bonding privilege." Charlton therefore decided to take a strong line when appearing later before a Senate subcommittee, for he wrote, "we may just as well tell the Yankee to go to hades and we will go to England."[25] Appearing before the subcommittee he justified Canada's reaction to the Dingley Bill because of the United States' denial of "geographical, racial, and business affinities" and because the proposed tariff approached a "declaration of commercial war." The two senators—W. B. Allison and N. W. Aldrich—agreed with this description, but explained that they could do nothing because they

23Laurier Papers, p. 11181, Charlton to Laurier, "Private," Jan. 26, 1897.
24*Ibid.*, p. 14197, "Confidential," April 27, 1897.
25*Ibid.*, pp. 14319–20, "Private," April 30, 1897.

were "tied up . . . by political conditions."[26] Charlton also plied Democratic members of the whole committee with statements on the probable economic effects of the bill on Canada.[27] In July the Dingley Bill became law without substantial alteration, and the Canadian preference proved to be but a gesture of retaliation, for the unfavourable balance of trade against Canada continued to grow.

III

In contrast to the failure of preference as a weapon of retaliation, it met with enormous domestic success, for without threatening Canadian business, it constituted a great low-tariff gesture. It was regarded, and to some extent advertised, as a measure of freer, rather than of imperial, trade. In theory any nation, even the United States, complying with its terms could take advantage of the Canadian preference.[28] The Conservatives trained their guns on this feature and dolefully prophesied how Belgium, Germany, and other countries, after readjusting their tariffs, would deluge Canada with their goods,[29] and make Canada a "slaughter market." By obligingly proclaiming the tariff a free-trade tariff, Conservatives doubtless helped keep the Liberal party united.

But the most spectacular success of the preference was its reception in Britain. What impressed Britain most was that the preference came from a notoriously high-tariff country, and that it was in such marked contrast to the proposed action of the United States; Englishmen, like Canadians, tended to regard the McKinley Tariff and the proposed Dingley Tariff as American attempts to crush their industry. It was no accident that Sir Wilfrid Laurier received the Cobden Medal in 1897 for freeing trade. The preference stressed Canada's loyalty and gave the country tremendous advertising in Britain and the national recognition Canadians craved. The Liberal Government thus had not only slaked free-

[26]*Ibid.*, pp. 14326–30, "Private," May 1, 1897. In reply to an expression of President McKinley's kindly feelings towards Canadians, Charlton observed that the Dingley Bill was no proof of that feeling "among American public men" (*ibid.*, p. 14333). See also two articles by Charlton, "American Trade Relations," *Can. Mag.*, IX (Oct. 1897), p. 504, and "Canada and the Dingley Bill," *North Amer. Rev.*, CLXV (Oct. 1897), pp. 418–30.

[27]He had "confirmed" from the Republican Senator G. F. Hoar that "good friends in Canada had advised them to avoid making concessions to Canada for the purpose of forcing the country into political union." Charlton replied that a "struck" Anglo-Saxon would resent it as much as any other Anglo-Saxon. Laurier Papers, pp. 14410–17, Charlton to Laurier, "Private," May 4, 1897. For a possible reference to the Canadian friends, see Queen's University Library, Walter Dymond Gregory Papers, Diary, Jan. 3, 1897.

[28]Sir Richard Cartwright, *Debates*, April 26, 1897, p. 1254.

[29]N. F. Davin (Conservative, Assiniboia), *Debates*, April 27, 1897, p. 1323.

trade desires; it had also robbed the Tories of their loyalty cry. The Tories had talked; the Grits had acted. In any case, it could easily be represented that Tory loyalty was selfish loyalty, for the Tories had demanded a reciprocal tariff.[30] Kipling's poem, "Our Lady of the Snows," which Canadians regarded as atrocious immigration propaganda,[31] and which was published shortly after the introduction of the preference, emphasized the imperial aspects of the preference: it reminded Canadians and Englishmen that Canada was mistress in its own house and suggested that the denunciation of the Belgian and German treaties had been delayed too long.

In offering a preference to Britain alone the Canadian Government knowingly violated these treaties, a violation which the Opposition denounced. In reply, Government leaders argued that they "were not born yesterday," knew what they were "about," and intended "to fight this point by all legal and constitutional means."[32] Although the measure was unprecedented, it was justified on grounds of Canada's importance, responsibilities, and increased rights. Even the cool effrontery with which the Canadian Government was forcing the British Government to abrogate resented restrictions of the treaties aroused enthusiasm in Britain. The London *Times* believed that obsolete arrangements in treaties should not prevent closer union.

The decision whether or not Britain would yield to this pressure depended on Canada's support by the Colonial Office. Less than two years previously the Colonial Secretary, Lord Ripon, because of the necessity of observing "international obligations" and preserving the "unity of the Empire," had returned a "no" to the request of the Colonial Conference of 1894 that the offending clauses of the two treaties be denounced.[33] The Foreign Office had learned from Belgium and Germany that these clauses could not be denounced without the termination

[30]T. D. Craig (Conservative, East Durham, Ont.) observed: "I do not think a man is better for constantly talking about his loyalty, but I believe I am expressing my honest sentiments when I declare that true loyalty to the Empire is loyalty to Canada, or that true loyalty to Canada is real loyalty to the Empire, and that the true way to build up the Empire is to build up Canada." *Debates*, April 27, 1897, p. 1367; see also T. S. Sproule, *ibid.*, April 28, 1897, p. 1422.

[31]See the amusing short debate in protest against this poem, *ibid.*, April 30, 1897, pp. 1546–50; see also J. Gordon Mowat, "Where Summers are Long," *Can. Mag.*, XII (Nov. 1898), pp. 3–10.

[32]Sir Richard Cartwright, *Debates*, April 26, 1897, pp. 1245, 1252–53. See also Laurier's summary in 1898 of the position of the Minister of Finance in the preceding year: ". . . he assumed the position that England had authority to denounce the treaties, or he could refuse the offer which we made to her"; *ibid.*, Feb. 4, 1898, p. 86.

[33]Arthur Berriedale Keith, ed., *Selected Speeches and Documents on British Colonial Policy 1763–1917* (London, 1918), II, pp. 156–64.

of the treaties as a whole. Therefore it argued against denunciation because the total British trade with Belgium and Germany in 1893 was estimated at £41,000,000 whereas the total trade with all the self-governing colonies only amounted to £35,000,000.[34] Oddly enough the Board of Trade was not moved by the possible loss of trade because, it argued, Belgium and Germany would continue to need British raw goods.[35]

When the rumour reached London of the proposed Canadian preference a month before the budget was brought down, the Foreign Office protested to the Colonial Office that Canada might force the abrogation of the treaties regardless of the benefits it conferred. But the Colonial Office gave the Foreign Office no satisfaction.[36]

On the introduction of the new tariff, the Governor General inquired of the Colonial Office on the reservation of the bill; he also reported that, if the Canadian tariff was found contrary to international treaties, the Canadian Government intended to request the denunciation of the treaties. In spite of the opposition of the Foreign Office and also, by now, of the Board of Trade, Chamberlain replied to Aberdeen that the bill need not be reserved; rather, Aberdeen should demand an undertaking that, if the Law Officers gave an adverse decision on the bill, Canada would abide by the treaties.[37] Canada agreed, and arranged for Louis Davies, with Edward Blake as counsel, to plead before the Law Officers.

Meanwhile in response to the Colonial Secretary's request for Canada's justification in offering a preference to Britain alone, a subcommittee of the cabinet, consisting of Sir Richard Cartwright, Louis Davies, W. S. Fielding, A. G. Blair, and Sir Oliver Mowat, protested that Canada could make such a tariff because Canada had had her "fiscal independence practically conceded" to her before the treaties with Belgium and Germany were made. In any case if Belgium and Germany granted Canada special privileges equal to those given by Canada they too might qualify under the reciprocal preference. If the Imperial Government were still not convinced of the foregoing justifications for the preference it should simply denounce the treaties.[38] Davies, who accom-

---

[34]C.O. 42/833, pp. 340–41, F.O. to C.O., Feb. 21, 1895.

[35]*Ibid.*, p. 700, Board of Trade to C.O., June 27, 1895, cited in C.O. minute of John (afterwards Sir John) Anderson, April 28, 1897.

[36]C.O. 42/852, p. 377, memorandum of Sir H. Bergue of F.O., March 30, 1897, Conf. F.O. Print, and p. 378, C.O. to F.O., April 1, 1897.

[37]C.O. 42/847, pp. 21–25, Aberdeen to Chamberlain, May 4, 1897; p. 47, paraphrase of cable, May 7, 1897, and Chamberlain to Aberdeen, "Confidential," May 10, 1897.

[38]C.O. 42/853, pp. 48–49, Conf. F.O. Print, May 12, 1897.

panied Laurier to the Diamond Jubilee, used some of these arguments before the Law Officers. A Colonial Office official minuted that Germany would not accept the Canadian contention that Canada's fiscal independence antedated the treaties. Chamberlain, however, minuted that he was "perfectly willing to risk the wrath & claims of Germany" because "the question of imperial policy involved in the Canadian preferential offer is so important."[39]

In the meantime Davies tried to obtain a further respite from the almost certain adverse ruling of the Law Officers by requesting an appeal to the Judicial Committee of the Privy Council on the legality of the matter. The British Government refused to permit this appeal, and on August 3, 1897, the Law Officers replied that the treaties were binding on Canada[40] and that the Canadian Government must reimburse importers for duties collected on goods from countries affected by the preference. Accordingly some thirty countries were now offered the preference, the United States being denied its advantage. A few days earlier, Lord Salisbury, in spite of many European protests against the Canadian action, made known Britain's intention of denouncing the treaties—a denunciation that took effect a year later on August 1, 1898. Thereupon the Canadian preference, now granted only to Britain, New South Wales, and the British West Indies, became unmistakably imperial.

IV

The policy of preference was brave and astute. It was of a piece with Laurier's bold affirmation of liberalism against the Ultramontanes in 1877 and his defiance of the bishops on the Manitoba school question in 1896. The preference kept the Liberal party united; and under its guise the party accepted protection.[41] It was a mark of approbation of Britain and retaliation against the United States appealing to the swelling pro-British, anti-American sentiment. It excited British public opinion, for despite the forcing of Britain's hand, the preference seemed a jubilee gift of a lower tariff on British goods, and it raised expectations among the British that contributed much to Laurier's successful visit to Britain during the Diamond Jubilee.

[39]C.O. 42/847, pp. 196–201, minutes of Anderson, June 2, 1897, and Chamberlain, June 3, 1897.
[40]C.O. 42/850, pp. 34, 41.
[41]*Man. Free Press*, April 24, 1897, edit., "The New Tariff."

5. Canada Turns to Imperial Unity

DISAPPOINTMENT with the United States action in passing the Dingley Tariff was succeeded in Canada by astonishment at British enthusiasm for the Canadian preference. This was quickly followed by the eagerness with which Canadians celebrated Queen Victoria's Diamond Jubilee. Several elements made up the Canadian response to that celebration. One was the defiance of the Olney doctrine implicit in proclamations of loyalty to the Queen—a defiance that coloured and heightened much of the other enthusiasm. The second was the veneration for the institution of monarchy, which Professor Morton has suggested is necessary for Canada's existence. The monarchy is the focus of personal allegiance, the form and the expression of national union, and a decisive fact of differentiation from the United States. Canada's governing principle of "peace, order, and good government" permits a sectional variety, provides a stability, and allows for a personal freedom sometimes lacking under the social compact theory of its neighbour, whose ideal of "Life, Liberty and the pursuit of Happiness" often results in egalitarianism and social atomization.[1]

In the third place, Queen Victoria excited among the mass of Canadians, not just an interested response, but a heart-felt enthusiasm. The Queen was held in deep veneration.[2] She was the quintessence of middle-class ideals and practices which, though being undermined, were still widely held in honour. She inspired celebrations, articles, poems, and the like, which in turn provided excuses for national self-congratulations on progress. The celebrations themselves consisted of military parades and reviews, assemblies of school children, patriotic speeches, unveiling

[1]W. L. Morton, "The Relevance of Canadian History," *Report of the Canadian Historical Association*, 1960, pp. 1–21.

[2]Queen's University Library, Walter Dymond Gregory Papers, Diary, April 30, 1897. See also Laurier Papers, p. 27876, Geo. A. Cox to Laurier, "Private," Nov. 8, 1898; in asking for a grant for the Victorian Order of Nurses, Cox observed: "The Dominion has not done anything of a national character in commemoration of Her Majesty's Diamond Jubilee."

of monuments, opening of parks, and banquets. In Winnipeg, for example, the enthusiasm having lasted more than two weeks, the *Manitoba Free Press* headed a Canadian news report: "Still Jubilating."[3] A. H. U. Colquhoun in Ottawa wrote to Denison in England that the Jubilee sentiment "absorbed attention," and the "trade aspect" pretty well disappeared; and a few days later reported the "extraordinary enthusiasm" of both the French and English.[4]

Public enthusiasm was also excited by the royal welcome Laurier was receiving in Britain. He had taken care that Canadians should be informed of his progress.[5] One of the purposes of his visit was to have the Belgian and German treaties denounced to avoid what would have been the ignominious failure of the preference.[6] His arrival and that of a contingent of 200 Canadians in Britain in the wake of British enthusiasm for Canadian preference provided an unparalleled opportunity for Laurier to enlist British support for denunciation and obtain recognition and advertisement of Canada. A unit of the North-West Mounted Police was also sent to make it "plain" that Canada was determined "to preserve law and order."[7] Chamberlain welcomed the Canadians' effort to make themselves known, not only for the economic benefit they might derive, but also for the awareness in Britain of the political and defensive strength they might bring to the British Empire. He attached the "utmost importance" to the reception of the colonial units for it was

[3]John T. Saywell, ed., *The Canadian Journal of Lady Aberdeen 1893–1898* (Toronto, Champlain Society, 1960), pp. 397, 401–4, June 29, 1897. The Jubilee celebration in Halifax also included the four hundredth anniversary of the voyage of John Cabot; *ibid.*, p. 403.

[4]Denison Papers, pp. 3249–53, June 26 and 30, 1897.

[5]Many Canadians had long been concerned that most news from Britain came via American news sources and from American pens and that Britain received little news of Canada: Beckles Willson, *The Life of Lord Strathcona and Mount Royal* (London, 1915), p. 476; Laurier Papers, pp. 14887–89, "Memorandum for J. Castell Hopkins regarding cable news service supplied to Canadian newspapers," prepared by A. H. U. Colquhoun; and *ibid.*, pp. 17672–78, W. S. Fielding (in London) to Laurier, Nov. 3, 1897.

[6]Cf. C.O. 42/846, p. 501, Aberdeen to Chamberlain, cable rec'd. March 19, 1897.

[7]*Debates*, April 13, 1897, pp. 846–47; and see *ibid.*, June 2, 1897, pp. 3239–41. For the difficulties caused by too many Canadians (800) wishing to be sent to the Jubilee, see C.O. 42/846, p. 608, also pp. 605, 609. See *ibid.*, pp. 213, 214, 218, for the War Office reaction to having to provide horses for the 26 officers commanding the 200 men, which included the parliamentary colonels—M.P.'s Tisdale, O'Brien (of the 1891 Parliament), Tyrwhitt, and Domville—who formed the "Political detachment Mr. Laurier's 'Bodyguard'" and presumably were among the "rare lot of *bounders* coming from Canada" (Lord Methuen to Sir W. A. Baillie-Hamilton, Chief Clerk of Colonial Office, "Private," no date—June 1897).

most desirable for them to "be encouraged to increase their forces, and to identify them with the general defences of the Empire."[8]

Chamberlain saw to it that the colonial premiers occupied a centre of attention; invited to visit the Queen at Windsor, they were made members of the Privy Council. Laurier alone received a knighthood, which was unsought and undesired. Lord Aberdeen and Sir Donald Smith (himself about to accept a peerage) planned this honour which, at the last moment, Laurier could not decline. Yet the acceptance of a knighthood honoured Canada and flattered its dominant mood, as Laurier was aware, though it aroused the opposition of the more egalitarian of his party.[9] The premiers were also invited to a "great and important national demonstration"—the review of the Royal Navy flauntingly drawn up in four lines each thirty miles long.[10]

Of the overseas visitors Laurier was a "tremendous favourite," for he had a "great personal charm . . . apart from his wonderful oratory."[11] Probably the latter was the most influential aspect of his visit. In France he rejoiced that he was French in culture, British in citizenship, and Canadian in nationality. In Britain he sounded four main themes concerning Canada: (1) that the preference was a free gift though its acceptance depended on Britain; "either Canada will have to retreat," he announced at Liverpool, "or England will have to advance";[12] he also artfully made an eloquent obeisance to free trade; (2) that the Dominion was a nation of a new type—a nation within the Empire; (3) that the growth of the colonies required changes in imperial organization, possibly in the direction of some sort of imperial parliament or council; and (4) that the Dominion was loyal to the Empire and intended to maintain "to the fullest extent the obligations and responsibilities as British subjects."[13]

[8]George Earle Buckle, ed., *The Letters of Queen Victoria*, 3rd series (London, 1932), III, p. 166, Baillie-Hamilton to Sir Arthur Bigge, Sec. to the Queen, May 28, 1897.

[9]Laurier Papers, pp. 15928–29, Chamberlain to Laurier, June 17, 1897; for opinions on Laurier's acceptance of a title, see *ibid.*, pp. 9200–400, *passim*; see also Maurice Pope, ed., *Public Servant: Memoirs of Sir Joseph Pope* (Toronto, 1960), p. 115.

[10]*Can. Sess. Pap.* (no. 19), 1898, p. 42, Chamberlain to Aberdeen, July 8, 1897, app. "G," "Commemoration of the Queen's Reign of 60 Years," in the Report of the Major-General.

[11]Pope Papers, Semi-Official Correspondence 1896–1898, docket 13J, John Anderson (Colonial Office official) to Joseph Pope, Aug. 31, 1897.

[12]O. D. Skelton, *The Life and Letters of Sir Wilfrid Laurier*, II (Toronto, 1921), p. 73.

[13]Minto Papers, vol. 19, p. 35, speech at Liverpool, June 13, 1897, cited in General Sir Edward Hutton, "A Narrative of Lord Minto's Career."

The Jubilee celebration was a tribute to Chamberlain's boldness, but the Colonial Conference held in conjunction must have seemed to negate its promise. The terms of Canada's acceptance of Chamberlain's invitation,[14] Laurier's public reference to the establishment of some kind of imperial council, and his advocacy in the conference of closer imperial relations inspired hopes of closer union among British imperialists, who were convinced that in Laurier they had "a very interesting and useful man."[15] Laurier had voiced a prevalent belief that Canada's existing relationship to Britain was unsatisfactory, the only alternatives permitted by the prevailing Austinian theory being independence or closer imperial relations. Hence both he and Chamberlain pressed the other premiers to follow Canada's lead and establish preferences. Laurier argued that such an act would "strengthen the bonds of Empire" and be "a great gain to the Imperial idea." He supported the interchange of Canadian and Imperial military units, which was already being carried out in Canada, and advocated the uniformity of equipment, drill, and weapons for the colonial and Imperial forces. Finally, while admitting the satisfactory nature of existing political relations, Laurier pleaded for eventual acceptance of colonial members in the British House of Commons.[16]

It was, however, easier to evoke sentiment than to transform it into concrete results. Thus the chief resolution of the conference, drafted by Laurier himself,[17] expressing satisfaction with "the existing conditions of things," was a decisive precedent for autonomy and a rebuff for Chamberlain's, and to some extent, Laurier's, own initial scheme of imperial centralization. The conference also recommended denunciation of the Belgian and German trade treaties that prevented inter-imperial tariff arrangements, and dealt with informal military agreements.[18]

[14]*Parliamentary Papers,* 1897, LIX (C. 8485, p. 9), p. 629: "The Sub-committee [of the Canadian cabinet] unite most sincerely in the hope that the result of the approaching celebration may be such as will tend powerfully to cement the union between the Mother Country and her Colonies, both socially and politically." Report of Committee of Privy Council, April 17, 1897, inc. in Aberdeen to Chamberlain, April 20, 1897.

[15]Cecil Headlam, ed., *The Milner Papers* (London, 1931), I, p. 113, Lord Selborne, Under-Sec. for the Colonies, to Sir Arthur Milner, "Confidential," July 6, 1897.

[16]C.O. Conf. Print, Misc., no. III, cited in Richard H. Wilde, "Joseph Chamberlain's Proposal of an Imperial Council in March, 1900," *Can. Hist. Rev.,* XXXVII (Sept. 1956), p. 231.

[17]Lucien Pacaud, sel. & ed., *Sir Wilfrid Laurier Letters to My Father and Mother* (Toronto, 1935), p. 117, Laurier to Ernest Pacaud, April 12, 1900.

[18]See below p. 72. For the formal resolutions of the conference see "Proceedings of a Conference between the Secretary of State for the Colonies and the Premiers of the Self-Governing Colonies at the Colonial Office, London, June and July 1897," *Parl. Pap.,* 1897, LIX (C. 8596).

On Laurier's return he received a triumphal welcome from his countrymen. Bonfires burned on the hillsides of the St. Lawrence, cheers greeted him from Quebec to Windsor, and the boards of trade in Toronto and Montreal banqueted him. Laurier's success had "flattered Canadian pride, and touched Canadian hearts," for he was regarded as a representative Canadian.[19] Public enthusiasm was excited not so much because of advertisement as because of recognition: Little-England disdain for the colonies seemed dead, and Canada was recognized as a separate entity from the United States.[20] In obtaining national recognition from Britain, Laurier had in effect made the Anglo-Canadian alliance explicit for Canadians and celebrated their membership in a powerful empire.[21] Not least, he had obtained, if not extracted, a political advantage in the denunciation of the Belgian and German treaties.[22]

II

By the fall of 1897 as a result of these developments, Canadians were generally embracing the idea of imperial unity. They were therefore prepared to accept many of the attitudes and much of the platform of the British Empire League. This was the first and decisive condition of the league's influence during the period. In the second place, the Canadian branch of the league had outgrown its partisan beginnings and become a national organization. We have seen its president, Colonel Denison, successfully wooing Liberals. He had shown extraordinary persuasiveness in inducing them not only to attend annual meetings in the Parliament Buildings at Ottawa, but also to share positions in the organization with Conservatives. His success points to the third reason for the league's influence, namely, his own skilful presidency. Indeed, the three leading figures in the league, Denison, Principal Grant, and Dr. (later Sir) George R. Parkin (1843–1921), constituted an influential trio, primarily because they symbolized current fears and resent-

[19]Hon. J. D. Edgar, *Canada and Its Capital* (Toronto, 1898), p. 204; and see Halifax *Chronicle*, Sept. 1, 1897, edit., "Welcome to Laurier."

[20]Cf. *Man. Free Press*, Jan. 1, 1898, edit., "Canadian products in England." The editorial explained that it was "only a few years ago that anything from this side of the Atlantic, even Canadian men and women, was American."

[21]*Ibid.*, June 14, 1897, "British Empire—One and Undivided," heading to three-column news story.

[22]Denison Papers, p. 3288, Aug. 6, 1897, G. R. Parkin to Denison: "Canada for the first time sets the tune for the Empire to dance to." Canadians also obtained other material advantages as a result of the Laurier visit. There was a general easing of the London money market for Canadian loans. Laurier Papers, pp. 17374–77, W. S. Fielding to Laurier, Oct. 23, 1897; and C.O. 42/860, p. 622, British Treasury to High Commissioner, July 23, 1898.

ments of the United States, but also because of their public prominence, forceful characters, and persuasive writings and speeches. Parkin stands somewhat apart from Denison and Grant; their chief concern was the maintenance of Canada, his the unity of the Empire, as the sub-title of his chief work indicates, *Imperial Federation: The Problem of National Unity* (1892). Of New Brunswick Loyalist stock, he had been a grammar school teacher and a paid propagandist for imperial unity in the late 1880's and early 1890's, especially in Britain, where Buckle of *The Times* declared that Parkin had "shifted the mind of England."[23] From 1895 to 1902 as principal of Upper Canada College, a preparatory school near Toronto, and as special correspondent of *The Times* in 1898, he exercised considerable influence in Canada. The prominence of such men in the league explains much of the attraction of its programme.

Two other elements of the imperial evangel seem to have attracted members: the first was an emotional faith in British statesmanship, institutions, and ideals; the second was a secularized missionary spirit, which imperial expansion at its best espoused. Imperialism was often associated with the idea of the "Redemption of Africa," by which was meant *inter alia* the end of slavery and the introduction of law and order. This aspect of imperialism may account for the considerable number of clergymen who paraded fashionable imperial views. Among the members of the league, for example, were a Roman Catholic archbishop and several Anglican bishops.

The league contained a representative and powerful cross-section of the socially prominent and the professional men of Canada; it was, in fact, a class organization of some of Canada's leading men, including educationists, journalists, and politicians.[24] Business men were less prominent in it than professional men. And it was implicitly an Anglo-Saxon organization, attracting few French Canadians.[25]

It was no accident that Toronto was the headquarters of the British Empire League. The city had had a stirring and anxious history: as York it had been burned by invading Americans in the War of 1812; it had been threatened by rebels during the Rebellion of 1837; it had been gripped by anxious tension during the Civil War and the Fenian raids. Like the rest of Canada it had repressed its fears and anti-Americanism

[23]Sir John Willison, *Sir George Parkin* (London, 1929), p. 85: his primarily imperial rather than Canadian interest is also shown by his appointment in 1902 as the first administrator of the Rhodes (Scholarship) Trust.

[24]Denison Papers, p. 3496, C. Freeman Murray, Sec., Headquarters Branch, to Denison, "Private," June 15, 1898; Denison prevailed on Lord Aberdeen, after his term as Governor General, to become a vice-president of the league.

[25]J. Israel Tarte seems to have been the only prominent French-Canadian member.

during the Venezuela incident, but its citizens had taken a leading part in 1896 in demanding rearmament of the Canadian militia and the repatriation of the old 100th Regiment.[26] The memory of historical anxieties, the city's exposure to Americanism, and the reaction of its citizens to the attractiveness of the American way of life seem to explain much of Toronto's ardour for imperial unity and its constant need to reassert its loyalty to Britain.[27] In such an atmosphere many other patriotic societies also flourished.[28] But Toronto was not simply important as a historical centre of loyalty; it was also Canada's second largest city, a city of great political, administrative, ideological, religious, and economic influence.[29]

A further reason for the league's influence was the support the Canadian and British branches gave to one another, though the Canadian branch had far more influence in Canada than the British in Britain, where the league was a partisan Conservative, and not a national, organization.[30] Until the Spanish-American War the two branches worked hand in glove; for example, the British branch joined the Canadian in support of the Navy League's request to the Admiralty to authorize establishment of a naval reserve in Canada; the Canadian branch supported the British demand for an insolvency law—a law which would permit British creditors equal rights with Canadian creditors to the assets of a Canadian bankrupt, which, because of proximity, the Canadian creditor obtained first. Neither branch achieved either of these goals during the period. After the Spanish-American War, British public opinion put the friendship of the United States first, whereas Canada stood adamantly on its rights against the United States. Conflicting national interests, reflected in the programmes and the influences on the two branches, began taking priority over imperial unity and wedged their hitherto mutual interests apart.[31]

[26]See below, pp. 185–87.

[27]See also John Foster Fraser, *Canada as It Is* (London, 1905), p. 40: Toronto's "patriotism is ever on the bubble." In contrast, note John Charlton's comment: "In my own constituency [North Norfolk, rural Ontario], the people are not influenced by the excitement which pervades great commercial, business and population centres" (*Debates*, Feb. 13, 1900, p. 366).

[28]For example, the United Empire Loyalists, the Irish Benevolent Association, St. Andrew's Society, and St. George's Society were founded or flourished during the period. The Sons of England, founded in 1874 in Toronto, reported in 1897 an increase in its membership of 2,100 largely native-born Canadians.

[29]Cf. the lack of encouragement Edward Blake's surmised aspirations to re-enter Canadian life received in the Toronto atmosphere of December 1897: Margaret .A Banks, "Edward Blake's Relations with Canada during his Irish Career 1892–1907," *Can. Hist. Rev.*, XXXV (March 1954), pp. 34–38.

[30]Denison Papers, p. 3438, Lord Rosebery to Denison, "Private," April 19, 1898.

[31]See *ibid.*, correspondence between Denison and C. Freeman Murray.

III

Although the British Empire League appeared to be an organization of considerable influence, its success was a passing phenomenon. We have already suggested the decisive limitation—favourable conditions. After "Black Week" when these conditions changed the league's influence waned. But even when an apparent success of the league in the period is analysed, it will be found to depend on powerful and interested external support. Whenever the league agitated as a pressure group with little support in the country the Government disregarded it. For instance, the Canadian Government did not yield to the demand for a naval reserve, because, in spite of British official and public pressure joining with that of the Canadian branches of the British Empire League and the Navy League, it lacked the support of a powerful interest in the country.[32] But whenever the league's agitation coincided with a considerable national, provincial, ideological, or material interest, the combination usually forced the Government to act.

We can see this principle illustrated in the provincial pressures on the federal government. These are always great but were particularly so during the early years of the Laurier régime. His espousal of provincial rights and invitations to three provincial premiers to join his cabinet necessitated yielding to provincial demands to a greater degree than usual. For example, he did not dare combat too vigorously the anti-American policies of the provinces of Ontario and British Columbia. He was afraid of losing power—a strange foreboding in view of the overwhelming number of Liberal by-election victories in his first term of office. He did not forget the unhappy consequences of the fiscal and ideological rigidities of the Liberal Government of Alexander Mackenzie. He was not prepared to sacrifice office for the sake of his basic aim of settlement with the United States, and he would yield to a powerful demand which he disapproved of rather than jeopardize his position. His immediate concern was the ebbing power of the Liberal Government of the province of Ontario.[33]

When Sir Oliver Mowat left the premiership of Ontario in 1896 his Government had been in power for 25 years. Already weakened in the election of 1894, its majority was reduced in 1898 to 11, in 1902 to 4, and in 1905 it expired in scandal. The lawyer A. S. Hardy and the teacher-lawyer G. W. Ross, who succeeded as premiers in 1896 and

[32]The evidence for the noisy agitation is scattered but some of it will be found in the Laurier Papers, Minto Papers, Hutton Papers, Denison Papers, and C.O. 42/850, 859, 866.

[33]The genuineness of his fears is shown by the decline of Liberalism in the federal election of 1900.

1899 respectively, were not the equals of the strong and able Mowat. But the conditions of Mowat's success had also changed. The "Presbyterian element" which formed the "backbone of the Liberal party in the Province of Ontario"[34] was weakening. The Presbyterian Church like other churches lost membership to the cults under the impact of biblical criticism and the growth of secularism.[35] Nor could Hardy or Ross pose as champions of provincial light against federal Conservative darkness; on the contrary the new Liberal Premier of Canada assumed that pose himself. With the federal political enemy gone, political partisanship declined[36] and the government's cohesion weakened. After 1896 the Ontario Government leaders, casting about for policies to maintain their fortunes, hit upon anti-Americanism and imperial unity.

We have seen that they had failed to persuade Colonel Denison to stand in the federal election of 1896. But they did not give up hope. In the following year Ross urged Laurier to support Denison because the "Liberal Party cannot afford to treat with indifference" the course of the British Empire League.[37] Laurier did so, and pursued an ostensibly pro-British policy and did not oppose a provincial anti-American policy. In fact, Willison described the policy of Laurier's administration during its first term as "peculiarly a Toronto and an Ontario Policy."[38]

Two anti-American questions agitated Ontario: alien labour and lumber. The Ontario Government could not constitutionally interfere with alien labour; it could with lumber. Accordingly in January 1898 it passed a law requiring all timber holders on Crown lands—75 per cent of whom were American—to manufacture saw logs into lumber before exportation to the United States.[39] This law was intended to force Congress to repeal the provisions on sawn lumber in the Dingley Tariff and satisfy an Ontario demand for retaliation. Although it failed to alter the tariff it brought satisfaction to the lumbermen of Ontario but embittered those of Michigan.

On the merits of the preference on British goods Ontario remained

[34]Laurier Papers, pp. 33514 and 33559–60, respectively, Laurier to Thomas Gibson, May 16, 1899, in reply to Gibson to Laurier, May 15, 1899.

[35]S. D. Clark, *Church and Sect in Canada* (Toronto, 1948), chap. VIII.

[36]Laurier Papers, p. 33395: "Old party issues are dying out," John Willison wrote to Laurier, "Private," May 8, 1899.

[37]*Ibid.*, p. 14005, "Personal," April 17, 1897.

[38]A. H. U. Colquhoun, *Press, Politics and People* (Toronto, 1935), p. 94, June 2, 1902.

[39]This so-called Ontario log export embargo law was legally known as "An Act respecting the Manufacture of Pine cut on the Crown Domain." The regulations were issued in December 1897, to take effect, after passage of the act, on April 30, 1898. For an account of the Canadian grievances concerning the lumber trade see speech of Senator C. A. Boulton, Canada, *Senate Debates*, March 10, 1898 (Conf. 7135, pp. 17–18, in Pauncefote to Salisbury, June 21, 1898).

cannily Canadian. When the retaliation implied in the preference had not modified the Dingley Tariff, Laurier's announcement that the preference was a "free gift" to Britain angered Ontario opinion[40] because the denunciation of the Belgian and German treaties was not regarded as the equivalent of the preference; it demanded a material *quid pro quo*. This was the issue in a Toronto by-election in the fall of 1897. Liberals apprehensively advised Laurier to emphasize Canada's new fiscal freedom and warned him not to count on Britain's granting Canada a preference because of free trade.[41] Accordingly Laurier informed Willison of Chamberlain's remark on the latter issue: Britain might agree to Empire free trade—which Canada would reject—but never to a preference on food. After some hesitation Willison published Chamberlain's opinion, which was confirmed in the British Parliament and contributed to the election of the Liberal candidate, George H. Bertram.[42]

In spite of unmistakable indications of British devotion to free trade and opposition to granting a preference to the colonies many Canadians, prompted by the tariff hostility of Americans, persisted in the belief that Britain would soon yield to colonial importunities. Thus George W. Ross, Minister of Education and vice-president of the "European Exporter's Association" in Toronto, complained to Laurier that the vagaries of the United States tariff made the Canadian export market unstable, and advocated exploitation of the British market.[43] On becoming a vice-president of the British Empire League (a tribute to Denison's persuasiveness and the league's influence), Ross made an important address on Canadian tariff relations proposing that trade be used to strengthen Canada's unity with Britain. He based this proposal on the expectation that Britain to strengthen itself would grant a preference to the colonies—an expectation quite belied by the facts. On the other hand he considered reciprocity with the United States to be dangerous because of past irritations and the feeling that Canadian dependence would "utterly mar the true spirit of Canadian nationality."[44]

[40]Laurier Papers, p. 16652, George H. Bertram to Laurier, Sept. 24, 1897; Joseph Pope deplored Laurier's "fatuous policy," because Chamberlain was "on the way to agreeing to a system of preferential trade" (Pope Papers, Diaries Private and Personal, Aug. 20, 1897).

[41]Laurier Papers, p. 16235, Denison to Laurier, Sept. 6, 1897; Denison Papers, p. 3296, Denison to Mulock, Sept. 11, 1897, and reply, p. 3298, Sept. 14, 1897.

[42]Sir John Willison, *Reminiscences Political and Personal* (Toronto, 1919), pp. 300–1; for a similar opinion of Chamberlain in 1896, see report of the meeting of the "Chambers of Commerce of the Empire" in London, inc. in R. W. Scott to Laurier, Oct. 4, 1897 (Laurier Papers, pp. 16912–15).

[43]Laurier Papers, pp. 17914–15, Nov. 13, 1897.

[44]"Preferential Trade with Great Britain and Reciprocity with the United States," Dec. 4, 1897 (Toronto, 1897), p. 11. Note also that Ross as Minister of

The Canadian Government's economic policy was subject to pressures not only from the provinces and the United States, but also from Britain. In the winter of 1898 Chamberlain intervened with Canada on behalf of the British West Indies. A royal commission on the economic state of the islands—the "Empire's darkest slum"[45]—had unanimously diagnosed the cause of their difficulties to be the inability of West Indian cane sugars to compete with bounty-fed European beet sugars, but had divided on the minority member's remedy of countervailing duties on bounty-fed sugars entering Britain. British free trade made this remedy impossible but perhaps Canada might be persuaded or induced to help out the islands.[46] Opportunity came early in 1898 when Canada offered to extend its preference to Britain and to colonies offering reciprocal advantages. On grounds of Canada's geographic proximity and of imperial cohesion, Chamberlain raised the question of including the British West Indies, hinting at an offer of a special steamer service between Canada and the islands. Canada's interest was tepid: the islands offered no economic equivalent to Canada's market. Furthermore Chamberlain must have known of the steamer services already existing. Nevertheless he next disclosed the existence of trade negotiations between the United States and the islands, which were eventually to fall through, but held out the prospect of a steamship subsidy. The Canadian Government was apprehensive, and promised a preference, but hoped that any prospective treaty would not harm Canada, a hope that Chamberlain satisfied.[47] Accordingly in April 1898 Canada granted not only the general preference to the British West Indies but also a special one on its sugars, an act of goodwill which was justified by the Minister of Finance on grounds of proximity, imperial cohesion, and Canada's possession of

---

Education introduced the celebration of Empire Day in 1898; see W. Sanford Evans, "Empire Day: A Detailed History of Its Origin and Inception," *Can. Mag.*, XIII (July 1899), pp. 274–79.

[45]The phrase is from Julian Amery, *The Life of Joseph Chamberlain* (London, 1951), IV, p. 234; for a sketch of the condition of the islands and Chamberlain's measures, see *ibid.*, chap. LXXXIV, "The West Indies and the Sugar War," and George Carrington, "Our West Indian Colonies," *Proceedings of the Royal Colonial Institute*, XXIX (1897–98), pp. 171–203. The Report is in *Parl. Pap.*, 1898, L (C. 8655).

[46]In 1883 a steamship line between Canada and the British West Indies was abandoned, but two steamship lines plied between them in the 1890's. See also C.O. 42/862, pp. 217–29, pamphlet, "Canada's Interests in the West India Islands issued by the Canadian Pacific Railway Co. 1897," and *ibid.*, pp. 233–47, Colonial Office report by Sydney Oliver, "Trade between the West Indies and Canada," April 25, 1898.

[47]C.O. 42/856, pp. 184–85, 242–43, 258–59, paraphrase cables between Aberdeen and Chamberlain from Feb. 10 to Feb. 25, 1898.

"some Imperial responsibilities" requiring a willingness "to lend a helping hand to those colonies."[48] In spite of great pressure Canada refused to join in granting a subsidy for another steamship line; a further preference to the British West Indies in 1900 was the most that would be conceded.[49]

IV

The foregoing analysis shows the complexity of the popular idea of imperial unity. It did not include the surrender of powers gained under responsible government to a super-government ruling the British Empire from London. In 1896 when John Charlton expressed this fear no one in Parliament bothered to answer him. Sir Wilfrid Laurier was apparently the only important political leader who tried to effect some kind of imperial constitutional change, though his position was consistent with his view of 1892: Canada's relations with Britain "must become either closer or looser."[50] In 1897 English Canadians obviously were coming closer to Britain, and he interpreted that affinity as a desire for a closer constitutional relationship. In the course of an inquiry from Denison on the possibility of Britain's adoption of a preference he volunteered the opinion that Britain would never adopt a preference "until the colonies are represented in the Imperial Parliament."[51] The reply from the most renowned Canadian imperialist must have surprised Laurier:

You say the battle cannot be won until the colonies are represented in the Imperial Parliament, and ask me whether I dissent from this. I hope we will win before this happens, but you have raised an important question, and you may be surprised at my saying that I think it would be well not to say much on that topic at present. You know I have been a most active worker for Imperial Federation for the last ten years in this country[.] I have addressed any number of large meetings, and have discussed the question everywhere. I find a general feeling even among the strongest Imperial Unity men against representation in the Imp¹ Parliament. The same feeling exists in Australia. We left the word Federation out of the title of our re-organized League in deference to that opinion in the Australasian Colonies. The fear seemed to be that the representation of each colony would be so small at present, that each would be controlled to [sic] much by the whole. The idea of Conferences agreeing to certain points in the meantime, has however been

[48]*Debates*, April 5, 1898, p. 3150.
[49]E. A. Benians, Sir James Butler, and C. E. Carrington, eds., *The Cambridge History of the British Empire*, III (Cambridge, 1959), p. 395.
[50]Cited in Skelton, *Laurier*, I, p. 364.
[51]Denison Papers, p. 3329, "Private," Dec. 24, 1897.

very popular because whatever would be done, would be done by mutual consent, and therefore not strain the bond of union.[52]

Laurier's puzzling pursuit of imperial constitutional reform had no popular support. In popular, or at least newspaper, understanding, imperial unity meant the orientation of Canadian policies and interests towards Britain rather than the United States. For example, the *Manitoba Free Press* described "Imperial defence" as another name for "Imperial Federation."[53] In 1897 it wrote that if Britain responded to Canadian preference it would constitute an important step towards imperial federation. In the next year Principal Grant envisaged a common postal rate for the whole Empire as "the actual federation of the Empire, so far as postal matters are concerned."[54]

Although the national entities of Britain and Canada remained constitutionally the same as before, the application of the phrase "Imperial unity" to the fulfilment of essentially national policies possessed political advantages. The erstwhile selfish nationalist could now pose as an unselfish Imperial Federationist—especially a Canadian—and with clear conscience could interfere in the essentially national concerns of the other state. For example, at the annual meeting of the Toronto Branch of the British Empire League in 1898, G. W. Ross described such interference: "I take the ground that we have just as much right to discuss imperial questions here as Englishmen have on the floor of Parliament." Citing a recently published article of Colonel Denison, he maintained that advo-

---

[52]Laurier Papers, pp. 19482–83, Jan. 1, 1898. Denison added: "Understand I myself would consent to an Imperial Parliament, although I think it would be premature at present, and that an Imperial Council would be better" (pp. 19483–84). How is Laurier's imperial flirtation to be explained? His official biographer suggests that "Laurier's formulas were never very formal" at best, and that in his first year in office, and during the Jubilee excitement, he often used words which "made the supporters of imperial federation count him a convert." But the responsibilities of office and the experiences of the South African crisis changed these views, if they had ever been very seriously held, and the "federation tack" was abandoned (Skelton, *Laurier* II, pp. 289–91). One could add to Skelton's explanation the fact that during the Diamond Jubilee he was courting English opinion to get the Belgian and German treaties denounced. But the puzzle remains to this writer. If Laurier's imperial council had been agreed upon at the Colonial Conference of 1897, an imperial institution would have been set up which no important Canadian would have approved. The writer therefore suggests that part of the explanation may also lie in Laurier's belief in Austinian theories of sovereignty and a penchant for a person of French culture to interpret English phrases like "imperial federation" literally.

[53]"Imperial Federation," March 28, 1896, edit.; cf. "Comrades in Arms," April 8, 1897, edit., on interchange of British and Canadian troops in Canada.

[54]"Current Events" by "G," *Queen's Quarterly*, V (April 1898), p. 329.

cacy of Britain's granting an imperial preference was not really a " 'question of trade, it is a question of the unity, of the consolidation of the empire.' "[55]

Consequently imperial unity often seems little more than Canadian nationalism writ large. As Principal Grant put it in 1898: "We are Canadian, and in order to be Canadian we must be British."[56] Few other Canadians would have made such a statement, having been soured by memories of the insensitivity of Little Englandism and the might-have-beens of Canadian history. On the contrary, however much they were angered at United States interference in Canada, Canadians enjoyed countless individual friendships with Americans, admired many of their ideals and practices, and made their country a model. Accordingly a repressed liking for much that was American and a repressed dislike for much that was British gave imperial unity a forced and artificial quality. But imperial unity was more than a mask for Canadian nationalism: it comprehended loyalty to British ideals and institutions and derived part of its strength from the potency of Anglo-Saxon racism and social Darwinism. So long as the essential weakness of British power in North America was not further exposed, the movement for imperial unity continued to grow in strength, and coloured the decisions of the Canadian Government and people at a time of crisis.

[55]*Globe*, April 15, 1898.
[56]"Current Events" by "G," *Queen's Quarterly*, V, p. 328.

6. Militia Reform, 1896-1898

THE VENEZUELA AFFAIR had demonstrated Canada's need for aid from Britain and for the reform of the militia. Canada's reaffirmation of its will to remain within the British Empire and Britain's gratified response and intention to support Canada implied a reciprocal obligation on Canada's part to defend Britain.[1] In rearming and reforming the militia Canada was simply accepting her defence obligations under responsible government.

But militia reform was complicated by several factors. Few Canadians, probably, wanted a really thorough military reform; they regarded it as a dangerous provocation of the United States. Reluctance to engage in whole-hearted defence measures contravened Canada's tacit defence alliance with Britain, the existence of which the crisis had disclosed. But in the capacity of military ally Britain could insist on military reform and, because she still enjoyed some diplomatic and military controls over Canada's defence, could make it difficult for Canada to resist. On the other hand, the colonial inferiority implied in those controls provoked nationalistic opposition to their exercise; they were regarded not as inherent in an alliance but as requests from a superior. Nevertheless the new Liberal Government, in spite of its principal aim of a general settlement with the United States, was committed to a modest military reform that contrasted with the virtual indifference of its predecessors.

I

The Minister chiefly responsible for militia reform was Dr. (later Sir) Frederick Borden (1847-1917), cousin of Sir Robert Borden. Having

---

[1]Cf. remark of Lieut.-Col. Sir George S. Clarke, former secretary of the Colonial Defence Committee: ". . . the defence of her long frontier cannot be left to Canada unaided, and so long as it is her free wish to remain a member of the Empire, she must be and she will be supported with the whole force at our disposal. To state this proposition is, of course, to proclaim the reciprocal obligations of the Dominion." "National Defence," paper read at the Royal Colonial Institute, Feb. 11, 1896, *Proceedings*, XXVII (1895–96), p. 137.

served for thirty years as a medical officer in the militia he knew its deficiencies. Interested largely in the details of administration rather than in larger policy, he was not a strong administrator who could withstand the pressures of able general officers commanding, the cabinet, or other interests. Improvements under him seem due less to his own administration than to pressure from general officers or the public. Nor was he a person of originality or intellect, for he mouthed the political commonplaces of the day. He was popular with militia officers, possibly because he was a "joyous old boy and something of a scamp," possessing "other qualities which for the sake of delicacy are usually called human."[2] Yet he enjoyed advantages over his predecessors: he was to have fifteen years in office, at a time of prosperity and of public and militia interest in defence.[3]

In the first years of his administration, Borden carried out a number of reforms. He revived annual training camps. He enforced the long-flouted rules of tenure: by April 1899 he had retired 52 of the 76 officers commanding in July 1897,[4] and thus had begun to "liberalize" what often were Conservative political machines. He removed the old and inefficient Major-General D. R. Cameron, son-in-law of Sir Charles Tupper, as Commandant of the Royal Military College, and replaced him by the able Colonel (afterwards Sir) Gerald Kitson (1857–1950). He also bore some responsibility for the setting up of provisional schools of instruction and of an officers' reserve, the appointment of the Committee on Canadian Defence, the interchange of Canadian and Imperial forces in Canada, and the dispatch of the Yukon Field Force.

The execution and administration of these measures, many of which were the uncompleted plans of previous general officers commanding, seem to have been the responsibility of the able and tactful quartermaster-general, Colonel P. H. N. Lake,[5] rather than of the easy-going General Officer Commanding, W. J. Gascoigne. Trusted by a previous Conservative Government, Lake was also charged by the Liberal Government with planning, purchasing, and shipping supplies to the Klon-

[2]Paul Bilkey, *Persons, Papers and Things* (Toronto, 1940), p. 101; see also Minto Papers, vol. 21, p. 174.

[3]Younger Canadian officers induced newspapers to take regular notice of the militia; see, for example, Hutton Papers, p. 399, Capt. Charles F. Winter to Hutton, "Personal and official," Sept. 7, 1898, and Public Archives of Ontario, Queen's Own Rifles Scrap Book 1897–1899.

[4]For a list of all lieutenant-colonels commanding, their regiments, ages, and length of command in July 1897, see *Debates*, April 27, 1899, pp. 2183–84.

[5]Probably his tactfulness was in part due to the fact that his mother was a Canadian. For an account of his military career, see Capt. J. F. Cummins, "Lieutenant-General Sir Percy Lake and Some Chapters of Canadian and Indian Military History," *Can. Def. Quart.*, III (April 1926), pp. 244–56.

dike for the Yukon Field Force. Apparently whenever Dr. Borden desired a professional opinion upon an important military matter he would by-pass Gascoigne and consult Lake. Lake was appointed to the Committee on Canadian Defence, but he did not succeed to Gascoigne's position, though persistent efforts were made to that end.[6] He was, however, appointed in 1904 as the first Chief of the Canadian General Staff.

His superior officer, Gascoigne, who succeeded the driving Herbert as General Officer Commanding, was plunged into political and military crises soon after his arrival in October 1895. For nine months he had to accommodate himself to four successive ministers of militia amidst the political intrigues of a dying administration, and for much of that time he was concerned with preparing plans for the defence of Canada. Perhaps these preoccupations at Ottawa habituated him to make infrequent inspections, a subject of criticism later. Nevertheless he early saw the need for authority to enforce discipline and requested a clearer definition of his powers in that regard. It is almost certain that the Minister made no reply to his request.[7] Anticipating a period of more stable and sympathetic interest from his fourth and Liberal Minister of Militia, Gascoigne now undertook to discipline officers. But he was frequently confronted with ministerial reversals of discipline, and in 1898 he resigned because of inadequate pay and probably also to force the Minister to support him in the removal of a colonel.[8] On the other hand, the British authorities, aware of the difficulties confronting a general officer commanding in Canada, by making Gascoigne commander at Hong Kong gave Canada an implied rebuke.[9]

II

While Borden's early activities as Minister suggested a little improvement, to the War Office and the British Government the condition of

[6]See below, pp. 137–38.
[7]D.M. 14457, memorandum of G.O.C. to Min. of Mil., Jan. 14, 1896. It is true that the Minister left office on the next day, but the policy of all ministers was to leave the powers of the general officer commanding on discipline indefinite.
[8]C.O. 42/865, p. 38, W.O. to C.O., Feb. 18, 1898; Public Archives of Ontario, Edward Blake Collection, Martin J. Griffin, Parliamentary Librarian, Ottawa, to Edward Blake, May 18, 1898; D.M. 16881. Cf. Gascoigne's support of the Minister: "Gen. Herbert was a very able man and had a free hand given to him by the Minister, and went on the principle that he could do a great deal, perhaps, off his own bat. I took the other view and in every case I have gone hand in hand with the Minister." Evidence before Public Accounts Committee re Domville and Barnes, April–June 1898, *Journals of the House of Commons, Canada*, 1898, XXXIII, app. 2D, p. 47. Cf. *Can. Sess. Pap.* (no. 105), 1898.
[9]See G 3, vol. 32, Chamberlain to Aberdeen, "Confidential," April 1, 1898: ". . . in view of the conspicuous success . . . I am sure your Ministers will agree" to allow General Gascoigne to remain until the expiry of his term.

the Canadian defence system was still one of incompetence and danger: Canada could not adequately defend itself, and the loss of Canada would be a catastrophe to imperial power. On the other hand British attitudes to the United States were very like those of Canada: war with the United States was unthinkable. Accordingly amid the crises of the period 1896–99 Britain's chief political interest in improved Canadian defence, apart from the unthinkable military contingency, was to accustom Canada to the possibility of participation in an imperial war.

The members of the new Salisbury administration were very sensitive to Britain's defensive needs,[10] and there gradually came into key War Office positions men of like sensitivity. Many of these political and military leaders enjoyed direct experience or close knowledge of defence conditions in Canada. The key figure of the administration—Joseph Chamberlain—knew the United States through his third wife and was acquainted with Canada through service on a fishery commission in 1887 and through friendship with Sir Charles Tupper and Lord Strathcona. The Secretary of War, Lord Lansdowne, had been Governor General of Canada in the 1880's; the new Commander-in-Chief, Lord Wolseley, had served in Canada in the 1860's and commanded the Red River expedition, on which the Adjutant-General, Sir Redvers Buller, had accompanied him. Major-General Sir John Ardagh, the head of the Intelligence Division, was a personal friend of Lord Lansdowne and a relative of Senator (later Sir) James R. Gowan (1815–1909), a prominent Canadian Conservative, with whom he was in intimate correspondence. This formidable team of associates exercised continual pressure for

---

[10]Sir Michael Hicks-Beach, Chancellor of the Exchequer, pooh-poohed Canada's eagerness to supply grain for a much discussed scheme to build granaries to guard against Britain's starvation in war (*Globe*, Jan. 20, 1898): Canada might better contribute to Britain's naval defence. Colonel Denison, echoing the complaint of Hicks-Beach, bore Tupper's attack, which he reported to Hicks-Beach. The latter replied forthrightly in a private letter. He had said that Canada had done nothing, not for imperial peace, but for the defence of her merchant marine, a fact that had nothing to do with the construction of the Canadian Pacific Railway or the maintenance of a militia. "And I absolutely decline to recognize" a British undertaking of 1865 "to do for all time, whatever the strength & growth of Canada might be, work which, as a 'nation,' she ought to do for herself. This is not the first time which it has seemed to me that Sir C. Tupper's view of the relations between the United Kingdom & Canada practically amounts to this—that Canada should 'take' as much as she can get, & 'give' as little as possible in return. That is a natural relation between the mother country & a young and weak Colony.—But when such a Colony has grown up, the Imperial connection can only be permanently maintained on the basis of equal contribution to the common good." Denison Papers, pp. 3427–28, "Private," March 24, 1898; see also other letters between Denison and Hicks-Beach, *ibid.*, pp. 3365–66, 3378–81, 3421; and *ibid.*, p. 3419, Lord Rosebery to Denison, "Private," March 11, 1898.

the reform of the Canadian defence system and the stimulation of closer military co-operation with Britain.

The many-pronged efforts to reform Canada's defences (in spite of the fact that Imperial policy seems occasionally to have been working at cross purposes) suggests co-ordination of a high order. In the general political sense Chamberlain appears to have been the co-ordinator, and to have supported most War Office proposals for reform. His strength lay, not in professional military matters, or even in military diplomacy, about which he probably knew little,[11] but in his recognition of the political use to which military reform might be put. On routine military matters he obtained advice from the Secretary of the Colonial Defence Committee, and more formal opinions from the committee itself and the Intelligence Division of the War Office. The division indeed undertook the task of looking after the problem of colonial defence forces.[12]

With his genius for organization and direction Chamberlain exploited every channel of influence: his own position and his powers of persuasion; the reinvigorated Colonial Defence Committee; the Committee on Canadian Defence set up in 1898; and other British officials, the chief of which were the new Governor General, Lord Minto, and the new General Officer Commanding, Colonel E. T. H. Hutton.

Chamberlain's direct personal interest ranged from apparent military minutiae to fundamental questions of imperial defence. On the one hand he intervened sympathetically against a War Office ruling on behalf of an over-age Canadian applying for a cadetship; on the other hand, he successfully enlisted Canadian aid in the South African War. In April 1897, at the request of the War Office and with the concurrence of the Colonial Office and Admiralty, he transmitted some correspondence sketching a plan for the transport of torpedo boats ($150' \times 15' \times 14'$) by rail in three or four days, depending on the distance, from the lower St. Lawrence River at Quebec to the Upper Lakes.[13] He drew the attention

[11]See Henry Spenser Wilkinson, *Thirty-Five Years 1874–1909* (London, 1933), pp. 227–28, and the Earl of Ronaldshay, *The Life of Lord Curzon* (New York, 1928), III, pp. 22–23.

[12]Cd.1790, qq. 537, 540–41; see also Countess of Malmesbury, *The Life of Sir John Ardagh* (London, 1909), pp. 366–68.

[13]Laurier Papers, p. 13713, Chamberlain to Aberdeen, "Secret," April 5, 1897. The main part of the correspondence (*ibid.*, pp. 13714–24, Oct. 1896–March 1897 between Capt. A. H. Lee and Sir William Van Horne) contained technical descriptions and drawings of the flat cars which would be used, and suggested that they could be constructed in five days by the Canadian Pacific Railway. The Committee on Canadian Defence observed that, while such a boat would be small (45 tons), its moral effect would be great (*Report No. II*, "Secret," p. 57). The reference to the cadetship may be found in G 1, vol. 312, pp. 63–65, inc. in C.O. to Canada, Sept. 23, 1896.

of the Canadian Government to Canadians who advocated measures that might bind Canada closer to Britain: for example, the repatriation of the 100th Regiment,[14] and the objections of Canadian petitioners to a proposal for a monument in Quebec City in honour of the American General Montgomery who fell in an attack on that city in 1775. He was thus to some degree representing and encouraging imperial opinions in Canada, which the Canadian Government often tried to ignore.

Of far more importance in creating, if not a common imperial military policy, at least a common military attitude, was Chamberlain's part in the Colonial Conference of 1897. Known for his support of colonial needs and devoid of the contemptuous Little-England view of colonies, Chamberlain in his introductory speech was able bluntly to remind his audience of colonial military deficiencies. He hinted that more of the tremendous cost of the British Navy should be borne by the colonies. Flatly denying the Canadian contention that British fleets were maintained "even mainly, for the benefit of the United Kingdom," he declared that most wars of the nineteenth century "had at the bottom a colonial interest." He warned Canada of the power of the United States, Japan, and Russia. Without Britain's "great military and naval power," Canada would be "to a great extent, a dependent country." Australia and South Africa could similarly be threatened. Existing colonial naval contributions were "absolutely trifling," though Britain did recognize the "Colonies as still children. . . ." Nevertheless, Britain would be glad to establish the principles of contribution. He warned of disorganized colonial defences, of the need for defence plans and for uniformity of military preparation. He also urged consideration of the possibility of the interchange of British and colonial forces.[15]

The formal military results of the conference must have disappointed Chamberlain; the informal results, however, were valuable. The conference heard from the Secretary of the Colonial Defence Committee the steps that should be taken in emergencies. It consented to submit local defence plans to the committee for comment.[16] It agreed that defence preparations required better training of officers, who might be assimilated, if necessary, into any imperial force. These proposals were almost a blueprint of many of the reforms undertaken by Canada in the next two years.

14See below, pp. 185–86.
15Part of opening speech, June 24, 1897, in Arthur Berriedale Keith, ed., *Selected Speeches and Documents on British Colonial Policy 1763–1917* (London, 1918), II, pp. 216–23.
16Regulation 167 of Queen's Regulation and Orders for the Army 1898 and J. F. Cummins, MS hist., "The Organization and Development of the Canadian Militia" (Historical Section, Can. Gen. Staff, 1932–36), pp. 234–35.

III

The first Colonial Defence Committee, composed of departmental representatives from the Admiralty and the War and Colonial offices, was set up in response to the colonial clamour for defence during the Russian panic of 1878.[17] When the next Russian panic occurred in 1885, the committee was revived and put on a permanent footing.[18] It now had a secretary whose duty was to study colonial defence problems, gather accurate information, and make recommendations for discussion by the committee. Upon approval a memorandum was printed and sent to the persons concerned. In 1886 its energetic secretary, Major G. S. Clarke (later Lord Sydenham of Combe), wrote a comprehensive memorandum on "Local Preparations to be made in anticipation of War,"[19] recommending the establishment of a local standing committee to organize "the resources of the Colony" and prepare a defence scheme, subject to Colonial Office annual approval and advice. These recommendations were carried out in all the colonies with the conspicuous exception of Canada, and code words were settled upon, for preparation and anticipation of war.

In the early 1890's the committee fell into the doldrums partly because its secretary trespassed on government policy,[20] but with the advent of Chamberlain it underwent a revival and became an important instrument of his policy.[21] To educate opinion in the colonies and in Britain it was called upon to draw up a memorandum, "Principles of

[17]D. Schurman, "Imperial Defence, 1868–1887" (doctoral dissertation, Cambridge, 1955), pp. 96–135. See also Donald C. Gordon, "The Colonial Defence Committee and Imperial Collaboration: 1885–1904," *Pol. Sci. Quart.*, LXXVII (Dec. 1962), pp. 526–45, and N. H. Gibbs, *The Origins of Imperial Defence* (Oxford, 1955).

[18]Schurman, pp. 232–35.

[19]This memorandum, no. 19M, Nov. 1, 1886, is in C.O., "Circular Secret," Nov. 19, 1886 (G 21, no. 165, Additional). It began with general remarks and continued with specific suggestions on telegraph cables, submarine mines, torpedo boats, etc., lights, buoys, and beacons, lookout stations and boat patrols, bombardment, coal, food, specie, personnel, armament, intrenchments, management of civil population, and local defence committees.

[20]Clarke met with officials of four departments of state, received valuable information from the Colonial Office, and enjoyed great "opportunities of trying to inculcate the broad principles at which I had arrived." Sydenham of Combe, *My Working Life* (London, 1927) p. 75.

[21]Cf. Conf. 7135, p. 62, Intelligence Division to F.O., Sept. 10, 1898, in which Sir John Ardagh suggested that a dispatch of Lord Herschell's "should be referred to the Colonial Defence Committee for report"; if this suggestion were approved "it would be convenient if the Colonial Office were requested to instruct the Committee to consider the despatch." This seems to imply that the Colonial Office could use the Colonial Defence Committee to bring matters the Colonial Office thought important before the Foreign Office, the War Office, and the Admiralty.

Colonial Defence," a subject which had hitherto been looked at piece-meal. The memorandum attacked suggestions for protecting places "that have no importance in the general strategic scheme of the Empire," a protection that was unnecessary because of the Admiralty's duty to maintain the supremacy of the sea. Well-trained troops, whose value depended on numbers and training, were to be preferred to unnecessarily elaborate fortifications. It was hoped that Canada would look after its own defences, that every colony would draw up a defence scheme, and that in time the colonies might assist the mother country materially. Chamberlain's accompanying letter expressed the hope that copies of the memorandum would circulate widely among the officials concerned.[22] This memorandum, modified slightly, but substantially the same, was sent again a year later.

Maintaining a general oversight over colonial defence, the committee commented freely on the state of Canadian defence, supporting recommendations for efficiency but avoiding those requiring expenditure. The objectivity of these memoranda and their sympathetic understanding of basic Canadian assumptions doubtless explain Lieutenant-Colonel J. F. Cummins' opinion that they had a "good deal of influence."[23] The committee commented on the report of the Department of Militia for 1896, noting that Canada had taken no action on an earlier recommendation for a defence committee and departmental services. It criticized militia expenditure of 1896 on *matériel* rather than on improved personnel. Although admitting a basic Canadian contention in its recognition of the "paramount importance to Canada of carrying out . . . costly public works," the committee looked to "better organization [rather] than to increased expenditure" for military improvements.[24] It made milder criticisms of the 1897 report and commended the interchange of units of the Permanent Force and British Regulars.[25]

A second type of memorandum concerned specific defence problems, some of which arose out of the Venezuela affair. At the end of 1896 the

[22]G 21, no. 165, Additional, "Confidential," no. 57M, May 29, 1896, in C.O., "Circular Secret," July 6, 1896. Except for technical details, the relevant sections will be found in Henri Bourassa, *Que devons-nous à l'Angleterre?* (Montreal, 1915), pp. 365–68. In his speech of Dec. 3, 1896, the Duke of Devonshire, Chairman of the Cabinet Committee on Defence, quoted extensively from this document.
[23]"Organization and Development of the Canadian Militia," p. 235.
[24]G 21, no. 165, Additional, "Secret," 165R, Dec. 31, 1896, inc. in C.O., "Circular Secret," July 31, 1897.
[25]*Ibid.*, "Secret," 190R, June 30, 1898, inc. in C.O., "Secret," Aug. 27, 1898. The War Office also made adverse criticisms: W.O. to C.O., "Secret," July 8, 1898, inc. in Chamberlain to Aberdeen, "Secret," July 14, 1898 (G 3, vol. 32).

War Office inquired about how best to spend £20,000 on artillery for the defence of Quebec, Montreal, and Kingston to give those cities a "chance . . . to hold out against an attack from the United States until reinforcements could arrive from England."[26] The committee replied that all the money should be spent on Montreal and that the War Office should be asked to present 9″ guns from Halifax for its defence, provided Canada find funds for the mountings. Even though the War Office offered further inducements, Canada made no move to accept the guns, which were apparently those requested by Gascoigne during the Venezuela crisis.

The committee also recommended avoidance of military dependence on the United States by careful consideration of "Canal Communication to the Great Lakes in relation to War." The committee concurred in an opinion reported in a committee of the House of Representatives in February 1896, that the superiority of the American merchant marine in the Great Lakes conferred a great advantage on the United States. This superiority could be minimized if Canada encouraged competition in the Great Lakes carrying trade and vigorously completed the deepening of the St. Lawrence River. But the canal would require "vigilant defence" to permit passage of Royal Naval vessels to Lake Ontario on the outbreak of war. On the other hand, a "Georgian Bay–Ottawa–Montreal Canal" would seem commercially profitable, in spite of rail and canal competition, and bestow great military advantages, especially in permitting a "disconcerting" counter attack during wartime. The Civil War had demonstrated that the "Northern States showed themselves especially sensitive on this point"; hence "it would be well to take avantage of their peculiar constitution [presumably concerning the distribution of powers] and endeavour to set the interests of a State against the interest of the commonwealth, and a threat against Chicago might accomplish this." If the committee's opinion on commercial prospects should prove true on "detailed examination," nothing should stand in the way of the construction of the canal because North America's "conformation," by making the Great Lakes accessible to the ocean, gave Canada "enormous advantages over the United States."[27] In the 1898 session of Parliament, the Ottawa supporters of the Montreal, Ottawa and Georgian Bay Canal Company requested a Canadian Government guarantee of 2 per cent on a $17,000,000 loan for the building of the

[26]G 21, no. 165, Additional, "Secret," 132M, March 17, 1898, inc. in C.O., "Circular Secret," May 5, 1898.

[27]*Ibid.*, "Secret," 128M, March 17, 1898, inc. in C.O. "Circular Secret," April 5, 1898. The U.S. committee report, no. 423, is in 54th Cong., 1st Sess. (Ser. no. 3458), Feb. 18, 1896.

canal. All kinds of arguments were advanced to justify the scheme, economic, historical, national, imperial, and strategic. The debate ended with the Premier's casting doubt on its predicted cost and commercial possibilities.[28] Although the possibility of a Georgian Bay–Ottawa River canal continued to figure in War Office thinking, the Canadian Government gave the idea no encouragement.

Perhaps the most influential of the committee's memoranda induced the British Government to make Esquimalt virtually an Imperial base, a step which Canada had long advocated. Concerning Canada's responsibility for the defence of Esquimalt under the 1893 agreement, which was about to terminate, the committee said the problem resolved itself into Canada's ability either to defend the base from an attack by one or two cruisers or to secure it against full-scale attack.[29] The Secretary of War agreed with the analysis and commented that it was preferable to spend money on the enlargement of the British Navy rather than provide the enormous sum required to secure Esquimalt against a possible United States attack; he therefore suggested the continuance of the lesser scale of defence under the 1893 agreement. Although the financial arrangements of that agreement had been adhered to, divided defence responsibilities between the Admiralty, the Dominion Government, and the War Office would result in "scandalous confusion" in wartime. Therefore he proposed that Canada should bear responsibility for the defence of Esquimalt under the command of an able Imperial officer borrowed for the purpose. Although he conceded that Britain should make further money contributions, yet he recalled that Britain would make no contribution for the defence of the Australian colonies.[30] The Admiralty, beyond reminding Chamberlain that Esquimalt was necessary for the defence of British Columbia, supported the views of the War Office.[31]

Chamberlain agreed with Lansdowne's analysis of the defence of Esquimalt but objected to the comparison with Australian colonies: Canada had to defend a long border. Furthermore, the base, as a coaling station, was as much Imperial as colonial, and Canada, if laden with the full costs, might abandon Esquimalt.[32] By March 1898 the Admiralty was more sympathetic to Canada's difficulties. It concurred in Chamber-

---

[28]*Debates*, May 31, 1898, pp. 6466–6510; also Laurier Papers, pp. 23576–82, evidence before the Canadian Senate, and C.O. 42/868, pp. 386–90. The proposal came up again in 1899 but nothing essentially new was added.

[29]For the 1893 agreement see above, p. 20; two memoranda, "Secret," 104M, and "Secret," 79M, are mentioned in C.O. 42/859, p. 410, Conf. C.O. Print.

[30]*Ibid.*, pp. 409–11, W.O. to C.O., "Secret," Oct. 29, 1897.

[31]*Ibid.*, p. 411, "Secret," Oct. 12, 1897.

[32]*Ibid.*, p. 412, C.O. to Admiralty and W.O., "Secret," Dec. 15, 1897.

lain's views, observing that with the value of British Columbia being enhanced by the discovery of gold, boundary disputes and other causes might "furnish the United States with a pretext for attempting to separate" British Columbia from the rest of Canada.

The upshot was a departmental conference in November 1898 among Colonial Office, War Office, Admiralty, and Treasury officials on the defence of the base. Among the reasons given for the inadequacy of the 1893 agreement was the presence in eastern Canada of the Permanent Battery; it was intended to be shipped to Esquimalt on the outbreak of war, but there were the dangers that the railway line would be cut in wartime and that local spirit would prohibit the government's removal of the battery westwards. In addition, Esquimalt was insufficiently garrisoned, the organization of the Permanent Force was deficient and too costly, and existing arrangements for the defence of the base were chaotic. The conference doubted Canada's ability properly to defend the base and noted that a unit of the Canadian Permanent Force would cost more than an equivalent Imperial force. It therefore decided that (1) the Imperial Government should assume full responsibility under War Office direction for a peacetime garrison of 322 Regulars and 623 local militia, (2) in view of Canada's special responsibilities for the protection of its land frontiers, it should pay £21,000 for half the annual cost of the Imperial garrison, £12,500 for half the prime cost of barrack accommodation, and £9,345 for the whole cost of the local militia; (3) "as a set off against the foregoing," Canada should be relieved of responsibility for the defence of the base in wartime, provided the militia garrison came under the commanding officer, and released from the obligation under the 1893 agreement to "maintain 100 permanent artillery" ready to go to Esquimalt; (4) after ten years Canada should assume full responsibility for the base.[33]

After some British pressure the Canadian Government agreed to these "very liberal proposals."[34] In July 1899 the Minister of Militia announced the terms of the agreement to Parliament. Except for his own comment that it cost more than the previous one, there was no debate. To make Esquimalt virtually an Imperial base like Halifax—an

[33]*Ibid.*, pp. 407–8, "Report of a Conference held at the Admiralty to consider the question of the responsibility for the Defence of Esquimalt in connection with the Garrison which, in the near future, will have to be provided for that place," Nov. 10, 1898; but cf. C.O. 42/873, pp. 257–58, W.O. to C.O., "Pressing & Confidential," Jan. 18, 1899.

[34]The phrase is in D.M. 17424, Chamberlain to Minto, "Secret," Feb. 1, 1899; the acceptance is in Laurier Papers, p. 215054, Minto to Chamberlain, cable, May 12, 1899.

ambition earlier hoped for—involved a surrender of control if not of sovereignty of a part of Canadian territory.[35] But Canada's dread of United States ambitions and pressures in the Yukon account for its acceptance and the silence in Parliament.

IV

The principal concern of the Colonial Defence Committee was to induce Canada to accept a committee to produce a comprehensive plan of defence, at which Canada had consistently balked. The Minister of Militia gave vague encouragement in 1888 and 1891, but the matter was dropped.[36] The Venezuela affair provided the committee with a good opportunity to broach the matter again. It reminded Canada of its need for a plan, the lack of departmental services, and the necessity of maintaining a strategic advantage until Imperial help arrived. The German victories of 1866 and 1870 showed the importance of a defence plan.[37] The Colonial Secretary in a dispatch in October 1896 and again at the Colonial Conference, also reminded Canada of the need for a defence plan. During the conference Dr. Borden in his visits to the Intelligence Division of the War Office was shown the book containing defence memoranda of all the colonies and his attention was drawn to the absence of "any defence scheme for . . . Canada." That visit, Borden later claimed, was the real start of the defence committee.[38] In early November 1897, Lieutenant-General A. G. Montgomery-Moore, the General Officer Commanding the Imperial Troops in Canada, impressed on Dr. Borden Canada's "confusion and helplessness" in wartime without a prepared scheme. "Dr. Borden in further conversation, said it might be well if I could bring my views before the Government," General Montgomery-Moore reported, and he subsequently wrote to Sir Wilfrid Laurier to the same effect.[39]

By January 1898 the War Office was in earnest. Lord Lansdowne, recalling an earlier memorandum, emphasized Canada's "own safety as part of her duty to the Empire." He was aware of "Canada's loyalty" and accepted the maintenance of a militia and recent expenditure on the "best modern armament" as proof of that loyalty. Yet Canada appreci-

---

[35]Cummins, "Organization and Development of the Canadian Militia," p. 176.

[36]G 21, no. 165, vol. V, report of Min. of Mil., Jan. 23, 1888, P.C. Despatches, 1141G, Jan. 24, 1888; see also *Can. Sess. Pap.* (no. 19), 1892, p. 9.

[37]G 21, no. 165, Additional, "Secret," 59M, March 31, 1896, inc. in C.O., "Circular Secret," May 14, 1896.

[38]*Debates*, June 25, 1900, p. 8246.

[39]G 21, no. 165, vol. VII, "Confidential," Nov. 3, 1897, inc. in P.C. 297, Feb. 25, 1898, inc. in Aberdeen to Chamberlain, "Confidential," Feb. 25, 1898; and Laurier Papers, pp. 10719–22.

ated neither the "vital necessity" of a plan, nor the liability to "as severe disasters . . . as France suffered . . . in the war of 1870."[40] Chamberlain added his emphasis; on February 5, the Governor General submitted a memorandum on the subject; two days later, Major-General Gascoigne formally approved the suggestion of a committee to prepare a defence plan and made detailed proposals. The visit of Lieutenant-General Sir Henry Wilkinson on February 24, 1898, to Lord Strathcona in London and the defence memorandum which he left with the Canadian High Commissioner suggest how desperately in earnest the British authorities were to obtain a defence plan.[41]

A few days later, with a flourish of magnanimous acquiescence, the Canadian Government at last approved the appointment of a defence committee and emphasized acceptance of all War Office recommendations.[42] Except for the reasons specified in the documents above, no other evidence is available explaining the acceptance of the committee. Nevertheless the Government could not have failed to see the intensity of British representations or the need for Britain's support in the Yukon. The committee consisted of varied experts: as chairman Major-General E. P. Leach, R.E., lately in command of engineers at Halifax and author of two reports on the defence of Montreal; an artillery expert, Lieutenant-Colonel J. C. Dalton, R.A.; the recent quartermaster-general of the Canadian militia, Major (Regular Army rank) P. H. N. Lake, an officer whom the Government would trust to represent Canadian interests; and a naval expert, Captain W. G. White, R.N. British authorities with some regret also agreed to the Canadian suggestion that two cabinet members be added—the Minister of Militia and the Minister of Marine and Fisheries.[43] The committee was instructed by the British Government to consider "the possibility of a closer connection between the Colonial and Imperial Forces, in pursuance of the policy which was discussed at the Conference of Colonial Premiers held last year," to

[40]G 21, no. 165, vol. VII, W.O. to C.O., "Secret," Jan. 8, 1898, inc. in Chamberlain to Aberdeen, "Secret," Jan. 20, 1898.

[41]*Ibid.*, memo of Gascoigne to Min. of Mil., Feb. 7, 1898, in P.C. 297, Feb. 25, 1898, and memo "Confidential" dated Feb. 24, 1898, inc. in Lord Strathcona to Min. of Mil., March 3, 1898 (R.G. 9, II B2 (71)).

[42]G 21, no. 165, vol. VII, P.C. Despatches, 703K, Feb. 28, 1898, inc. in Aberdeen to Chamberlain, "Secret," Feb. 28, 1898.

[43]*Ibid.*, P.C. Despatches, 982K, July 1, 1898, inc. in Aberdeen to Chamberlain, "Confidential," July 6, 1898. The Minister of Marine and Fisheries, Sir Louis Davies, could not have played much part in the committee's labours, since for much of the time he also served as a Canadian delegate to the Joint High Commission. The two men were officially added to the committee only a month before the end of its labours (C.O. 42/858, p. 723, P.C. Despatches, 1057K, Oct. 18, 1898).

examine the defence resources in Canada, "to draw up and submit to the Minister of Defence" a defence scheme based on existing resources, report on organization, equipment, armament, the mobilization of existing forces "entering fully into all points in which the forces of the Dominion can be rendered more efficient," and "what more complete scheme of Defence could be established" if the changes recommended were adopted.[44]

V

Even though a committee might examine the state of Canadian defences, under existing conditions little further military progress was immediately possible in Canada; more forceful men than General Gascoigne and Lord Aberdeen as General Officer Commanding and Governor General were essential.[45] Two such men arrived in August and November 1898, Major-General (later Sir) Edward T. H. Hutton and Governor General Lord Minto. No matter how able the men, however, their success depended on public acceptance of their leadership, and this in turn depended largely on the continuance of anti-American resentments. These not only continued but intensified. In the Dingley Tariff Canadians had seen United States indifference to Canada; in the Yukon gold rush they were to see United States interference.

[44]G 21, no. 165, vol. VII, "Instruction to Committee on Military Matters in Canada," inc. in Chamberlain to Aberdeen, "Secret and Confidential," July 29, 1898. The committee went by several titles: "Committee on Military Matters in Canada," "Defence Commission," "Defence Committee," "Defence Scheme Committee," and "Committee on Canadian Defence, 1898"—its title on the official report.

[45]For two examples of Canadian military Cassandras in 1898 see Capt. Charles F. Winter, "Canada's Share in Imperial Defence," *Can. Mag.*, X (Jan. 1898), pp. 199–207, and Capt. Wm. Wood, "In Case of War," *ibid.*, XI (June 1898), pp. 93–100.

7. The Open Door in the Yukon

THE PERIOD between Laurier's return from the Queen's Jubilee and the opening of the Joint High Commission a year later was marked by two important political developments: United States insistence on the open door in the Yukon and the events leading to the Joint High Commission. It is not the purpose of this chapter to consider in detail the adventuresome, economic, or social characteristics of the Yukon gold rush, but to analyse its bearing on Canadian-American relations and on Canadian nationalism.

I

The Klondike gold rush was the most spectacular of that series of Northern Pacific gold rushes that began in California, continued in British Columbia, and concluded in the Yukon.[1] The gold strike touched off a world-wide epidemic of "Klondicitis"; especially affected was the city of Seattle, which enjoyed a commercial boom as headquarters of a leading Yukon supply company, equipping and transporting thousands of miners in many a "crazy craft" to Alaska.[2] To reach the Klondike most easily the miners had to sail past the mountainous and bewrecked coast of British Columbia and Alaska, cross American-occupied territory, scramble up a steep and treacherous pass, and, after building a boat in sub-arctic weather, sail down a formidable Yukon river to the gold fields near Dawson City. It was a perilous trip for city gold hunters, hundreds of whom perished in the attempt. Yet spectacular fortunes were made. It was reported that the winter's effort of one miner yielded $400,000 and that two miners from Halifax, Nova Scotia, made $85,000 each. The total value of the gold mined in the Yukon jumped almost tenfold, from $2,500,000 in 1897 to $22,275,000 in 1900.[3]

[1]H. A. Innis, *Settlement and the Mining Frontier*, part II of vol. IX of *Canadian Frontiers of Settlement*, ed. W. A. Mackintosh and W. L. G. Joerg (Toronto, 1936), p. 178.

[2]S. B. Steele, *Forty Years in Canada* (London, 1915), p. 289; Pierre Berton, *The Klondike Fever* (New York, 1958), p. 107.

[3]*Annual Report of the Mineral Production of Canada, 1926* (Ottawa, 1926), p. 117, cited in Tansill, p. 171.

The gold fever infected Canada from coast to coast. Newspapers carried reports of the gold rush and large advertisements for mining outfits and railway transportation. Canadians gloated over the world-wide attention their country was receiving. But they soon discovered that, although the Yukon was a Canadian treasure trove, Americans were managing, for a variety of reasons, to get most of the treasure. One reason was the little-challenged historical occupation of the Alaska Panhandle by the United States under the Anglo-Russian Convention of 1825. This narrow strip of territory jutting down from the main part of Alaska fenced in the gold-bearing territory of Canada from the sea. Its occupation by the United States, together with the difficulties of access to the Yukon region, made it possible for Americans to deny Canadians free entry to their own territory. Another reason was the threatening jingoistic attitude which had already found expression in the Venezuela crisis and was soon to help carry the United States into the Spanish-American War and effect the annexation of Hawaii. This feeling had a particular intensity in the Western states, in the envy of what Westerners called the greedy British control of mineral-bearing lands in Alaska.[4] In fact the Yukon was under, not British, but Canadian jurisdiction, but Canada was in effect identifying itself with Britain in the guise of imperial unity and had to bear the obloquy which such identification entailed. In the third place, the city of Seattle provided most of the wealth, experience, shipping, supplies, and energy. Finally, the thousands of individualistic Western miners, many of them criminal characters, who poured into the Klondike exhibited a ruthless, "first come, first served" attitude.[5] The United States administration could exercise some control over this mob of miners and the powerful Western interests behind them by letting them have their own economic way and preventing Canadians enjoying economic advantages over Americans in the Yukon, that is, by pursuing a policy of the "open door."[6]

II

The Canadian Government was well aware of the pressures from the Western states on the United States Government and of the danger to

[4]Cf. resolution of the House of Representatives of the State of Washington in 1895, cited in F. W. Howay, W. N. Sage, and H. F. Angus, *British Columbia and the United States* (Toronto, 1942), p. 369.

[5]As Clifford (afterwards Sir Clifford) Sifton (1861–1929), Minister of the Interior, wrote to a Western Liberal M.P. in August 1897: ". . . one of the principal ideas western men have is that it is right to take anything in sight provided nobody else is in ahead of them." John W. Dafoe, *Clifford Sifton in Relation to His Times* (Toronto, 1931), p. 153.

[6]For a suggestion of this attitude, see President McKinley's annual message to Congress, Dec. 6, 1897, *Foreign Relations*, 1897, p. xxviii.

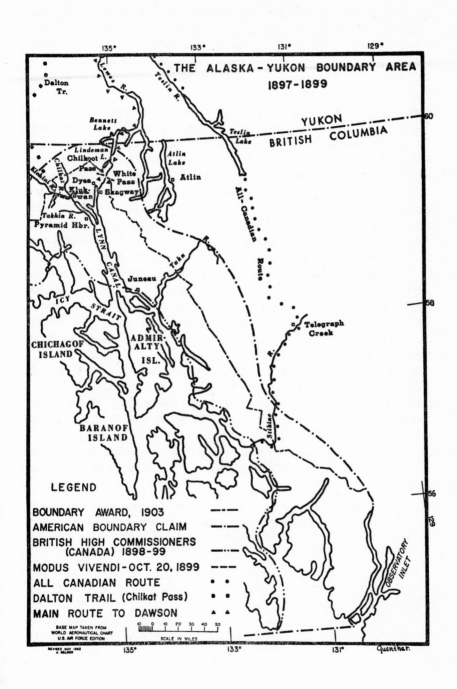

THE ALASKA - YUKON BOUNDARY AREA
1897-1899

LEGEND

BOUNDARY AWARD, 1903	— — —
AMERICAN BOUNDARY CLAIM	————
BRITISH HIGH COMMISSIONERS (CANADA) 1898-99	—·—·—
MODUS VIVENDI-OCT. 20, 1899	– – –
ALL CANADIAN ROUTE	• • •
DALTON TRAIL (Chilkat Pass)	▪ ▪
MAIN ROUTE TO DAWSON	▲ ▲

BASE MAP TAKEN FROM
WORLD AERONAUTICAL CHART
U.S. AIR FORCE EDITION

SCALE IN MILES

REVISED MAY 1962
J. GELOCK

Canadian interests in the Yukon, and it tried to avoid policies that would weaken the influence of the administration over those states. The United States Government for its part was disposed to be accommodating to the obvious needs of the Yukon. For example, in July 1897 the Canadian Commissioner of Customs telegraphed direct to the Assistant Secretary of the Treasury to inquire if Canadian goods might "pass from Juneau, Alaska, to Yukon frontier without payment customs duties if parties pay for United States' officers accompanying goods." The Treasury Department agreed, and went a step further by suggesting Dyea, and later agreeing to Skagway, the two closest harbours to the Yukon, as sub-ports of entry.[7] By such a request Canada was recognizing United States sovereignty over the Panhandle, and even seemed to be recognizing the extreme American interpretation of the Anglo-Russian Convention of 1825: that the boundary should be not less than ten marine leagues (about 35 miles) from the coast at any point. When the local United States authorities early in January 1898 hoisted the Stars and Stripes near the Union Jack "three miles down from the head" of Lake Bennett, that is, beyond the ten-league claim, the Canadian police demanded an explanation, and "after some parleying the flag was lowered and an apology tendered."[8] The attempt to assert this territorial claim alarmed the Canadian Government, and on January 29, 1898, it anxiously cabled the Colonial Office that the summits of the passes were the "furthest inland limit which the United States could possibly establish." It reported that it had repeated its instructions to the Canadian police and customs officials to set up "posts and collect duties at these summits," having just learned of the United States claim "down Lakes Lindeman and Bennet [sic]." The possibility of trouble from "nearly all in gold-mines," who were United States citizens, and the impossibility of reaching the area through Canadian territory rendered the difficulty acute. Fifty policemen and supplies were in the passes and "more are going forward":

When disputes are made known at Washington, it is possible United States' authorities may forbid further Canadian goods or men being sent through Skagway or Dyea. My responsible advisers therefore suggest that no communication be held with United States' authorities on this subject for eight

---

[7] *A.B.T.*, III, pp. 373–74, Appendix to the British Case . . . , John McDougald, Commissioner of Customs, to W. B. Howell, Asst. Sec. of the Treasury, telegram, July 22, 1897, and replies, July 22, 23, 1897; *ibid.*, pp. 374–75; and cf. *Foreign Relations*, 1897, pp. 327–29.

[8] Conf. 7161, p. 22, F. Turner, police officer, to George F. Stelly, collector of customs, Jan. 4, 1898, inc. in C.O. to F.O., March 2, 1898. Turner's letter is important as a description of conditions on the border.

days, so as to enable the latest men and supplies to pass through unhindered [a request Britain complied with].

The importance of avoiding any concession to unjust territorial claims cannot be overestimated. A large influx of United States' miners is now beginning, and difficulty of maintaining Canadian authority will be increased by questions of disputed jurisdiction. The entire boundary line is unsettled, and a concession at one point would be probably the signal for similar unfounded claims along the whole boundary line.[9]

Accordingly, on February 13 the posts were erected and on February 25 dues were collected at the summits of the White and Chilkoot passes,[10] boundary claims Washington had been informed about in the previous year.

Professor C. C. Campbell asserts that this sudden reinforcement was prompted by a rumour of an American military force gathering at Portland bound for Skagway.[11] That may have been a factor, but in view of the attempts of local United States officials to enforce extreme boundary claims and their subsequent reactions to the establishment of the posts, its alarm does not seem excessive. No official protest was made from Washington but local United States customs officials refused to recognize Canada's presence at the summits and ordered the convoys accompanying Canadian shipments to proceed to Lake Bennett twenty miles further on. "The idea of an American convoy escorting Canadian goods through British territory was too much for the police at the Summits," wrote Z. T. Wood, the local superintendent of police, in his annual report, "and convoys were politely but firmly impressed with the necessity of returning to Skagway or Dyea as soon as they reached our camps."[12] Apparently as a result of having been thus halted, the officer commanding American troops at Dyea at the end of March sent an official request to Canadian police officers "to cease exercising jurisdiction at the summits of Chilkoot and White Passes and at Lake Lindeman." The Canadian Government protested to Chamberlain at this assertion of jurisdiction and at the manner of making it.[13]

[9]*Ibid.*, pp. 1–2, Aberdeen to Chamberlain (ca. Feb. 1, 1898), inc. in C.O. to F.O., "Confidential," Feb. 2, 1898. See also Marjorie Pentland, *A Bonnie Fechter* (London, 1952), p. 129, Laurier to Aberdeen, Jan. 1898; and C.O. 42/856, pp. 113–14, F. H. Villiers to E. Wingfield, Jan. 31, 1898.

[10]The police suffered severely from the weather; see reports of several North-West Mounted Police superintendents and inspectors in *Can. Sess. Pap.* (no. 15), 1899, III.

[11]Campbell, pp. 74–75, and Dafoe, *Clifford Sifton*, pp. 214–15.

[12]*Can. Sess. Pap.* (no. 15), 1899, III, p. 47; see also Sifton Correspondence, letter book, vol. 226, pp. 104–8, to Maj. J. M. Walsh, N.W.M.P. Commissioner, Yukon District, "Personal," March 26, 1898.

[13]Conf. 7161, p. 70, Aberdeen to Chamberlain, undated cable (before April 7, 1898), inc. in C.O. to F.O., "Confidential," April 7, 1898.

These violations of presumed Canadian sovereignty made the Government reconsider the unofficial permission it had previously given to a unit of the United States Army to distribute relief in the Yukon. Because of a widespread belief that Yukon miners would face starvation in the winter of 1897–98[14] President McKinley had suggested in his annual message to Congress in December the possibility of relieving their suffering,[15] and Congress had passed an act authorizing expenditure of $200,000 by the Secretary of War for that purpose.[16] At that time the Canadian Government had unofficially consented to the transport of supplies accompanied by a "reasonable" American "escort" and a "Canadian officer."[17] But early in February in response to the official request Canadian authorities, no longer fearing starvation because of the energy of the Mounted Police, stipulated the same terms imposed by the United States on Canadian police passing over the Panhandle: Canada was to provide the police escort, arms were to be packed in the baggage, and, a later stipulation, American soldiers were to wear civilian dress.[18] In spite of a warning from Chamberlain against giving the United States a pretext for refusing passage of additional Canadian troops Canada stuck to its guns. After some protest the United States accepted the stipulations, but in April abandoned the "American Relief Expedition."[19]

An armed relief expedition might well have been the signal for American miners to seize the Yukon. Even apart from any such direct incitement, many of these men, bred in the traditions of frontier lawlessness,

[14]Laurier Papers, pp. 17112–14 (copy). Inspector C. Constantine of the N.W.M.P. reported to Commissioner Herchmer at Regina, Oct. 14, 1897, that "in all probability" there would be deaths from starvation: *Debates,* Feb. 16, 1899, pp. 624–25; Innis, *Settlement and the Mining Frontier,* p. 187.

[15]*Foreign Relations,* 1897, p. xxviii.

[16]*Ibid.,* 1898, p. 359. The act, signed on December 18, 1897, empowered the Secretary of War to purchase, transport, donate, or sell the necessary stores, supplies, and materials for the "relief of people who are in the Yukon River country or other mining regions of Alaska. . . . *Provided,* That with the consent of the Canadian Government first obtained, the Secretary of War may cause the relief . . . to be extended into Canadian territory."

[17]*Ibid.,* p. 360, Sir Julian (afterwards Lord) Pauncefote (1828–1902), British Ambassador to United States, to John Sherman, Sec. of State, Dec. 27, 1897. On the invitation of R. A. Alger, Sec. of War, Sifton had gone to Washington to give information enabling United States officers "to extend relief to starving people of the United States" (*Debates,* Feb. 15, 1898, p. 583).

[18]*Can. Sess. Pap.* (no. 79), 1899, pp. 19–20, McDougald to A. R. Milne, collector of customs, Victoria, B.C., Feb. 2, 1898, and *ibid.,* p. 21, Feb. 11, 1898; Conf. 7161, p. 4, Aberdeen to Chamberlain, undated cable, inc. in C.O. to F.O., "Confidential," Feb. 5, 1898; C.O. 42/861, pp. 493–94, Conf. F.O. Print, William R. Day, Asst. Sec. of State, to Pauncefote, Feb. 16, 1898, and Pauncefote to Sherman, Feb. 17, 1898, inc. in Pauncefote to Salisbury, Feb. 18, 1898.

[19]Conf. 7161, p. 75, Day, Acting Sec., to Pauncefote, April 6, 1898, inc. in Pauncefote to Salisbury, April 8, 1898.

were dangerous desperadoes, guilty of murder and armed violence. Under "Soapy" Smith and his gang, murder and robbery reigned in Skagway, a city which a Mounted Police superintendent described as "little better than a hell on earth."[20] Furthermore the 1890's were the years when the doctrine of "Manifest Destiny," of which the Yukon gold rush and border scuffles were an expression, revived. The Minister of Finance declared that in 1897 the American press assumed that "American miners who were going in there [Yukon] were going in to occupy American territory, and that if any one attempted to interfere . . ., their rights as American settlers would be asserted. That was the common cry of American newspapers."[21] In February 1898 the Minister of Justice wrote grimly to his brother that if "western border men" seized power, "as they did at Texas," the American Government "would certainly not afford us, nor could we expect them to do so,—facilities for regaining the country."[22] That fears of this kind were not groundless is indicated by "another Texas" in the annexation of Hawaii in 1898 and by the discovery of a conspiracy to seize the Yukon in 1901.[23]

From 1894 to 1897 Canada had dispatched police in small numbers to the Yukon: they had had to assert their authority twice. But where hundreds of miners had arrived before 1897, thousands came afterwards.[24] The Yukon soon gained the reputation of being one of the most law-abiding mining camps in the world, but for a time the situation was dangerous. In November 1897 Commissioner Walsh recommended that 200 troops be sent to the Yukon to reinforce the police,[25] and early in March 1898 a similar suggestion came from Britain: the Colonial Office enclosed a warning about the perils of the Yukon by the British Admiral of the North Pacific Station, who advised that with the dispatch of American troops the Canadian forces should be "largely increased to resist the United States pretensions."[26] On March 17, therefore, the

---

[20]*Can. Sess. Pap.* (no. 15), 1899, III, p. 4. Cf. also the fact that the 1890's were the years when the greatest number of lynchings was reported in the United States.

[21]W. S. Fielding, *Debates*, April 17, 1899, p. 1642; see also *Globe*, Feb. 11, 1898.

[22]University of Western Ontario Library, Mills Papers, letter book no. 1, p. 642, David Mills (1831–1903) to Daniel Mills, Feb. 18, 1898, and p. 599, Feb. 1, 1898; see also "G" in *Queen's Quarterly*, V (April 1898), p. 328.

[23]Campbell, pp. 242–44.

[24]Laurier Papers, pp. 224427–30, memorandum of Fred White, Comptroller, N.W.M.P., Feb. 3, 1897 (to Laurier); cf. S. B. Steele on police experience from 1894 to 1896, in *Forty Years in Canada*, pp. 288–89.

[25]*Can. Sess. Pap.* (no. 38B), 1898, p. 31, written about Nov. 25, 1897.

[26]G 3, vol. 32, and Conf. 7161, p. 20, Rear-Admiral H. B. Palliser to Admiralty, Jan. 25, 1898, inc. in Chamberlain to Aberdeen, "Confidential," March 2, 1898. The Admiralty took the threat seriously; see above, p. 76.

Government informed the British Ambassador at Washington and the Colonial Secretary of the decision to send 200 Canadian troops to the Yukon "to assist in the maintenance of order."[27] Permission for the troops to pass through American territory under an agreement of the previous year was granted with surprising alacrity in less than a week: American authorities might well have raised difficulties, but they merely stipulated that arms and munitions be carried as baggage across American-held territory.

The professed object of the "Yukon Field Force" was to strengthen the Mounted Police. But when the Minister of Militia referred to the presence of the four companies of American regulars in Alaska, two of them at Skagway—the total estimated at between 300 and 400 men— little doubt could exist as to the other purpose of the force.[28] The Canadian troops, consisting of about 200 officers and men of the Permanent Force, were officially authorized on March 21 and made a hazardous journey not unlike the Red River Expedition of 1870,[29] via the Stikine River over land and down a tributary of the Yukon River to the Klondike. The virtual necessity to ship most of the supplies for the force by an American transportation company up the Yukon River through Alaska shows Canadian dependence in the area on the United States.[30]

III

The maintenance of boundary claims and internal authority was largely a government matter. Public concern was fixed on the unfortunate ability of Americans to deny Canadians any economic advantage in possession of the Yukon. This fact exasperated and angered Canadians, and explains much of the anti-American mood in 1898–99.

Canadians widely resented the American acquisition of the outfitting, supply, and shipping trades.[31] Vancouver and Victoria were particularly galled at the predominance of Seattle. Some blame rests on Canadians

[27]Laurier Papers, p. 214966, telegram, and Conf. 7161, p. 38, Aberdeen to Chamberlain, cable, March 17, 1898.
[28]*Debates*, May 4, 1898, p. 4795; at the end of August a battery of 225 men left San Francisco to man the forts on the Yukon River (Conf. 7161, p. 99).
[29]R. C. Fetherstonhaugh, *The Royal Canadian Regiment 1883–1933* (Montreal, 1936), pp. 67–73.
[30]*Debates*, May 13, 1898, pp. 5498–5518.
[31]*Globe*, March 9, 1898, edit., "Yukon Outfitting," and Laurier Papers, p. 19051, resolution of Hamilton Board of Trade, Dec. 24, 1897. Newspapers contained many advertisements concerning the gold rush: see advertisement headed "Klondike!" demonstrating merits of Vancouver as a port of debarkation, Halifax *Chronicle*, Feb. 1, 1898.

for their self-distrust and lack of energy.[32] On the other hand Canadians could only lament the existence of American navigation laws which forbade British ships carrying goods between a Pacific west-coast port and an Alaskan port. They protested angrily at Western officials delaying the unloading of British ships at Skagway. After the abolition of that abuse Canadian ships[33] were frequently harassed by close subjection to United States customs regulations which the United States ships were often permitted to evade.[34] What most angered Canadians was having to pay convoy fees of up to $9.00 per day on mining outfits purchased in one part of Canada for use in another and transported in bond across the Panhandle to the summits of the passes or even beyond. Yet Canada had suggested them. Complaints brought the suggestion that United States customs duties should be paid, a procedure bringing more convenient repossession of the outfits. The effect of the payment of fees or duties by Canadians after Americans paid Canadian duties on American outfits entering the Yukon was to place Americans on terms of economic equality with Canadians. At the end of December 1897 Sifton visited Washington and unofficially came to an agreement with the Secretary of the Treasury, Lyman J. Gage, to eliminate convoy fees, and the problems convoys produced, but the agreement was not put into effect because of the "violent political pressure" of the Western interests to place the trade in American hands.[35] Resentment against the convoys reached such a pitch that the Victoria and Toronto boards of trade and other commercial groups even demanded that the Minister of the Interior order the Mounted Police to block the passes to Americans. Sifton warned a Victoria newspaper owner that any such "high-handed proceedings" might jeopardize the whole movement to the Yukon and lose millions to Canada.[36]

The Minister, however, issued mining regulations requiring American miners to obtain Canadian miners' certificates personally at Victoria, Vancouver, or Dawson. The American Secretary of State, John Sherman,

[32]Cf. Victor Ross, *A History of the Canadian Bank of Commerce* (Toronto, 1922), II, p. 192.

[33]*A.B.T.*, III, p. 375, W. B. Howell, Asst. Sec. of the Treasury, replying to request of R. W. Scott, Acting Min. of Customs, on August 20, 1897, that Canadian vessels be given the "same rights as vessels of United States" to "enter at Skagway."

[34]*Can. Sess. Pap.* (no. 52), 1899, p. 58; but cf. Conf. 7161, pp. 31–34, Pauncefote to Salisbury, Feb. 28, 1898.

[35]Dafoe, *Clifford Sifton*, pp. 160–62, and Laurier Papers, p. 17043, clipping of letter in Kingston *News*, Oct. 1, 1897.

[36]Sifton Correspondence, letter book, vol. 226, p. 696, June 1891–Dec. 1899, Sifton to William Templeman, "Personal," Jan. 26, 1898. These commercial bodies even demanded that the Relief Expedition be stopped.

complained of this inconvenience. He argued that the United States had opened the sub-ports of Dyea and Skagway "prompted by the belief that it was the purpose of the Canadian Government to meet the efforts of this government to promote the development of new gold-fields."[37] He objected to the 24-hour delay of two ships at Victoria awaiting miners' licences—one ship incurring a loss of over $1000. Sifton was not moved by this "open-door" appeal. To put off complying with the request, he even argued that the provision of miners' licences was not discretionary but a statutory matter.[38] He prolonged this inconvenience as long as possible to try to compel the United States to put its new customs regulations into effect. Not until April 16, 1898, did he agree to issue certificates at Dyea and Skagway,[39] but the United States did not implement its regulations until mid-May.[40]

Thus the United States could encumber the most convenient routes across the Panhandle and on the 1800-mile trip up the Yukon River through Alaska—the essential route for the conveyance of heavy supplies in summertime. To avoid these encumberances Sifton and his Yukon subordinate, Commissioner Walsh, sought an alternative route, and thought the so-called "All-Canadian" route a feasible substitute.[41] Under the Treaty of Washington, 1871, Canada enjoyed navigation rights subject to reasonable laws and regulations on the Stikine River, which flowed across the Panhandle. About 150 miles up this river, a railway in Canadian territory might be built from Telegraph Creek to Lake Teslin, about 200 miles distant. Thence came a difficult and dangerous journey down tributaries of the Yukon River to the gold fields.

In January 1898 the Government let a contract to the Mackenzie and Mann railway interests to construct a narrow-gauge railway between Telegraph Creek and Lake Teslin.[42] This contract made Mackenzie and

---

[37]Conf. 7161, p. 23, Sherman to Pauncefote, Feb. 19, 1898, inc. in Pauncefote to Salisbury, Feb. 21, 1898; see also C.O. 42/862, pp. 46, 63–64.

[38]C.O. 42/862, p. 46, Conf. F.O. Print, Feb. 26, 1898, and p. 63, March 25, 1898; see also C.O. 42/861, p. 459, Feb. 19, 1898, all from Sherman to Pauncefote.

[39]C.O. 42/857, p. 89, P.C. Despatches, 811K, April 16, 1898.

[40]Among the pretexts for delay was a demand for Canadian provision of accommodation for United States customs inspectors at the summits of the passes. Only one was authorized (Conf. 7161, p. 39).

[41]*Can. Sess. Pap.* (nos. 30, 66a), 1898, and (no. 79), 1899, for reports on routes to Yukon; for a report by Walsh see *ibid.* (no. 38B), 1898; there was also much propaganda for an overland route from Edmonton.

[42]If the development of the country warranted it, it was intended to continue the railway south to Canadian coastal territory (memorandum of Min. of the Interior, Feb. 28, 1898, P.C. 489, Feb. 28, 1898, in C.O. 42/856, p. 301). Other syndicates were also interested in gaining the contract; see Laurier Papers, pp. 18936–40 and 20062, and *Can. Sess. Pap.* (no. 30B), 1898.

Mann personally liable, gave them 25,000 acres of land per mile of railway (the blocks of land generally selectable anywhere in the Yukon and west of the Mackenzie and Liard rivers, and interspersed with blocks of Crown land) and required the completion of the railway by September 1898. While the Government gave no subsidy it agreed that for five years no American railway from Alaska in the Lynn Canal area should be extended into the Yukon.[43] Under existing conditions, the "All-Canadian" scheme seems to have been the best practicable one, speedy, protecting the Government from loss, and Canadian in construction and ownership. Two of the more independent and perspicacious members of Parliament—one Liberal, John Charlton, and the other Conservative, Sam Hughes—approved the contract. Both agreed that the railway was a gamble, owing to the probable quick exhaustion of placer-gold, as actually occurred within a few years. Charlton clearly expounded the Government's nationalistic position: nobody denied that other routes were better commercially, but "national considerations compelled the Government to disregard the natural advantages of these routes and to build a line on Canadian territory which will enable us to be independent of foreign control and foreign interference."[44] But the route suffered a fatal defect: it was not "All-Canadian." Although Canada enjoyed treaty rights on the Stikine River in American-occupied territory, its free use depended on United States goodwill.

There were many protests from the Canadian public against the plan, partly because of the hastiness of the arrangements, the need for which the public could not be expected to grasp, and especially because of the apparent monopoly and land-grant provisions of the contract. One writer described it as a "seemingly hasty, very shady, one sided arrangement."[45] The battle raged more than a month in the House of Commons. Opponents placed greatest weight on the alleged peril of another railway monopoly; Sir Charles Tupper, at first inclined to support the Government, partly because of a personal financial interest, was forced in caucus and especially by Toronto newspaper editors to oppose the bill.[46]

[43]*Debates*, Feb. 16, 1898, pp. 645–52.

[44]*Ibid.*, March 10, 1898, p. 1642; Hughes's remarks are *ibid.*, Feb. 18, 1898, p. 756.

[45]Laurier Papers, p. 20414, W. D. D. Gauthier to Sen. C. A. P. Pelletier, Feb. 7, 1898; also p. 20723, W. W. B. McInnes (Liberal, Vancouver, B.C.) to Laurier, Feb. 17, 1898.

[46]John T. Saywell, ed., *The Canadian Journal of Lady Aberdeen 1893–1898* (Toronto, Champlain Society, 1960), Feb. 28, 1898–July 1898, pp. 457–58; W. F. Maclean (*World*, Conservative, East York), *Debates*, Feb. 4, 1898, pp. 93–100, and Feb. 21, 1898, pp. 844–55, and Ross Robertson (*Evening Telegram*, Conservative, East Toronto), *ibid.*, Feb. 8, 1898, pp. 248–52.

Nor, opponents argued, should the railway magnates be permitted to prospect for gold. Sifton, under whose aegis the bill was sponsored, emphasized that Bonanzas and Eldorados were rare and that experience showed "it costs more to take the gold out than the gold is worth after it is taken out."[47]

The bill had also to face a powerful American lobby against it. One Hamilton Smith, purporting to represent British interests but almost certainly representing American interests, offered to build an alternative route to the Yukon. His object was to delay the passage of the Mackenzie and Mann bill. Having failed in the House of Commons, the same lobbyist, according to the Minister of Justice, induced the Senate to vote the bill down.[48] The Senate's Conservative majority was also moved by extreme partisanship.

In an effort to prevent Canada's using the Yukon railway to evade the open door, the United States Senate introduced provisions into the Alaska Homestead Bill empowering the Secretary of the Treasury to regulate the transshipment of goods from ocean to river vessels at the mouth of the Stikine River. The conditions were that Canada (1) abandon exclusive transportation privileges between Alaska and the Yukon and British Columbia, (2) permit Canadian railways to connect with American ones in Alaska, (3) admit free into Canada mining outfits up to 1,000 pounds in weight, (4) remove unequal restrictions on the issue of mining licences, (5) permit United States fishing vessels, contrary to the Treaty of 1818 and the *modus vivendi* of 1888, to purchase bait and supplies and transship fish in bond to the United States, and (6) generally let the United States enjoy most-favoured-nation trade treatment.[49]

Canadians were angry at these provisions. Even Sir Richard Cartwright, the most pro-American member of the cabinet, warned that if the "Government or the people of the United States should attempt to violate a solemn treaty" it would be Canada's and Britain's duty to take

[47]*Debates*, Feb. 16, 1898, p. 665. To what extent was the timing of the announcement of this contract—the day before the dissolution of the Ontario legislature—and the intensity and length of the Yukon Railway debate affected by the current Ontario provincial election? See *ibid.*, pp. 356, 1132.

[48]U.W.O. Library, Mills Papers, letter book no. 1, pp. 942–43, Mills to Rev. Dr. Dewart, April 2, 1898; see also Laurier Papers, p. 12409, Laurier to Strathcona, cable, Feb. 24, 1898, for an inquiry concerning Hamilton Smith's "disreputable tactics"; also *ibid.*, pp. 12412–13, 20775–76, and 20931, and *Can. Sess. Pap.* (no. 30C), 1898.

[49]C.O. 42/861, pp. 445–46, paraphrase telegram, March 7, 1898, inc. in F.O. to C.O., "Confidential," March 7, 1898; the bill was no. 660, H. R. 5975.

action to secure Canada's rights.[50] On the other hand, the Senator look-ing after the bill later informed Pauncefote that if "Canada should aban-don policy of railway monopoly and secure liberty to connect Canada with Alaska railways," bonding privileges would be granted, and he implied that the other offensive provisions would be abandoned.[51]

It seems odd that the Canadian Government did not foresee American retaliation. When the contract was let in January, the Government was still trying to avoid actions which by provoking American opinion would force the American Government into policies inimical to Canadian inter-ests. It trusted in treaty right and the integrity of the McKinley adminis-tration to respect that right. But the purpose of the Mackenzie and Mann railway was to circumvent American insistence on the open door. The uproar which the railway bill caused in Canada, the introduction of the opposing bill into Congress, and the actual and potential threats to Canadian boundary claims and sovereignty alarmed the Canadian Government. It therefore sought a promise from the United States Treasury that goods would be permitted to be freely transshipped at the mouth of the Stikine. The Treasury of course would not commit itself. The Minister of Justice invoked international law for the enforce-ment of this right in a protest to the Colonial Office: he argued that navigation rights on rivers implied the necessary subsidiary rights, an opinion which the Law Officers upheld.[52] The Government called on Britain to protest against the congressional bill but to no avail. The defeat of the Yukon Bill in the Canadian Senate, however, made a protest unnecessary; the United States Senate withdrew the blatantly anti-Canadian provisions of the Alaska Homestead Bill and the Treasury issued fair transshipment and bonding regulations on May 3, 1898.

There was deep bitterness in Canada at the defeat of the railway bill, particularly in the province of British Columbia. British Columbia inter-ests sought to arouse eastern interests to support the construction of a

[50]*Debates*, March 7, 1898, p. 1327.

[51]C.O. 42/861, p. 601, Pauncefote to Salisbury, paraphrase cable, March 26, 1898, inc. in F.O. to C.O., "Immediate and Confidential," March 28, 1898. Already a railway was about to be built from Skagway up the White Pass (Innis, *Settlement and the Mining Frontier*, pp. 213–14 and n. 1), and prohibition from its joining a Yukon railway would have impaired it economically.

[52]C.O. 42/856, pp. 306–8, memorandum of Min. of Justice, Feb. 27, 1898, inc. in P.C. 489, Feb. 28, 1898; for a general justification of the railway policy see memorandum from Min. of the Interior, Feb. 28, 1898, *ibid.*, pp. 299–305; for the Law Officers' opinion see L.O. to Salisbury, April 23, 1898, in C.O. 42/862, pp. 192–93, and for their earlier less favourable views on the Canadian position see C.O. 42/861, pp. 461–77.

Canadian railway.[53] The British Columbia premier offered Laurier what was understood to be $4000 extra per mile to give to a railway if the Dominion Government would introduce another bill.[54] Laurier declined, arguing that there was little ground for believing that the Canadian Senate would support a new railway bill. He must also have seen that the action of the United States Congress would render any such railway commercially useless.

IV

In spite of its frustration, the Canadian Government was anxious to avoid an explosive incident that might endanger Canadian authority in the Yukon and hazard Canadian prosperity; a threatened Canada offered few attractions to miners, investors, or settlers. A boundary settlement, however, would avoid the hazard. Unfortunately the Anglo-Russian Convention of 1825, under which the boundary was to be determined, was ambiguous. The United States had inherited Russian rights when Alaska was purchased in 1867, but remained cool towards Canadian proposals of a boundary settlement. By 1898, when the gold rush made the width of the Panhandle a matter of vital importance, all that had been accomplished was a joint Canadian-American survey of the disputed area, which had been agreed upon by convention in 1892 and completed in 1895.

The convention of 1825 laid down that a range of mountains which was said to parallel the coast constituted the boundary; the Canadian-American survey demonstrated the existence of no well-marked range of mountains, though Canada had claimed that such a range existed. According to the convention, if there was not a well-marked range the boundary was to be drawn ten leagues parallel to the sinuosities of the coast. A line exactly parallel to the bays, fiords, and inlets of that rugged coast would make such a boundary ridiculously twisting and

[53]Laurier Papers, pp. 22378, 22728, 23675, 24122. The *Man. Free Press* of June 10, 1898, in an editorial, "The Yukon for Americans," argued, *inter alia*, in support of an all-Canadian railway, that there was little point in having resources "if the advantage from developing them is borne off by another country." The Lynn Canal Railway would get the trade. "That is not what this country wants. We want if possible to get something out of the Yukon, first because it is our own territory and next because it is a great expense to us."

[54]Laurier Papers, p. 22546, telegram, J. H. Turner to Laurier, April 15, 1898; cf. *ibid.*, pp. 22545 and 22547. For a sketch of the Yukon Railway affair from another point of view, see G. R. Stevens, *Canadian National Railways* (Toronto, 1962), pp. 85–86.

complex, and it was therefore generally recognized that any boundary should follow the general trend of the coast. But what did the word "coast" mean? Canada contended that the coast meant a line drawn along the ocean shoreline of the innumerable islands close to the mainland; the United States that it meant a line joining the tidewater limits of the heads of bays on the continent itself. The Canadian contention would result in a disjointed boundary allowing Canada access to an inlet from the sea; the American would make for a continuous land boundary requiring Canada to cross American territory before reaching the sea. In addition, Canadians argued that the boundary was to be no more than ten leagues from the coast, and the Americans, that it was to be no less than ten leagues.[55]

Canada's case was weak because Russia and the United States had been in effective, and largely unchallenged, occupation of the coast line.[56] In 1897 this right of occupation was reinforced by a vast inrush of population behind which were the enormous vested interests of the Pacific west coast. Thus the "object" of the United States policy, in the words of Joseph Pope, the Under-Secretary of State in Canada, was "to let things drift until they acquire a title by prescription."[57] In opposition to the American case largely built on long possession, Canada relied on a juridical interpretation of the convention of 1825. It saw the whole boundary in dispute. In practice, however, the dispute centred on three areas: first, the marking of the 141st meridian from the Arctic Ocean to the edge of the Panhandle;[58] second, the beginning of the boundary at the southern end of the Panhandle, which remained undetermined until the settlement of 1903 but scarcely figured as a problem during the period of this book; and third, the chief Canadian interest, the boundary across the Panhandle near the passes at the end of the Lynn Canal. It was the United States attempt to enforce an extreme American claim, and Canada's complaint to Britain, that raised the latter question in January 1898. Chamberlain advised the settlement of a boundary south of Mount St. Elias, and Laurier in

[55]Conf. 7161, p. 52, C.O. to F.O., April 7, 1898.
[56]Most of the maps confirmed the American contention; cf. also the charge of the Conservative N. F. Davin, that a map issued by the Department of the Interior, apparently in 1898, contained the same boundary that the United States was contending for (*Debates*, March 24, 1899, p. 363).
[57]Pope Papers, Semi-Official Correspondence 1896–98/A-C, docket 19a, Pope to John Anderson (C.O. official), Feb. 26, 1898.
[58]Conf. 7161, p. 10; a convention, signed Jan. 31, 1897, was to locate the boundary north of Mount St. Elias on the meridian. It was never ratified by the Senate, but this undefined boundary caused no trouble.

reply proposed a commission of three to determine that part of the boundary.[59]

In the meantime, Canadian policy hardened towards the United States. Official Canada had been disposed to accept official United States policy at face value. As late as mid-February Sifton and Laurier both acknowledged possession of the Lynn Canal by the United States, which indeed had never been challenged by Canada.[60] But the days of being directly pleasant to Uncle Sam were succeeded by days of unaccommodating indirection through John Bull. On February 28, 1898, in a memorandum to the Colonial Office the Canadian Government protested against the United States attempt to enforce its claim of a subport on rightfully Canadian territory—presumably near Lake Bennett. It urged Britain to enter into negotiations with the United States on the matter.[61] From this time on the official Canadian attitude assumed that Britain could force the United States to come to a boundary agreement satisfactory to Canada.[62] Washington had been consulted regarding the Laurier suggestion of the appointment of three commissioners under the convention of 1892 to settle the permanent or a temporary boundary. The Canadian Government balked, however, at a temporary boundary being determined under that convention because it contemplated the settlement of a permanent boundary. The settlement of a temporary boundary under such an instrument would be construed as an admission that the description of the topographical features in the boundary treaties were "impracticable," in other words the boundary would not be decided on the basis of a legal interpretation of the treaty. Hence a provisional boundary should be arranged informally between the British Ambassador and the State Department; a temporary line should be drawn at the summits of the passes or at the watershed between the rivers flowing into the Yukon and the northern end of the

[59]Laurier Papers, p. 214970, Chamberlain to Aberdeen, "Secret," Feb. 2, 1898; Laurier's undated draft cable, Feb. 18, 1898, *ibid.* (and Conf. 7161, p. 9), suggested France as a third power.

[60]*Debates*, Feb. 11, 16, 1898, pp. 407 and 619–20 respectively, cited in Tansill, pp. 165–66.

[61]C.O. 42/856, pp. 349–51, 356–57, respectively, memoranda each dated Feb. 28, 1898, in P.C. 490, Feb. 28, 1898.

[62]Pope Papers, Semi-Official Correspondence 1896–1898/A-C, docket 19a, Pope to Anderson, Feb. 26, 1898: "You ask me in one of your letters why we don't settle the Alaska Boundary question. I think I should ask you that question—Why doesn't H.M. Govt. insist upon something being done? The Yankees are bent upon delay. They won't agree to anything we propose, not even the purely scientific determination of the 141st meridian. Their object being to let things drift until they acquire a title by prescription. In the meantime they are administering the disputed territory, and have nothing to gain by settlement."

Lynn Canal.[63] The State Department widened this suggestion, which had been narrowed to include the summit north of Dyea only, to take in the two adjacent passes—the White and the Chilkat.[64] The Canadian Government accepted the temporary boundaries at the summits of the White Pass, connected with Skagway, and of the Chilkoot Pass, connected with Dyea. It rejected the summit of the Chilkat Pass on the Dalton Trail connected with Pyramid Harbor because Canada was in possession of territory closer to the Lynn Canal than the Chilkat summit, which was more than ten marine leagues from salt water. It suggested instead the junction of the Klehini and Chilkat rivers as the temporary boundary, one of the essential landmarks of the agreement of October 20, 1899; it demurred against the appointment of official commissioners to mark the boundaries; officers "on the spot" would be satisfactory.[65] These documents constituted an unofficial agreement for the temporary boundary at the summits of the White and Chilkoot passes.

In May 1898 tension relaxed; the American Relief Expedition had been abandoned and American customs officers by taking up their posts at the summits of the passes close to Canadian officers eliminated the need for expensive convoys. Canada's resolution and Britain's support partly explain the relaxation, but most decisive was American recognition of the "friendliness shown to" the United States "by Great Britain in the war with Spain."[66]

V

The late John Bartlet Brebner suggested that in the age of imperial expansion, with territory being seized in many parts of the world, there was doubt as to Canada's ability to survive alone.[67] It is even more difficult under those circumstances to imagine Canada keeping the Yukon.[68] Even as part of the British Empire, could Canada have kept

[63]C.O. 42/857, pp. 26–28, P.C. Despatches, 764K, March 28, 1898.

[64]C.O. 42/856, p. 605, Aberdeen to Chamberlain, paraphrase telegram, March 31, 1898; tentative State Department acceptance in C.O. 42/862, p. 150; Pauncefote to Salisbury, paraphrase telegram, April 20, 1898, and official acceptance, *ibid.*, pp. 279–80, Conf. F.O. Print, Pauncefote to Salisbury, cable, May 10, 1898.

[65]*A.B.T.*, III, pp. 377–78, Report of the Privy Council, June 27, 1898.

[66]Washington *Post*, April 28, 1898, inc. in Pauncefote to Salisbury, April 28, 1898 (Conf. 7161, p. 83).

[67]*North Atlantic Triangle* (New Haven, 1945), pp. 245–46.

[68]Sifton asserted in reply to Tupper, who, he said, had urged the Government to "wave the bloody shirt and say we would have nothing to do with these grasping Yankees": "He would have found that he did not own the country in six months or so if he had followed that policy" (*Debates*, Feb. 15, 1898, pp. 588–89).

the Yukon from the United States if Canada had been able to enforce exclusive economic privileges for Canadian nationals in the gold fields? The result would surely have been an explosion of resentment forcing not only the opening up of the Yukon but also its seizure. The United States ability to enforce the open door in the Yukon probably prevented its political loss to Canada. But Canada's inability to deny equal economic rights to Americans entering Canadian territory produced a jingoistic intransigence in Canada that boded ill for Laurier's hope of an extensive settlement of difficulties with the United States.

8. The Background of the Joint High Commission

UNITED STATES INDIFFERENCE to Canadian interests and Canadian resentment of that indifference were the barriers to Laurier's hope of establishing friendly relations with Canada's neighbour. His strategy, therefore, was to bide his time until either country's need to settle a particular problem with the other might provide the opportunity of raising the issue of a general settlement. Opportunity came in the fall of 1897 when the United States sought a settlement of the fur-seal question.

I

For nearly two decades after the purchase of Alaska, American interests had enjoyed a virtual monopoly in catching fur-seals off the Pribilof Islands in the Bering Sea. In the late 1880's Canadian sealers intruded by catching seals in the open sea, a practice called pelagic sealing. Their actions cut into the American company's profits and the United States Treasury receipts, and threatened the extermination of the seals. Under company pressure the United States seized a number of Canadian vessels and fined or imprisoned their officers. Britain protested against these seizures and actions and the assumption that the Bering Sea was a *mare clausum*, and threatened to send warships to protect the sealers.[1] Eventually an arbitration treaty was signed, and the arbitrators in 1893 decided at Paris against the United States and laid down five-year regulations to preserve the seals. The decision was resented by the United States, but the stipulation that the regulations were to be reviewed every five years gave the American sealers renewed opportunities to harass the pelagic sealers.[2] On the accession of the McKinley administration, General John W. Foster (1836–1917), former Secretary of State, was appointed special "fur-seals commissioner,

[1]Tansill, pp. 314–15, and Col. George T. Denison, *The Struggle for Imperial Unity: Recollections & Experiences* (London, 1909), pp. 151–54.
[2]Campbell, pp. 82–83.

plenipotentiary," and Canada and Britain were now subjected to a diplomatic onslaught on the question of fur-seals. Foster accused the British Government of bad faith in refusing to carry out the terms of the Paris award—an accusation apparently true and published.[3] Although there were many professions of compassion for the seals, the Secretary of the Treasury in September 1897 let it be known that if Canada did not agree to accept $500,000 to give up pelagic sealing, all the seals would be branded, and, if Canada remained obdurate, exterminated.[4]

Foster convened three conferences virtually concurrently. At the first Japan, Russia, and the United States agreed to refrain from pelagic sealing for one year provided Great Britain did likewise. Britain declined. The second, consisting of American, British, and Canadian experts, concluded that there was no fear of the extinction of seals. Neither of these conclusions appealing to Foster, he invited Sir Louis Davies and Sir Wilfrid Laurier to a third conference at Washington, and proposed to them the convening of a conference on outstanding Canadian-American differences, provided Canada suspend pelagic sealing for one year. Canada refused; a one-year suspension would simply destroy an already weakened Canadian industry.[5] Foster next proposed to Britain the appointment of three naturalists from Britain, Canada, and the United States to make binding regulations. Canada would consent only on terms unacceptable to Foster: a mixed commission should be convened at once "to settle if possible all questions in dispute" and the decisions of the naturalists should be both "unanimous" and "subject to approval of mixed Commission. . . ."[6]

On March 10, 1898, the coming struggle with Spain eased the situation. Pauncefote, taking advantage of presenting General Gascoigne at the White House, observed to the President that Foster's conditions prevented the establishment of a mixed commission.[7] The President agreed in principle to such a commission and authorized a preliminary investigation into its possibilities. But for two months Canada delayed sending a delegate to a preliminary conference, almost certainly until the United States eased bonding regulations in Alaska.[8]

[3]Tansill, pp. 355–56.

[4]Laurier Papers, pp. 16642–43 (copy), Wm. Stead to Lady Aberdeen, Sept. 24, 1897; for the complete letter and commentary see Bingham Duncan, "A Letter on the Fur Seal in Canadian-American Diplomacy," *Can. Hist. Rev.*, XLIII (March 1962), pp. 42–47.

[5]For important letters exchanged, see *Can. Sess. Pap.* (no. 39), 1898, pp. 1–5; see also C.O. 42/848, pp. 359, 362, and C.O. 42/854, pp. 436–38.

[6]C.O. 42/856, p. 235, Aberdeen to Chamberlain, paraphrase cable, draft, Feb. 16, 1898.

[7]Conf. 7135, pp. 1–2, Pauncefote to Salisbury, "Confidential," March 10, 1898.

[8]Laurier Papers, p. 214983, Aberdeen to Pauncefote, May 16, 1898.

From May 25 to May 30 a preliminary conference was held at Washington to settle the agenda, procedure, and structure of a joint high commission. The five principal subjects on the agenda were naval vessels on the Great Lakes, fur-seals, North Atlantic fisheries, reciprocity, and the Alaska boundary.[9] Laurier instructed Davies to seek an "immediate appointment of tribunal of experts"[10] to locate the Alaska boundary, but Davies could only obtain in the protocol a statement of settlement "by legal and scientific experts if the commission shall so decide, or otherwise."[11]

In the meantime, the "hands-across-the-sea" mood of the Spanish-American War had led to the settlement of claims against the United States for seizures of Canadian sealing vessels in the late 1880's. Two commissioners appointed under a convention signed February 8, 1896, made a decision on December 17, 1897, to award Canada $473,151.26. In the following April Henry Cabot Lodge introduced into the Senate the necessary appropriation bill, which in June was unanimously approved by the Congress.

II

The indirect benefits Canada derived from the Spanish-American War require a more careful examination of the influence of the war itself on the Dominion. The underlying causes of the Spanish-American War were much the same as those of the Venezuela incident: the "psychic crisis" of the 1890's, popular movements of reform, and a sense of national self-assertion which was particularly fostered by a small imperialistic élite of politicians, publicists, and intellectuals, with Theodore Roosevelt as the spearhead, who considered the United States to be lagging in the competition among nations.[12]

In February 1895 rebellion against Spain broke out in Cuba, an island long regarded as being in the sphere of United States interest. The outbreak found Americans in an aggressive mood. A Cuban junta was established in New York, and poured supplies and money into the

[9]The conference members were John Kasson, John W. Foster, Sir Julian Pauncefote, and Sir Louis Davies; for an account of the conference see "Protocol of the Conference at Washington in May, 1898 . . . ," in William M. Malloy, comp., *Treaties, Conventions, International Acts, . . . between the United States of America and Other Powers 1776–1909* (Washington, 1910), I (no. 5646), pp. 770–73, and Conf. 7135, pp. 6–8.

[10]Laurier Papers, p. 224885, Laurier to Davies, telegram, May 28, 1898.

[11]Malloy, *Treaties*, p. 771.

[12]Richard Hofstadter, "Manifest Destiny and the Philippines," in Daniel Aaron, ed., *America in Crisis* (New York, 1952), pp. 173–85. A general confirmation of the Hofstadter thesis will be found in Perry E. Gianakos, "The Yanko-Spanko War" (doctoral dissertation, New York University, 1961).

island. Seventy-one filibustering expeditions set out, twenty-seven of which successfully landed; the United States stopped thirty-three, and Spain five. Spain had good reason to complain of the United States attitude: of American professions of humanity, of recognition of the insurgents by Congress, and of Congress' insistence on concessions from Spaniards but not from rebels. In spite of Spanish helplessness, Spain could not, out of national pride and fears for the dynasty, allow the struggle to go by default.[13] The explosion of the *Maine* in Havana harbour precipitated the jingoistic desire for war—a desire nurtured by American traditions, ideologies, and the provocations of the yellow press. In April Congress, caught up in the frenzy, declared war.

No American interest of such scope could escape Canadian attention. In the early years of the rebellion Canadians generally approved of the Spanish position. Gradually, however, reports of Spanish atrocities swung Canadian newspapers—most of them Liberal—over to the American side. Nor did reports in Canada of "A Satanic Spirit" in the yellow press which demanded war delay this swing.[14] The lingering doubts of most English Canadians were overcome by increasing anarchy in Cuba and by British sympathy for the American cause.[15]

With the approach of war Britain and Canada were benevolently neutral towards the United States: Britain because it desired friendship and Canada because it sought a settlement.[16] Neutrality, however, involved Canada directly. Early in April 1898 Canada granted permission to four United States revenue cutters to pass through the canals to the ocean. On the outbreak of war two weeks later the Foreign Office and the Law Officers of the Crown weighed the possibility of rescinding this permission, in order to maintain Canada's neutrality under article VI of the Treaty of Washington of 1871. Canada and Chamberlain objected: Canada had given the permission to avoid "ill feeling" and Chamberlain was "extremely anxious" to avoid the appearance of "an unfriendly enforcement of the laws of neutrality against" the United States.[17] The voyages were completed without incident.

---

[13]A. E. Campbell, *Great Britain and the United States 1895–1903* (London, 1960), pp. 127–30 and 130, n. 1.

[14]Edit., Halifax *Chronicle*, March 26, 1898; see also *Globe*, comment on March 1, 1898: certain men would profit not "by stopping . . . but in supplying bullets."

[15]William N. H. Whitely, "Canadian Opinion on American Expansionism 1895–1903" (master's thesis, Queen's University, 1952), pp. 68–75.

[16]For a public statement of the official Canadian position see *Globe*, April 18, 1898; but cf. *Mail and Empire*, April 22, 1898, edit., "Canada's Neutrality," which stated, "Let us mind our own business."

[17]C.O. 42/857, pp. 111–14, C.O. to F.O., "Immediate & Confidential," draft, April 23, 1898; *ibid.*, pp. 106–10, 153–56; C.O. 42/862, pp. 157–58; and R. B. Mowat, *The Life of Lord Pauncefote* (Boston, 1929), pp. 209–10.

There was no doubt, however, that Canada's neutrality was violated by at least one of the two members of the staff of the Spanish Embassy in Washington, Juan du Bosc and Ramon Carranza, who arrived in Canada from the United States early in the war. They were at first met with curiosity and courtesy; Sir Oliver Mowat, the Lieutenant Governor of Ontario, hesitated to invite them to dine with the Governor General and Lady Aberdeen because of "national considerations,"[18] but Colonel Denison, who had been involved in anti-Northern activities during the Civil War, did not hesitate to invite them to his home.[19] Two days later du Bosc, who had been first secretary of the embassy, lectured in Massey Hall, Toronto, at the inaugural meeting of the Canadian Branch of the British Red Cross Society. To an audience of about 1500, which included Most Rev. John Walsh (Roman Catholic Archbishop of Toronto), the Premier of Ontario, Goldwin Smith, and Dr. Parkin, du Bosc outlined the Spanish position in the war, and concluded his address with a warning to Europe, Mexico, and Canada: ". . . if the United States should triumph whose will be the next turn?"[20]

Du Bosc's anti-American speech, which does not seem to have been repeated, was contrary to the pro-American but officially neutral policy of the Government. Early in the war Laurier offered his good wishes to the Acting Secretary of State.[21] He later wrote to a supporter: "Our sympathies are strongly with the United States; but you know very well that officially, we have to be absolutely neutral."[22] Yet much English-Canadian opinion during the war appears to have been pro-Spanish and anti-American. A member of Parliament expressed the hope of many Canadians that the United States would "get a little bit of a spanking to begin with," because of its poor treatment of Canada, an utterance deplored by both Laurier and Tupper.[23]

Pro-Spanish sympathies dwindled, however, when American agents exposed a Spanish attempt to set up a spy system in Canada. In late May Canadian newspaper readers were entertained by accounts of Spanish spies pursued by American agents in Canada seeking evidence of espionage. The Chief of the United States Treasury Secret Service, John E. Wilkie, boasted that one of his agents, posing as a health inspector,

---

[18]Laurier Papers, pp. 22979–85, Mowat to Laurier, May 2, 1899. The invitation does not seem to have been extended.

[19]Denison Papers, Diary, p. 272, May 1, 1898.

[20]*Globe* and *Mail and Empire*, May 6, 1898, and George Sterling Ryerson, *Looking Backward* (Toronto, 1924), pp. 120–21.

[21]Laurier Papers, pp. 23131–32, W. R. Day to Laurier, May 7, 1898.

[22]*Ibid.*, p. 22972, to W. D. Gregory, May 19, 1898.

[23]William McCleary (Conservative, Welland, Ont.), *Debates*, May 18, 1898, pp. 5792–95.

had stolen an incriminating letter from the Montreal lodging of the former Spanish diplomats. In the letter Carranza, who had been the naval attaché, informed the Spanish Minister of Marine that he had been left in Montreal "to look after the spy service, which I have organized, or, I had better say, am establishing here."[24] The British Ambassador to Washington satisfied himself as to the authenticity of the stolen letter, which he was shown, and was informed of the manner of its acquisition.[25]

The stealing of the letter was of course equally a violation of Canadian neutrality and of British law, and the Foreign Office considered prosecuting an American detective for alleged complicity in the theft. Pauncefote did not relish the duty of making a remonstrance; fortunately for Pauncefote, Salisbury minuted: "If we prosecute the man on confidential information given to us by the United States Government, we must not expect ever to receive confidential information again. I would certainly drop the matter."[26] Chamberlain, informing Canada of the purloined letter, reported it as having been "intercepted" in the United States. He also relayed the opinion of the Law Officers of the Crown that if the facts were as alleged both Carranza and du Bosc should be asked to leave the country.[27]

The delay in their expulsion turned on the absence, or at least the uncertainty, of the law regarding the expulsion of aliens. The Minister of Justice, relying on a House of Lords decision in 1842, offered the legal opinion that the Crown had no right of expulsion for no law existed.[28] The Canadian Government therefore raised the question with the Colonial Office whether, since Canada had "no Alien Act now in force," the power of expulsion resulted "from the Common Law, or from Imperial legislation."[29] This exposure of Britain's legal vulnerability produced bluster among the lower Colonial Office officials. One actually minuted that if Carranza were not withdrawn he should be turned out of

---

[24]The letter, Carranza to José Gomez Inay, dated May 26, 1898, and the American boast are in the *Globe*, June 6, 1898.

[25]*Mail and Empire*, June 7, 1898, and C.O. 42/862, pp. 600–1, Pauncefote to Salisbury, June 10, 1898, inc. in F.O. to C.O., "Secret," June 30, 1898.

[26]Mowat, *Lord Pauncefote*, pp. 210–11.

[27]C.O. 42/862, p. 437, Chamberlain to Aberdeen, paraphrase cable, June 6, 1898. Lord Salisbury argued that they should be expelled because of a "purpose inconsistent with the neutrality of this Country": *ibid.*, p. 438, F.O. to C.O., "Pressing and Confidential," June 6, 1898.

[28]*Creole Case*; Laurier Papers, pp. 24180–83, opinion of David Mills, June 9, 1898.

[29]C.O. 42/857, p. 360, and Laurier Papers, p. 215005, Aberdeen to Chamberlain, paraphrase cable, June 9, 1898.

Canada by an act of state, put on an English-bound ship, or carried off by a captain of a gunboat dispatched to Montreal for that object. Another, armed by the Lord Chancellor's opinion that the prerogative right to expel existed and should be exercised even at the "risk of its being held not to exist," suggested a peremptory telegram to Canada ordering his expulsion—a suggestion disapproved of by his chief.[30] The Foreign Office, fearing diplomatic repercussions, requested the Colonial Office not to send further instructions to Canada on the matter without prior Foreign Office consultation.[31]

Accordingly the Colonial Office informed Canada of the Law Officers' belief that the prerogative power existed and that in the Carranza case the power should be exercised. It lamely concluded that before arresting him the British Government was requesting the Spanish Government to withdraw him.[32] This request was unsuccessful.[33] In the end expulsion depended upon the action of the Canadian Government itself. In spite of the fact that there was some opposition from Quebec, Carranza and du Bosc had to be expelled if the forthcoming Joint High Commission were to succeed. Finally on June 30 Laurier gave orders for their departure: Carranza, on the ground that he had intended to set up a spy system, and du Bosc, "from evidence in our hands" that he was an accomplice; the evidence was never produced, however.[34] Carranza's abuse of asylum justified his expulsion, if not legally, at least politically. The circumstantial evidence against du Bosc, however, made the legality of his expulsion dubious. His English lawyers threatened, but never brought, suit for damages against the British Government.[35]

[30]The last half of the proposed telegram, however, tamely ordered "in event of refusal" an immediate report. Minutes of John Anderson, H. Bertram Cox, and E. Wingfield, Under-Sec., respectively, all dated June 9, 1898, C.O. 42/857, pp. 359–60. For two Canadian opinions on the legality of the expulsion, see W. Martin Griffin, Toronto, "Colonial Expulsion of Aliens," 33 *Amer. Law Rev.* (1899), pp. 90–96, and A. H. Marsh, Toronto, "Colonial Expulsion of Aliens: An Answer," *ibid.*, pp. 246–53.

[31]C.O. 42/857, pp. 363–65, T. H. Sanderson to E. Wingfield, June 11, 1898.

[32]Laurier Papers, p. 215010, Chamberlain to Aberdeen, cypher telegram, June 12, 1898, and C.O. 42/862, p. 480.

[33]C.O. 42/862, pp. 487–90, 500, 512, 525, decyphers of telegrams passing between Salisbury and H. Drummond Wolff from June 10, 1898, to June 16, 1898.

[34]Laurier Papers, pp. 24674–75, Laurier to H. C. Saint Pierre, June 30, 1898.

[35]"Really we expelled him because he was believed to be associated with Carranza both having been colleagues at Washington, and if the one was organizing a spy system it was pretty fair inference that the other was in the plot too" (C.O. 42/871, p. 380, minute, H. B. Cox, May 12, 1899). The lawyer later offered to submit the matter to arbitration but the Government stood its ground and the matter fell through. C.O. 42/867, pp. 31–40, 47–51; C.O. 42/871, pp. 379–98; and C.O. 42/874, pp. 625–28.

On the whole, neutrality was a governmental rather than a popular interest. Except for the spy question popular interest centred in the excitement and drama of war. Hundreds of Canadians enlisted in the United States army, many of them probably militiamen moved by adventure and the prospect of American citizenship.[36] There was an avid interest in war news: Canadian newspapers dispatched special correspondents to a war zone for the first time, and Canadians purchased war mementoes such as pictures of warships, heroes, episodes, and the like.[37] But the war was short; and the large amount of news in journals at the beginning soon dwindled except for descriptions of important battles. Moreover, Canada was not a participant but an entertained onlooker in the "Yanko-Spanko" war.[38] The Halifax *Chronicle* noted that "A war . . . is . . . like a theatrical performance, in which the belligerent forces are the actors and the nations of the civilized world the spectators."[39]

The thrill that the war engendered is also shown in the popularity of war pageants and military tattoos. In September 1898, of all the "spectacular performances" at the annual Toronto Industrial Exhibition, " 'The Bombardment of Santiago' " was described as easily the "most beautiful and interesting."[40] In the following year at the Halifax Exhibition "Next Week's Thrilling Spectacle" was to consist of "The Afghan War" depicting Lord Roberts' march to Kandahar.[41] The absorption in thrills of war could not help but predispose Canadians to participation in war itself—a predisposition fed by envy of American participation in a war that seemed short, cheap, and glorious.[42] The war also created a more sympathetic interest in the United States for Canadian problems,

[36]The writer has seen no estimate of the total number in the American forces but if the number of references to enlistment is a guide, it must have been considerable. One estimate affirms that more than one-third of some Montana regiments were Canadians: Richard Jebb, *Studies in Colonial Nationalism* (London, 1905), p. 110, n. 1. Another estimate said half the soldiers of an Illinois regiment killed in the Santiago Campaign were Canadians: W. D. Gregory to E. F. Baldwin, Oct. 11, 1898, Walter Dymond Gregory Papers, Queen's University, letter book, p. 188.

[37]Dr. Fred Landon of the University of Western Ontario recalled the wearing of "Remember the Maine" buttons (interview, July 22, 1946).

[38]Phrase used by the *Globe* of London, England, and cited in the Denison Papers, p. 3501, Freeman Murray to Denison, "Private," June 15, 1898.

[39]Edit., "Lessons of the War," July 23, 1898.

[40]*Globe*, Sept. 1, 1898.

[41]Halifax *Chronicle*, Sept. 20, 1899. "The Nile Expedition" was staged in the Queen's Theatre of Montreal in 1896: A. S. McCormick, M.D., typescript, "The Victoria Rifles of Canada, 1861–1914" (Akron, Ohio, 1960), p. 11.

[42]I am indebted to Dr. Fred Landon for this suggestion (interview, July 22, 1946).

not primarily on Canada's account but because of the rise of Anglo-American friendship.

III

A recent student of Anglo-American relations, A. E. Campbell, maintains that racial feeling was the most important ingredient in Britain's friendliness towards the United States. In the crisis preceding the war Britain's diplomatic policy was not essentially different from that of the other great powers. None of them wished to offend the United States, either by acting on behalf of Spain or by condemning the United States. When the war broke out, however, the sympathy of British public opinion for the United States stood out in marked contrast to continental opinion, and American opinion responded in gratitude, for Britain was believed to have averted the formation of a coalition of powers against the United States. When the possibility of annexation of the Philippines arose British opinion also abetted the United States because it was believed that American expansion would benefit Britain. Americans were regarded as Anglo-Saxons following Britain's expansionist example.[43]

Canadians did not fail to observe this reorientation or its significance. The *Globe* cited approvingly the opinion of the New York *Commercial Advertiser* which pointed out that the collaboration of the two powers "'excludes continental intervention in American concerns and limits continental invasion of British Imperial rights.'"[44] Canadians also saw that collaboration rested on considerable popular support. The sale of thousands of buttons bearing the Union Jack intertwined with the Stars and Stripes induced the *Globe* to inquire bewilderingly: "What day is this that has dawned upon Anglo-Saxons?"[45] Canadian enthusiasm temporarily expressed itself in a greater friendliness for American societies. It is noticeable that the Orange Grand Lodge, one of whose chief principles was loyalty to the Crown, should welcome the 1900 meeting of its Triennial Council in the United States.[46] Representatives of the Michigan Masons also met at Toronto.

Though these manifestations of friendliness were welcomed, many Canadians could not forget the decades of hostility; a cartoon depicted John Bull requesting to be allowed to heap coals of fire on Uncle Sam's

---

[43]A. E. Campbell, *Great Britain and the United States 1895–1903*, pp. 140–55.
[44]April 26, 1898.
[45]May 6, 1898.
[46]*Ibid.*, June 1, 1898. The Triennial Council represented the Orangemen of Great Britain, the Colonies, and the United States.

head while from the latter's pocket bulged the Senate bill that would harm Canada's Yukon trade.[47] Many examples can be found of an antagonism which a year later hardened into a rejection of American policy. For the moment, however, Anglo-American friendship provided Canada with an opportunity for settlement of outstanding difficulties.

IV

In spite of the advantages of Anglo-American friendship Canadians entered the Joint High Commission in an ambivalent and unhopeful mood. Canadian reluctance was partly due to a confidence born of prosperity. But it also was born of expectations of continued British support, which was fortified in 1898 by an agreement to introduce imperial penny postage. The British Empire League had advocated the measure in Canada and J. (later Sir J. Henniker) Heaton had been its leading advocate in Britain since 1886.

In 1893 the Chancellor of the Exchequer had pledged the introduction of imperial penny postage when finances permitted and the colonies assented. At the Colonial Conference of June and July 1897 Chamberlain virtually invited the colonies to offer penny postage "to bind together the sister nations," for, he believed, Great Britain was "quite ready to make any sacrifice of revenue" for imperial penny postage.[48] With the precedent of Canada's success in imposing imperial preference on the British Government, William Mulock, the Canadian Postmaster General, accepted the invitation. Apparently largely on Mulock's initiative Canada accepted on Christmas Day 1897 letters for delivery in the British Empire at 3¢ per ounce instead of 5¢ per half ounce.[49] Imperial penny postage now became a domestic issue in Britain, as was doubtless intended; the British Post Office on behalf of some of the colonies refused to accept such mail, but proposed a conference, which on Mulock's insistence was made governmental.

With the powerful support of Chamberlain Canada got its way at the conference. Mulock was advised by Chamberlain to request an imperial postage rate of 2¢ per half-ounce instead of the 3¢ per ounce and to stand resolute on his request.[50]

At the opening of the conference Britain advocated 2*d.* per half-ounce and Canada 1½*d.* per ounce. At the next meeting Mulock came

[47]*Ibid.*, March 16, 1898.
[48]*Parl. Pap.*, 1897, LIX (C. 8596, p. 13), p. 642.
[49]Laurier Papers, p. 17933, Mulock to Laurier, "Confidential," Nov. 15, 1897.
[50]*Ibid.*, p. 24947, Mulock to Laurier, July 9, 1898.

closer to the British proposal by advocating, seconded by Cape Colony and supported by Natal, a rate of 1*d*. per half-ounce. He justified the reduction of the rate by five main arguments: (1) the practical closure of the American market turned Canada to Britain, and cheap postage was of "greatest importance" for immigration; (2) the breakdown of former colonial systems emphasized the inexpediency of treating a colony as a "foreign country"; cheap postage would bring great strength to the Empire at little cost; (3) the Chancellor of the Exchequer had made a pledge in 1893 and the Colonial Secretary had supported it in 1897; (4) the Australian colonies should not hamper the proposals of Canada, which had made sacrifices for imperial trade unity; and (5) the denial of cheap postage would produce "grave disappointment."[51]

The British Postmaster General, the Duke of Norfolk, soon observed that the conference had not been called "to propound a policy, but to elicit opinions" and asked the Permanent Under-Secretary of the Post Office, Sir Spencer Walpole, for technical information. Walpole, while sympathizing with lower postal rates and imperial considerations, opposed the Canadian scheme as too costly, and he declared that Britain would renew the offer of 2*d*. per half-ounce letter.[52] At this point Chamberlain intervened, and his communication "with the Chancellor of the Exchequer and the Duke of Norfolk" as reported to Laurier appears to have clinched the matter, for Britain now joined with Canada, Cape Colony, and Natal to agree to establish imperial penny postage at 1*d*. per half-ounce.[53]

The new postal rate would materially benefit only a few Canadian interests. A prominent Ontario lumberman reported to Mulock complaints about the proposed 2¢ postage to Britain as contrasted with the 3¢ local rate. Such people argued that the Canadian Government was "conferring all their favours upon foreigners." These included Americans because under an 1874 Canada–United States postal agreement each country accepted for delivery the mail of the other at its domestic rate. Canada delivered mail from the United States at the domestic rate of 2¢.[54] Accordingly when the 2¢ imperial penny postage was

[51]Laurier Papers, pp. 24951–56, Conf. Post Office Print (proof), "Conference on Postage with the British Empire"; quotations on pp. 24955 and 24956, respectively.
[52]*Ibid.*, pp. 22957–58; cf. Howard Robinson, *The British Post Office: A History* (Princeton, 1948), p. 423.
[53]*Ibid.*, pp. 24795–96, Chamberlain to Laurier, July 7, 1898, and p. 29797, reply, Sept. 2, 1898.
[54]*Ibid.*, p. 28439, John Waldie to Mulock, Nov. 29, 1898; see also *ibid.*, p. 28259, "copy," unsigned letter on *Globe* letterhead (probably from J. Willison) with fewer details to Mulock, "Private," Nov. 21, 1898.

inaugurated on Christmas Day 1898, Canada's domestic rate was re- duced to 2¢ per ounce and that to the United States one week later. The special stamp issued to celebrate the occasion, which Goldwin Smith called a "painted lie,"[55] bore a map of the world with the British Empire in red and the proud imperial boast, "We hold a vaster Empire than has been."[56]

V

Penny postage disclosed something of Canada's ambivalence to im- perial unity. The spirit in which it entered the Joint High Commission discloses something of its ambivalence towards the United States. The prospect of such a conference excited little enthusiasm among Cana- dians. In Parliament one member reminded the House that the American was a hard negotiator, another that the existing Canadian-American friendship might be temporary, and the Premier, though aware of Can- ada's opportunity, recalled to members past uncordial attitudes of the United States, but hoped they would be forgotten.[57] In private Laurier wrote that Canada had received "a warm welcome and some cool pro- posals."[58] Prosperity, trust in Britain, faith in the future, and the advan- tages they already held seemed to convince Canadians that they had time on their side and could wait.[59]

By contrast Chamberlain wanted Canadian and American differences settled and early tried to spur on Canadians to "expedite prepara- tions."[60] But his sense of expedition would not be at the price of the destruction of imperial unity. Thus it was probably on Chamberlain's decision that Canada was permitted to select four out of the five dele- gates as contrasted with one out of five at Washington in 1871, though the latter conference was concerned with Anglo-American as well as

[55]*Debates*, March 20, 1899, p. 74. For a sceptical analysis of these postal changes see Queen's University Library, Walter Dymond Gregory Papers, letter book, pp. 289–90, W. D. Gregory to J. A. Wayland, "Private and Personal," Jan. 12, 1899.

[56]Cf. George Earle Buckle, ed., *Letters of Queen Victoria*, 3rd series (London, 1932), III, pp. 315–16, Minto to Queen Victoria, Dec. 4, 1898.

[57]*Debates*, June 10, 1898, George H. Bertram, p. 7691, and Sam Hughes, p. 7696; Laurier, June 1, p. 6611.

[58]O. D. Skelton, *Life and Letters of Sir Wilfrid Laurier* (Toronto, 1921), II, p. 126.

[59]*Globe*, edit., "The Quebec Conference," July 30, 1898, and John Charlton, "The Commission's Work—Counter Influences," *Can. Mag.*, XIII (May 1899), p. 14.

[60]Conf. 7135, p. 10, Chamberlain to Aberdeen, "Secret" telegram, June 17, inc. in C.O. to F.O., "Confidential," June 21, 1898; see also C.O. 42/862, p. 457, minute of Chamberlain, June 13, 1898.

Canadian-American problems. Secondly, its able and aggressive English leader, Lord Herschell, saw himself as the counsel for Canadian interests,[61] a position of diplomatic advantage to Canadians who would thus not have to bear American antagonisms. In the third place, Chamberlain requested a memorandum of Canadian views, which formed the basis of Lord Salisbury's "observations" to the British delegates. Their precision contrasted with the general vagueness of the United States memorandum.[62]

Chamberlain also supported Canada when Newfoundland forced the inclusion of its representative, bringing the number of delegates to six. By invoking the principle of unity of action which Canada had itself invoked against the Newfoundland–United States Trade Convention of 1890, Newfoundland confronted Britain and Canada with the alternative of inclusion in the British delegation or separate negotiations with the United States. Britain and Canada yielded, but Chamberlain insisted that the Newfoundland delegate support Canada except where Newfoundland's own interests of trade and fisheries were at stake.[63]

The choice of Canadian delegates also suggested a desire for successful negotiation: Laurier himself and Sir Louis Davies, his most trusted political emissary; Sir Richard Cartwright and John Charlton, erstwhile advocates of commercial union, a fact well known in Canada and the United States. Charlton, "popularly known in Canada as the 'member from Michigan' "[64] with an itch to rush into print and to confuse the national interest with his own private lumbering interest, turned out to be an

[61]In a speech at a banquet in Toronto honouring him, Lord Herschell declared: "I can assure you that my best powers, such as they are, will be devoted to serving Canada and the interests of Canada upon the mission in which I am engaged. I shall argue your case as earnestly, and as strenuously, and further your interests as far as I can, as ardently as if I were myself a native born Canadian." *Globe*, Sept. 15, 1898.

[62]Conf. 7135, pp. 33–37, Canadian memorandum, P.C. Despatches, 978K, July 4, 1898, inc. in Aberdeen to Chamberlain, "Secret," July 5, 1898, inc. in C.O. to F.O., "Confidential," July 16, 1898; and cf. C.O. 42/858, pp. 26–27. See Conf. 7135, pp. 24–30, July 19, 1898, for Salisbury's observations, and *ibid.*, pp. 46–48, United States memorandum (undated), inc. in Pauncefote to Salisbury, Aug. 9, 1898. On the question of the necessity of ratification of treaties by colonial legislatures, see Herschell to Salisbury, Oct. 11, 1898 (Conf. 7135, pp. 101–2, and replies, *ibid.*, pp. 107, 110).

[63]Conf. 7135, p. 40, Salisbury to Pauncefote, "Confidential," cable, July 25, 1898; *ibid.*, pp. 20–21, J. S. Winter and Alfred B. Morine to Chamberlain, July 2, 1898, inc. in C.O. to F.O., July 7, 1898; Canada managed to secure the selection of Winter rather than Morine (Laurier Papers, pp. 24801–3 and 25486); cf. Pope Papers, vol. 39 (letter book no. 3), p. 73, J. Pope to R. Boudreau (sec. to Laurier), Jan. 24, 1898.

[64]Campbell, p. 88.

embarrassing colleague. Laurier excluded from the delegation two experts—the most inflexible Canadian nationalists—Clifford Sifton, the Minister of the Interior, and David Mills, Minister of Justice and professor of international and constitutional law.

If the attitude of Canadian public opinion to prospective negotiations be described as national disinterest, that of the United States might be described as national indifference, especially as the diplomatic and military pressures inclining the United States towards Britain had gone. The closest expression to a national interest was the public reaction that forced the United States Senate to reconsider its refusal to pass an appropriation of $50,000 for the expenses of the commission.[65] In spite of the Senate's coolness, President McKinley's support of the commission and the selection of a strong delegation suggest that its members could have induced Congress to approve the decisions of the commission. The delegation consisted of Senator Charles W. Fairbanks as chairman, Senator Charles J. Faulkner, John W. Foster, Congressman Nelson Dingley, Chairman of the Ways and Means Committee, T. Jefferson Coolidge, and John A. Kasson.[66] The choice of Fairbanks as chairman caused surprise,[67] but he appears to have resembled McKinley in character, being equable and affable, and whatever sharpness Foster might display, formal relations between the two countries would remain cordial.

When the President affirmed that anyone who took a " 'pronounced stand' " on any question should not be a member, Sir Louis Davies had high hopes for Foster's exclusion.[68] Pauncefote, who would have heard from Davies, on his own initiative protested to Secretary Day against the rumoured appointment of Foster. Foster had been responsible for an offensive dispatch in May 1897 and in the previous winter's negotiations his language had been "insolent, discourteous and even threatening";[69] his appointment would be "fatal to the harmony of the Com-

[65]Campbell, p. 87, n. 86; Canada's expenses to March 1899 were $33,666.80 (Pope Papers, vol. 69, p. 282).

[66]Senator Faulkner succeeded Senator George W. Gray, who resigned to go as a delegate to the Spanish-American peace conference in Paris.

[67]Lady Aberdeen wrote: "We do not quite understand why he was placed in this position as he is one of the junior Senators & the others did not altogether seem to look upon it as natural." John T. Saywell, ed., *The Canadian Journal of Lady Aberdeen 1893–1898* (Toronto, Champlain Society, 1960), Nov. 19, 1898, p. 475.

[68]Laurier Papers, p. 224853, Davies to Laurier, May 25, 1898.

[69]For a detailed description of this incident, see C.O. 42/854, pp. 637–38, in Conf. F.O. Print, C. F. Adam (first secretary in the Washington Embassy) to Pauncefote, "Confidential," Nov. 23, 1897, inc. in Pauncefote to Salisbury, "Confidential," Nov. 23, 1897.

mission." Pauncefote's action in making an indictment of this kind is a testimony to Washington's respect for his astuteness and courage and to Canada's good fortune.[70] A few days later Day defended Foster's appointment: his exclusion would be "bitterly resented" and might even endanger relations between the two countries. Futhermore his attitude had changed: he was under the "immediate control" of the State Department and had been "talked to" by the President about being more liberal.[71] Foster was certainly not responsible for the adamant United States stand. But he was a convenient scapegoat of obstructionist Americanism, and especially if Canadians intended to repudiate the United States they had to take Foster at his nationalist face value.[72]

Yet Canada entered the conference with some hope. The round of festivities introduced by Canada at Quebec and reciprocated by the United States at Washington suggests the possibility that Canada hoped to repeat the coup of Lord Elgin, who "floated" the reciprocity treaty (1853) "through on champagne."

[70]C.O. 42/862, pp. 473–75, Pauncefote to Salisbury, "Secret," May 31, 1898.

[71]*Ibid.*, pp. 567–68, Pauncefote to Salisbury, "Secret," June 9, 1898, inc. in F.O. to C.O., "Secret," June 23, 1898.

[72]But Joseph Pope wrote that Foster's "bark was always a good deal worse than his bite." Maurice Pope, ed., *Public Servant: The Memoirs of Sir Joseph Pope* (Toronto, 1960), p. 91.

9. The Joint High Commission, 1898-1899

CANADIANS had long complained that their interests had been sacrificed on the altar of Anglo-American friendship. They could not make this complaint of the Joint High Commission, because no treaty was negotiated at all. The majority of the members of the British delegation were Canadians, its leadership rested in the hands of the brilliant English advocate Lord Herschell, who was guided by Canadian wishes, and it received much British support.

The sessions at Quebec lasted from August 23 to October 10, 1898, and at Washington from November 10, 1898, to February 20, 1899. The commission opened with the election of Lord Herschell as President and quickly organized itself into some thirteen committees.[1] The first few meetings in Quebec were largely exploratory and marked by goodwill on each side. Serious negotiations did not begin until after the Republican victory in the November congressional elections. On minor and rather technical subjects decisions were soon reached and by December several articles of agreement were drafted.[2] Of the five subjects of national concern[3] four were closely associated with one another, so far as Canada was concerned, with possibilities of bargaining: Bering Sea sealing, North Atlantic fisheries, reciprocity, and the Alaska boundary. The fifth—war vessels on the Great Lakes—does not appear to have figured in bargaining of this type.

I

Under the Rush-Bagot Convention of 1817 the United States and Great Britain were each permitted a naval force of four 100-ton naval vessels, one on Lake Champlain, one on Lake Ontario, and two on the

[1]For a list of the committees and their personnel, see Conf. 7135, p. 78.
[2]See *ibid., passim.*
[3]Two other issues almost reached a national status—alien labour (*ibid.*, p. 95) and the bonding question (*ibid.*, pp. 36, 46–47, 74–75, 194–95, 208); see also Laurier Papers, letters to and from Sir William Van Horne in 1898.

Upper Lakes; the armament of each vessel was not to exceed one 18-pounder gun. Although the letter of the convention had several times been violated—notably in the 1890's when a 685-ton vessel armed with four 6-pounder guns was put into service on the Upper Lakes—both sides generally adhered to its spirit. A new factor entered with the rise of the modern United States Navy. Great Lakes shipbuilders clamoured to build warships, a clamour which Secretary of State Blaine supported in 1892 and which prompted the Canadian Government to raise the question whether "the British Government is disposed to enter the competition with the United States for naval supremacy on the lakes."[4] Although pressure on the Navy Department to permit bids grew,[5] it was resisted. In 1898 the Colonial Defence Committee wrote a memorandum concerning American warships on the lakes.[6] In the same year Canada had permitted United States revenue cutters to pass through the canals, but was concerned to avoid upsetting the balance of power.

Canada's policy at the Joint High Commission was that the "severity of the restrictions" of the convention should be maintained.[7] The United States in its memorandum did not wish to violate the convention's spirit, but recognized, in Senator Fairbanks' words, that both sides had "temporarily violated" the agreement owing to "changed circumstances." He therefore proposed to modify the existing agreement by substituting training for armed vessels and permitting the construction of warships "under proper regulations and restrictions, for use on the ocean."[8] In reply to Herschell's demand for instructions, Salisbury cabled the opinions of the Colonial Defence Committee, which opposed the first, agreed with the second, and proposed an increase in the size of the armed vessels to 300 tons, each with a 6-pounder gun.[9] On December 2, Herschell recommended the acceptance of the United

---

[4]P.C. Despatches, 1184H, June 28, 1892.

[5]For a reference to a rejection by President Cleveland, see C.O. 42/862, p. 580, Pauncefote to Salisbury, June 11, 1896, in F.O. to C.O., "Confidential," June 27, 1898.

[6]Laurier Papers, p. 214928, "Secret," no. 127M, March 9, 1898; for a discussion of Great Lakes defence problems from an American and a British point of view see Lieut. J. H. Gibbons, U.S.N., "The Great Lakes and the Modern Navy," *North Amer. Rev.*, CLXVI (April 1898), pp. 437–47, and C.O. 42/859, pp. 418–35, copy of report of Capt. W. G. White, R.N., to Sec. of the Admiralty, Nov. 29, 1898.

[7]Conf. 7135, p. 37, Report of the Privy Council, July 4, 1898, inc. in Aberdeen to Chamberlain, July 5, 1898; Salisbury's observations were essentially the same.

[8]*Ibid.*, p. 47, and pp. 61–62, Herschell to Salisbury, Aug. 29, 1898; and cf. pp. 50–52, "Secret," Aug. 22, 1898.

[9]*Ibid.*, p. 72, Sept. 19, 1898, "Memorandum by the Colonial Defence Committee, Secret," Sept. 16, 1898, inc. in C.O. to W.O., "Secret," Sept. 19, 1898.

States proposals. The 1817 agreement should be annulled; two training vessels with two 4″ guns and four of lesser calibre and six revenue cutters each with one 6-pounder rapid-firing gun should be substituted for war vessels; naval vessels might be completed one at a time without being "rendered available for war" and sent through the canals.

Herschell warned that because of pressure from the lake states the alternative would be a demand for at least four training vessels.[10] Though lukewarm, Britain gave its consent. Chamberlain observed:

The agreement is not satisfactory but it is the best we can get & we should do no good by standing out for more. Canada is becoming stronger & must take care of herself. She will have to avoid courses of offence to her great neighbour, but it is important to foresee & provide for all the contingencies of the future in North America. For the present our object sh. be to clear away subjects of irritation.[11]

The rumour of this agreement—especially the provision of the right of American vessels to pass through the canals—excited an angry attack in the *Globe* from Colonel Denison under the rather thin pseudonym of "Canadian." Denison had already warned Laurier in July of the "madness" of permitting United States war vessels to use the St. Lawrence, though it had not been "madness" during the Spanish-American War; and he admitted, too, that Canada probably could not prohibit the United States building dockyards and arsenals and thus could not avoid being at United States mercy in wartime.[12] In the letter to the *Globe* he denounced altering the agreement of 1817 as a concession to friendship with the United States, because "we have had our rights and interests sacrificed time and again by Imperial statesmen to secure the problematical friendship of the United States."[13]

Laurier calmly and suavely tried to remind Colonel Denison of a few strategic facts of Canada's life: "You seem to assume that Great Britain has the power to prevent the United States from building ships on the lakes, & that if she withholds her consent, that will be the end of it." On the contrary the United States could "use her shores as she pleases," and after giving six months' notice to denounce the conven-

---

[10]Conf. 7135, pp. 117–20, Herschell to Salisbury, "Secret," Dec. 2, 1898.
[11]C.O. 42/864, pp. 384–85, minute, Dec. 25, 1898.
[12]Laurier Papers, p. 224948, "Private," July 23, 1898; Willison informed Laurier that if the right were given to pass United States war vessels through Canadian canals, Denison, Grant, and others would "stump" against the Government (*ibid.*, p. 26824, "Private," Sept. 28, 1898).
[13]*Globe*, Dec. 5, 1898; see also Laurier Papers, pp. 225086–87, Denison to Laurier, "Private," Dec. 8, 1898.

tion, she could build as many ships as she liked and "fill the lakes with war ships of every description." Which was better, to permit this situation to develop or to modify the convention of 1817 so as to limit the number of vessels and provide for their prompt dispatch to the sea? He urged Denison "to ponder over all these aspects of a most painful question," and concluded that he intended to be guided by the advice of the "Naval Defence Committee" (the "Colonial Defence Committee"?).[14] In spite of Denison's earlier boast of his "military education"[15] he had to admit that there was force to Laurier's argument, but he warned again of the political temper of the people who wanted "to see the negotiations broken off."[16]

Laurier was blunter to his friends: he complained that the attitude of the "jingo press" was "sheer nonsense."[17] He plied Willison with unanswerable arguments.

I would have supposed that it would have been preferable to have them out of the lakes than in the lakes. Of course, if we keep them from building ships in their own waters, that would be the easiest solution of all, but, if you believe that the American people with their new policy of expansion, are to be prevented from using for that purpose, their own shore, either on the Atlantic, on the Pacific, or on the interior waters, to the full extent of their territorial sovereignty, I very much fear that you fail to consider the present temper of public opinion in the United States.[18]

The argument might have been unanswerable but so were the political facts. Willison warned him that to put this right into a treaty and to sell out pelagic sealing "without any substantial concessions to Canada to counterbalance, will involve you in very serious political losses, if not in the defeat of the Government." One should not be afraid "to face popular clamour" on a "great question" but why "imperil the Government in order to make a treaty at Washington?"[19]

14Denison Papers, pp. 3638–43, "Private," Dec. 13, 1898; Laurier must have known of the existence of the Colonial Defence Committee. Did he for nationalistic reasons dislike its name?

15Laurier Papers, p. 224948, Denison to Laurier, "Private," July 23, 1898.

16*Ibid.*, pp. 29039–42, "Private," Dec. 28, 1898: ". . . I don't think this temper is confined to either political party."

17*Ibid.*, p. 28654, "Private and Confidential," Dec. 8, 1898, Laurier to George H. Bertram, M.P.

18*Ibid.*, pp. 28809–10, Dec. 17, 1898.

19*Ibid.*, pp. 19035b–f, "Private," Dec. 27, 1898; Willison also wrote that he was voicing not simply the "sentiment of Toronto," but that of Ontario. The people would not listen to "your arguments." He was "astonished at the letters" received "even from old Commercial Union Liberals, against concessions to Washington."

II

The United States resolve to prevent pelagic sealing, which its memorandum reiterated, was the occasion for the Joint High Commission. But if Canadians were to give up the practice they demanded compensation for the sealing fleet and for the surrender of the national right of sealing. Davies had informed Laurier in May that even a *"moderate & reasonable* compensation" for a year would make the sealers political enemies.[20] The official British observations proposed, as an equivalent to forgoing the right of pelagic sealing, an "equivalent commercial concession" and compensation for sealing vessels.[21]

Once Canadian sealers learned of Canada's intention of abolishing pelagic sealing, passions rose and the British Columbia Attorney General hurried to Quebec to protest.[22] Laurier eventually had to yield on this question but it was other pressures that forced him to do so. In the meantime the fur-seals committee (Fairbanks, Foster, Herschell, Davies) had discovered that Foster was their only member well versed in this matter, and they adjourned in order to send experts to Victoria for information.[23] By December the United States delegates thought Canada deserved little compensation; the industry was on its last legs, the outcome of its own malpractices in sealing. On the other hand, Lord Herschell, following a British naturalist's report, had contended that the herd though diminished was not being exterminated, but was in a state of equilibrium, whence profits from pelagic sealing would continue. Furthermore, if all the sealing vessels were dumped for sale on the Canadian market they would be practically worthless, and if they were to become the property of America, they would become valuable. For, as he had written earlier, abolition of pelagic sealing would give the United States a "practical monopoly" and save it onerous policing duties costing $150,000 annually, duties normally shared with British ships but in 1898 left to them alone.[24] The Canadian sealer had as much right to complain as the Gloucester, Massachusetts, fisherman, whose attitudes determined those of the American delegation. The surrender of one's livelihood required reasonable compensation otherwise the "vehement hostility of the sealers . . . would spread widely throughout Canada, and

---

[20]*Ibid.*, p. 224876, "Private and Confidential," May 27, 1898.
[21]Conf. 7135, pp. 24–26, and *ibid.*, p. 46 (for United States memorandum).
[22]Campbell, pp. 91–92.
[23]*Ibid.*, p. 91, W. Chauncy (later Sir W. Chauncy) Cartwright, sec. of British delegation, to F. A. (later Sir F. A.) Campbell (F.O. official), Oct. 10, 1898.
[24]Conf. 7135, p. 63, Herschell to Salisbury, Sept. 2, 1898.

might endanger the existence of the present Canadian Government and the ratification of the Treaty."[25] By February 1899 the United States offered $500,000 for the sealing fleet, the sum unofficially suggested in September 1897, and for national compensation agreed to give an unspecified percentage of the receipts on all seals beyond the estimated 20,000 seals that would be caught annually off the Pribilof Islands if pelagic sealing continued.[26] These proposals, which were substantially those carried out in 1911, would have been approved by Congress in 1899.

III

The North Atlantic fisheries problem in 1898 concerned American vessels fishing off Canada and Newfoundland, which, far from their New England bases, had to put in to British ports for bait.[27] According to the *modus vivendi* of 1888 Americans had been permitted to purchase bait provided they paid a licence fee of $1.50 per ship ton. About one-third of the ships evaded taking out a licence, a provision which before 1898 was "enforced with extreme leniency."[28] Threats to enforce strictly were empty because of previous lax enforcement, presidential authority to exclude Canadian and Newfoundland fish from the United States market, and the dwindling importance of the North Atlantic fisheries. Perhaps, however, the privilege of purchasing bait could be exchanged for the abolition of the tariff on fresh fish.

Accordingly the British delegation (Davies, Winter, and occasionally Herschell) tried first to negotiate on the basis of the legal rights of the convention of 1818, which excluded American ships from rights enjoyed under the *modus vivendi* of 1888. But the United States said rights under the convention had become obsolete because of the admission of foreign ships in 1830 to Canada and Newfoundland ports. Thus there was no legal right to sell licences. No progress having been made, the British delegation called on the United States delegation (Faulkner and

[25]*Ibid.*, p. 129, Herschell to Fairbanks, "Confidential," Dec. 21, 1898, inc. Herschell to Salisbury, Dec. 22, 1898; Herschell added that the British delegation was constantly being reminded that the two-thirds ratification requirement of the Senate made an arrangement impossible even if approved by the United States delegation itself. "May I not in fairness ask that our position should also sometimes be taken into account?"

[26]*Ibid.*, pp. 155–56, Herschell to Salisbury, Feb. 7, 1899; C. C. Tansill says that the offer was raised to $600,000 and that the percentage was 7½. There seems no confirmation of these figures in available British documents.

[27]P. T. M'Grath, "The Atlantic Fisheries Question," *North Amer. Rev.*, CLXVII (Dec. 1898), pp. 729–30.

[28]Conf. 7135, p. 101, Herschell to Salisbury, "Confidential," Oct. 11, 1898.

Coolidge) to make suggestions. It refused. Thereupon at the end of November Herschell saw Fairbanks privately on the failure to come to a fisheries agreement when feelings for Britain were said to be so favourable: it "seemed strange" that it was "more important to conciliate a single town"—Gloucester, Massachusetts—than to "insure a satisfactory settlement with Britain."[29] At that time Fairbanks acknowledged the force of these representations. Massachusetts senators were powerful: Hoar would not approve a treaty like the one he had helped reject in 1888, and Lodge thought Gloucester "a nursery of seamen" for the navy and a future congressional district for his son-in-law.

The British delegation, realizing that the United States purchase of Canadian and Newfoundland bait was a valuable bargaining point, proposed throwing open these ports on three conditions: (1) that the British right to issue licences be based not on treaty right but sovereignty, (2) that American vessels be excluded from bays with entrances of less than a specified width, and (3) that the United States lower tariffs on Newfoundland minerals and Maritimes agricultural products. The United States delegation agreed to the first two, but opposed the third.

Would Newfoundlanders and Maritimers have supported such an agreement? Herschell wrote that fishermen of the area had been taught to value their privileges, and that Davies and Winter would not have signed a treaty involving their abandonment without important tariff concessions.[30]

IV

Canada's failure to use fish to bargain its way into American markets paralleled its failure to use the other natural products of the forest, soil,

[29]*Ibid.*, p. 115, Herschell to Salisbury, Nov. 25, 1898; Gloucester did not want a settlement (C.O. 42/864, pp. 306–8, Sir Louis Davies to Pauncefote, inc. in Pauncefote to Salisbury, "Confidential," Nov. 5, 1898, inc. in F.O. to C.O., Nov. 25, 1898); the *Globe* reported that Gloucester fishermen hoped to displace Canadian and Newfoundland codfish in Cuba and Porto Rico (Nov. 12, 1898).

[30]Conf. 7135, p. 155, to Salisbury, Feb. 7, 1899. Lodge's phrase is in letter to Henry White, Jan. 7, 1899, Tansill, p. 91. Is the foregoing account the whole story of North Atlantic fisheries? In an article, "Work of the Joint High Commission" by an anonymous writer, "A Canadian Liberal," in *North Amer. Rev.*, CLXVIII (May 1899), p. 619, the following statement appears: "It is pretty certain that the free importation of fresh fish from the Maritime Provinces is already largely secured by clandestine arrangements, fresh fish being transferred from Canadian vessels at sea to fishing vessels from the United States, which go out with scanty provisions and speedily return with phenomenal catches." As there is good reason to believe this article was written by John Charlton, it is probably true. See below, p. 200, n. 11.

and mine. Except for a fairly strong ideological concern among leaders of the two countries, little popular or vested interest for reciprocity existed in either country.[31] Interest in Canada was largely a nostalgic yearning for the reciprocity era of 1854–66. But reciprocity on those terms was irrelevant to the conditions of 1898–99. The United States might open its markets to Canada's natural products, but would Canada open its to United States manufacturers? Prosperity and the substitute market in Britain suggested that Canada could do without the United States. Furthermore, past treaties with the United States were now being regarded as surrenders,[32] and many Canadians objected that to woo the United States for reciprocity gave the impression that Canada's economic existence depended on United States economic sufferance.[33] Both sides lacking a compelling national concern, special interests armed with acceptable nationalistic pretexts exerted pressures without much opposition. Whenever a rumour of a reciprocity agreement was noised abroad each delegation was "almost overwhelmed by protests and deputations."[34]

Three other considerations hampered negotiations for a successful trade treaty. The first was the Canadian intention not to offer genuine tariff concessions. Canadians believed that the United States need to settle the fur-sealing and the North Atlantic fisheries problems would make the Americans offer substantial concessions. Secondly, the United States resented Canada's failure to extend the preference to American products, and wanted to make that extension the condition of a lower tariff on Canadian goods.[35] Thirdly, as indicated in a statement of Sir Richard Cartwright to the commission, Canada believed that an "equitable and permanent arrangement" between Canada and the United States would result in vastly increased trade even though Canada now bought more per head than any other United States customer. Admittedly, high tariffs created conditions making "free trade" difficult. "In principle, however, the nearer the Canadian Provinces could be assimilated to the general system of interstate commerce, the more quickly

[31]For a detailed account of reciprocity negotiations at the Joint High Commission see also Charlton Papers, Diary and MS "Autobiography and Recollections," in the library of the University of Toronto.

[32]Laurier Papers, p. 28447, Sifton to Laurier, "Personal," Nov. 29, 1898, and pp. 26067–69, Arthur S. Hardy to Laurier, "Private," Aug. 29, 1898.

[33]Montreal *Gazette*, Sept. 18, 1897, and *Globe*, Oct. 20, 1898.

[34]Conf. 7135, p. 100, Herschell to Salisbury, "Confidential," Oct. 11, 1898; but cf. absence of opinion from the Maritimes (Laurier Papers, pp. 27424–25, Laurier to Sen. L. G. Power, Oct. 27, 1898); for an important statement of Canadian manufacturing and trading opinion see Laurier Papers, pp. 26947–49, "Confidential Memorandum . . . of the Board of Trade (Toronto) . . . ," Oct. 3, 1898.

[35]Campbell, pp. 96–97.

trade would develop on both sides of the frontier."[36] Perhaps Cartwright's statement prompted Dingley's offer of a *Zollverein* to Laurier, an offer that alarmed the secretary of the British delegation, W. Chauncy Cartwright, who reported to the Foreign Office that "Canada would be closed to us as well as the U.S." and that such an arrangement would "be a step to annexation!"[37] Laurier of course rejected it; the Liberal party had been defeated once on that issue.

Of the items considered by the reciprocity committee (consisting of Faulkner, Dingley, Kasson, Sir Richard Cartwright, Charlton, and Davies) perhaps the most important, and certainly the most controversial, was lumber. Following the non-enforcement of the federal law of 1897 restricting the export of saw logs, the Ontario Government had passed the so-called Ontario log export embargo law, requiring Canadian manufacture into sawn lumber of timber cut on Crown lands. Like fishermen who hoped for "free fish for free fishing," Ontario lumbermen hoped for "free lumber for free logs." They believed that the Michigan demand for free logs would force down the American tariff and permit importation of Canada's sawn lumber free or at a low tariff.[38] The restrictive law infuriated Michigan lumber interests which possessed extensive forest stands in Ontario. They threatened to file suit for damages of $400,000 against the Ontario Government. They protested to the Secretary of State that they had an "absolute right" of renewal of licences because the grant was of a "perpetual character" and that the Ontario law amounted to "confiscation." In a supplemental letter they suggested in effect that the Ontario law should be "disapproved" by the Dominion.[39] The Secretary of State pressed for disallowance or discussion of the question at the Joint High Commission. The Canadian Government retailed the first request to the Ontario Government: its Premier and Attorney General, Arthur S. Hardy, established that the law was clearly within provincial jurisdiction and not subject to disallowance.[40] Nevertheless Ontario's attempt to force concessions by retali-

[36]Conf. 7135, p. 75, Herschell to Salisbury, Sept. 20, 1898.
[37]W. Chauncy Cartwright to F. A. Campbell, Oct. 10, 1898, cited in Campbell, p. 101.
[38]Laurier Papers, p. 26796; R. W. Scott wrote to Laurier, Sept. 27, 1898, that an export duty on spruce logs "will force the American people later on to come to our terms."
[39]Conf. 7135, pp. 13–16, Messrs D. M. Dickenson, Robert Lansing, and others, to W. R. Day, June 11 and 13, 1898, inc. in Day to Pauncefote, June 15, 1898, inc. in Pauncefote to Salisbury, June 17, 1898.
[40]*Ibid.*, pp. 54–57, "Memorandum of the Attorney-General" (no date), in Report of the Privy Council, Aug. 3, 1898, inc. in C.O. to F.O., Sept. 3, 1898. John Charlton was accused by Ontario lumberman of trying to induce the Minister

ation failed; Ontario lumbermen overlooked the power of new lumber interests in Wisconsin and Minnesota. By December the British delegation realized that Canada could not obtain major lumber concessions from the United States.

Similar vested interests prevented the free exchange of coal. Central Canada, New England, and the Pacific Coast states would all benefit by import from mines in the adjoining area of the other country. An agreement was actually made for the progressive reduction of duty on bituminous coal over a three-year period. It failed: Nova Scotia coal producers refused to give up the certainties of the Montreal market for uncertain advantages in New England.[41]

V

Canadian delegates entered the Alaska boundary negotiations in the belief that Canada had a poor case. Both sides had taken American ownership of the Lynn Canal for granted; nor did Britain take the Canadian case any more seriously. The unchallenged occupation of the Panhandle and of the Lynn Canal area was the strongest title of the United States. To allay bitterness and preserve the peace Laurier hoped for a permanent boundary settlement or a temporary line giving Canada a port on the Lynn Canal.[42] A strong Pacific Coast opinion existed against making the latter concession. Shipping and exporting interests of Seattle reaping enormous profits and the North American Commercial Company dreading a Canadian port closer to sealing waters than Victoria were unwilling that the United States surrender control of the Lynn Canal area.

At the beginning of the conference Lord Herschell presented Canada with an argument to bolster its case on the Lynn Canal. Indicative of previous Canadian acquiescence in United States predominance was Herschell's discovery that Canada's case was "neglected" for he "found

---

of Justice to declare the Ontario law *ultra vires*. "In this he was the active agent of Michigan saw-mill owners." (Laurier Papers, p. 25201, "Personal & Private," July 21, 1898; see Laurier's defence of Charlton, *ibid.*, p. 25203.) A number of Quebec firms attempted to obtain an embargo for spruce lumber and pulp (Laurier Papers, pp. 26590, 26728, 28423).

[41]Conf. 7135, p. 211, memorandum by W. Chauncy Cartwright, March 25, 1899. This is only one incident that suggests that the death of the powerful Nelson Dingley early in January 1899, while unfortunate for the commission, was not an important factor in it failure.

[42]*Ibid.*, pp. 35–36, Canadian memorandum, July 4, 1898, inc. in Aberdeen to Chamberlain, "Secret," July 5, 1898, inc. in C.O. to F.O., "Confidential," July 16, 1898.

that it had not been thoroughly studied or thought out by any Canadian official."[43] Herschell argued that the word "océan" had replaced "mer" at certain points in the treaty of 1825, the obvious purpose being to distinguish the ocean proper from the salt water inlets. Secondly (not really a new point), the boundary could not follow the excessive convolutions of the winding coast but only its general trend.[44] These arguments disconcerted the American delegation: they would have yielded to Canada the upper reaches of the Lynn Canal and reduced American territory in Alaska to a "few jutting promontories," as Secretary Hay wrote resentfully.[45] Senator Fairbanks blandly disregarded Herschell's inconvenient argument by making an offer which assumed United States ownership of the Lynn Canal. Let Canadian ships in the Lynn Canal freely land goods and be transported without duty across Alaska. Lord Herschell testily retorted that Canada did not want to be given the use of her own ports.[46]

In December bargaining began in earnest; Herschell offered everything in the Lynn Canal to the United States except Pyramid Harbor and a strip connecting it with the interior; alternatively, the boundary should be settled by arbitration except that, whatever the decision, Dyea and Skagway would go to the United States and Pyramid Harbor to Canada. In reply Fairbanks offered Canada jurisdiction but not sovereignty over Pyramid Harbor for 50 years and the right of British ships to land equally with Americans. Canada foolishly rejected this offer for the American delegates overlooked that it permitted British vessels to carry between United States ports and Pyramid Harbor. But the offer leaked out, the American delegates accusing Sir Richard Cartwright's son, then in Skagway, as the one responsible.[47] But even if the storm of opposition to the proposal on both sides had not burst then, it would only have been postponed. The legislature of the state of Washington passed a memorial in vehement terms against giving Canada a port.

43*Ibid.*, p. 100, Herschell to Salisbury, "Confidential," Oct. 11, 1898; Campbell uses the word "neglected," p. 105.

44Campbell, p. 107; in the "Confidential Memorandum by Mr. Cartwright on some of the Questions submitted to the Anglo-American Commission" the following appears: "Senator Gray, who was on the Committee at Quebec, admitted quite recently, in a private and confidential manner, that he thought our case a strong one." (Conf. 7135, p. 215).

45William Roscoe Thayer, *Life and Letters of John Hay* (Boston and New York, 1915), II, p. 205, Hay to White, Jan. 3, 1899.

46Campbell, p. 108.

47Pope Papers, Diary, "Anglo-American Joint High Commission at Quebec and Washington 1898–1899," Feb. 11, 1899.

Protests of western shippers at the threat to the carrying monopoly forced the American delegation to withdraw the offer referring to British shipping. But Canadians kept demanding sovereignty of Pyramid Harbor, for it had become a symbol of national ambition.

VI

Meanwhile public doubt concerning the course of the Joint High Commission kept mounting, a doubt which Laurier shared.[48] Distrust of British policy, though not of British power, constituted one of its sources. Britain's power was unmistakably demonstrated over France at Fashoda in the fall of 1898. This demonstration seemed to imply that Britain need not give way to the United States, though it appeared that the policy of friendship to Americans dictated doing so. The apparent disregard of Canadian interests implied in such a policy bore too close a resemblance to traditional Little-England disregard of Canadian loyalty.[49]

For example, in December 1898 President McKinley announced the United States ambition to build an inter-oceanic canal in Central America, an ambition requiring the abrogation of the Clayton-Bulwer Treaty of 1850 between Britain and the United States. The treaty provided that both countries should facilitate the construction of a canal and prohibit its exclusive use or fortification. Under the assumption of the existence of imperial unity Canada hoped that these treaty rights could be exchanged for Canadian demands on the Lynn Canal. On February 4, 1899, the British cabinet supported the settlement of the Alaska boundary and the modification of United States navigation laws as the price of abrogation of the Clayton-Bulwer Treaty. But on February 17, F. H. Villiers of the Foreign Office informed Henry White, United States chargé in London, that Britain intended to yield on the Clayton-Bulwer Treaty when public opinion permitted.[50] British press

---

[48]Cf. his speech at Kingston, Ont., *Globe*, Oct. 19, 1898.

[49]Canadians seemed curiously apathetic about the Fashoda affair, which was amply reported in the Canadian press. Though there was some French-Canadian reaction (John T. Saywell, ed., *Canadian Journal of Lady Aberdeen 1893–1898* (Toronto, Champlain Society, 1960), Nov. 19, 1898, pp. 481–82) and some attempts were made to pit English and French Canadians against one another, English Canadians were indifferent, interested in their own imperialism in the Yukon and in the outcome of the Joint High Commission. The affair provided Britain with the opportunity of raising the question of Canadian military participation overseas; see below, pp. 188–91.

[50]Campbell, pp. 133–35, and Tansill, p. 179.

suggestions that this should be done in the interests of Anglo-American friendship called forth a Canadian rejoinder from David Mills.[51] Furthermore Chamberlain's attachment to Canada began to seem doubtful, for he was ardently wooing United States friendship in speech and in an article written for *Scribner's* in December 1898.[52]

These actions suggested that Canadian interests would be sacrificed to the United States, as eventually they were. But few prominent Canadians in 1898 would have admitted that Britain when confronted by an adamant United States had no alternative but to yield. Britain had to give way on the inter-oceanic canal, however; Pauncefote reported that the United States would never permit the joining of the Isthmian canal and the Alaska boundary questions in one treaty.[53] The Venezuela incident also demonstrated that Britain lacked the power in the Americas to withstand the United States. Canadians were reluctant to face this fact, because of its implications for their national existence. They preferred to contemplate Britain as an old world-wide power, whose resources they fondly believed could be mobilized in America.

British authorities, aware of Canada's doubts about Britain's firmness towards the United States, strove to reassure Canadians.[54] Chamberlain pointed to the fact that the majority of delegates on the Joint High Commission were Canadians as evidence of Britain's good faith, and to Herschell's role as Canada's counsel. But the truth was the Canadians did not want to accept the implication of national responsibility which the Canadian majority on the Joint High Commission implied. Indeed none of the Canadian commissioners concerned himself with an over-all view; they trusted Herschell and left the over-all management of the negotiations in his hands.[55]

But although these doubts of Britain's fidelity in support of Canada against the United States were only occasionally expressed, the longer negotiations with the United States continued and the more rumours of unacceptable agreements leaked out, the more anxiety grew that Canada was being forced into yielding to the United States. A cry went up

[51]*Globe*, Feb. 8, 1899; see also two articles on "The Nicaragua Canal and the Clayton-Bulwer Treaty," in *Can. Mag.*, XII (March and April 1899), pp. 385–91 and 480–81.

[52]Rt. Hon. Joseph Chamberlain, "Recent Developments of Policy in the United States and Their Relation to an Anglo-American Alliance," XXIV, pp. 674–82.

[53]Conf. 7340, p. 1, Pauncefote to Salisbury, cable, Feb. 9, 1899.

[54]Minto Papers, letter book no. 1, p. 60, Minto to Lansdowne, "Private," Jan. 27, 1899; and cf. C.O. 42/864, pp. 364–65.

[55]C. O. 42/871, p. 246, minute of John Anderson, April 22, 1899.

against making a treaty without great benefits, but in the prevailing mood this really meant no treaty at all. Liberal leaders cautioned Laurier of the danger of submitting a treaty to Parliament. Willison warned Laurier that without "substantial advantages" the "best treaty would be no treaty."[56] The second-in-command of the Ontario Government, George W. Ross, wrote: "All our anxiety here is for the country and the Liberal party. To offend the Canadian sentiment at the present moment is a more serious thing than to offend the Tory sentiment. Toryism we can control; Canadianism we cannot. It is stronger among our own people and far more sincere than among our opponents."[57]

Until the end Laurier carried on a strong rearguard action to beat off demands to come home without a treaty. In January he deprecated *Globe* and Tory belligerency towards the United States: "There is a feeling in Ontario today among our friends that I could make myself a hero, by abruptly breaking off negotiations & proudly coming back to Canada, thus showing to the Americans that we are made of some stern stuff."[58] In one of his rare philosophic observations he vindicated to Sifton his willingness to abolish pelagic sealing: "It is the true part of statesmanship to act with some courage and in prevision of future events."[59]

But pressure from Canada was relentless. Early in February Sifton, Mills, Fielding, and A. G. Blair, Minister of Railways, forced the summoning of a ministerial conference on commission matters in New York, to which Laurier, Davies, and Cartwright travelled from Washington. The four opposed any settlement without a sovereign port on the Lynn Canal and demanded an unattainable degree of reciprocity.[60] Their attitude emphasized the truth of Lord Herschell's January statement to Senator Fairbanks:

> ... unless we can defend on their merits, as a fair settlement, by themselves ... the result[s] arrived at, we can only do so if we can point to concessions made in other parts of the Treaty which will make it palatable. You would be, I am sure, the first to regret that the net result of the Treaty should be

---

[56]Laurier Papers, p. 28849, "Private," Dec. 20, 1898.
[57]*Ibid.*, p. 29029, "Private," Jan. 9, 1899; cf. *ibid.*, p. 29024, Dec. 27, 1898.
[58]Willison Papers, pp. 17874–75, Laurier to Willison, "Private," Jan. 7, 1899.
[59]Sifton Correspondence, p. 46675, "Private and Confidential," Jan. 28, 1899.
[60]Pope Papers, Diary, "Anglo-American Joint High Commission," Feb. 4, 1899. Laurier would have been kept fully informed of the state of the cabinet and Canadian sentiment by the periodic visits of Sifton, Fielding, and Tarte to Washington; cf. *ibid.*, Jan. 18, 1899.

to turn out of office my colleagues—the representatives of a party which has been condemned by not a few as too friendly to the United States. The consequences would be disastrous to the relations of the two countries.[61]

It is doubtful whether the United States delegates had any concern for the fate of the Canadian Government.

On February 3, the day before the cabinet meeting and possibly partly prompting it, the United States made a substantial reciprocity offer on minerals, coal, and lumber, and put on the free list many articles made of wood.[62] This offer may have been made partly to conceal the United States embarrassment at its withdrawal the next day, owing to west coast pressure, of the December offer to permit British ships to carry between American ports and the Lynn Canal area. The Canadian delegation rejected the offer; they doubted its firmness, thought the duties too high, and could not be persuaded by Herschell to resist the "unreasonable pressure" of their Ottawa colleagues.[63] Canada's action suggests the setting up of impossible demands as a pretext not to make a treaty.

The Alaska boundary offer withdrawn and reciprocity rejected, it was now to Canada's interest to terminate the commission in such a way as to preserve the Government's power, maintain national unity, and avoid offending the United States. To break off on reciprocity would be to disturb Government supporters; to break off on the Alaska boundary would cause less disunity.[64] The possibility had crossed Laurier's mind late in December,[65] but the decision, reached by February 8, 1899, must have been made reluctantly.[66] Laurier wavered, unwilling to make the actual break almost to the day of termination. The British secretary noted that at the last session Laurier was "burning with suppressed

[61]Conf. 7135, p. 198, "Private," Jan. 24, 1899, inc. in Cartwright to Salisbury, "Confidential," March 3, 1899. Herschell added that he was "still looking forward to the fulfilment of the President's words: 'You must have something that you want' " (*ibid.*, p. 199).

[62]Tansill, pp. 454–56, Fairbanks to McKinley, Feb. 3, 1899. Joseph Pope called this offer an "ultimatum"; Pope Papers, Diary, "Anglo-American Joint High Commission," Feb. 4, 1899.

[63]He used arguments "for the best interests of Canada, even if Imperial interests were wholly excluded from consideration" (Conf. 7135, p. 156, Herschell to Salisbury, Feb. 7, 1899).

[64]Arnold Haultain, *Goldwin Smith, His Life and Opinions* (London, 1913), p. 79. On February 1 the Canadian delegation discussed the free coal question, and to the surprise of Sir Richard Cartwright and John Charlton, Sir Louis Davies and Sir Wilfrid Laurier opposed it (Charlton, "Autobiography and Recollections," p. 847).

[65]Laurier Papers, p. 29038, Laurier to Charlton, "Private," Dec. 24, 1898. But Laurier apparently crossed out the idea before sending it to Charlton.

[66]Conf. 7135, pp. 156, 199.

fury."[67] Nevertheless on February 12 Herschell had cabled Salisbury that "a crisis . . . seems imminent" and requested permission to adjourn negotiations. Two days later the cabinet gave permission.[68]

By February 8, the United States delegation had been made aware of the British delegation's probable intention to rest all negotiations on the "success or failure . . . of the Alaska Boundary question."[69] This was embarrassing in view of United States conduct in the Venezuela affair. The United States delegation, however, hoped to salvage something from the subjects agreed upon in principle. As Canadian public opinion was adamant on the Alaska question, the American delegates, suspicious because much arbitration had gone against the United States, presented a series of proposals on that subject. The conditions of the arbitration tribunal and the exclusions of the subjects to be arbitrated were, however, unacceptable to the British delegation.[70] The British delegation's counter proposals were equally unacceptable. To meet United States objections, its final proposal tried to take account of justice and equities but without stating that Dyea and Skagway belonged to the United States.[71] The United States would not accept such an arbitration treaty unless the two places were specifically named. But Canadian opinion would not have accepted that condition unless Pyramid Harbor was also specifically named, a condition equally unacceptable to United States opinion. The United States final proposal was an arbitration commission of three on a side, Dyea and Skagway to be American—a method by which the United States could not lose and by which it might win, as it was to do in 1903. Upon this note the conference officially adjourned. The communiqué issued announced its unlikely reconvocation in the following August and summarized fairly the Alaska boundary differences.[72] Thus the conference ended in failure, and Canada bore the brunt of that failure, for British and American public opinion was by and large

[67]Campbell, p. 116, W. Chauncy Cartwright to F. A. Campbell, Feb. 24, 1899.
[68]Conf. 7135, pp. 152–53.
[69]Conf. 7135, p. 199, Fairbanks to Herschell, "Private and Confidential," Feb. 9, 1899, inc. in W. Chauncy Cartwright to Salisbury, "Confidential," March 3, 1899.
[70]The memorandum and correspondence passing between the two delegations between Feb. 9, 1899, and Feb. 11, 1899 are *ibid.*, pp. 164–67, inc. in Herschell to Salisbury, Feb. 17, 1899.
[71]*Ibid.*, pp. 174–77, and cf. *ibid.*, p. 216.
[72]Campbell, p. 116, W. Chauncy Cartwright to F. A. Campbell, Feb. 24, 1899. In form the last two weeks were very polite, but the last two months had shown an undercurrent of friction. For example, Herschell stated to Fairbanks in his letter of Dec. 31, 1898, that "where we differ as to the respective rights of the two countries, the contention of the United States is always the correct one, and . . . the British claim is always without any foundation" (Conf. 7135, p. 192).

indifferent. While officialdom in Britain thought little of Canada's Alaska boundary case, in the United States Canada was regarded as a nuisance troubling Anglo-American relations.

VII

Why then were the negotiations suddenly broken off? The necessity for cabinet members to return to Ottawa to prepare for the parliamentary session was one reason. Laurier's belief—or at least excuse—that Canada could obtain a treaty on some subjects whenever she desired one was another.[73] More important was the inadequacy of Lord Herschell's leadership. He was a gentleman lawyer and not an accomodating politician. According to W. Chauncy Cartwright, one of his great mistakes was devoting himself so exclusively to Senator Fairbanks, a "weak man," rather than to Foster and Kasson "who after all are the leading men of the Commission" and one "might say of the permanent service." Furthermore, Cartwright commented, the "Fosters are not in the best society," and if Herschell "had devoted himself to them, invited them often to meet swells, they would have appreciated it."[74] Both Herschell and Laurier also pinned too much faith on McKinley, who blandly promised to use his influence on the commissioners. The American delegation accused Herschell of aggressive legalism, but it does not seem to have compared to Foster's calculated offensiveness.[75] Although Herschell broke off negotiations to hasten a settlement, this seems to have been done rather from despair than as a tactic, and he appears to have lacked a sense of timing and political acumen. Yet his Canadian colleagues thought highly of him.

The decisive reason was of course the intransigence of Canadian opinion which forced the British delegation to pursue an inflexible policy. This intransigence was based on three miscalculations: on time being on Canada's side, on the country's strength, and on British imperial power. The Canadian imperial tail was trying to wag the

[73]Denison Papers, p. 3683, Laurier to Denison, "Private," Feb. 23, 1899: "But we have the trump card in our hands, for we will not reassemble unless we reassemble on our own terms in advance conceded. The Americans must give way; they cannot maintain the position which they have taken."

[74]Pope Papers, Diary, "Anglo-American Joint High Commission," Feb. 21, 1899, as told to Joseph Pope.

[75]*Ibid.*, March 1, 1899; Herschell told Pope "of a shindig he had with Foster at the Conference & how in subsequently alluding to it he referred to Mr. Foster's remarks on the occasion, 'which had the appearance of being offensive.' Mr. Foster interrupted, 'They were meant to be offensive,' said he. This amused though I think rather surprised his L⁴ship."

British national dog. This policy, however, could only end in humiliation. Time was not on Canada's side and the combined strength of Canada and Britain had not withstood the United States in the Venezuela crisis. Furthermore the rejection of proposals virtually agreed upon gave the United States a plausible grievance that Canada had entered upon negotiations with no intention of making a treaty. This was not true. Canada's assertion of a neglected claim in the Lynn Canal area also gave grounds for the charge of a "manufactured case."[76] A year earlier Henry White had complained to Senator Lodge that only under compulsion would Canada change her views because the necessary type of "control over Canada is beyond the power of any British Government."[77] Lodge was to be quite willing to see that compulsion meted out.

[76] Henry Cabot Lodge to Henry White, Jan. 7, 1899, cited in Campbell, p. 105.
[77] March 5, 1898, Tansill, p. 164, and cf. p. 360.

10. General Hutton and the Canadian Militia

WHILE THE SESSIONS of the Joint High Commission were proceeding, important militia reforms were being undertaken. The British Government had long hoped for militia reform in order that Canada might better defend itself and, if necessary, render overseas aid. The appointment of a new general officer commanding and a new governor general went far to fulfil this intention. The next three chapters will trace the contribution of the general officer commanding.

I

The office of general officer commanding had come into existence in 1875. It succeeded to the duties of the office of the adjutant-general, which had held command of the militia since 1855.[1] Section 37 of the Militia Act of 1886 required the general officer commanding to be at least a "Colonel" of the "regular army, charged, under the orders of Her Majesty, with the military command and discipline of the Militia. . . ." The term "command" was defined in Queen's Regulations and Orders for the Army, which had full authority in Canada save when in conflict with Canadian Regulations and Orders. These had legal force in the Dominion not by any vague colonial, imperial, or prerogative rights, but by virtue of re-enactment in section 82 of the Militia Act itself.

In theory, these regulations made his powers similar to those of the British commander-in-chief. In practice, the organization at Canadian headquarters resembled that of Britain before the 1850's, when the civilian War Office constitutionally checked the military Horse Guards. But efficiency and democratization placed many civilian duties in military hands in one War Office, but under the civilian control of the

---

[1] For the origin of the office and duties, see C. W. de Kiewiet and F. H. Underhill, eds. *Dufferin-Carnarvon Correspondence 1874–1878* (Toronto, Champlain Society, 1955), pp. 17–20, *passim*, Lord Dufferin to Lord Carnarvon, "Private," March 26, 1874.

Secretary of War. In Canada the reverse process occurred: the civil branch at headquarters absorbed many duties of the military branch. A new general officer commanding therefore usually suggested reforms to bring Canadian headquarters into line with War Office organization. Although most of them were eventually carried out, initially they were regarded as unsympathetic British interference in Canadian affairs.

All generals agreed on the basic needs of the militia: longer and more regular periods of training and hence more funds. On failing to win these from the government, most of them proposed a drastic curtailment in the number of militiamen drilled, in order to ensure sufficient training. Although most left Canada under a cloud, nearly all contributed some important accomplishment, and their unfulfilled plans usually bore fruit under their successors.[2] In spite of apathy within the militia and political opposition, collectively they probably accomplished much.

The fundamental cause of friction was the attempt of generals to overcome Canadian inertia in matters of defence. They naïvely thought Canadians desired military efficiency and reform. In theory they did; in practice the desire was usually drowned in public indifference, need for economy, and interest in patronage. The generals believing themselves possessed of the statutory power of "military command and discipline," endeavoured to introduce order but found the minister disregarding this power and interfering in the pettiest detail of military administration. When friction inevitably broke out, vague charges of disobedience or undefined charges of unconstitutionality were made against them. To avoid further trouble, most generals suggested a closer definition of their duties. This suggestion met with no response from the governments, determined to retain rights of control and dismissal. Militarily Canada wanted to be let alone, and wanted the right to be let alone.

The same essentially national friction may be detected in the discordant relationships between generals and members of the militia. The Canadian militia respected able general officers: Selby Smyth, Herbert, Hutton, and Dundonald. But these were the very men with whom independent and vociferous Canadian nationalists and government officials would likely clash. The nationalists would complain, and often justly, of

[2]The names and the period of office of the eight general officers commanding were as follows: Sir Edward Selby Smyth, 1874–80; A. G. Luard, 1880–84; Sir Frederick W. Middleton, 1884–90; Ivor J. C. Herbert (later knighted and still later created Lord Treowen), 1890–95; W. J. Gascoigne (later knighted), 1895–98; Edward T. H. Hutton (later knighted), 1898–1900; R. H. O'Grady-Haly, 1900–2; Earl of Dundonald, 1902–4. On Selby Smyth, see Capt. J. F. Cummins, "General Sir Edward Selby Smyth, K.C.M.G.," *Can. Def. Quart.*, V (July 1928), pp. 403–11; on the Earl of Dundonald, see *My Army Life* (London, 1926), chaps. XV–XXVIII.

a general's lack of tact, perhaps the result of insular ignorance, contempt for the colonial Canadian, or a calculated method of discipline. The three rather indolent and easygoing generals—Middleton, Gascoigne, and O'Grady-Haly—inspired no such genuine respect, and except, for the last, also exhibited tactlessness and ignorance. In the last analysis the friction between generals and Canadians grew out of a national resentment that Canada's colonial inferiority and strategic dependence required the presence of a British general.

Part of the reason for the poor calibre of some general officers was their small salary. In 1880 the Canadian Government cut the salary in half, from $8,000 to $4,000 a year,[3] a reduction which might explain the selection of an officer such as A. G. Luard. The third Salisbury Government at least made repeated efforts to coax the Canadian Government to increase the salary.[4] Lord Lansdowne even proposed to the Treasury that because the position was "of such peculiar importance from an Imperial point of view" the Imperial Government should make up the deficiency. The Treasury greeted this suggestion with heavy irony. It thought "of proposing to Parliament a Grant-in-Aid to Canada under a special subhead of the Colonial Services Vote, for the purpose of enabling that wealthy and powerful dependency to pay a proper salary to the chief of its militia. But such a course," it added, was "not one to be seriously contemplated."[5] General Gascoigne's resignation, partly the consequence of his low salary, provided the final impetus to press the Canadian Government to grant an increase.[6] In the May 1898 debate on the grant of a $2,000 allowance a year extra (which was "more than we expected," commented John Anderson[7]) no one disputed the

[3]For the first year the unfortunate officer was allowed to keep his half-pay, but thereafter even that was taken from him (C.O. 42/850, pp. 164–65, W.O. to Treasury, Sept. 9, 1897). For Treasury and War Office disdain for colonial government employment of army officers settling in the colonies, see Cd. 1790, qq. 8122, 8126.

[4]See C.O. 42/850, p. 162, G. Lawson to Edward Wingfield, Sept. 22, 1897, Lord Lansdowne quoting Lord Wolseley to the effect that Sir Wilfrid Laurier "might, under the influence of the Jubilee, give way to pressure" for a higher salary, but admitted he would be reluctant.

[5]*Ibid.*, p. 165, W.O. to Treasury, Sept. 9, 1897, and p. 164, Treasury to C.O., Sept. 11, 1897.

[6]C.O. 42/865, pp. 38–39, W.O. to C.O., Feb. 18, 1898; Lord Lansdowne urged that Gascoigne should obtain some of this increase retroactively, *ibid.*, pp. 91–92, W.O. to C.O., March 29, 1898, and John Anderson of the Colonial Office minuted: "Lord Lansdowne apparently has not much hope of getting what he asks for. He knows Canada too well for that." *Ibid.*, p. 90, March 30, 1898. Chamberlain also made the same unsuccessful request.

[7]C.O. 42/850, p. 414, Aberdeen to Chamberlain, March 10, 1898, and minute, March 10, 1898.

statement of a former Conservative Minister of Militia that for Canada to obtain a "thoroughly qualified commanding officer" a salary increase was essential.[8]

II

In contrast to his predecessors and successors, Major-General E. T. H. Hutton (with the British Army rank of colonel) enjoyed enormous advantages: a public opinion resenting United States policy and turning to Britain for aid, a government committed by public pronouncement and private acknowledgement to militia reform, and the many-pronged support of the Imperial authorities. During the first three months of his appointment he probably had a freer hand than other general officers commanding to influence the Minister and to carry out his own policy, for he began his term of office under a virtually senile Deputy Minister, Colonel Eugene Panet.[9] Hutton was a soldier of a "brilliance only too rare," a military innovator with a carefully thought-out policy, and a great army organizer. He was a masterful and "charming-mannered" personality and a first-rate speaker. He had also recently obtained military experience in a self-governing colony as commandant of New South Wales troops.[10]

Educated at Eton, Hutton entered the army at the age of eighteen. He was a member of the "Wolseley School," served with distinction in several African campaigns, graduated from the Staff College at Camberley, and was the chief inspiration of the Mounted Infantry movement. In 1893 he took charge of New South Wales forces, whose military condition had been unfavourably reported upon by Major-General (afterwards Sir) Bevan Edwards in 1890 and by a royal commission in 1892. With the assistance of these reports and Australian fears of the rise of Japan, Hutton began the creation of federal defence by reorganizing the New South Wales force to enable it to fit into an Australian defence scheme.[11]

[8]*Debates*, May 5, 1898, p. 4943, David Tisdale (Ontario, Conservative). Tisdale also read into the record the letter of the Secretary of War, who *inter alia* considered it "very desirable, as a matter of Imperial policy," to obtain a "general officer on the active list of the British army." *Ibid.*, p. 4942. The whole debate is *ibid.*, pp. 4930–46. See also D.M. 15087.

[9]For some of the politics involved in the retirement of Panet, which occurred on Dec. 7, 1898, and the appointment of Lieut.-Col. L. F. Pinault, see Laurier Papers, pp. 25888–92, Borden to Laurier, "Private," Aug. 20, 1898.

[10]*Times* (weekly ed.), Aug. 16, 1923, p. 180, obituary. For the phrase on his "brilliance," see Charles E. W. Bean, *Official History of Australia in the War of 1914–1918* (Sydney, 1921–29), I, p. 71.

[11]Sir Charles Lucas, ed., *The Empire at War* (London, 1921), I, pp. 141–44; see also Warren Perry, "Military Reforms of General Sir Edward Hutton in New

After his return to Britain in 1896 his concern for imperial defence increased as he observed the lack of any practicable imperial defence policy, the prospect of war in South Africa, and German and French army manoeuvres of 1897. Hutton was one of a considerable group of critics who doubted the adequacy of imperial defence.[12] At the Diamond Jubilee he received encouragement from two of Laurier's speeches in which it was affirmed that French Canadians would remain British and that Canada would render what help it could if Britain were in danger.[13]

Hutton interpreted these speeches as tacit support for a plan of co-operative defence which would require Canadian participation. His long-held ambition to be General Office Commanding in Canada, an ambition that had received encouragement from General Herbert, was now about to be fulfilled. With the help of his friend Major-General Sir John Ardagh, Director of Intelligence, he made an official application, which was accepted in September 1897. Meanwhile, he made a careful study of Canadian military problems and obtained a considerable knowledge of Canadian public opinion through study of Canadian newspapers. Doubtless moved by his New South Wales experience, Hutton added his voice to the pressure for the appointment of a Canadian defence committee, but opposed his own selection as chairman so that its conclusions might appear independently to uphold his own.[14]

His address in April 1898 to the Royal Colonial Institute, "A Co-operative System for the Defence of the Empire," was also preparation for his Canadian command. He suggested that imperial defence be based on an "offensive-defensive alliance." He advocated applying the principles of Australian defence co-operation to the Empire: each part of the Empire would provide for its own "passive defence" and help the "active defence" of the Empire as a whole. The following principles should apply to the whole scheme: (1) the mutual guarantee of all parts, (2) guarantee of sea supremacy by the Imperial Government, (3) a vigorous offensive potential. There would also be a defence agreement

---

South Wales, 1893–96," *Australian Quart.*, XXVIII (Dec. 1956), pp. 65–75, and George Cathcart Craig, *The Federal Defence of Australasia* (London, 1897), pp. 167–69, *passim*. For a hostile description of the "Wolseley Gang," see Lieut.-Col. Frederick Ernest Whitton, comp. and ed., *The History of the Prince of Wales's Leinster Regiment* (Royal Canadians) (Aldershot, 1924), I, pp. 101–2.

[12]Cf. Sir Charles Wentworth Dilke and Spenser Wilkinson, *Imperial Defence* (London, 1892).

[13]Hutton Papers, pp. 860–61, 1794–96, speeches, June 13 and 18, 1897.

[14]*Ibid.*, pp. 1712–18, "My Command in Canada August 1898–February 1900," and *passim*.

and council. The details of the scheme were necessarily vague because of their confidential nature,[15] but that very fact gave Hutton wide scope to follow whatever policy he thought practicable. Indeed in his leave-taking of officials in the War and the Colonial offices, Hutton appears to have pictured himself not as a subordinate receiving instructions but as an independent general announcing a policy in the presence of superiors whose tacit support he could thereafter claim.[16] His subsequent policy in Canada bore out this picture of himself.

Whether or not Hutton's superiors agreed with his views, the War Office had decided that his abilities were what Canada required in its next general officer commanding. It resisted tremendous pressure for the appointment of Major P. H. N. Lake as Gascoigne's successor. As early as November 1897 when Lake was appointed second in command of his regiment, the Governor General, the Canadian Government, the Minister of Militia, and the General Officer Commanding Imperial Troops all urged a postponement of Lake's departure from Canada. The Colonial Office joined in this unanimous testimony. "It is a pity," John Anderson minuted, "that we shd lose Major Lake. His extraordinary tact has proved of the greatest service in handling Canadian politicians."[17] The Colonial Office "fought the matter" as best it could but the War Office argued that Lake was too junior and his appointment would produce friction, and that no one beneath the rank of colonel should be selected.[18] Aware of Canada's disgruntlement Chamberlain apparently gave the Canadian Government an opportunity to reject Hutton. But having recently pressed for the long-delayed appointment, it could hardly do so, though Aberdeen once more reminded Chamberlain:

[15]*Proceedings of the Royal Colonial Institute*, XXIX, 1897–98, pp. 223–58. Hutton was also invited to address military members "in committee" of the House of Commons on the question (Hutton Papers, p. 1785).

[16]Hutton Papers record interviews in July and August 1898, pp. 3–5, 22–23, 26–29, 955–57, 959–63.

[17]C.O. 42/848, pp. 461–62, Nov. 13, 1897, and see *ibid.*, pp. 473 and 480. After Gascoigne's resignation Aberdeen telegraphed again: ". . . it is almost impossible that any other officer cd. be found however distinguished combining Lake's Canadian experience and other special qualifications. I entirely concur in this view." (To Chamberlain, paraphrase, rec'd. May 18, 1898, C.O. 42/857, p. 289.)

[18]C.O. 42/865, p. 170, minute of John Anderson, June 2, 1898; p. 171, W.O. to C.O., May 31, 1898; and pp. 173–75, Chamberlain to Aberdeen, draft, "Confd.," June 4, 1898. Colonial Office support of Lake and pressure on the Foreign Office— that is, on Lord Salisbury—to have Gascoigne rewarded by being made chairman of the Committee on Canadian Defence suggest friction between the Colonial Office and the War Office, though probably not only because of Canadian affairs (C.O. 42/857, p. 145, C.O. to F.O., "Secret and Immediate," May 11, 1898).

"Their own wish was clear to have Lake apptd."[19] Hutton had too much support for his appointment to be revoked, but he had to bear the initial brunt of official Canadian vexation.

III

Hutton was helped in his reforms by a new Governor General, Lord Minto (1845–1914). A nephew of a British Prime Minister, Lord John Russell, he was educated at Eton and Cambridge. Upon graduation he joined the Scots Guards, but soon resigned, and until 1876 devoted his life to sport—especially horse-racing—and volunteer soldiering. With a characteristic intensity, he became a daringly successful gentleman jockey—the only jockey in the Grand National Steeplechase to break his neck and survive. His racing experience gave him a first-hand knowledge of all classes of men, knowledge of decisive importance in the coming era of democracy.

His career as a jockey perforce ended, he concentrated upon soldiering. Upon the advice of his close friend, Wolseley, he helped to organize and command the Border Mounted Rifles. In the Russo-Turkish War of 1878, Minto (then Lord Melgund) was a war correspondent for the London *Morning Post* and collected information for the Intelligence Division of the War Office. In the next year he served on Lord Roberts' staff in Afghanistan. In 1882, he was wounded in the Egyptian campaign. In the following year he married Mary Grey, daughter of Queen Victoria's secretary.

Most important for his future experience as governor general was his service from 1883 to 1885 as military secretary to an old Eton schoolfellow, Lord Lansdowne, Governor General of Canada. In this position he handled defence correspondence and came into close contact with Canada's defence system. He was appointed in 1884 to a committee consisting of the Minister and Deputy Minister of Militia, the General Office Commanding, and himself to investigate, sort, and assess a vast mass of documents that concerned coastal defences.[20] This experience gave him a historic, imperial, and strategic view of Canada's defence problem. He was chiefly responsible for the organization in August 1884 of the 400 voyageurs—Canadian rivermen—sent to help

---

[19]C.O. 42/858, p. 198, Aberdeen to Chamberlain, paraphrase telegram, July 27, 1898. For Sir John Macdonald's opinion to Lord Knutsford, Aug. 18, 1890, on the need for Canada's voice in the appointment of a general officer commanding, see Macdonald Papers, vol. 530, pp. 156–57.

[20]See valuable material in Minto Papers, part III.

Lord Wolseley in his unsuccessful attempt to rescue General Gordon at Khartoum in 1884–85,[21] and in February 1885 Canadian enthusiasm to offer volunteers for the Sudan gave him an insight into problems in overseas participation.[22] He also had the experience of seeing Canadian militiamen in action when he served as Chief of Staff under General Middleton in the North-West Rebellion of 1885. On his return to Britain in 1885 he pursued a life of reading, writing, and volunteer soldiering. His one attempt at election to Parliament as a Liberal Imperialist in 1886 met defeat. Two years later he became Brigadier-General of the Scottish Lowland Brigade. Repeated requests for him to serve as umpire in sham battles and his official attendance at the French Army manoeuvres in 1890 suggest a considerable military reputation.

In the autumn of 1898 he became Governor General of Canada, a surprise appointment because of his minor administrative experience.[23] But he had a claim to a political office for St. John Brodrick (after wards Lord Midleton) had obtained the position of Under-Secretary of War for which Minto had been considered in 1895. Brodrick seems to have been one of Minto's foremost advocates;[24] others included Lord Wolseley, Lord Lansdowne, and his brother-in-law, Lord Albert Grey, who was a personal friend of Joseph Chamberlain.

An analysis of Lord Minto's governor generalship first requires an examination of Lord Aberdeen's resignation from office, which he publicly explained was for private and domestic reasons. Canadian public opinion interpreted his resignation as recall,[25] for it quickly followed that of Gascoigne. In his joint autobiography with his wife, Lord Aberdeen denied that he was prematurely recalled and his denial has been accepted by Professor Saywell.[26] The present writer, however, is still

[21]C. P. Stacey, "Canada and the Nile Expedition of 1884–85," *Can. Hist. Rev.*, XXXIII (Dec. 1952), pp. 320–24.

[22]Arnold Haultain, coll., *Goldwin Smith's Correspondence* (Toronto, 1913), pp. 166–69, Melgund to Goldwin Smith, "Private," March 1, 1885.

[23]Cf. Laurier Papers, pp. 224985–86, Strathcona to Laurier, "Confidential," Aug. 13, 1898.

[24]Minto Papers, vol. 12, p. 92, St. John Brodrick to Lord Minto, "Confidential," June 30, 1898. There is perhaps a hint in Earl of Midleton, *Records & Reactions 1856–1939* (London, 1939), pp. 92–93, that Queen Victoria may have supported Minto's candidacy.

[25]Cf. P.A.O., Blake Papers, Martin J. Griffin (Parliamentary Librarian, Ottawa), to Edward Blake, May 18, 1898.

[26]*"We Twa": Reminiscences of Lord and Lady Aberdeen* (London, 1925), II, pp. 134–37, and John T. Saywell, ed., *The Canadian Journal of Lady Aberdeen 1893–1898* (Toronto, Champlain Society, 1960), pp. xxxii and 455–56. Professor Saywell writes that Aberdeen's "estates needed his supervision and his falling income could no longer bear the steady drain of his Canadian office" (p. xxxii).

puzzled. Aberdeen in a letter to Laurier put quotation marks around the word "resignation,"[27] and a Colonial Office minute on a communication from Aberdeen crossed out the word "absolutely" in the phrase "absolutely no truth" that he was being recalled.[28] Moreover, Laurier's rather effusive reply makes a point of saying that Aberdeen was not being prematurely recalled.

Assuming that he was recalled, why would Chamberlain wish to do so? In the late nineteenth century the duties of a governor general were to represent the Crown and the British Government. According to his lights Aberdeen had performed the first task fairly well. He had entered into the life of Canada and had tried to bring the two races closer together. But his actions during the waning Conservative régime, though constitutional and receiving the approval of Chamberlain, produced acute controversy. Sir Charles Tupper carried on a personal vendetta against him, ostensibly because of his failure to approve of his post-election appointments.[29] There was considerable criticism by the civil service and the public of Aberdeen's delays in making up his mind and of his absences from Ottawa, though Laurier did not find all the absences disagreeable.[30]

Aberdeen represented the British Government far less well. Whenever a subject interested him and his wife, he was capable of energy and subtlety; otherwise a laissez-faire and indiscriminate indolence seems to have pervaded his actions. The Colonial Office frequently complained of lack of guidance. For example, when General Gascoigne's desire to be relieved of his duties was reported, Lord Aberdeen sent no indication of the Minister of Militia's attitude to an increase of pay for a

[27]Laurier Papers, p. 23267, May 13, 1898; the word "resignation" may refer to Chamberlain's use of it in cypher telegram (May 13, 1898, G 3, vol. 32).

[28]C.O. 42/857, p. 323, John Anderson, May 30, 1898; cf. minute of Lord Selborne, Parliamentary Under-Secretary (June 6, 1898): "He is thin-skinned to an absurd degree by nature I agree" (*ibid.*, p. 322). Aberdeen was requesting publication of a dispatch generally supporting him against Tupper in 1896. If Aberdeen was not being prematurely recalled, it might appear that an effort was being made to make it appear that he was, but if so, why?

[29]Cf. P.A.O., Blake Papers, Martin J. Griffin to Edward Blake, Nov. 7, 1898, and April 5, 1899.

[30]Laurier Papers, p. 10014, Laurier to Aberdeen, draft, "Private and Confidential," Dec. 23, 1896. After informing him of the completion of negotiations concerning the Manitoba school question Laurier commented: "I did not think it advisable to trouble you with this matter while you were away from the seat of Government. As things were proceeding very smoothly, there was no occasion for your active participation." Cf. Maurice Pope, ed., *Public Servant: Memoirs of Sir Joseph Pope* (Toronto, 1960), pp. 106–9, 112–13; *Man. Free Press*, Aug. 22, 1898, edit., "The Governor General," and Aug. 1, 1898, edit., "Lord Aberdeen's Footsteps."

general[31] though the Colonial Office had written frequently of the matter. During the events of the Diamond Jubilee he indiscriminately dispatched patriotic effusions to the Colonial Office for Queen Victoria. The Colonial Office became angry and hinted that discrimination be observed; and when he still did not get the hint and sent a piece of embroidery to the Queen, it was peremptorily ordered sent back.[32] Thus from a Colonial Office point of view the dignity of the office was being lowered and its powers allowed to atrophy.

The contrast between Aberdeen and Minto was marked. Was the friction Minto produced in his first year of office partly the result of a revival of practices followed by Lord Lansdowne? Sir Louis Davies, for example, complained when Minto asked to see the evidence for a Privy Council order. Minto justified this request to Laurier: "I thought I was only acting in the usual manner adopted by my predecessor in the way of ordinary routine."[33] It might be inferred that Aberdeen had not demanded to see that kind of evidence. Nor did an English newspaper's remark that Minto ought to give Canada " 'vigorous rule' " help his position.[34] It has therefore been assumed that Lord Minto was a constitutional ignoramus. But he had served under Lord Lansdowne and had read carefully Alpheus Todd's *Parliamentary Government in the British Colonies*—one of the standard constitutional works of the time. In judging his constitutional actions harshly, later critics, blinded by the ideological view of responsible government, have failed to note the practices of responsible government in the late 1890's. In most internal matters the governor general acted as a constitutional monarch, but on many external matters he was still a viceroy acting on his own discretion as a representative of Britain's imperial policies. Minto himself expressed this as a distinction between imperial and Canadian matters;

[31]C.O. 42/865, pp. 37–38, minute of John Anderson, Feb. 21, 1898: "If he has not taken the trouble to discuss the matter with them he ought to have done it." For an undiscerning summary of the events of the spring session of 1896 see C.O. 42/838, pp. 983–93, Aberdeen to Chamberlain, "Secret," April 29, 1896.

[32]C.O. 42/847, p. 52, Chamberlain to Aberdeen, "Confidential," June 8, 1897.

[33]Laurier Papers, pp. 31386–89, March 13, 1899.

[34]*Globe*, Aug. 4, 1898; see also *ibid.*, Dec. 19, 1898, edit., "Why not a Canadian?" The mistake of the English writer who hoped that Lord Minto would give Canada "strong government," coming soon after Jubilee enthusiasm, the *Globe* argued, showed a danger of misinterpreting Canada's enthusiasm. "India requires a strong government. Canada most emphatically does not require strong government, except such as is given by representatives of the Canadian people elected at the polls. And our conception of the growth of the empire is not that Canada shall become more like India, but that India shall become more like Canada; the ideal being not a group of dependencies governed from one central point, but a league of self-governing communities."

on the former he asserted himself and on the latter he simply offered an opinion.[35] The practical difficulty of Minto's position was that the prevailing idea of imperial unity was blurring the distinction.

Furthermore, his strong support of Imperial military policies made him an object of dislike. But he was the military expert, knowing Britain's strategic needs and the details of Britain's and Canada's military administration. His ministers knew virtually nothing of efficient military administration, for their interest was usually political patronage. His military knowledge, combined with a "strong will with a conciliatory address,"[36] enabled him to carry the Minister of Militia with him during the first year of Hutton's work. Sir John Macdonald had predicted in 1885 that one day Minto would become Governor General, and his Imperial masters later rewarded him with the chief pro-consular office, the vice-royalty of India, in 1905; Lord Minto was obviously something more than a "combination country squire and heavy dragoon."[37] A re-examination of his policies and accomplishments shows the absurdity of such a view.

Lord Minto arrived about three months after Hutton, in November 1898. They had been schoolfellows at Eton, brother officers in the Egyptian campaign of 1882, associates in the Mounted Infantry Movement; they saw eye to eye on the need for militia efficiency and the elimination of politics from military affairs. In one of his earliest speeches in Canada Lord Minto indiscreetly affirmed his old friendship with Hutton and in effect condemned "political influence" in the militia,[38] an indiscretion in relation to Hutton which he did not repeat. Minto's chief assistance to Hutton came from his expert military knowledge and position as Governor General. This enabled him, when necessary, to intervene with the Government on Hutton's behalf.

IV

A cool Canada greeted Hutton. The virtual imposition of his appointment on the Dominion and his arrival at Quebec during the inaugural

---

[35]Minto to G. R. Parkin, Sept. 26, 1904, "Private," Frank H. Underhill, "Lord Minto on His Governor Generalship," *Can. Hist. Rev.* XL (June 1959), p. 124.
[36]Hutton Papers, p. 794, "The 4th Earl of Minto: An Appreciation," Dec. 12, 1918.
[37]J. W. Dafoe, *Laurier: A Study in Canadian Politics* (Toronto, 1922), p. 77.
[38]*Globe*, Dec. 15, 1898. Note that behind the scenes Minto was largely responsible for inducing all classes of Canadians to give more than £1,000 for the Gordon Memorial College in Khartoum (Minto Papers, letter book no. 1, pp. 116–17, Minto to Lord Kitchener, "Private," June 13, 1899; see also *ibid., passim* for 1898–99; Mills Papers, University of Western Ontario Library, *passim* for 1898–99; Militia Orders 24 and 43 (5), March 1899).

meetings of the Joint High Commission must have been unforgettable reminders to Laurier of Canada's weakness and military dependence on Britain. The reception of the militiamen was no warmer; they seem to have been moved by the contempt into which Gascoigne appeared to have brought the position of general officer. When Hutton opened the Rockcliffe Rifle Range at Ottawa, he was greeted with a stony stare. Undaunted he was determined to reform the Canadian militia. In his first interview with the Minister of Militia he warned that there was to be no politics in the militia. The Minister, "startled" by Hutton's "boldness" and "emphatic declaration of opinions so pronounced,"[39] nevertheless agreed that it was his policy too, though it could not be accomplished at once. To this Hutton agreed. For the first six months Hutton's relations with Borden and the cabinet seem to have been comparatively amicable. When opposition to Hutton began, Borden saw his task as trying to appease the two factions of the cabinet, one of which favoured and the other opposed defence improvement—a task he did not relish.[40]

Although there had been many recent military improvements, Canada lacked a military policy, and this Hutton determined to supply. His policy may be summarized as follows: (1) to imbue both militia and public with a sense of military purpose, (2) to accustom Canadians to the idea of participation in an imperial war, (3) to reform and train the force, (4) to reorganize headquarters.

The first two aspects of his policy concern what today would be called propaganda activities. Hutton set about to identify himself with the needs and aspirations of the militia. To overcome inertia he strove on his first inspection tour to awaken a wave of "military enthusiasm and patriotic ardour."[41] He gave statements of his policy to the press in order that the public should be given correct reports of the "changes and reforms contemplated,"[42] and he made use of his gifts of social

[39]Hutton Papers, pp. 1720, 1723, "My Command in Canada: A Narrative"; and *ibid.*, p. 1044.

[40]Lord William Seymour, G.O.C. Imp. Troops, wrote to Hutton, March 19, 1899, that some members of the ministry were more "Democratic & opposed to Military" reform "than the others." Seymour wrote that the opponents included Laurier, Sifton, Tarte, Blair, and Patterson; and the supporters included Cartwright, Davies, Fielding, and Borden (Hutton Papers, pp. 177–78). The latter group probably also included Mulock and Mills. The writer is inclined to doubt whether Sifton in 1899 was opposed to militia reform. See also below, n. 49, of this chapter.

[41]Minto Papers, vol. 21, p. 94, copy to Sir Richard Harrison, "PRIVATE AND CONFIDENTIAL," April 7, 1899.

[42]Quotation from Minto Papers, vol. 19, p. 39, "A Narrative of Lord Minto's Career." One newspaper item was a paper Hutton had delivered in England on "Our Comrades of Greater Britain," which was reproduced on the front page of the Saturday *Globe*, Nov. 26, 1898. To arouse military interest he also introduced the tattoo, which was entertainment in the form of military exercise.

grace and of oratory, an art to which he was addicted and in which he was fatally gifted. Lieutenant-Colonel H. J. Grasett, Chief of Police in Toronto, who had several opportunities to observe him, wrote that he was a "most pleasant man to meet socially," and that as a public speaker he made "the best speech I ever heard a soldier deliver. He is fluent, logical and interesting being listened to with the closest attention by his audience."[43]

In his speeches he attempted to evoke within his listeners a sense of national pride in the militia. His first important "national" address was delivered to officers in Toronto. In it he emphasized that military affairs were approaching a "crisis." He assumed that "a good army, a national army, must be one which is apart from party, and which sinks all individual views, be they political or religious, in the general welfare of the country."[44] Evidently emboldened by the response to his speeches, Hutton began to speak with increasing frankness. After a church parade in London he took advantage of the "deplorable" condition of the 7th Fusiliers to lecture the citizens on the shortcomings of their battalion, and announce its thorough reconstruction.[45] In February, in the presence of two ministers, Dr. Borden and Israel Tarte, he linked the militia to national purposes, which he suggested were more than economic. One of Canada's responsibilities, he declared, was the creation of "that military and martial spirit on which every great nation depends. No nation was ever great on agriculture or pastorage alone. History teaches that to become great a nation must be martial."[46] Asked for a precise definition of "national army" Hutton described it in terms of structure: it was a force complete in all arms.

By March 1899, he was becoming bolder and more critical, probably because he believed he had carried the bulk of the militia with him and was confident of public support, a confidence which the reception of his annual report would seem to have confirmed. At the first annual ser-

---

[43]Gowan Papers, in possession of Prof. E. G. R. Ardagh of Toronto, Grasett to Sen. James R. Gowan, July 5, 1899.

[44]*Can. Mil. Gaz.*, Oct. 18, 1898. Hutton's first important speech on technical matters was printed separately, "1898 Address by Major-General Hutton, C.B., A.D.C. to H. M. the Queen . . . at His First Inspection of Military Districts during September and October, 1898" (Hutton Papers, pp. 1051–64).

[45]*Can. Mil. Gaz.*, Nov. 1, 1898. Nearly two months after this lecture 16 officers were retired (all but three of the total number), and in February 1899 the battalion was disbanded and reconstituted, as it had been once before in 1889. Hutton had to agree to Borden's recommendation that the tenure of the incumbent officer commanding be extended for one year, which later seems to have been extended to three. *Globe*, Dec. 29, 1898; G.O. 16, Feb. 1899; A.G. 78325 and 77858; and Hutton Papers, p. 1236.

[46]*Globe*, Feb. 13, 1899.

geants' banquet in Toronto, to which officers were invited, he again spoke. He began by emphasizing the unity of the Permanent Corps and the militia, and the importance of sergeants, artfully reminding them that "deference was due to the officers, even though some of them might not be as proficient as desirable." Then he warmed to his favourite subject—the national army:

By "national" the Major General said he meant Canada as a whole, English and French speakers as one unit. A national army to me as a soldier, the General proceeded, does not mean what we now have in Canada. I have several times referred to it as an army, but it has not yet been placed on that footing, though, thank God, it will be soon. (Loud applause) An army consists of a complete military machine. To be capable of defence it is a simple matter comparatively, but it must also be capable of offensive defence. It must not only have the fighting stuff, but it must have the brain power to deal with it, the administrative department to supply it with food, to move it from one point to another, to treat it in sickness and disease, to pay it in the field, to supply it with arms and equipment. None of these departments exists in Canada. I am sorry to tell you that you gentlemen who represent the fighting units are at the present time, from my point of view, and from that of all Generals and staff officers who have to do with the movements of troops in the field, in a state of temporary paralysis. But what we are all determined to do, officers and men alike, is to render to Canada the best she can demand, to give her, as far as possible, an ideal army which shall be capable, not only of the defence of Canadian soil, but of participating, when necessary, in the defence of the empire. (Cheers) . . .
I feel this, . . . that the time has arrived for Canada, not to rely so much on the strong arms of the old country, but to assume the responsibilities essentially hers as a young and vigorous nation. (Loud and long continued applause.)[47]

The calculated audacity of this speech must have made it enormously effective. In it there appeared a skilful blending of all the main themes of Hutton's programme: the criticism of inadequate officers and inadequate administration, the state of "temporary paralysis" of the Canadian militia, the appeals to Canadian pride, the possibility of Canada's helping the Empire, and the criticism of Canada's overdependence on Britain.

A few days later, a letter to the *Globe* signed "Officer" criticized Hutton's communications and speeches. If these were not authorized, the writer stated, someone should forbid them or else the " 'national army' will not only be temporarily but permanently 'paralyzed'. . . ."[48] The contents of this letter, references to a "breach of regulations" and

---

[47]*Globe*, March 4, 1899. The headings to this news account were "CANADA'S MILITIA / Maj. Gen. Hutton Says it / is Temporarily Paralyzed / HOPE FOR THE FUTURE."
[48]Letter dated March 11, 1899, *Globe*, March 13, 1899.

to the "authority of the Minister," and the dates of writing and publication make it likely that the letter was written by Lieutenant-Colonel D. A. Macdonald, Director of Stores at headquarters, who was a "Liberal and in close touch with Borden." In a "private" letter, dated March 11, 1899, to the newspaper's editor, the *Globe*'s Ottawa correspondent enclosed an "anonymous" letter reflecting "Borden's opinion" for publication in the *Globe*.[49] Evidently Hutton assumed in his relations with Borden, as he assumed in those with his British masters, that statements made to those in authority, if unanswered, were tacitly approved. Thus his barbs concerning a "crisis" and "temporary paralysis" had already appeared in his letters to Borden. Hutton's justification was the need for reform. "No colonial government, however strong," he wrote to the President of the Colonial Defence Committee, "will undertake reform unless outside opinion presses it upon the arena of practical politics."[50]

A few weeks later, Hutton's reference to his "mission" provided the General Officer Commanding Imperial Troops, Lord William Seymour, with an opportunity to pass on Borden's hint that Hutton spoke too much and pressed the Government too hard: " 'Some of the Ministry are too Democratic to like extreme "Militarism" to which they think General Hutton's speeches able as they are tend.' "[51] Hutton replied in effect that he had been misreported and that his statement was an answer to Ontario press remarks that he had come to Canada "to reorganize the Canadian troops on a War Office basis." He had accordingly stated that "the mission . . . was to do the best I could in the interests of Canadian Defence. . . . The recommendations which I had made . . . I alone am responsible for, etc., etc., it was for the Canadian Government and the Canadian people to decide upon their merits."[52] Thus Hutton

---

[49]"The enclosed letter is written by Col. Macdonald of the Department. The Minister is very angry at the way Hutton has been going on and has remonstrated with him. . . . My impression is that Hutton will not last long as he has succeeded in antagonizing not only the Minister the Department and Headquarters Staff but a large body of militia officers throughout the country." George Simpson to John Willison, Willison Collection, pp. 27628–29.

[50]Minto Papers, vol. 21, p. 94, copy, to Sir Richard Harrison, "PRIVATE AND CONFIDENTIAL," April 7, 1899.

[51]Hutton Papers, p. 184, Seymour to Hutton, "Private," April 13, 1899, and Minto Papers, vol. 22, p. 201, Seymour to Laurence Drummond (Mil. Sec. to Gov. Gen.), "Private," March 29, 1899. A month before Seymour's letter to Hutton—March 13, 1899—Hutton had written to Dr. Parkin that Dr. Borden was most anxious to carry out the recommendations of Hutton's annual report; he added: "I have the good will of the Cabinet, but as you know in our Colonies it is 'Public Opinion' only, which forces on big national measures, & it is you and those like you who are above all to lead and educate the latter." Parkin Papers, pp. 3839–40.

[52]Hutton Papers, pp. 186–87, Hutton to Seymour, "Private," April 18, 1899.

regarded himself as the expert adviser and the instrument of the national policy approved by the Government.

After years of neglect most of the militia seem to have been enthusiastic, but why was the public also moved by Hutton? In contrast to the prevailing imperialistic mood, the strength of Hutton's appeal lay in its national and moral ideas. Principal Grant, who together with Dr. Parkin gave him strong support, wrote that he was "glad . . . that you are from the first stimulating Canadian national spirit."[53] Loyalty to a national moral ideal above the religious and political factionalism appealed to Protestant Canada.[54] What national moral ideal had Canada ever stood for? Even Hutton's covert sneer at Canadian economic progress carried a moral appeal. Lord Minto later observed that much as one admired Hutton's high standard of public morality, "here it was impossible to stuff down people's throats. . . ."[55] In the jingoistic atmosphere of 1899, however, Hutton's secularized evangelicalism was irresistible. The Colonial Secretary "noticed with the greatest satisfaction the growth of public opinion in regard to Defence. We seem at last to be making some impression."[56]

In contrast to his success with English Canada, Hutton failed to arouse enthusiasm in French Canada. Neither the contemporary English feeling for closer union with Britain nor antagonism to the United States touched French Canada. On the contrary, after 1885—the date of Louis Riel's execution—French Canada tended to regard English Canada as its enemy. The purchase of war material after the Venezuela affair was explained in Quebec during the election of 1896 as "spending money to send our children to war to fight for the British Empire."[57]

Hutton was not daunted by French-Canadian apathy. He ascribed the low condition of the militia to treatment by the authorities "either with a cold indifference or with positive contempt."[58] He used the same

[53]*Ibid.*, p. 459, March 10, 1899.
[54]Cf. the reaction against extreme political partisanship after the mid-nineties: the number of independent candidates in the federal electon of 1896, the Liberal Government's impatience that the Toronto *Globe* and Toronto *Star* were not sufficiently partisan, and John Willison's resignation from the *Globe* to edit the Toronto *News*, which was to be non-partisan.
[55]Minto Papers, letter book no. 3, p. 80, to Lord Hopetoun, Gov. Gen. of Australia, "Private," Dec. 15, 1901.
[56]Minto Papers, vol. 14, p. 17, Chamberlain to Minto, "Private," May 8, 1899, and Parkin Papers, p. 3882, Minto to Parkin, May 10, 1899.
[57]J. G. H. Bergeron (Conservative, Beauharnois), Sept. 29, 1896, *Debates*, pp. 2243–44. This election broadside may be found in Henri Bourassa, *Que devons-nous à l'Angleterre?* (Montréal, 1915), pp. 363–65.
[58]Hutton Papers, p. 977, Hutton to Chamberlain, "Confidential," July 28, 1898. Hutton also complained that French-Canadian officers lacked energy, and their instructors did not speak French.

methods in French Canada as in English Canada. He combined appeals
to half-forgotten military traditions, such as that of Colonel de Sala-
berry, with criticisms of the existing state of the militia. At a banquet in
honour of Israel Tarte, Minister of Public Works, Hutton, speaking in
French, appealed to the "essentially martial . . . origin" of the French
Canadians, criticized their failure to participate in the militia, and
appealed to the Church and landowners to assist him.[59] In the summer
of 1899, Archbishop Bruchési celebrated "high Mass with great solem-
nity & pomp" at La Prairie Camp near Montreal, and, according to
Hutton, made an excellent short address to the troops. Much progress
could be made, Hutton believed, if the "interest and goodwill of the
Priests could be secured."[60] He had already issued orders that Permanent Force officers and militia officers aspiring to higher commands
should be able to speak both French and English, but the Government,
although approving of the principle, did not enforce the ruling.[61]
Although he seems to have been personally popular with the French-
Canadian militia,[62] upon the outbreak of the Boer War French-Canadian
leaders singled him out for political attack.

[59]At St. John's, Quebec, *Globe*, Feb. 13, 1899.
[60]Minto Papers, vol. 15, p. 30, Hutton to Minto, June 28, 1899.
[61]Minister of Militia, *Debates*, July 27, 1899, pp. 8631–32.
[62]See Col. Oscar C. Pelletier's laudatory estimate of General Hutton in
Mémoires, souvenirs de famille et récits (Québec, 1940), pp. 307–8.

11. Militia Plans and Reforms, 1898-1899

THUS FAR the analysis of Hutton's actions has centred on his moral and national appeal rather than on specific improvements. His aim was to use the sentiment evoked to achieve reforms in the militia. These were set forth so clearly to the public in his annual report that public pressure overcame the government's normal indifference. The report was invulnerable to government attack, too, because it paralleled the second part of the report of the Committee on Canadian Defence.

I

The two-volume "secret" report of the Committee on Canadian Defence was a detailed and critical account of the palsied state of the Canadian forces with many a gibe at Canada's defencelessness.[1] In contrast to the piecemeal recommendations of the Colonial Defence Committee, *Report No. I*, "Secret," contained a mobilization plan to meet an immediate attack from the United States. In the first two months of war the committee did not believe that sudden raids by small forces would be serious; the attack would be first made in the area of Montreal, "the key of the Canadian defence." Within two months, however, 50,000 American troops would be mobilized and would likely attack five other places: at Quebec, on the St. Lawrence canal system, and across the rivers of Niagara, St. Clair, and Sault Ste Marie. If Quebec city, lacking in "suitable defence," fell "assistance from Great Britain would be practically lost." To meet the advance Canada could put 36,000 men into the field at once, but lacking experienced staff officers it would need to have at least 137 British staff officers on the spot at

---

[1]*Report No. I,* "Secret," and *Report No. II,* "Secret." There exists a third (unprinted) report. C.O. 42/865, p. 370, Maj.-Gen. E. P. Leach to W.O., Nov. 17, 1898: "The third report called for, being one in which the co-operation of Imperial troops is of necessity involved, will, for obvious reasons, be forwarded direct to the War Office."

the beginning of war; if Canadian officers initially organized troops it would be difficult for British to supersede Canadian officers because of "jealousy and ill feeling." The committee drew the moral of Canada's need for staff officers. Mobilization tables were drawn up to assign Canada's militia to the "field Forces"—Montreal, St. Lawrence, Niagara, St. Clair, New Brunswick—and to the garrisons of Montreal and Quebec.[2] The Montreal Field Force, made up of local units from Quebec, Ontario, the Maritimes, and even Manitoba, was the largest. But the ability of those forces to take the offensive depended, first, on rapid mobilization, increased strength, the existence of departmental organization, and the presence of Imperial officers, and second, on the delaying of American forces "by a counterstroke delivered . . . upon another portion of the American Continent" not otherwise defined.[3] The committee warned that Canada's unpreparedness equalled that of the United States during the Spanish-American War, and that American military authorities had learned much from that war.

The committee then outlined essentially makeshift measures to meet a sudden attack, the actions which the non-existent headquarters staff and departmental services should take. It suggested the immediate creation, and defined the duties, of supply and service departments; recommended the immediate procurement of necessary supplies, the distribution of the Lee-Enfield rifles, and the acquisition of more artillery, some of which "can be obtained from Halifax for the asking."[4] It also suggested enlisting the help of the Canadian Pacific and Grand Trunk railways in building earth-works, listed defensive works in the Montreal area to be built, and outlined mobilization laws and regulations to be put into effect under certain contingencies.

Report No. I, "Secret," concerned measures to meet a sudden threat; *Report No. II,* "Secret," measures for the future. It contained careful discussions of nearly all phases of Canadian defence: the assimilation of British and Canadian forces; the powers of the general officer commanding; the staff; the permanent force; the active militia; increased armaments; reserves of supplies; maintenance of fortifications; departmental services; the formation of a naval militia; the Royal Military College; a formation of reserves; certain miscellaneous matters such as Central Military Stores, the Government Cartridge Factory, the need for a Georgian Bay canal; and certain appendixes elaborating on issues raised in the text.

The year 1898 probably marks the end of the period in which Canada could have been defended against American attack for a few

---

[2]*Report No. I,* "Secret," pp. 1–46.
[3]*Ibid.,* p. 49.   [4]*Ibid.,* p. 77.

months. The growing local superiority of the United States fleet in the western Atlantic combined with other pressures on the British Empire would soon make impossible effective British aid to Canada. Nor in 1898 could a section of the United States be neutralized as in the War of 1812, for the Civil War had made a nation out of a federal union and demonstrated that the United States could be one of the most powerful military nations of the world. Militarily, therefore, the defence of Canada against the United States was rapidly becoming hopeless. Politically, on the other hand, Anglo-Saxon racialism, the growing awareness of the parallelism of many British and American political and economic interests, and British support of the United States in the Spanish-American War seemed to make defence plans unnecessary. In moments of anger between the United States and Britain, Canada's policy has usually been to play political possum.

Assuming that Canada was defensible, an assumption military and political leaders accepted, the committee's plan had several weaknesses. In a sort of preface to the report, Lord Minto objected that its strategical considerations were those of an earlier day—the defence of eastern Canada. No provision was made for the defence of the West.[5] Hutton criticized *Report No. I*, "Secret," wherever it differed from his own report: its failure to mention aid to Britain and the erroneous assumption that Canada's defence could be based on non-existent administrative departments, which would take months to create. Nor could Canada depend on British staff officers who in a crisis would be needed in Britain. But Hutton in general praised *Report No. II*, "Secret," as supporting his own analyses and proposals. Finally, the hypothetical question might be raised, whether, if the plan could have been explained to Parliament, it would have been willing to double the annual militia budget and vote $22,500,000 on capital defence costs, even though $17,000,000 of it was for a Georgian Bay–Ottawa River Canal.[6]

The Canadian Government transmitted the report to England without comment and refused to make a "formal acknowledgement" to the committee's military members, who complained of neglect.[7] Nevertheless,

[5]*Ibid.*, pp. v–vii, Minto to Chamberlain, "Secret," April 5, 1899.

[6]*Ibid.*, pp. viii–xiii, memorandum of G.O.C. to Min. of Mil., "Confidential," May 30, 1899, and app., May 15, 1899. Except for the cost of the bituminous coal (half the amount imported in 1898) the figure of $22,500,000 consists of the sum of the estimates supplied but not summarized by the committee.

[7]Minto Papers, vol. 12, p. 153, Leach to Sir Montagu Ommanney (Under-Sec. of the Colonies), March 1, 1901, inc. *ibid.*, p. 152, Ommanney to Minto, "Private," April 6, 1901. See also *ibid.*, vol. 9, p. 90, Min. of Mil. to Gov. Gen., May 17, 1901. Leach had testified to the cordial assistance of its Canadian members, Borden and Davies (P.C. Despatches, 1223K, Dec. 20, 1898).

despite the Government's caution, the report did set up a standard by which military conditions in Canada could be measured. Its independent opinions strengthened those in harmony with Hutton's annual report, and made it more difficult for the Government to stand in the way of military improvements.

II

Hutton's report[8] gave an equally outspoken account of the deficiencies of Canadian defence. Part I presented a "Narrative of Events in 1898," and part II, "Proposals for the Current Year, 1899." Interlarded with the narrative and the proposals were criticisms and unflattering comparisons with the military practices in other parts of the British Empire.

In a sense both of these parts were comprehended in part III, "General Report and Recommendations dealing with the Military Situation in Canada." In five pages and less than 4,000 words Hutton gave a brilliant, coherent, logical diagnosis of the failings of the Canadian defence system, and recommended a cure. The "existing condition of the military forces of the Dominion," he wrote, was "unsatisfactory in the extreme." These formed not "an army . . . but a collection of military units without cohesion, without staff, and without those military departments by which an army is moved, fed, or ministered to in sickness." Its inefficient state was the result of lack of a general staff, administrative departments, corps of engineers, and sufficient stores. The standard of military efficiency was thus quite inadequate by the two "Principles Governing the Defence of Canada . . . (a) The defence of Canadian soil," and "(b) The power to participate in the defence of the British Empire." As a nation, Canada had the "responsibilities of self defence" and public opinion seemed determined "to uphold at all costs the integrity of the empire." For the actual defence of Canadian soil, Canada needed garrisons to protect "strategical centres" and "well

[8]*Can. Sess. Pap.* (no. 19), 1899, pp. 23–42, part II, "Report of the Major General" in "Report of the Department of Militia and Defence for 1898"; for the writing of the report see "My Command in Canada: A Narrative," Hutton Papers, pp. 1728–30; see also Parkin Papers, pp. 3822–25; on March 5, 1899, Hutton enclosed a proof of his report to Parkin and informed him of one sent to Principal Grant. "The Report involves most important military issues," he wrote, "based upon those national & imperial principles of which you are so widely known as one of the Pioneer Exponents. I have endeavoured to put the military situation in such a light that, without giving offence, it may appeal to Public Opinion. I have every reason for being most hopeful, & confidently look forward to the support of the Gov[t] as well as of my kindly Minister D[r] Borden."

trained, carefully organized, and thoroughly equipped" field troops ready for action "at the shortest notice."[9]

The changes needed to establish "a Canadian Army" included, first, a redefinition of the power of the general officer commanding to remove friction between the military and civil branches of the Militia Department; an appendix set forth in detail the readjustment which would enlarge the general officer's powers. Secondly, the militia force should be transformed into a militia army, not by an increase in strength, but by the creation of administrative departments. To be practicable, however, these required militia units of uniform size. Finally, military stores and buildings should be improved. The conclusion to part III and to the whole report emphasized Canada's immediate defensive needs, the costs of the proposals, and the fulfilment of a national obligation. "Success in modern war" necessitated "organization during peace," for Canada possessed 3260 miles of frontier "contiguous to a foreign State" and paid "less per head" for defence "than any other country in the world." Yet with only a small increase of $130,000 above the preceding year's estimates, his departmental proposals could be effected, though a larger outlay would be required later. The report swept on to a triumphant national conclusion.

> The creation of a Militia army upon the lines indicated will transform the existing militia units into a Military Force, which shall in some degree at least be worthy of the Canadian nation, and be equal to maintaining the rights and liberties of the Canadian people. It will be, in its true sense, a National Army, and will, as such, be able not only to defend inviolate the integrity of Canadian soil, but it will be capable of contributing to the military defence of the British Empire in a manner and with a power which will place Canada in a position of unparalleled dignity and influence among all the possessions of the Crown.[10]

Nowhere could Canadians find in shorter scope a better description of the state of the Canadian militia. Comprehensible by anyone of reasonable intelligence, it was designed to inform and awaken the public.[11] The whole report was printed separately as well as for the

[9]At this point Hutton emphasized the necessity for the establishment of a "Naval Militia Brigade" on Lakes Erie and Ontario (*Can. Sess. Pap.* (no. 19), 1899, p. 40). Minto had cautioned Hutton against making such a reference before publication of the report (Minto Papers, letter book no. 1, p. 78. Minto to Lord Wm. Seymour, April 18, 1899).

[10]*Can. Sess. Pap.* (no. 19), 1899, p. 42. His military report for 1899 is commonplace.

[11]Parkin Papers, pp. 3842–43, Hutton to Parkin, March 13, 1899: "You must excuse me and not put it down to personal vanity when I ask you to read with the utmost care Part III of my report. I have bestowed much & deep thought upon every line, & every syllable."

Sessional Papers, and was reprinted in whole or part by the press. Its brilliant and blunt quality made it the subject of widespread comment in Canada, Britain, and the United States.[12] Except for attacks in the rural press, which misinterpreted Hutton's plans for a national army as desiring "to create a small but expensive standing army,"[13] the report was favourably received by the militia and the public, and by both parties in Parliament. This reception astonished even Hutton himself. Arthur H. Lee, British military attaché at Washington, who had recently served on the Royal Military College staff, wrote to him: ". . . Tupper is also apparently on your side—it looks as if wonders would never cease! I think you must have hypnotised them all!"[14]

Why was part III, a "State Paper of really vast Imperial moment," to use Hutton's words,[15] so generally accepted in Canada? In the first place, no one could deny the truth of its description of defence conditions nor, secondly, the explicit affirmations of Canadian defence purposes. Thirdly, the report appeared under exceptionally favourable circumstances: it coincided closely with the rebuff of the United States at the Joint High Commission, and the fear thus produced turned Canadians to Britain for support. The Government now faced a public report which in essentials agreed with the secret report of the Committee on Canadian Defence.

The coincidence of the two reports was to a considerable extent a matter of design, for Hutton had pleaded with War Office officials not to select him as a member of the Committee on Canadian Defence in order that the committee's conclusions might be independent of his own. Although he deliberately did not read the committee's report until after writing his own, he had discussed the committee's problems "in direct collusion" with its members.[16] While Hutton proposed to use the similarities between the reports to justify his own plans, Dr. Borden announced that whenever differences existed, he proposed to follow the committee's advice.[17]

[12]*Globe*, March 28, 1899, and April 11, 1899, edit., "A Militia Army"; see also Hutton Papers, p. 522, [Sir] W. C. Van Horne to Hutton, April 7, 1899; *ibid.*, pp. 1734–35, "My Command in Canada: A Narrative," and D.M. 17385.
[13]*Can. Mil. Gaz.*, May 2, 1899.
[14]Hutton Papers, p. 485, May 2, 1899.
[15]*Ibid.*, p. 1731, "My Command in Canada: A Narrative."
[16]Minto Papers, vol. 15, pp. 15–16, to Minto, March 30, 1899.
[17]Lieut.-Col. J. F. Cummins, MS hist., "The Organization and Development of the Canadian Militia" (Historical Section, Can. Gen. Staff, 1932–36), pp. 245–46; the writer has not been able to trace this statement which Cummins says was made in Parliament.

III

It was one thing to write and read reports, another to contend with the chaos described. The "truly deplorable" conditions nearly caused Hutton to despair, as he opened his heart to his friends in correspondence.[18] Unlike his predecessor, who usually remained closeted in Ottawa, Hutton learned of conditions at first hand through his inspection tours, which had as one object to identify himself with the militia. His energy, knowledge, and ability, his attention to detail, and his appreciation of the needs of the force deeply impressed officers and men, who responded enthusiastically to his demands. A Toronto adjutant asserted that Hutton knew more of the internal economy of a regiment than any general he had known previously.[19]

Hutton held "levées (of the whiskey & soda type)" on his first tour so that he came to know personally the leading militia officers in eastern Canada.[20] Periodically he also met with local commanding officers in the expectation that local difficulties should be raised. On the first tour he discussed such topics as (1) more advanced formations of troops at training camps, (2) the need for central armouries for the new Lee-Enfield rifle, (3) the proposal to attach a drill instructor to each battalion at summer training camp, (4) clothing, (5) booting, and (6) messing. The tour culminated in November 1898 in a four-day conference at Ottawa on much the same subjects, attended by district officers commanding and inspectors of calvary and infantry.[21]

His general criticisms and suggestions were prudent and practical. To improve the battalions he induced the Minister to readjust instructional allowances, in order to eliminate abuses, and take account of regimental expenses not provided for. He suggested changes in the establishments, disbanding, amalgamation, and raising of units of troops. In general, however, he preferred not the raising but the reorganization of battalions. He also proposed a better-instructed staff, "an improved system of organization," and "a higher degree of military training" for the instructional camps of 1899.[22] He described the artillery standard as

[18]Hutton Papers, pp. 1046–49, Hutton to M. Nathan, Sec., Col. Def. Com., Jan. 9, 1899.

[19]John A. Cooper, "Editorial Comment," *Can. Mag.*, XII (Nov. 1898), p. 82; for a report on one of Hutton's inspections, see *Globe*, Oct. 13, 1898.

[20]Hutton Papers, p. 1045, Hutton to M. Nathan, Jan. 9, 1899.

[21]For a list of some 25 topics discussed, see *Globe*, Nov. 17, 1898, and Hutton Papers, pp. 1727–28, "My Command in Canada: A Narrative."

[22]*Can. Sess. Pap.* (no. 19), 1899, p. 25.

inadequate, though officers and non-commissioned officers had already been sent to England for artillery training. Hutton wrote a strong memorandum to Borden emphasizing that in the meantime a technically qualified officer was needed to provide Canada with its own instructional staff so as to avoid reliance on the Imperial service.[23] Rifle shooting lacked sufficient ammunition, rifle ranges, and a musketry course. He complained that citizens tended to look upon rifle shooting as a sport rather than a duty, a tendency encouraged by the Dominion Rifle Association.[24] The Permanent Force was particularly lacking in artillery and musketry skills.

On the other hand, he was "much impressed by the general excellence of the permanent force," a tribute largely due to General Herbert's energy. But the instruction it offered was "purely elementary," not from lack of zeal but "want of opportunity," for the force was engaged continually and lacked relaxation. To improve its instructional ability Hutton recommended two furloughs in 1899, and the return of the Field Force, made up of members of the Permanent Force, from the Yukon. He also arranged for the Permanent Force to be concentrated at Ottawa in 1899 for a month and a half for annual drill, where it received expert instruction from a Scots Guards drill sergeant. Hutton opposed the interchange of Permanent and Imperial garrison units, for the latter could not undertake the instructional duties of the former.

Hutton was more sympathetic to Permanent Force officers than was the Committee on Canadian Defence. As in the case of the Permanent Force in general, he attributed the deficiencies of the officers to overwork and lack of time to take more advanced instruction. Accordingly he proposed that promotion and salary increases should be contingent "upon a higher standard of professional knowledge."[25] He also recommended that senior officers should receive a greater salary increase than junior officers. The salary of a Permanent Force officer was less than one-third that of the equivalent American officer and about one-half that of the equivalent British officer.[26] General Hutton, and at least

[23]D.M. 17333, Jan. 17, 1899; see also A.G. 77711, 77892, 78607. For other aspects of artillery problems, see A.G. 79279 and 79277. Until the latest artillery was available Hutton was persuasive in suspending the purchase of artillery. (Hutton Papers, p. 1304, Hutton to Sir George Clarke, March 1, 1899.)

[24]*Can. Sess. Pap.* (no. 19), 1900, p. 23; Hutton himself, Lord Minto, Lord Strathcona, and others gave prizes for proficiency in musketry.

[25]But officers were allowed two and a half years to qualify from Jan. 1899 (A.G. 78454 and G.O. 75, 1899).

[26]A.G. 78290, memorandum of Maj.-Gen. Com. to Adj.-Gen., Jan. 16, 1899, and *Debates*, May 8, 1899, p. 2708.

General Herbert before him, recommended pensions for these officers: "It is universally recognized that it is not to the true interest of any State to abandon its public servants, be they soldiers or civilians, to want or poverty-stricken old age after having extracted from them years of faithful service."[27] In Parliament, Lieutenant-Colonel Sam Hughes introduced a motion, probably as a result of this statement, supporting a pension for members of the Permanent Force. When Hughes incidentally referred to the argument of those opposing the granting of pensions, who asserted "let these fellows just save up their money," he was interrupted with "hear, hear." When such an attitude existed, little could be done, though the Minister promised to look into the matter.[28]

IV

In a country like Canada where the dollar was the chief symbol of value, officers needed compensatory prestige if able and energetic men were to be attracted to the military profession. The Governor General tried to increase their prestige by attending professional military gatherings, making occasional speeches, and magnifying the social position of officers by inviting them to functions "on account of their military rank."[29] Hutton too made great efforts to encourage them. Unlike his predecessor, he espoused the cause of officers' associations, and, indeed, used them as sounding boards for his own ideas. Offered the presidency of the newly formed Field Officers' Association of the Militia, he used this position, together with that of General Officer Commanding, to merge the association with the Canadian United Service Club, which apparently had become the organization of the Permanent Force officers. He thus hoped to eliminate the friction between the Permanent Force and volunteer militia officers. He commended the Dominion Artillery Association and the Dominion Rifle Association in letter, speech, and annual report. At one meeting of the Artillery Association, for example, he congratulated artillerymen on their zeal, and, though deploring their low standard of technical efficiency and lamenting the obsolete guns that most exercised with, took advantage of the occasion to suggest a school of musketry.[30] To confer "a distinction" upon "selected officers," honorary aides-de-camp to the Governor General

[27]*Can. Sess. Pap.* (no. 19), 1899, p. 37.
[28]*Debates*, May 8, 1899, p. 2710. The whole debate is *ibid.*, pp. 2706–24.
[29]John Buchan, *Lord Minto: A Memoir* (London, 1924), p. 130, Minto to Wolseley, April 21, 1899.
[30]*Can. Mil. Gaz.*, Feb. 21, 1899, and *Globe*, April 6, 1899; see also A.G. 78544, and Minto Papers, vol. 17, p. 7, Hutton to Minto, Jan. 15, 1899.

were appointed.[31] Hutton modified the conditions for the appointment of honorary lieutenant-colonels, specifying that thereafter appointees should be of "high standing in the State" or have given "distinguished service in the Field."[32] To implement this change required considerable resistance to the pressure to appoint local worthies.

More crucial for defence was the quality of training, especially of militia officers. Hutton encouraged the able young officer in his studies and training, and by promotion.[33] He apparently tried to supersede regulation 75 of Regulations and Orders which laid down as a general rule that promotion was by seniority, by two general orders: G.O. 105, 1898, inaugurated an "Unattached List" in order "to facilitate the transfer of officers of one corps to another without sacrifice of militia rank," and G.O. 20, 1900, required officers seeking command or second-in-command of a militia corps to pass an examination for "Tactical Fitness to Command," though its implementation was postponed at least until the end of 1900. In training militia officers Hutton had an advantage over his predecessor in the existence of an improved Royal Military College under an able new commandant, Lieutenant-Colonel (later Major-General Sir) Gerald C. Kitson (1857–1950). Hutton noted its "good discipline," "satisfactory standard" of education, good clothing and quarters, and "high moral tone and *esprit de corps*," but he lamented that, although the college provided many officers for the Imperial forces, the Staff and Permanent Force did not receive the benefit of its training.[34] Nor did the college make as great a contribution to militia training as possible. Part of the explanation might be, as the Commandant complained, that militia officers were "in most cases so ignorant, that we have to start them with 'Vulgar Fractions.' "[35] Under Hutton's stimulus, however, the numbers attending courses at the college or elsewhere were much increased.

Hutton placed strong emphasis on improving discipline within the militia, enforcing strict obedience to existing laws and regulations: the Militia Act, Regulations and Orders, relevant parts of the Army Act, and Queen's Regulations and Orders.[36] To gain respect for rank and to

---

[31]G.O. 1, Jan. 1899.   [32]G.O. 112, Dec. 1898.

[33]Note the facet of his philosophy that "every man has his own future in his own hands . . .": Hutton to Lieut.-Col. Holmes, D.O.C. London Dist., April 20, 1899, Hutton Papers, p. 1364; and cf. *ibid.*, p. 1066.

[34]*Can. Sess. Pap.* (no. 19), 1899, p. 30.

[35]Hutton Papers, p. 346, Kitson to Hutton, Aug. 20, 1898.

[36]Note Hutton's order that all non-commissioned officers and men attached to schools of instruction should come under the discipline of the Army Act (C.S.O. to O.C., Royal Regiment of Canada, Infantry, March 16, 1899, A.G. 79717).

make training more efficient, Hutton sought to have the expert Imperial officers on loan to Canada given seniority to all officers of similar rank. This was the apparently literal interpretation of section 50 of the Militia Act of 1886; but because of implied national inferiority, Canadian authorities had interpreted the section as referring only to militia colonels serving with Regular colonels (that is, on manoeuvres with Imperial forces at Halifax, for example), not to officers lent by the Imperial Government and holding appointments under the Canadian Government.[37] In 1896, the War Office issued a regulation laying down seniority over local officers of the same rank to Imperial officers with local rank granted by the Queen.[38] Since, however, Canadian Regulations and Orders had legal force when in conflict with Queen's Regulations and Orders, the regulation was inoperative in Canada.

Hutton, therefore, put pressure on the War Office to promote in Britain newly appointed Imperial officers to the local rank of full colonel, which would automatically have given them superior rank to Canadian lieutenant-colonels, the highest rank. Because the Imperial officers affected were usually majors, the War Office was reluctant to give them two steps in local rank. With his usual directness, and to the resentment of Canadian officers, Hutton attempted to give Imperial officers precedence over militia officers of the same rank on the ground of appointment by the Queen and of literal interpretation of section 50 of the Militia Act. Lieutenant-Colonel Sam Hughes probably brought the matter to an issue by refusing to obey an order of Lieutenant-Colonel F. G. Stone, the Imperial expert in command of Canadian artillery. Lord Minto later observed to Lord Landsdowne that it would have been preferable to have continued the old office of Inspector, for the appointment of an Imperial officer to command the cavalry "raised a great deal of jealousy on the ground of putting Impl. officers over the heads of Canadians."[39] Hutton's solution in August was to cancel the relevant general order, and, to ensure seniority, he placed the names of Lieutenant-Colonels Kitson and Stone in November 1899 at the head of the militia list. The latter action appears to have prompted the Minister to protest the cancellation of the general order. Hutton defended his action on the ground of the repugnancy of the general

[37]Section 62 of Regulations and Orders 1879 interpreted as above the similar section of earlier militia acts. See also Maurice Ollivier, comp. and ed., *Colonial and Imperial Conferences 1887–1937* (Ottawa, 1954), I, p. 58.

[38]Queen's Regulations and Orders 1898, reg. 3, iv.

[39]Minto Papers, letter book no. 2, p. 93, "Private," Aug. 24, 1900; Minto thought Hutton agreed with this before he left.

order to section 50 of the Militia Act and insisted that the two Imperial officers could not be deprived of the seniority which "Imperial rank confers on them."[40] The cancelled regulations were not restored until after Hutton's departure from Canada; and in 1901 the Law Officers of the Crown, to whom Hutton had suggested the matter be referred, agreed with the Canadian contention.

Hutton himself set an example of the good officer. In one of his early speeches he announced: "I know my business. I expect you to do your duty; and, as a brother officer, I shall help you all I can."[41] Fearless in carrying out his own carefully thought-out plans, he exhibited a manner calculated to inspire fear. Several Canadian officers, in common with Australian officers, complained that Hutton filled them with terror. Accustomed to command and to be obeyed, he endeavoured to infuse the same spirit into commanding officers. He thrust responsibility on the able officers and hoped that they would exhibit the quality of energy. The burden of disciplining recalcitrants was placed on the shoulders of the usually easy-going district officers commanding, many of whom Hutton discovered "lacked confidence in asserting their authority."[42] At least two balked at this uninviting task. One of them justified his failure to inspect regiments on the ground that but a short time was available and added: "I may say that the ruling, that an Inspecting Officer must be senior is new to me, and has never, to my knowledge, been before laid down in Canada."[43] In a confidential comment Hutton rejoined: ". . . there are likely to be many changes made . . . under my command which are new to that officer. It is his duty to endeavour to carry out the principles & customs of H.M. service quite irrespective of whether they have been customary in Canada or not."[44] When another district officer commanding questioned one of Hutton's decisions regarding the ineligibility of an officer for an unattached list, Hutton flatly commented: "Please inform DOC No. 11 that I am not accustomed in giving decisions upon questions involving discipline to state my reasons to officers whose duty it is to obey."[45]

[40]D.M. 18714, memo of Maj.-Gen. Com. to Dept. Min. of Mil., Nov. 23, 1899, and Militia List 1899, pp. 20, 22, Oct. 1, 1899. Note also the technicality of local rank being granted by the (London) *Gazette*, which Hutton requested of Sir Evelyn Wood in Kitson's case (Hutton Papers, p. 66, Sept. 1, 1899).

[41]*Can. Mil. Gaz.*, Sept. 6, 1898; see also introduction of Viscount Wolseley, Commander-in-Chief, in Queen's Regulations and Orders 1898, p. ii.

[42]Hutton Papers, p. 1358, Hutton to Borden, "Private," April 12, 1899; see also *ibid.*, p. 52.

[43]A.G. 86071, D.O.C. Mil. Dist. No. 1 and 2, to C.S.O., Nov. 22, 1899.

[44]*Ibid.*, Nov. 30, 1899.

[45]A.G. 82076, note in Hutton's handwriting pasted on letter of D.O.C. Mil. Dist. No. 11, to C.S.O., June 16, 1899; Lieut.-Col. Gregory had already com-

V

Hutton thought that influences undermining mutual trust, such as gross patronage, must be eliminated from the force. To lay down the rule was easy; to enforce it required a persistent and prolonged struggle. Political patronage connected with cleaning out furnaces or contracting for food and other supplies at summer training camps or for the Yukon Field Force scarcely interested him, though acrimonious political wrangles occurred in Parliament on such subjects. Hutton did, however, offer strong resistance to the location of a large military establishment to the east, rather than the strategic west, of Toronto.[46]

Appointments and retirements in a force too often honeycombed with the worst kind of politics were the prime interest of Hutton. As the militia had lost its purpose in the 1880's and 1890's, militia battalions often tended to become political machines. When lieutenant-colonels had political ambitions, votes of militiamen might be decisive in getting and keeping power. Hence many militia officers became influential public figures, a condition shared with Britain.[47] If a militia officer commanding became a member of Parliament, his political position could reinforce his military position, and vice versa. Moreover, as a battalion's lesser appointments and promotions became political its divergent party complexion appears to have made it a hive of intrigue. Not surprisingly, an American critic in 1884 described the Canadian militia as "a kind of military Tammany."[48] When the commanding officer's political power depended on his men's goodwill, or when officers intrigued with one another, discipline was bound to suffer. Apart from political considerations, a disciplined militiaman might leave his battalion in a huff, and a disciplined officer, accompanied by his local member of Parliament, might interview the Minister of Militia to moderate or eliminate the disciplinary measure.

The Minister's official policy, at least up to 1898, permitted if it did not encourage an aggrieved officer to appeal beyond the decision of the general officer commanding. Asked by George E. Foster to outline the procedure if an officer demanded an investigation of charges made by him against his commanding officer, Dr. Borden replied: "In the first

plained of sharing a room with Lieut.-Col. Peters because "I would not feel free to entertain my friends" (A.G. 85806, "Personal," Dec. 1, 1898; and see also A.G. 86211).

[46]Hutton Papers, pp. 246–49, Hutton to Borden, "Private," Sept. 2, 1899; see also A.G. 78266.

[47]A British general complained that militia colonels in Britain were "very influential people" (Cd. 1790, q. 4637).

[48]Cited in C. P. Stacey, *The Military Problems of Canada* (Toronto, 1940), p. 63.

instance, the matter will go as one of routine to the General. If the officer aggrieved did not get satisfaction from that quarter, if an investigation were refused, then he would have the right to appeal to the civil head of the department, to the Minister. . . . I think it would be open to any officer to appeal direct to the Minister."[49]

Under such circumstances the enforcement of discipline was difficult. Obviously too, a parliamentary colonel was in a strategic position to frustrate disciplinary measures. To be disciplined or to lose his militia position might threaten not only his parliamentary seat, but also the power of the Government. Parliamentary colonels, if guilty of infractions of discipline, could protect themselves by making vague charges against a general's lack of tact or his alleged unconstitutional actions. In fact the Minister's refusal to uphold the general's discipline of officers commanding helped bring about the resignation of Hutton's predecessors, Herbert and Gascoigne. Hutton's successful disciplining of two parliamentary colonels, the Liberal, James Domville, and the Conservative, Sam Hughes, undoubtedly played a part in the cabinet decision that forced Hutton's recall.

Hutton had seen the maleficent effect of politics in New South Wales. He thought that without its elimination there could be no militia worthy of Canada. His formal leave-takings of the War and Colonial offices specified his intention of eliminating politics and envisaged the prospect of friction in the process. Letters to his superiors and overseas friends are peppered with denunciations of their ill effect. Although Borden professed agreement with Hutton's goal his statement in Parliament did not mean that he would always be adamant in the face of political pressure. Hutton appears generally to have been upheld on less important matters or removals.[50] But his determined onslaught upon politically important personages brought him into conflict with the Government.

VI

Hutton's most important pre-war disciplinary action was the retirement of Lieutenant-Colonel (later Senator) James Domville (1842–1921), at the time a Liberal member of Parliament from New Brunswick and officer commanding the 8th Hussars.

[49]*Debates*, May 5, 1898, p. 4945; see also *ibid.*, April 18, 1896, p. 6735, and Hutton Papers, p. 341.
[50]But cf. Hutton's rebuke to a D.O.C. referring "a matter of discipline in a private capacity to the Minister of Militia," in C.S.O. to D.O.C. Mil. Dist. No. 7, Jan. 25, 1899, A.G. 78881; cf. also A.G. 78511, and Laurier Papers, pp. 18420–22, Borden to Laurier, "Private and Confidential," Nov. 29, 1899.

Domville was a formidable opponent, with much political support. Two military influences assisted his election as a Liberal in 1896 (he had been a Conservative member from 1872 to 1882): his position as officer commanding a cavalry regiment, and publicity in April 1896 from an offer of service in the reconquest of the Sudan, for which Chamberlain gave effusive thanks.[51] His parliamentary career from 1896 to 1900 was subject to much controversy. In the spring of 1897 he illegally put in a claim for $300 rental for the regiment's armouries. By pressure on the Deputy Minister and with the approval of the Acting Minister of Militia, Sir Richard Cartwright, Domville received and cashed a cheque for $300[52] and went to the Diamond Jubilee.[53] On his return the Auditor General discovered the irregularity of the cheque. In the spring of 1898 the Public Accounts Committee heard evidence damaging to Domville's reputation;[54] Domville himself was in the Yukon at the time. In the meantime other charges of irregularity were made against Domville by his second-in-command, Lieutenant-Colonel Alfred Markham, and placed before Parliament in the 1898 session by George E. Foster, deputy leader of the Conservative Opposition and a bitter opponent of Domville. General Gascoigne stated that these charges were not fully substantiated, but neither were they fully investigated.[55]

[51]C.O. 42/838, pp. 690–92, draft, C.O. to W.O., April 20, 1896.

[52]*Journals of the House of Commons, Canada*, 1898, XXXIII, app. 2D, evidence before Public Accounts Committee re Domville and Barnes, April–June 1898. Originally money for the care of arms had been allocated to squadron leaders of the regiment, but in 1892 on the authority of documents he could not find, Domville obtained full control of the distribution of the funds of the whole regiment (*ibid.*, 1898, *passim*). In the fall of 1896 after the election General Gascoigne in effect regularized the procedure by recommending that the 8th Hussars be placed on the same basis as a city corps, that is, that all payments should be made direct to the officer commanding.

[53]As a member of Parliament Domville was one of the "political" officers accompanying Laurier. Canadian officers were lodged but not boarded at Britain's expense until July 3, 1897. A month later Domville, who had prolonged his stay in England to attend to mining business, was the only one of the " 'political' or sham colonels," as the Colonial Office put it, to have the "face to put forward . . . a preposterous claim" for board and lodging for the extra period—a claim which was of course rejected. C.O. 42/855, p. 235, minute by W.S.B.-H., Aug. 11, 1897. See also Baillie-Hamilton's side-note comment, "I have paid over £100 for quarters at various hotels for these warriors," *ibid.*, p. 238. See also Laurier Papers, pp. 16500–2, and letter July 30, 1897, cited in *Debates*, March 10, 1898, pp. 1701–2.

[54]*Journals*, 1898, XXXIII, app. 2D, p. xiii.

[55]Gascoigne suggested that the charges be dropped since Markham himself was under a cloud (to Adj.-Gen., March 10, 1898, A.G. 77703); but see A.G. 64836 containing précis of "Charges against Lt-Col Domville" by Markham.

Six months before Hutton's arrival the first steps were taken to retire Domville, who had been seventeen years in command of his regiment. Already in October of 1897 General Order 90 had been issued limiting the tenure of all officers commanding to a period of five years, though in some cases it might be extended to eight; and Borden stated his intention of enforcing the order as strictly as possible. When Domville received notice of his retirement he protested to Laurier against the application of the rule to him. He accused Markham of political intrigue (which was almost certainly true) and warned of the peril to his political position if he were retired:

From a political standpoint it is suicidal, the Regiment and the connections cover a vote of at least five hundred now, and the votes of the future of those that may be brought into the Regiment. It controls all the patronage of the Regimental Camp at Sussex, buildings, stables, armoury, forage and rations.
Whilst I have never made political use of the position it is quite capable of being turned to account against us as a heavy political factor. This power is proposed to be placed in the hands of my most bitter political opponent who worked all he and his paper could against myself and you and your friends. I refer to the "Sun" newspaper of St. John of which he is part owner and business manager. It is detrimental to my position in the Country and allows those opposed to me to use it against me.[56]

Borden commented on this letter that tenure was a departmental matter, that Markham was entitled to his brevet lieutenant-colonelcy, and that Domville overemphasized the political importance of the regulation; in any case he could not be exempted from it.[57] Apparently Domville's protest was not uninfluential, for in April 1898 the local District Officer Commanding recommended a three-year extension. This recommendation was not officially acted upon,[58] but Domville ignored requests by the Adjutant-General and Hutton later in the year for his retirement.

In late November, in order to enforce Domville's retirement, Hutton ordered the transfer of regimental supplies to Markham as Domville's successor. Domville was absent without leave at the time; on his return, at his order his representative illegally entered Markham's armouries and recovered some of the supplies.[59] The bitterness between the two men was such that the new District Officer Commanding recommended the retirement of both, and their replacement by the third-in-command.[60]

[56]Laurier Papers, pp. 20811–15, Feb. 16, 1898.
[57]*Ibid.*, pp. 20750–52, Borden to Laurier, "Private," Feb. 18, 1898.
[58]A.G. 77703, copy, Lieut.-Col. Geo. J. Maunsell, D.O.C. Mil. Dist. No. 8, to Adj.-Gen., April 1, 1898, and Minto Papers, letter book no. 1, pp. 112–13.
[59]A.G. 77703, Markham to Lieut.-Col. F. L. Lessard, Jan. 4, 1899.
[60]*Ibid.*, D.O.C. Mil. Dist. No. 8, to C.S.O., "Confidential," Jan. 7, 1899.

Hutton acknowledged the faults of both, but he was reluctant to retire Markham, for apparently he was a competent officer and had served as President of the Cavalry Association. Domville meanwhile complained to Hutton about Markham's replacing him and reminded him of Borden's promise of an extension of tenure, a promise, according to Hutton, that Borden had never made.[61]

Nevertheless, Borden, who up to this time had supported Hutton in the affair, persuaded him to postpone Domville's retirement until after the New Brunswick elections on February 18, 1899, and, the elections over, still refused to give the necessary permission. The Government was undoubtedly under pressure from Domville. He had informed Laurier that he would take action in the forthcoming session of Parliament to maintain his political position, but that such action "must not be construed as any hostility on my part against the Government."[62] One of his efforts, the introduction of an amendment to the Militia Act which would have drastically curtailed the power of the General Officer Commanding, was apparently intended to assist Borden, but the Government gave no support to the amendment and it was withdrawn.[63] Domville's main courses of action in the session, however, were to embarrass the Minister by asking awkward questions about the transfer of regimental arms and to revive the charges made against him by Markham and Foster, which he now requested be considered by the Public Accounts Committee.[64] Domville's purposes in raising this issue were apparently to confuse the personal charges made by Markham and Foster with public charges of irregularities, and to make it appear that he desired to clear himself before the committee. In fact he put off appearing before it as long as possible.

Hutton brought matters to a head by two steps taken on his own initiative: he placed Domville on " 'leave of absence . . . pending his retirement under regulations,' "[65] and he tried, though unsuccessfully, to persuade Foster to withdraw the charges against Domville. These independent actions were deeply resented by Borden, and he now put pressure on Hutton to cancel the leave and the retirement completely. Hutton refused; in a long indictment to Borden he set out the facts of the case, explaining the serious effects political pressure was having on

[61]*Ibid.*, Domville to Hutton, Jan. 5, 1899, and memorandum, G.O.C. to Dep. Min., Jan. 11, 1899.
[62]Laurier Papers, p. 31154, Domville to Laurier, March 9, 1899.
[63]*Debates*, June 1, 1899, p. 4055.
[64]*Ibid.*, April 19, 1899, p. 1840.
[65]*Ibid.*, May 10, 1899, p. 2899.

the discipline and good name of the militia. If Domville was not retired, Hutton concluded, he would himself resign.[66]

This letter, together with other documents and correspondence in the case, was considered by the cabinet. Hutton was in a strong position, partly because of his own popularity in the country,[67] and also because of Canada's dependence on Britain in the Alaska boundary dispute. Moreover, Minto, although conceding to Borden that he had grounds for dissatisfaction over some of Hutton's actions, considered the military procedure correct, and took a strong stand with the cabinet: if the Government wanted Domville's tenure extended, Minto would demand the reasons, that is, would insist on Domville's resignation.[68] Minto therefore prevailed upon Laurier to consider Hutton's letter as a private rather than an official communication,[69] and suggested as a solution that Borden require Domville to state in writing the date of his appearance before the parliamentary inquiry, his command meanwhile being extended for the intervening period and regimental stores re-transferred to him; at the conclusion of the inquiry he was to be gazetted out. Minto amplified the details of the conditions in his next letter to Borden two days later.[70] Apparently distrusting Borden's ability to withstand Domville's pressure, Minto warned Hutton to keep in touch with him to "ensure case remaining in my hands."[71]

[66]Hutton Papers, pp. 904–15, May 31, 1899. *Inter alia* Hutton denied that in granting leave he "assumed power that was vested in the Governor General in Council." He also observed: "I need hardly bring to your notice a fact which, unfortunately, is too well known throughout the Empire, that Canadian troops have been subjected to the criticism that political influence has been allowed to interfere with the discipline and good order of the Force. I understood from you, when assuming command, that political influence would not be allowed under the new Government, to weigh against the discipline and good order of the Force." He hoped that Borden would consider the good name of the militia. For a statement defending the legality of Domville's position, see undated and unsigned memorandum in D.M. 17487.

[67]Minto Papers, letter book no. 1, p. 107, Minto to Hutton, June 3, 1899.

[68]*Ibid.*, p. 114, Minto to Borden, "Private," and p. 112, Minto to Hutton, "Private," June 9, 1899. Minto warned Hutton to use the greatest tact and avoid unguarded expressions (p. 113).

[69]Laurier Papers, pp. 34277–83, 34269–76, Minto to Laurier, "Private," two letters on June 7, 1899.

[70]Minto Papers, letter book no. 1, pp. 114, 115, Minto to Borden, "Private," June 9, June 11, 1899, respectively. The second letter (copy in Laurier Papers, pp. 34452–55) omitted a condition made on June 9 that if the inquiry were unduly prolonged Borden would place Domville on leave once more or gazette him out. Note that Minto advised Hutton to accept the proposal, the alternative suggested by Laurier being the withdrawal of Hutton's letter to Borden (p. 113, "Private," June 9, 1899).

[71]*Ibid.*, p. 127, Minto to Hutton, "Private," June 28, 1899.

Although Borden agreed to Minto's arrangement, and Minto and Hutton thought they had won a great victory in purifying the militia,[72] Borden triumphed on the question of Domville's successor. Hutton ordered the transfer of regimental arms and stores back to Domville, but Markham balked until the end of July at carrying out what must have been a humiliating order. On August 7, 1899, the Public Accounts Committee reported, summing up the evidence and unanimously condemning the transaction and the parties concerned; on the next day, "under further consideration," it gave Domville as a gentleman, officer, and member of Parliament a clean bill of moral health.[73] His resignation should now have taken place under the terms of the agreement, and Hutton intended that Markham should succeed for the period of the summer training camp. But Borden insisted tht Markham should succeed for one week only. In mid-August, Domville was retired, Markham succeeded for the week and was then transferred to the reserve, and the third-in-command, Major H. M. Campbell, became officer commanding.[74] Hutton had thus to give way in some measure, although he had, with Minto's assistance, succeeded in his main purpose and had benefited the militia ethically and administratively. But the clash with the Minister had strained his relations with the Government, and his victory, even though partial, had demonstrated once again that, militarily at least, Canada was not a sovereign state.

[72]Hutton Papers, p. 77, Hutton to Sir Redvers Buller, June 18, 1899, in which Hutton mentioned his deep gratitude for Minto's support in the "desperate battle."
[73]*Journals*, 1899, XXXIV, app. 1, pp. x–xiii, and *Journals*, 1899, XXXIV, p. 528.
[74]G.O. 84 and 85, Aug. 1899. Alone among the units, the 8th Hussars did not receive summer training in 1899. Domville was defeated in the election of 1900.

12. Headquarters Reform

ONE OF THE CHIEF TARGETS of criticism in both Hutton's report and the report of the Committee on Canadian Defence was the administrative branch of the army. In the early nineties, Canada's militia headquarters bore too close a resemblance to a militia post office and centre for the distribution of patronage. One of Hutton's principal reforms, therefore, was to lay the groundwork for an efficient headquarters organization.

I

The Committee on Canadian Defence had insisted on the need for trained senior officers, for Canadian officers lacked experience in commanding large forces. Although Canadian troops had occasionally been brigaded,[1] extensive manoeuvres of troops either in Canada or Britain were almost unknown at that time. In November 1898 Hutton wrote a memorandum on the need for a general staff, which he described as "the primary condition for an efficient military administration." He proposed "to form, and carry out, a Course of Instruction . . . at the Royal Military College."[2] Twelve officers completed this officially approved four-month course under the Commandant, Colonel Kitson. These same officers also gained experience by taking part under Hutton's personal guidance in a "most successful" three-day staff ride in the Niagara Peninsula against a prospective enemy from the United States.[3]

[1] Alice R. Stewart, "Sir John A. Macdonald and the Imperial Defence Commission of 1879," Can. Hist Rev., XXXV (June 1954), q. 3848, p. 132.
[2] D.M. 17169, Nov. 4, 1898; see also Can. Sess. Pap. (no. 19), 1899, pp. 32–33; cf. ibid., p. 25, and Globe, Nov. 25, 1898.
[3] Minto Papers, vol. 15, pp. 21–22, Hutton to Minto, May 28, 1899; cf. also detailed instructions for staff ride in Militia Order no. 50, April 4, 1899. Hutton planned similar staff rides near Montreal and Windsor for 1900 and 1901. Note also Capt. A. H. Lee's lecture to those officers "upon the capabilities of the American army for action against Canada." C.O. 42/871, p. 173, extract from military attaché's report at Washington, inc. in F.O. to C.O., "Confidential," March 29, 1899.

The results of this staff training, other regular and special training courses, and the assistance of some 42 Royal Military College cadets go far to account for the success of the summer training camps in 1899. Like his predecessors Hutton failed in an attempt to have the training period extended from 12 to 16 days, but he saved time by having the camps prepared beforehand and living arrangements improved. Because camps lacked adequate musketry ranges, Hutton proposed the use of a small rifled barrel—called a Morris Tube—which was fitted inside a regular service rifle to fire small calibre bullets at miniature targets.[4] Commanding training camps in person, he cut out all frills and worked the men *"very* hard,"[5] and they in turn responded eagerly to real soldiering. His decisive innovation was the embodying of all the militia: in the last two days of camp instruction the city corps came to camp to take part in divisional manoeuvres with the rural corps. Thus the Canadian militia was being converted into a self-contained army, and its officers given the opportunity to command large bodies of men.[6] The thoroughness of the training in the summer camps impressed Canadian public opinion and newspapers both in Canada and the United States.[7]

II

Canadians might well be proud of the successful training camps of 1899, but they were largely the result of the masterful ability of a great personality. Hutton's administrative successes were not unlike those of a great mediaeval king, whose accomplishments, if not institutionalized, would collapse under a weakling successor. To ensure the continuance of his reforms, Hutton instituted changes at the rather indolent headquarters. In the early 1890's there had been a few improvements; a quartermaster-general and other officers had been added to the headquarters. But criticisms continued unabated; for example, the flouting

[4] A.G. 78544, memorandum of Maj.-Gen. Com. to Min. of Mil., Jan. 17, 1899.
[5] Gowan Papers, in possession of Prof. E. G. R. Ardagh of Toronto, Lieut.-Col. H. J. Grasett to Sen. James Gowan, July 5, 1899.
[6] Cf. Lieut.-Col. Sam Hughes's description of old time-wasting brigade drill: ". . . men became disgusted, standing, waiting, doing nothing but swearing; . . . Vide some old Brigade orders, 'Fall in' 1.30, Brigade markers, or, out at 1.30: posted 1.45, Corps to march on markers at 2. parade come to attention 2.30, and it was usually 3 before all could be ready. To my mind, fifteen minutes after 'Fall in' sounds, each battalion or corps should be at or near its place in Brigade." Hutton Papers, p. 1105, Hughes to Lieut.-Col. C. E. Montizambert, D.O.C. Mil. Dist. No. 3 and 4, Nov. 29, 1898; cf. *Debates*, July 10, 1899, pp. 7063–65.
[7] *Globe*, June 21, 1899, edit., "The Annual Camps"; cf. *Can. Mil. Gaz.*, July 4, 1899, and Hutton Papers, pp. 1738–40, "My Command in Canada: A Narrative."

of General Orders by Generals Herbert and Gascoigne[8] and arbitrary actions of both General and Minister, especially in matters of patronage.[9] General Hutton's aide-de-camp vividly described the utter chaos after Gascoigne had let things drift: "Clerks, politicians and civilians seem to do everything, without the knowledge of anybody. For instance half the drill ground [location unspecified] had been sold to a pork factory, without the General knowing a word about it, or being consulted at all."[10]

One reform was insistence on proper routine. Hutton protested to the Deputy Minister, for example, that a Colonial Office document marked "Secret" had "passed to the Military Branch under open cover."[11] He introduced innovations to free him from routine: he appointed a chief staff officer in whose name correspondence and routine might be conducted, and inaugurated a system of personal orders called Daily Militia Orders, issued twice a week, which made political interference more difficult. He justified these orders to the Deputy Minister as saving correspondence, as universal in other armies, and as his "own orders as General Officer Commanding to the Troops under my command." Two months later when their importance became evident, the Minister requested that both he and the Deputy Minister should see them before issue. Hutton only partly agreed to the Minister's request.[12] Furthermore to ensure remaining in full control of the military branch and to avoid interference by the civil branch, Hutton forbade his subordinates to consult the Minister without his permission, and if they had to do so, to report back to him.

His most important innovation was the inauguration of administrative departments. When British Regulars left central Canada in 1871 administrative departments ceased though their existence was implied by the Militia Act. Neither the need for them in the North-West Rebellion of 1885 nor the representations from Britain moved the Canadian Government to set them up. Pressure increased after the Venezuela incident. The memorandum of the Colonial Defence Committee, prin-

[8]Lieut.-Col. James R. McShane, *The Dominion Militia Past and Present* (1896), p. 6, and *Can. Mil. Gaz.*, Feb. 2, 1898.

[9]Cf. evidence of Dep. Min. of Mil. before the Public Accounts Committee, re Domville and Barnes, app. 2D, *Journals of the House of Commons, Canada,* 1898, XXXIII, pp. 35–36; cf. also David Tisdale, *Debates*, April 3, 1900, p. 3110.

[10]"The stores are full of the funniest old guns," he continued, "(on old wooden step carriages) and boarding pikes." He also described Hutton's efforts to restore order (to his brother, Maj. Morison Bell, Oct. 12, 1898; sent to Hutton, Jan. 12, 1907, Hutton Papers, p. 148).

[11]D.M. 17424, "Secret," Oct. 22, 1899.

[12]D.M. 17308, Dec. 30, 1898, Jan. 10, 1899; cf. *ibid.*, April 14, 21, 1899, and *Globe*, Jan. 27, 1899.

ciples of "Colonial Defence," ascribed the "greatest importance" to departmental services, otherwise the "smallest operation in war becomes impossible," though in peacetime much could be done "without expenditure by mere registration" of required personnel and sources of necessary supply, transportation, and labour.[13] The first volume of the secret report of the Committee on Canadian Defence emphasized Canada's dire peril in wartime without administrative departments; the second volume analysed the need more deeply. Hutton pressed for their formation in a strong memorandum[14] and in his annual report. The big advantage of pressing for this reform was its importance and cheapness.

Canadian physicians had shown spasmodic interest in the creation of a militia medical department and in 1898 a stretcher-bearer company had been established at Halifax. In June 1899 Hutton obtained consent for the establishment of a Militia Army Medical Corps and the authorization of four additional bearer companies and four field hospitals. The regulations for the required Medical Service, the General Order (62) stated, "contemplate the formation from the existing Military Units of two complete Divisions of Infantry, two Cavalry Brigades, and two independent Brigades of all three Arms, the establishments for which will be found in the War Establishments (War Office) 1898." This "most far-reaching Order . . . promulgated from Headquarters for some years," wrote the *Canadian Military Gazette*[15] implied the creation of other departmental services. But Hutton saw a deeper significance, as he jubilantly enclosed a copy of this General Order to Minto. He stressed the "enormous importance . . . of the Preface. . . . It is the official recognition of the necessity & of the intention for reform of the Canadian Militia upon an Army basis. . . . Candidly I hardly expected that the Gov^t would accept all my bill."[16] It is, however, doubtful whether the Government saw its significance.[17]

III

The significance of the proposed reorganization of the department controlling transport and supply was seen, however. It would affect the existing stores branch under the deputy minister. In 1887 transport

[13]G 21, no. 165, Additional, "Confidential," 57M, May 29, 1896, inc. in C.O., "Secret Circular," July 6, 1896.

[14]D.M. 17126, memorandum of Maj.-Gen. Com. to Dep. Min. of Mil., Jan. 9, 1899.

[15]July 14, 1899.

[16]Minto Papers, vol. 15, p. 25, June 9, 1899; for his efforts towards setting up an Army Veterinary Department, see A.G. 79273.

[17]Cf. Minto Papers, letter book no. 2, p. 284, Minto to Sir Montagu Ommaney (*sic*), "Private," May 7, 1901.

and supply in England had been removed from the control of a civil official, the surveyor-general, and placed under the control of the commander-in-chief. In Canada, on the contrary, as the secret report of the Committee on Canadian Defence explained, supply and transport remained under civil control; "the Minister of Militia and Defence controls both the latter branches, and is referred to upon every minor detail in connection with them, including the issue from stores of every article, however small."[18]

The Committee on Canadian Defence criticized stores arrangements. It emphasized that the general officer commanding should have the "custody and control of the issues of all stores," and prepare annual requirements subject to the minister. He should also have custody of all fortifications, barracks, and lands. The committee and Hutton both recommended the enlargement of the Government Cartridge Factory to make Canada more independent in wartime.[19]

Borden recognized the need for changes at headquarters, and in his first letter to Hutton requested him "to look into the system (or want of it) now in vogue in the civil branch & give me the benefit of your advice." Two days later he made the same kind of complaint to Laurier, but threw the responsibility on the aged Deputy Minister: "Colonel Panet is no longer able to fill the position. I do not think it would be possible for me to go on with his branch of the service in the condition in which it is, for any considerable length of time. The mistakes that are constantly being made, the forgetfulness and carelessness that are displayed, are insufferable."[20] In reply Hutton suggested a stricter definition of duties and especially increased accommodation. The Minister worried too much about military detail; the usual practice was "for a General to be responsible for the issue, care, & amount of Military Stores & Equipment," which was "a purely technical & professional matter." Much blunter in an official memorandum a month later, he asserted that the existing system "from a Military point of view" was

[18]*Report No. II*, "Secret," p. 11, and J. B. Atlay, *Lord Haliburton* (Toronto, 1909) chaps. I-IV; for the duties of the Canadian equivalent of the surveyor-general, the director of stores, see Regulations and Orders for the Canadian Militia 1887, regs. 754–62; reg. 754 reads as follows: "The Director of Stores and Keeper of Militia Properties is responsible to the Minister of Militia and Defence for all clothing, Militia Stores and properties committed to his charge, and under whose sole authority he acts with regard to their safe keeping, issue, and disposition."
[19]*Report No. II*, "Secret," pp. 11–13 and 73–74 and *Report No. I*, "Secret," pp. 68–69.
[20]Hutton Papers, p. 217, Borden to Hutton, Aug. 19, 1898, and Laurier Papers, p. 25890, Borden to Laurier, "Private," Aug. 20, 1898.

"chaotic and pregnant with friction in peace and disastrous in war or national emergency." In November 1898 he made representations about disorganization in the stores department, which with the Minister's permission he had inspected in each district. He condemned severely the lack of proper precautions in handling ammunition; one building was not even fireproof. For the sake of "public safety, if not of military efficiency," the stores branch should come "under the supervision and control of skilled officers."[21]

In his annual report too Hutton was critical of the custody and issue of military stores; it was "contrary to universal military precedent elsewhere, to economy, and to military efficiency for the custody and issue of military stores to be in the hands of a civil department."[22] Criticizing the lack of regimental stores space, gun sheds, and armouries, he recommended a $30,000 appropriation for the construction or enlargement of these stores. He particularly recommended the construction of adequate stores for the cities of Toronto, London, and Ottawa, and of many drill halls and armouries.[23] He suggested too that the military branch should have custody of and issue clothing.

Included in the 1898 report of the Department of Militia was the Report of the Director of Stores, Lieutenant-Colonel D. A. Macdonald. Macdonald, who Hutton believed lacked the necessary military and technical knowledge, carried on a counter attack against Hutton's recommendations. He affirmed that "under the authority of . . . the Minister" and "in the interest of the Public" the stores branch was charged with the custody, care, and issue of *matériel*. The purchase of these stores was based on "absolute necessity . . . from personal knowledge of the wants of the force and not based on any estimate supplied by its officers." Yet he complained the military branch had never laid down any "estimate of probable requirements for any given period." In effect he admitted that the relationship of the two branches was unsatisfactory. Concurring in the need for more storage space, he could argue plausibly that stores duties were "carried out as satisfactorily as possible under existing circumstances." Appearing as part of the report of the new Deputy Minister, Lieutenant-Colonel L. F. Pinault, Macdonald's report may be interpreted as meeting his superior's approval and designed to oppose Hutton's plans.[24]

[21]Hutton Papers, pp. 220–21, Borden to Hutton, Aug. 26, 1898; *ibid.*, pp. 226–27, memo of G.O.C. to Min. of Mil., "Confidential," Oct. 6, 1898; *ibid.*, pp. 1223–24, G.O.C. to Borden, "Private," Nov. 2, 1898; A.G. 79316, Feb. 14, 1899; and cf. A.G. 85805, Nov. 8, 1899.
[22]*Can. Sess. Pap.* (no. 19), 1899, p. 28.
[23]*Ibid.*, pp. 35–36.   [24]*Ibid.*, pp. 1–2.

That the transfer would increase safety and efficiency, and accord more closely with British precedent, seems unquestionable, but it would drastically curtail the Deputy Minister's powers, for he would have been left only with procurement of supplies, parliamentary finances, and audit. Hutton wrote to the President of the Colonial Defence Committee that there was "a good deal of opposition to the transfer of stores in question, now in civil custody, to military administration."[25]

Available evidence suggests that after the Domville affair relations between the General and the Minister began to cool. Hutton had aspired to be the sole military adviser to the Minister, but the Minister now, apparently, began taking advice from the Deputy Minister on purely military matters.[26] The Deputy Minister and his supporters were apparently in strong opposition to Hutton's plans and policies, as they undoubtedly were to those of his near successor, Lord Dundonald, the last General Officer Commanding.[27]

IV

In all his actions Hutton was convinced that he was acting strictly within the letter of the law and the spirit of the constitution. In a letter intended for Laurier at the time of his recall, he wrote:

It has been my constant aim to keep within the sphere laid down as that of the military command of the troops, in accordance with the Statute. The role of the Officer in command of the Militia is as clearly indicated in the Militia Act, and in Regulations and Orders for the Militia, 1898, Para. 3, as are the powers of the Minister of Militia.

The General Officer Commanding is charged with the promotions, appointments and discipline of the troops, and in administering my command in these respects I have made every effort to meet the views and wishes of the Minister, so far as I was able to do so, compatible with what I conceived to be my duty, and the interests of the Force.[28]

But the few Canadians who had expressed opinions upon the matter, including at least one expert on Canadian military law, reasoned otherwise. On the basis of the principle of responsible government, con-

[25]Minto Papers, vol. 21, pp. 95–96, copy to Sir Richard Harrison, "PRIVATE AND CONFIDENTIAL," April 7, 1899.
[26]Hutton Papers, p. 1526, Hutton to L. F. Pinault, Sept. 10, 1899; cf. ibid., p. 1486, Hutton to Borden, draft, Aug. 11, 1899.
[27]Cf. Col. C. F. Hamilton, "The Canadian Militia: The Change in Organization," Can. Def. Quart., VIII (Oct. 1930), p. 97.
[28]Hutton Papers, p. 922, unsent letter, Feb. 6, 1900; cf. ibid., pp. 1797–98, also "My Command in Canada: A Narrative."

sidered ideologically rather than pragmatically, they argued that Hutton had acted unconstitutionally. In their minds, the test of responsible government seems to have been the constitutional right of members of a government to give a governor general unpalatable advice—the right to "misgovern" themselves, as Sir John Macdonald put it. Pragmatically this right of "self-misgovernment" was not exercised at once, but it was gradually acquired by pressure, request, co-operation. The Canadian Government was often only too glad, as in the period of this volume, to submit as a colony to British imperial power. Sometimes Britain put considerable pressure on Canada to assume responsible government duties of defence. Resentment against this pressure appears to imply that Canada envisaged sovereignty as a kind of irresponsibility. Whatever the actual status of Canada, many Canadians ideologically held that responsible government meant abject obedience of a general officer commanding to Canadian authorities.

Lord Minto's public reference to "military machinery" being "entirely unhampered by political influence"[29] perhaps prompted inside talk in Ottawa on the alleged unconstitutional actions of Hutton and Minto.[30] Possibly this reference induced the Toronto *Globe* to write a long editorial defining the positions of the governor general, the militia, and the general officer commanding, which was probably a warning to Minto and Hutton in view of the quasi-official status of the *Globe* as a Government organ. The editorial also gave the current ideological theory of responsible government on defence very clearly, its apparently impeccable logic being maintained by avoidance of a careful analysis of the historical evolution, constitutional practice, and strategic necessities of Canadian defence. Canada wanted not " 'strong government' " but responsible government, the editorial declared. "At Confederation Canada became to all intents and purposes a self-governing nation" and took over the control and the expense of the militia. Except for an increase in cost, scarcely any administrative change took place in the control of the militia. A British Army officer still commanded the Canadian militia and after the withdrawal of British Regulars from Quebec in 1871, British troops still garrisoned the Halifax Naval Base,

---

[29]*Globe*, Dec. 15, 1898.

[30]Cf. Willison Collection, pp. 27625–26, "Private," Nov. 24, 1898, George Simpson, *Globe*'s Ottawa correspondent, to John Willison; Simpson reported that Hutton had refused to approve the appointment of a new medical officer for a military school, and had also induced Minto to refuse approval; but Borden insisted because of rights of responsible government, and the Governor General gave way. Cf. Minto Papers, letter book no. 1, p. 2, Minto to Borden, Nov. 21, 1898.

the British Navy still patrolled Canadian waters, and Britain still provided the diplomatic support upon which Canada's existence depended.
But, the editorial continued, the efficiency of the militia rested with
Parliament and the people. The Militia Department, however, differed
from other departments in having an "Imperial officer in command of
the Canadian Militia," whose duties were "ill-defined." He was "virtually responsible to nobody," for his appointment rested with a body
thousands of miles away and not with the body controlling and maintaining the force. The "true remedy," the editorial concluded, was to
introduce more responsible government and to appoint a Canadian
general officer commanding.[31] The occasional suggestion of a Canadian
general officer met with some public support, but militia officers were
opposed because of the possibilities of dissension. The Government
almost certainly believed that an Imperial general officer provided "a
link that binds the Imperial government to this country."[32]

But although Canadians generally seem to have desired a British
rather than a Canadian general officer, contemporary and most later
critics have held that the general officer was constitutionally a virtual
"rubber stamp" of the Minister of Militia.[33] Many of the generals
apparently came to acquiesce in this subservience. Coming to Canada
with high hopes they believed themselves possessed of powers similar
to those of the commander-in-chief in England. Upon discovering lack
of support for militia reform, Hutton's two predecessors at least tried
to induce the Government to define the general's duties more clearly
—a mandatory obligation under section 40 of the Militia Act.

At least as far back as the governor generalship of Lord Stanley an
attempt had been made to clarify a general officer's duties. Lord Stanley
wrote in 1888 that it had been understood that the positions of the
minister of militia and the general officer commanding paralleled those
of the secretary of war and the commander-in-chief. But changes in
British army administration had not been followed in Canada.

---

[31]"Why not a Canadian?" Dec. 19, 1898.

[32]E. G. Prior (Victoria, B.C., Conservative), *Debates*, June 25, 1900, pp.
8261–62.

[33]One of the best contemporary accounts is Lieut.-Col. W. E. Hodgins, "The
Law Applicable to the Militia of Canada," *Canadian Law Times*, XXI (April
1901), pp. 169–88. One of the best modern accounts will be found in Col. C. F.
Hamilton, "The Canadian Militia: The Change in Organization," *Can. Def.
Quart.*, VIII (Oct. 1930), pp. 95–97. A similar point of view will be found in
the works of John S. Ewart, Henri Bourassa, Oscar D. Skelton, John W. Dafoe,
etc. The opposite view may be found in John Buchan, *Lord Minto: A Memoir*
(London, 1924), pp. 144–49, and Earl of Dundonald, *My Army Life* (London,
1926), p. 195 and *passim*.

The result is that the G.O.C. Militia, who has, as an Imperial officer, to guide himself by the Queen's Regulations in the exercise of duties which would appear to be unquestionably assigned to him by Statute and Regulations, finds himself unable to act, in consequence, either of a want of proper definition of his duties, or on account of a custom (which appears to have grown up without written authority), of submitting every detail, however small, for the personal approval of the Minister.

Stanley therefore suggested that sections 36–40 of the Militia Act should be amended, and that an order-in-council should be passed, based on the Imperial Order-in-Council of February 21, 1888, to correspond to recent changes in Britain. This suggestion would have brought clarification of the duties of the general officer.[34] Five years later (1893), the Minister of Militia had been prevailed upon to recommend doing this. Some months later Major-General Herbert submitted a requested memorandum on the duties and responsibilities of the general officer, somewhat elaborating Lord Stanley's suggestions.[35] Nothing came of either the Minister's recommendation or Herbert's memorandum.

With a few minor changes and some additions, Herbert's proposals appeared as an appendix to Hutton's annual report of 1898 and formed the basis of his suggestions for the reallocation of duties at headquarters. Hutton's plan provided for a military branch directly under the general officer commanding who would control seven military departments, the heads of which, reporting to him, would be as follows: adjutant-general, quartermaster-general, assistant adjutant-general for artillery, engineering officer, director of stores, chief paymaster, director-general of medical staff. On the other hand, the chief accountant, the chief of the contract department, and the superintendent of the manufacturing department would report to the deputy minister as head of the civil branch.[36] Nothing was done to implement these suggestions until Lord Dundonald's time.

To have defined the powers of the general officer commanding in this way would have brought about their enlargement—a development quite contrary to the ambitions of a Canadian Government. While the Government had already closely defined the adjutant-general's and the quartermaster-general's duties, it refused to define the general officer's, though it desired his prestige and the potential British power his presence

---

[34]G 21, no. 165, Additional, "Notes of Governor General Stanley on the position of the General Officer in 1888," also printed in *Report No. II*, "Secret," app. C., pp. 78–90.

[35]*Ibid.*, pp. 80–82, Memorandum of Herbert to Min. of Mil., "Very Confidential," Oct. 2, 1893.

[36]*Can. Sess. Pap.* (no. 19), 1899, pp. 55–56, app. G.

in Canada signified. During Hutton's régime there is some evidence
that the Government desired, as Lord Dundonald put it, a "dumb
General,"[37] a role which Hutton had no intention of playing. On the
contrary, in the absence of the definition of his duties, section 82 of
the Militia Act specified that the relevant sections of the Queen's Regulations and Orders with the necessary changes applied in Canada.
Although the secret Committee on Canadian Defence had observed
that this section had "practically been allowed to become a dead
letter," a few pages later it held that the British regulations were still
in force by virtue of the Canadian Militia Act.[38] Hutton boldly interpreted this section of the Act in his report not as dead letter but as
living law.[39] Law, past recommendations, and necessity required the
clear definition of duties, he argued.

Because of Canada's need for Britain's support, the Government
dared not argue that section 82 had become a dead letter, and that
Hutton was acting unconstitutionally in assuming that the section meant
what it said. The Government did not, for example, support Domville's amendment of the Militia Act to make the general officer commanding legally subordinate to the minister.[40] On the other hand, Lord
Minto, while affirming the constitutional supremacy of the Government
over the general, held that the "G.O.C. is sent as a military expert on
whom they [the Government] are expected to rely for professional
advice."[41] When, therefore, a general, anticipating acceptance of his

[37]*My Army Life*, p. 221; for a definition of the duties of the adjutant-general,
quartermaster-general, assistant adjutant-general for artillery, and deputy-assistant
adjutant-general (later abolished), see G.O. 6, Feb. 1897.

[38]*Report No. II*, "Secret," pp. 7, 11, respectively.

[39]*Can. Sess. Pap.* (no. 19), 1899, p. 41; probably the most important of the
Queen's Regulations and Orders for the Army 1898 in this connection was reg.
156; see also A.G. 77015; cf. D.M. 20762, Capt. A. Benoit, Sec., Dept. of Mil.,
to Jas. P. Taylor, June 23, 1899: "It is a matter of doubt to me whether the Bill
of 1868 intended to give the Major General the Command of the Militia in the
sense which has been adopted by all those officers since, thus creating constant
trouble with the Department proper. The functions of this officer, if continued in
Canada, should be clearly defined because I have observed that whenever one of
the Major Generals came to find out the real meaning of the word Command he
asked for permission to return to the Imperial Army, but it is generally considered, I believe, all over the country that the function could be suppressed by
obtaining instead the occasional service of the Imperial Officer Commanding Her
Majesty's Troops at Halifax to make inspections of the Militia (the Dominion
Government paying his expenses) and make a report to both the Imperial authorities and the Dominion Government, a thing which has never been done but which
I can vouch was the intention at the time of the Bill of 1868."

[40]D.M. 17500.

[41]Minto Papers, letter book no. 1, pp. 355–56, to Wolseley, "Private," March
17, 1900.

advice and obedience to his command, found himself often disregarded and his position virtually usurped by a minister, friction was inevitable. Dr. Borden complained to the Commandant of the Royal Military College in May 1898 that generals "always wanted to assume command too much."[42] Of course they did. What self-respecting and expert general wanted only to fulfil the Canadian Government's symbolic need for national security?

On the other hand, the statutory powers of the quasi-independent office of general officer commanding were becoming unworkable, and resented by Canadians. That this office in Canada, and the analogous offices of commander-in-chief in Britain and commanding general of the army in the United States should all have been given up at about the same time—1903-4—and the office of chief of the general staff substituted was significant of an inherent difficulty in the office itself, apart from changing strategic conditions. Under the new arrangements these governments obtained full control of the army; at the same time the establishment of a general staff ensured that the representations of the leading officers would be heard by government leaders.

V

If Hutton was acting strictly within the letter of the law and the spirit of the constitution, accusations of unconstitutionality would appear to mask other objections. What were these objections?

It should be emphasized that for the first six months Hutton and the Government agreed amicably; in the next six months there was an increasing discord; and in the last, the Government was looking for an opportunity to get rid of him. In his first year it is astonishing what the Government accepted: the annual report, the staff course, and the beginning of administrative departments. In the early months, Borden showed a genuine respect for what Hutton was doing, in February 1899 Tarte spoke publicly in warm terms of him.[43]

For much of the friction Hutton himself was to blame. He had been frequently warned, and indeed repeated the warning to Lieutenant-Colonel Stone, not to press the colonies but only to lead them. He himself was amazed at the success of the annual report, which he admitted

---

[42]Hutton Papers, p. 341, Kitson to Hutton, May 17, 1899.

[43]*Can. Mil. Gaz.*, Feb. 21, 1899; cf. *Globe*, Feb. 13, 1899. But as the Militia Department, hitherto one of the most abject in Ottawa, crept into the limelight as a result of the General's energy, its regular officials apparently became jealous of his success and wished to share it (cf. Laurier Papers, p. 34272, Minto to Laurier, "Private," June 7, 1899).

was among the frankest any government had ever received, and the degree of acceptance of his suggestions. Unfortunately for Hutton he ascribed his successes to his own efforts and not sufficiently to the exceptionally favourable circumstances. Hence, instead of exercising greater restraint, he pressed his programme harder than ever, and became the victim of his own success. Dr. Borden had hinted through Lord William Seymour that Hutton should not press too hard. To which Hutton replied to Seymour: *"The difficulty is to go in advance just so far as to lead so as to be followed, and not to go so far as to frighten or bewilder those who should follow!"* Nevertheless Hutton kept pouring a stream of suggestions upon Dr. Borden.[44] Nor did Hutton take hints regarding his dangerous "inclination to oratory."[45]

But Hutton's absorbing zeal, which was responding to Canada's jingoistic mood, was a decisive condition of his success. His organizing ab'lity impressed all who knew him. His verve, energy, and courage, and his vision of a militia worthy of a mighty Canada, skilfully described not in imperial but in national terms, swept Canadians off their feet. In view of the general volatility of American policy in the 1890's, no Canadian would plausibly argue that Canada ought not to possess an efficient defence system. The dispatch of the field force to the Yukon in 1898 and Laurier's parliamentary hint as to why it should be kept there in 1899 showed Canada's defensive requirements. Hutton was thus implementing what Canadians professed their country needed, and indeed he advocated nothing that the Government had not tacitly accepted.

His moralistic manner, however, repelled as well as appealed. Borden was nettled at Hutton's continued harping on politics. Borden had a legitimate complaint, for the Government had promoted Sam Hughes, a Conservative, to lieutenant-colonel in 1897. Borden also challenged Hutton's assumption that politics played no part in War Office appointments.[46] Repeated complaints of much "promotion by nepotism" during the Boer War cast doubt upon any such view.[47] Insistence on a non-

[44]Hutton Papers, p. 187, "Private," April 18, 1899; see also lists of "Outstandings," that is, items that Dr. Borden had not fully considered, held over, or ignored during each month (A.G. 79016), and " 'Interview Dr Borden & Gen. Hutton Sunday 24/9/99 4–5 P.M. Victoria Chambers,' " ("Strictly Confidential," Hutton Papers, pp. 251–53).

[45]Minto also wrote to Lord Hopetoun, Gov. Gen. of Australia: "He is inclined to speak on every occasion . . . he is eloquent & words bubble out" (Minto Papers, Dec. 15, 1901, "Private," letter book no. 3, p. 80).

[46]Speech at dinner in honour of Maj. (later Sir) Percy Girouard, *Can. Mil. Gaz.*, Sept. 19, 1899.

[47]Cd. 1790, q. 4246; see also qq. 4674, 4703, and 9435.

political Canadian force owing loyalty to the highest national ideals was in accord with traditional British Army views, but was also an Imperialist conceit, an attempt to impose on others what was carried out with moderate success at home. The Government seems to have turned the charge of politics against the General. In his efforts to have the best available men as officers in the militia, Hutton possibly chose more Conservatives than Liberals, because there were more Conservative officers, and ideological considerations inclined Conservatives to greater loyalty to the Queen.[48] Conservatives also used Hutton's criticisms of the militia, as the Liberals used those of Herbert, for their own political advantage. Efficiency, however, was Hutton's criterion for the militia.

Hutton's lack of tact constituted another complaint. As General Officer Commanding-in-Chief of the Commonwealth of Australia (1901–4) he bruised many feelings. Clear-cut evidence of tactlessness in Canada is lacking. On the contrary during his first year he was extraordinarily adroit in his management of both government and public opinion. Although Hutton said many blunt things in Canada, he probably did not say, as a Canadian senator alleged, that he had overturned the Government of Sir George Dibbs in New South Wales in 1894; but he may have said that the militia had played a part in the Government's downfall.[49] If so, he came close to making a threat. Moreover it seems certain that he said indiscreet things to bully Sam Hughes into silence. These remarks took place in August and September 1899[50] when success seems to have gone to Hutton's head. His increasing influence with press and public was then illustrated by the request to open the Toronto Exhibition. Welcomed by a large crowd, he received a "most flattering address."[51]

The truth was that the essentially political leadership which the quasi-independent and statutory office of general officer commanding

[48]Cf. Richard Tyrwhitt (Conservative, South Simcoe, Ont.), *Debates*, April 3, 1900, pp. 3113 and 3108; cf. also *Globe*, Sept. 8, Sept. 12, 1899, for rumoured objections of Dr. Borden to five Conservatives as honorary aides-de-camp.

[49]Actually the Dibbs Government fell largely because of an unpopular protectionist policy (memorandum of Miss Ida E. Leeson, Mitchell Librarian, Sydney, Australia, to writer in 1943). For the alleged statement of Hutton, see R. Scott, Senate *Debates*, March 20, 1900, p. 207, c. 2, and Hutton Papers, pp. 1754–56, "My Command in Canada: A Narrative."

[50]See below, pp. 229–31; note also Hutton's awareness of the militia as "a most important factor in the electorate, & one which can be ignored by no Government however strong" (Hutton Papers, p. 35, Hutton to Sir Coleridge Grove, Jan. 9, 1899).

[51]*Ibid.*, p. 1741, "My Command in Canada: A Narrative."

had enabled an Englishman to win for himself in Canada before the South African War was a challenge and a provocation to the Government's own authority, its interpretation of the constitution, and its nationalism. The Government ignored the degree to which public support of Hutton's ideas and policy was the result of resentment of the United States, and consequent orientation towards Britain, which it itself had encouraged. Hutton's actions were not contrary to the practice of responsible government, but they were contrary to the ideological interpretation of responsible government that developed after the South African War.

Moreover Hutton was a masterful person whose persistent energies grated on a Government that was becoming conscious of its national power and resentful of the colonial inferiority which the necessity, presence, and actions of a British general officer implied. Furthermore, Hutton was taking seriously a part of Canadian life that few Canadians had ever taken seriously. The Canadian Government did not wish its tacit and repeated professions concerning defence taken completely at face value. No one likes a profession rebutted; still less does he like its insincerity exposed. The Government wished to reform the Canadian militia in its own way and at its own speed. Political conditions justified a degree of caution foreign to Hutton's nature and understanding. The policy of a representative government, when confronted with conflicting points of view, is often to make only professions and gestures of a policy. The basic assumptions of Hutton and the Government also contradicted one another. He thought in terms of war, they of peace; Hutton was moved by apprehension of Britain's future international position; they saw preparation for war as a threat to the material development of the country and to their implicit pacifist ideology.[52]

But beneath all the Government's objections was the decisive one— Hutton's success. It could plausibly hold Hutton responsible for militia improvement, elimination of politics, and especially, participation in the South African War.

[52]Hutton's phrase "National Army of Canada" invited the retort of "No Standing Army." The phrase smacked of the professional and class superiority of the British Army officer in contrast to the amateur Canadian officer dwelling in a self-consciously proud pacifist environment. This convenient phrase began to be used against Hutton, but his propensity to oratory suggested changes not contemplated. Halifax *Morning Chronicle*, Sept. 21, 1899, edit., "No Standing Army," and *Man. Free Press*, March 28, 1899.

13. Efforts to Commit Canada to Military Aid

SINCE the Jameson raid informed persons had foreseen a war in South Africa, an area of vital strategic significance. To guard against the kind of international threat that had developed during the raid British imperialists sought to bolster Imperial prestige and power by developing the military unity of the British Empire. Attempts were made to induce each self-governing colony to commit a token force, which by fighting beside Regulars would demonstrate that the British Empire was militarily one. In the spring of 1899 there seemed good prospects of token participation from Canada, because of the Dominion's contribution to imperial unity, the strength of her imperial sentiment, and the success of Hutton's militia reforms.

I

Both the War Office and the Colonial Office had long sought a military commitment from Canada. Their officials tried to induce the Canadian militia (1) to accept the authority of the General Officer Commanding the Imperial Troops in Canada and to "associate" Canadian and Imperial forces in combined Imperial and militia exercises at Halifax and Esquimalt, (2) to repatriate the 100th Regiment, (3) to interchange Canadian and Imperial forces, and (4) to commit Canadian forces for overseas service.

The first effort may be best understood in relation to the command of Imperial troops in British North America. Up to 1871 the British general commanded thousands of regular troops, and, it was understood, in wartime the Canadian militia as well. But in peacetime he exercised no official authority over the militia nor received the intelligence upon which the Canadian Government would base its decision concerning participation in a war. On the withdrawal of British troops from central Canada in 1871, the British general in effect commanded only the Regular troops of the Halifax garrison, and though the Militia Act of 1868 repeated the provision (s. 61) of the Province of Canada militia acts that he might command the militia in wartime, he still was not officially concerned in peacetime. Although his power was diminished, his prestige remained high because of his rank—lieutenant-general—and because he served as administrator of Canada during the absence from Ottawa of the governor general. In the early 1890's the Governor General proposed that the formal powers of this officer be limited to the command of the Halifax garrison, a proposal which would have magnified the power of the general officer commanding the militia.[1]

The decline in the scope of the Imperial command seems to have been temporarily reversed by the international crises of the nineties, and the mediocrity of the incumbent militia general Gascoigne, and the energetic ability of the Imperial officer, Lieutenant-General (later Sir) A. G. Montgomery-Moore. The latter, for example, informally advised the Governor General on the Imperial aspects of Canadian defence, for he received information direct from the War Office. He also took advantage of his position to make representations to the Canadian Government on the inefficiency of the Canadian militia units charged with supporting the Halifax garrison. He thus emphasized the association of Canadian and Imperial forces.

At the outset the same powers were exercised by Montgomery-Moore's successor, the rather weak, naïve Lord William Seymour, who assumed command in May 1898. Until the middle of 1899 a cordial relationship prevailed between Generals Seymour and Hutton, who were old friends. In March 1899, however, Seymour read the report of the Committee on Canadian Defence, which suggested that the powers of the Imperial general might be increased by exercising authority over the militia general and by rights of inspection over the militia itself. The Canadian Government would never have agreed to these suggestions, as Minto and Hutton well knew, for they would have placed the militia under the command of an officer not appointed by itself.[2] Seymour, however, began to magnify his powers by commenting on Hutton's militia policy. He proffered advice to the Governor General on the Imperial aspects of Canadian defence, the kind of advice given to Lord Aberdeen. Lord Minto refused this advice but accepted Hutton's instead. Seymour's irritation at Lord Minto's refusal was aggravated by the

[1]Endorsed, "Very Confidential. Memo: of H. E. Lord Stanley to Sir J. Macdonald urging definition of duties of Imp and Dominion Mil Commanders. 2nd April, 1891" (Confidential Material 1891–1899 from C. 1670); see also C. W. de Kiewiet and F. H. Underhill, eds., *Dufferin-Carnarvon Correspondence 1874–1878* (Toronto, Champlain Society, 1955), pp. 64–67, *passim*.

[2]Minto Papers, vol. 21, pp. 98–99, copy, "PRIVATE AND CONFIDENTIAL," Hutton to Sir Richard Harrison, Pres. of Col. Def. Com., April 7, 1899.

action of Hutton's Chief Staff Officer, Colonel Hubert Foster, in prohibiting examination of a secret defence report, which the War Office had suggested Seymour should look at in Canada. In June he became angry when Hutton declined to submit reports on Imperial officers serving in Canada, which the War Office had instructed Seymour to obtain. Hutton justified his action by an analogous defence situation in Australia. He also advised the Minister of Militia against accepting Seymour's suggestion of the fortification of the port of Lunenburg in Nova Scotia. These were severe rebuffs for a mere colonel to offer a lieutenant-general, and one instructed by the War and Colonial offices prior to leaving Britain, as Seymour had been.

Lord Minto now intervened. On August 3, 1899, he wrote a long letter to Seymour defending Hutton's and Foster's actions. He argued that the commands of the militia and of Imperial troops in Canada were separate and should remain so: it was impossible for Imperial officers serving under the Canadian Government to be subject to the general officer commanding the Imperial troops. Any idea that Seymour was Hutton's " 'Military Commander-in-chief of the Army,' " was contrary to custom.[3] The Secretary of War, evidently contrary to the position of other War Office officials, supported Minto's contention. No Canadian Government, Lord Lansdowne argued, would allow its army of 40,000 men to "become an appanage of the Halifax Command."[4] General Seymour now tried to enforce his presumed authority by sending a peremptory telegram to the Governor General ordering Hutton to make reports on Imperial officers serving in Canada. The telegram, however, was simply returned. The continuance of the quarrel between Seymour and Hutton later became public; and in mid-1900 Seymour, realizing that he lacked War Office support, resigned.

The War Office also tried to obtain direct control over a Canadian

[3]Minto Papers, letter book no. 1, pp. 141–45, Minto to Lord William Seymour, "Confidential." The following important constitutional statement by Lord Minto appeared in this letter (*ibid.*, p. 143): "It is necessary to recollect that this is a self-governing Colony, that the command-in-chief of its Military Forces is vested in the Governor General as representing The Queen, not of course as an executive Command, but as the constitutional Head of the State—that the Colony has its equivalent to the Secretary of State for War in its Minister of Militia & Defence, under whom is the G.O.C. the Militia & other Imperial Officers lent by the Imperial Govt. to Canada but paid for by Canada, & subject by Act of Parliament to the discipline & regulations laid down in that Act, & to the orders of the Governor-in-Council. There is no reference whatever of any connection as regards command between Imperial Officers lent to the Colony & the G.O.C. Her Majesty's Troops in Canada."

[4]Minto Papers, vol. 12, p. 15, Lansdowne to Minto, "Private," August 21, 1899.

unit by the repatriation of the 100th Regiment of the British Army and the interchange of Canadian and Imperial forces. In 1858 the 100th Regiment had been raised by Britain as completely Canadian in personnel for service in the Indian Mutiny, but had long since lost all but a sentimental connection with Canada. As a result of an editorial in the *Canadian Military Gazette* early in 1896 which declared that "the Dominion should be willing to devote more of her sons as well as of her means towards the armed forces of the Crown,"[5] Canadians from all over the Dominion, but principally from Toronto, signed a printed petition, dated May 8, 1896, praying that the 100th Regiment be repatriated. The Secretary of War replied that he was favourable to the suggestion as tending "to foster a connection between the Regular Army and the Militia Forces of Canada" and further commenting on the "strong feeling of sympathy already existing between the Mother Country and the Dominion." But, he inquired, did the scheme command provincial and Dominion support, and were barracks available locally?[6] Neither the federal, provincial, nor municipal governments contemplated financial support for the scheme; nor was the General Officer Commanding the militia willing to sacrifice part of the militia appropriation.

Meanwhile the Secretary of War, apparently wishing to obtain some concrete results from the agitation in Canada, sought permission to enlist Canadians in the 1st Battalion of the Leinsters, part of the old 100th Regiment, which had been stationed in Canada for that purpose. This battalion of Irish Roman Catholics, "although nominally raised in Canada, was really recruited in Liverpool," most of the men getting bounties costing £7,000.[7] Although the Canadian Government permitted Canadians to enrol the experiment was a failure; neither the officers, aggrieved by the sudden transfer of the battalion to Halifax, nor the Roman Catholic Irish privates welcomed Canadian recruits. The pay moreover was too small[8] and garrison duty unattractive.

[5]Notes, "History of the 100th Regiment," by the editor, in J. Castell Hopkins, ed., *Canada: An Encyclopaedia of the Country* (Toronto, 1898), IV, p. 466B; cf. G.O. 5, Sec. I, 1888, and also de Kiewiet and Underhill, *Dufferin-Carnarvon Correspondence 1874–1878*, pp. 95–96, 133, 154–55, and Lieut.-Col. Frederick Ernest Whitton, comp. and ed., *The History of the Prince of Wales's Leinster Regiment* (Royal Canadians) (Aldershot, 1924), vol. I, pp. 123–30.

[6]D.M. 14889, W.O. to C.O., Nov. 3, 1896, inc. in C.O. to Gov. Gen., Nov. 9, 1896; the petition itself may be found *ibid.*

[7]Hutton Papers, p. 56, Sir Evelyn Wood, Adj.-Gen., to Hutton, April 4, 1899; cf. Denison Papers, pp. 3672–75, Wolseley to Denison, "Private," Jan. 19, 1899, and pp. 3711–14, reply, April 10, 1899.

[8]Hutton Papers, pp. 945–49, memo for Min. of Mil. by Maj.-Gen. Com., Feb. 11, 1899; for an explanation of the grievances of the Leinsters, see Whitton, *History of Prince of Wales's Leinster Regiment*, I, pp. 123–30, and cf. pp. 373–81.

From the War Office point of view a more hopeful development seemed the interchange of Canadian and Imperial forces. In 1897 a company of Permanent Infantry at Fredericton, New Brunswick, was interchanged with an Imperial garrison company at Halifax; in 1898 a company of garrison artillery at Quebec was similarly interchanged with an Imperial artillery company at Halifax. The Colonial Defence Committee had also long supported such a scheme.[9] The Colonial Secretary cherished the hope at the Colonial Conference of 1897 of a similar interchange between regiments in Britain and Canada; they might even fight side by side. Sir Wilfrid Laurier had then supported this suggestion. A year later Chamberlain formally suggested Britain's having the "option of employing Colonial units . . . on Field Service abroad" and invited the Canadian Government's opinion. Hutton condemned the scheme ostensibly because Canada could not do without the Permanent Field Batteries, which formed part of an instructional, rather than a field service, unit.[10] The Canadian Government was, however, prepared to diffuse information concerning enlistment in the British Army and requested a supply of recruiting posters!

Meanwhile plans for the interchange of forces and for the repatriation of the 100th Regiment tended to become confused. George Wyndham, the Under-Secretary of War, wrote a long "private" letter to Sir Wilfrid Laurier, informally sounding him on the repatriation scheme and on the further possibility of Canada's supplying a "distinctly Canadian force to the Army of the Empire."[11] In spite of the Canadian Government's continued coolness, in August 1899 the War Office now making no mention of plans for interchange, eagerly produced another official and fantastic scheme, that a Canadian regiment serve in the British Army for seven years and five in the reserve (or three in the Army and nine in the reserve).[12] With the threat of war in South Africa steadily increasing, the implication that the scheme was a device to induce participation could scarcely have been missed. Fortunately for the Canadian Government, General Hutton, in spite of reminders to him

[9]Confidential Material from C. 1670, Montgomery-Moore to W.O., Jan. 8, 1897; cf. D.M. 17032; G 21, no. 165, Additional, Remarks by the Colonial Defence Committee, "Secret," 190R, June 30, 1898, inc. in C.O., "Circular Secret," Aug. 27, 1898; *Globe*, Feb. 11, 1898; and cf. C.O. 42/865, pp. 387–89.

[10]G 3, vol. 32, Chamberlain to Aberdeen, "Confidential," Aug. 3, 1898; Minto Papers, vol. 15, p. 18, copy Hutton to Borden, Oct. 7, 1898; the latter raised other objections.

[11]Laurier Papers, pp. 30140–47, Jan. 31, 1899.

[12]D.M. 17763; they were to be paid 1*s.* per day and 3*d.* messing allowance (W.O. to C.O., Aug. 3, 1899, inc. in Chamberlain to Minto, "Confidential," Aug. 8, 1899, C.O. 42/873, p. 376).

in private letters from Chamberlain, in effect advised against the scheme, for at the prevailing high wage level few recruits would enter such a regiment at 1s. *per* day.[13]

In both of these schemes the War Office and the Colonial Office were endeavoring to get direct control of a Canadian military unit. These schemes and policies were practically impossible and politically embarrassing to the Canadian Government. While Lord Minto believed that Canada would dispatch troops in an "Imperial emergency" he had "long thought the maintenance in Canada of any Dominion troops, Reserve or otherwise, engaged for foreign service on certain eventualities however remote is an impossibility."[14]

The War Office scheme of " 'one Army under one control' "[15] would have meant practically the repudiation of Hutton's scheme of a national army, complete in all arms, fighting as one unit with other colonial national units, together making up a combined imperial force. Canadians resented the Little-England view of the colonies as necessary evils, a view which they thought was implied in the British desire to assimilate colonial forces into one imperial army. Hutton, more acutely aware than most British officers of the world-wide dangers to British imperial power, wanted fighting colonial forces, not symbolic ones. Canada's enormous national pride in the contingent that set sail on October 30, 1899, from Quebec to Cape Town indicates Hutton's awareness of the essentially national nature of imperial unity in Canada.

II

Britain had thus failed to obtain a Canadian unit automatically committed to fight as part of an imperial force. In the meantime an event had occurred which enabled Britain to raise the abstract question of participation but in so oblique a manner that its implications apparently escaped Canada. During the Fashoda incident Sir John Fisher, Admiral of the British fleet in the Western Atlantic, in co-operation with Lord William Seymour, made plans for the seizure by the regular forces at Halifax of the French islands of St. Pierre and Miquelon in the Gulf of the St. Lawrence and the islands of the French West Indies. The plan

13*Ibid.*, memo of Maj.-Gen. Com., "Confidential," Sept. 25, 1899; in spite of further reminders, the Canadian Government declined to move in a scheme for further interchange of troops (*ibid.*, P.C. Despatches, 1555K, Nov. 10, 1899).

14Minto Papers, letter book no. 1, p. 21, Minto to Major Palliser, Dec. 30, 1898; cf. Hutton Papers, p. 28, Hutton's interview with Lord Lansdowne, Aug. 3, 1898.

15Richard Jebb, *Studies in Colonial Nationalism* (London, 1905), p. 286.

involved the immediate garrisoning of the Halifax fortress by the Canadian militia.[16]

The important result of this plan was Lord Minto's comment on the possible use of Canadian troops: ". . . it would in fact be a new departure asking for Canadian Militia to serve outside the Dominion against the troops of a European country which had made no attack directly on Canada."[17] The Admiralty and the War Office, perturbed by this legal bar and by the need for " 'power to move Canadian troops beyond the frontier,' " which " 'for strategical reasons' " was " 'essential to the defence of Canada in the event of War with the United States,' " desired Lord Minto's interpretation of section 79 of the Militia Act to be reconsidered.[18] This section laid down that Her Majesty might call out the troops within or without Canada in time of war or insurrection.[19] In requesting Laurier's opinion on the matter, Minto explained that his own opinion concerned war not with the United States, for he thought the militia could be moved across the border, but with a European power. As for section 79 of the Militia Act, he held that its "true" interpretation concerned the question, not whether the Queen had the literal right to call out Canadian troops " 'within or without Canada,' " but whether British military authorities were justified, under section 79, "in reckoning *officially* upon the availability of Canadian troops outside the Dominion in case of war with a European power." The raising of that subject provided the occasion to broach the question of an offer of troops, for Minto was "inclined" to draw a distinct line "between the official calling out by the Queen of Canadian troops for foreign service (i.e., outside the American continent)—and the offer of Canadian troops by the Dominion which I feel certain would be enthusiastically made if the Empire was threatened."[20]

To the Governor General's surprise, the Prime Minister, after con-

[16]Admiral Sir R. H. Bacon, *The Life of Lord Fisher of Kilverstone* (London, 1929), I, pp. 118–19; see also Minto Papers, vol. 22, part III, pp. 165–68, Seymour to Minto, "Secret," Nov. 9, 1898, and Hutton Papers, pp. 90–91, 655–57, 673–74.

[17]Minto Papers, letter book no. 1, p. 3, Minto to Seymour, "Confidential," Nov. 22, 1898.

[18]Minto Papers, vol. 1, p. 8, cited in Seymour to Gov. Gen., "Secret," March 20, 1899.

[19]Subsection 1 of section 79 of the Militia Act, Revised Statutes of Canada, 1886, c. 41, reads as follows: "Her Majesty may call out the Militia, or any part thereof, for active service either within or without Canada, at any time when it appears advisable so to do by reason of war, invasion or insurrection, or danger of any of them."

[20]Laurier Papers, pp. 31714–16, Minto to Laurier, "Confidential," March 25, 1899.

sulting the cabinet, which followed the advice of the Ministers of Justice and Militia, interpreted section 79 of the Act literally. The cabinet held that the Imperial authorities had an "undoubted" right to move the militia "to any part of the world in time of war," though Laurier warned of the inadvisability of moving French-Canadian troops, without qualifying the "right of the Imperial Government to do so." Apparently to make certain of the Government's opinion, Minto read to Laurier the interpretation of the section by Sir John Macdonald, that the Canadian Government could not send militia out of the country. But Macdonald's interpretation in no way altered Laurier's view. Minto ironically commented that the Government no doubt felt "quite safe in their opinion, as there is not a single Regiment of the active Militia of the Dominion capable of being sent as a Regiment on foreign service."[21]

By this time (March 1899) the Fashoda affair had been resolved, and with it the threat of hostilities between France and England. But in June the collapse of the Bloemfontein Conference foreshadowed war in South Africa; and Lord Wolseley made the first suggestion of preparations in anticipation of war, among them the furnishing of contingents by Canada and the Australasian colonies.[22] In the same month Chamberlain thanked the Canadian Government for its "patriotic interpretation of the Act." Chamberlain explained that the question had arisen over the doubt as to the

legality of employing Canadian troops for the occupation of islands in which Canadian interests are directly concerned and that it appeared . . . necessary to contest this opinion, not with any view of employing such troops in another hemisphere, (gladly though their aid would be welcomed should an opportunity arise) but because the basis of the defence of Canada proper in time of war with the neighbouring Power rests on the possibility of moving Canadian troops across the frontier.[23]

The possibility of the British authorities ordering out the Canadian militia was incredible, and even if they had, they would have done so only after consultation with the Canadian Government. As yet there was no question of war "for Canada's defence," which appears to have been first officially raised in Laurier's statement of October 4, 1899.[24] The timing of the interpretation suggests, too, Canada's need for continued

[21]Minto Papers, vol. I, pp. 20–23, March 27 and 29, memo and comment on conversation with Laurier on March 27, 1899, "on meaning of the 79th Para of Militia Act"; for Macdonald's letter of Feb. 10, 1885, see C. P. Stacey, "John A. Macdonald on Raising Troops in Canada for Imperial Service, 1885," *Can. Hist. Rev.*, XXXVIII (March 1957), pp. 37–40.
[22]Cd. 1789, p. 16, minute of Lord Wolseley to Lord Lansdowne, June 8, 1899.
[23]G 3, vol. 33, Chamberlain to Minto, "Secret," June 5, 1899.
[24]See below, p. 235.

British help against the United States in view of the friction from the breakdown of the Joint High Commission and the unsettled Alaska boundary.

III

Of the Canadian advocates of participation in any imperial war, the most persistent was Lieutenant-Colonel (later Hon. Lieutenant-General Sir) Sam Hughes (1853–1921). Descended of a line of soldiers on both sides of his family, he grew up in a poor farming area seventy miles east of Toronto. His unfinished autobiography seems to indicate the not very happy childhood of a rebel.[25] A streak of rebelliousness pursued him to the end of his days. While limiting his administrative and political effectiveness, it gave him popular strength, for an awakening Canadian democracy shared many of his characteristics. Sir Robert Borden, Canada's Prime Minister from 1911 to 1920 and a cousin of Dr. F. W. Borden, described Hughes as at times a man of sober ability, but at others so eccentric as to seem out of his mind,[26] a judgment amply borne out by the evidence of this period. No doubt his eccentricities explain the public failure to take him seriously.[27] But history has too often taken him at his eccentric and not at his sober value; it cannot write off as a foolish nonentity a man who stirred up interest in the militia, advocated Canadian participation in Empire wars, was partially responsible for the recall of General Hutton, became Minister of Militia, and dispatched the first troops in the War of 1914.

Educated at the Toronto Normal School and the University of Toronto, Hughes taught English and history successfully for eleven years at the Toronto Collegiate Institute School (later Jarvis Street Collegiate Institute).[28] Finding his scope as a teacher limited, in 1885 he bought the *Warder*, a newspaper in Lindsay, a town some seventy miles northeast of Toronto. One of the newspaper's themes was imperial unity, the roots of which may perhaps be found in Hughes's military background and militia interests, studies in English and history, and contemporary interest in wider political unions.[29] He also fought the commercial union movement and rejected money offers to change his

[25]In Private Papers of Sir Sam Hughes, in the possession of Mr. Justice S. H. S. Hughes, of Toronto, Ontario.

[26]Henry Borden, ed., *Robert Laird Borden: His Memoirs* (New York, 1938), I, pp. 462–63.

[27]Brig.-Gen. Charles F. Winter, *The Honourable Sir Sam Hughes* (Toronto, 1931), p. 7.

[28]Cf. Willison Collection, p. 40208, George Simpson to A. H. U. Colquhoun, Jan. 21, 1932.

[29]*Debates*, May 1, 1899, pp. 2339–40. As a teacher he painted the map of Canada, Great Britain, and Ireland, a "bright, brilliant red" (*ibid.*, p. 2340).

newspaper's policy.[30] For him the British Empire, because of its size, traditions, and principles, became a sort of god worthy of man's highest veneration and (like the United States for many other Canadians) a field for frustrated Canadian endeavour. He thus exhibited a typically imperial characteristic of trying to accomplish in faraway fields what could not be accomplished at home. Practically his imperialistic measures were essentially nationalist: imperial preference, "Colonial Assistance in Empire Wars," and the like.

The Lindsay area also provided an opportunity to enter politics, for which he had many assets: the gift of remembering names, a sympathy for those suffering personal injustice,[31] prominence in secret societies, sport, and militia affairs, and the influence of his newspaper. Accordingly, when elected as a Conservative in 1892, he was returned until his death nearly thirty years later. Actually Hughes was never a loyal Conservative; he was rather a vociferous Canadian nationalist masked as a British imperialist. In 1898, he supported the Liberal Government's "All-Canadian route" to the Yukon.[32] He was on friendly terms with such Liberals as Sir Wilfrid Laurier and Dr. F. W. Borden, who reciprocated his friendship. The Liberal Government made him lieutenant-colonel, supported him in his quarrel with General Hutton, and appointed him a military adviser to the technical Imperial Military Conference at London in 1909. During his own incumbency as Minister of Militia in World War I, Conservatives complained of his partiality for Liberals.[33]

Another source of Sam Hughes's influence was the friendship and ardent backing of the multi-millionaire Lord Strathcona, who doubtless welcomed Hughes's support to make him leader of the Conservative party in 1896[34] and who like Hughes cherished imperial unity. At Lord Strathcona's expense, Hughes and his family visited Britain for the Diamond Jubilee. At his expense, too, it was arranged with Joseph Chamberlain that Hughes should go to Australia and New Zealand in the year 1897–98, as a kind of unofficial imperial agent to advance his own plan of "Colonial Assistance in Empire Wars."[35]

Hughes's chief interest was military. He had long served in the Canadian militia, had taken part in the Fenian Raid of 1870, and studied

[30]MS autobiography, p. 35.

[31]*Debates*, Aug. 9, 1899, pp. 9963–64.　　　　　　　　[32]*Globe*, Feb. 19, 1898.

[33]Paul Bilkey, *Persons, Papers and Things* (Toronto, 1940), p. 160.

[34]Beckles Willson, *The Life of Lord Strathcona and Mount Royal* (London, 1915), p. 428.

[35]MS autobiography, p. 46; cf. Sir John Willison, *Sir George Parkin* (London, 1929), chap. IV, "The Australasian Mission."

military tactics and history. He had been offered but had rejected the position of deputy minister of militia in 1891, and that of adjutant-general in 1895. He had made personal offers of service in imperial wars. The plan of "Colonial Assistance in Empire Wars" in effect called for his leading Canadian troops. When the news arrived in 1898 that Sir Herbert Kitchener was about to begin the reconquest of the Sudan, Hughes enthusiastically suggested to Sir Wilfrid Laurier that a body of Canadians be made ready for acceptance by Britain. Even if Britain would not pay for them "surely the Canadian Govt. can easily send one man—i.e., myself!" Laurier replied that he was referring the matter to the Militia Department.[36] In July 1898, Hughes wrote directly to Joseph Chamberlain with suggestions "as to the raising of a Canadian regiment by him."[37] He had already suggested that the Permanent Infantry Battalion be sent on active service.

A high point in his offers of aid to Britain came when he moved a resolution on May 1, 1899, that in view of increased Canadian trade and in order "to perfect the union" of Britain and her colonies and maintain the "commerce, prestige and integrity of the British Empire," Great Britain should be authorized to enrol a brigade of Canadians for "Imperial service abroad," and permit Canadian seamen to serve in the British navy.[38] His motion was prompted by reports of New South Wales Lancers "under pay of the New South Wales Government" being sent to England for training and a New Zealand regiment volunteering for duty in Samoa.

Hutton, believing that this type of committed colonial force was impossible, and that any Canadian aid should be national not individual, perhaps used dubious constitutional arguments to dissuade Hughes from introducing his motion. But Hughes, fancying himself a constitutional expert, refused, and introduced his speech with an analysis of precedents on his constitutional rights to do so. As for the motion itself, Hughes explained that the plan called for giving Great Britain "authority" to enrol 5,000 Canadians for service anywhere in the world from five to seven years at Britain's expense. At the end of the period, the Canadian Government should provide each man with 160 acres of land, a cottage, and other farm necessities. His chief justification for the scheme was that he had looked forward to the day "when Canada shall form an integral portion of the British Empire." In trade, that union

[36]Laurier Papers, p. 24359, "Personal," June 18, 1898, and p. 24365, June 28, 1898.
[37]D.M. 16203, Chamberlain to Aberdeen, July 27, 1898.
[38]*Debates*, p. 2335.

was developing but he could "look forward still further. . . . to an alliance between them on political lines. . . . Shoulder to shoulder" Britain and her colonies would present to the world "a solid phalanx which no combination of nations can break."[39] Moreover, Canada should help Britain, because Britain had helped Canada. But why encourage Canadians to leave Canada when they were needed at home? Hughes answered that young Canadians would serve in foreign armies anyway. As for his incitement of a jingoistic spirit, jingoism had helped maintain peace. Finally Canadians would not serve in the 100th Regiment under British officers, but only under their own.[40]

A Conservative raised most of the objections that Hughes had already tried to answer. Canadians were "a peace-loving people . . . engaged in the industrial pursuits of life."[41] Canada's need of manpower, the inconsistency of the scheme, the harm to a man's industrious habits, and doubt as to the encouragement of the "military spirit" all suggested that Hughes's scheme would not benefit Canada. His aim "may be in the interests of the Empire in many ways, but I do not think it is in the interests of the development of Canada." Britain already had the authority to enlist men, argued another member and Dr. Borden. The latter also spoke against the "spirit of militarism."[42]

The debate illustrated the general lack of interest in a peacetime military commitment, though it aroused discussion in the English press.[43] It showed, too, that prevailing military attitudes in Canada were still basically colonial in contrast to Hughes's incipient nationalism. Hughes recognized that Britain would never call out Canadian troops without Canada's official approval. Yet on a specific issue English Canada was to force the Government officially to offer troops five and a half months later.

IV

Concerning the complex origins of the South African War little need be said, for British justifications of the war did not much influence Canadian sentiments favouring participation. A brief statement of its origin must therefore suffice.

---

[39]*Ibid.*, May 1, 1899, pp. 2337–38 and 2342; in attempting to prevent Hughes from introducing the resolution Hutton may have been influenced by the opinion of the Secretary of War that "an officer in active command . . . should not, in future, sit in Parliament" (*Parl. Deb.*, Aug. 30, 1895, 4th series, XXXVI, p. 1251).
[40]*Debates*, pp. 2342 and 2338–47.
[41]*Ibid.*, p. 2347, T. S. Sproule.
[42]*Ibid.*, pp. 2347–51.
[43]C.O. 42/868, pp. 592–93, minute of C. P. Lucas, June 12, 1899.

The underlying cause of the war was the replacement of an imperialism of veiled power by one of open coercion. This transformation was
the result of the change in the balance of power in South Africa: the
gold mines gave the Transvaal economic hegemony, and the completion
of the Delagoa Bay Railway gave it freedom from encirclement by
Rhodes and deprived Cape Colony railways of more than 45 per cent
of the Rand traffic. The new position of the Transvaal tempted Rhodes
and Jameson into the fiasco of the Jameson raid. Chamberlain and
Salisbury did not know of this filibustering expedition but they did
know of a prospective revolution among the Uitlanders which, it was
understood, Rhodes and the British High Commissioner in South Africa
intended to support *after* its successful outbreak. The outcome of the
raid was the virtual supremacy of the Transvaal in South Africa, its
heavy rearmament, and the rally of the Afrikanders in South Africa to
its protection. But Chamberlain, Selborne, and later Milner chose to
ignore the virtual destruction of Imperial influence in South Africa and
to rely on the discredited Rhodes and the Uitlanders, whose captives
they became. Although it is true that Selborne foresaw the alternative
in South Africa of "another Canada or another United States," he professed to believe that "another Canada" was possible because the
protection of Britain was needed on account of "international rivalries"
and against the "external pressure" of Germany and France.[44] Chamberlain and Salisbury probably also held the opinion that Transvaal
independence would not last long. Finally Chamberlain, Selborne,
Milner, and Rhodes were haunted by the prospect of a twentieth-
century Britain unable to assert its power against the United States and
Russia; Chamberlain thought that imperial federation was necessary for
the maintenance of British power, and the union of South Africa constituted a prerequisite for that federation. By the end of 1898 British
efforts to check the predominance of the Transvaal in South Africa
having failed, Milner and his South African supporters in 1899 took
advantage of Kruger's concessions in the complicated franchise issue by
making greater demands and manoeuvring Chamberlain into a position
where he found himself committed to force.

[44]C.O. memorandum, March 30, 1896, to Salisbury, drafted by Selborne and
largely quoted in Ronald Robinson and John Gallagher with Alice Denny, *Africa
and the Victorians: The Climax of Imperialism in the Dark Continent* (New
York, 1961), pp. 434–37. The sketch of the origin of the South African War in
the text generally follows chap. XIV of the foregoing book ("South Africa: Another Canada or Another United States?" pp. 410–61), and Richard H. Wilde,
"Joseph Chamberlain and the South African Republic 1895–1899," *Argief-jaar-
boek vir Suid-Afrikaanse Geskiedenis* (Archives Year Book for South African
History), 1956, I, pp. 1–158D.

Was war with the Transvaal so unwelcome as the foregoing interpretation suggests? Was not Chamberlain's chief justification for Canada's, and presumably Australasia's, participation in a South African war imperial solidarity? Would he not welcome the anticipated solidarity resulting from imperial participation as bringing Britain the strength needed to meet the coming challenge of the United States and Russia?

V

How much did Canadians know of the South African situation? O. D. Skelton has suggested that Canadians were ill-informed if not actually misinformed.[45] No question exists that much of the news and comment in the English-speaking press cabled from London and South Africa was tendentious. Directly and indirectly, most of it came from sources controlled by Rhodes's interests in South Africa.[46] While it truly emphasized the threat to British power in South Africa, it also reflected the sentimentalized hatred of the Boer and suggested patriotic self-righteousness. A posture of power was assumed in headings such as "BRITAIN IN EARNEST."[47] Revenge for the Boer victory at Majuba Hill in 1881 was also a frequent theme of reports. As war drew nearer, many pro-Boer dispatches received sceptical headings, references appeared to Boer mistreatment of natives, to a Dutch conspiracy, in which there was some truth, and to denials that capitalists were behind the war. Outright propaganda from Rhodes's interest also appeared in such stories as "BRITISH AGENT REPORTED ASSASSINATED."[48] Many dispatches affected to look upon the coming war as a triumphant victory parade. The apparently responsible Agent General of Natal in London declared that, after two months, fighting would be over.

Kill 500 of them [Boers] and all that would remain for England to do would be to send a few shiploads of crape [*sic*]. . . .
This is not optimistic twaddle, but an opinion based upon my experience in campaigns against the Boers.[49]

The strident note in this kind of bravado often ill concealed a fear that the war might be long and exhausting.

The tendentious quality of much of the cabled news and comment

---

[45]*Life and Letters of Sir Wilfrid Laurier* (Toronto, 1921), II, pp. 87–90; see also *Acadian Recorder*, Aug. 29, 1899, edit., "Will there be war?"
[46]J. A. Hobson, *The Psychology of Jingoism* (London, 1901), pp. 107–24; see also Sir William Butler, *An Autobiography* (London, 1911), pp. 392ff.
[47]*Globe*, July 12, 1899.
[48]Heading, *ibid.*, Oct. 12, 1899.
[49]Sir Walter Peace, *ibid.*, Sept. 28, 1899.

was, however, no mystery. Its unreliability occasionally was cited.[50] Only a little more than a year earlier the informed Canadian would have learned of the power of the yellow press in the Spanish-American War.[51] Moreover, the discerning reader could find a more reasoned account of the South African situation in the weekend press, long *Globe* editorials,[52] the *Canadian Magazine, Queen's Quarterly*, and some of the religious periodicals.[53] Canada also possessed an authority on international affairs, David Mills, Minister of Justice, who during the South African War published an able analysis of British policy in Africa entitled *The English in Africa* (Toronto, 1900). The pro-Boer case was presented in occasional letters to the press, in Goldwin Smith's *Weekly Sun*, and in the French-Canadian press. In July 1899 the influential supporter of imperial unity, Rev. Principal G. M. Grant, sympathized with the Transvaal in its national right to be free, a freedom guaranteed by Britain, the right freely to manage its own internal affairs, and its distrust of the Uitlanders and British officials because of their dealings with the Transvaal.[54] Thus a Canadian in 1899, even if reduced to newspaper and magazine fare alone, could have found a clear picture of both sides of the South African question.

But the problem of South African news is not its bias but its influence. It certainly enlarged the total amount of imperial news and contributed to Canada's vicarious participation in exciting struggles. Its cumulative effect undoubtedly entranced Canadians and predisposed them to participation in war. The use of such remarks in the Canadian press as "Our Empire," "What we have we hold . . . in North America or in South Africa,"[55] and so on, is some indication that Canadians felt themselves at one with the British Empire. But in a comparable period the amount and intensity of South African news was far less than Spanish-American news in the Canadian press.[56] Whereas Americans had undergone an intense three-year bombardment Canadians underwent a mild three-month barrage. In total, therefore, South African news probably had little effect on Canadian participation.

[50]Rev. Burford Hooke, Sec. of Congregational Colonial Missionary Society, *ibid.*, Sept. 11, 1899; cf. A. H. U. Colquhoun, "Current Events Abroad," *Can. Mag.*, XIII (June 1899), p. 183.
[51]See above, p. 102 and cf. p. 106.
[52]See Sept. 16, 20, 23, and 26, 1899.
[53]Marion V. Royce, "The Contributions of the Methodist Church to Social Welfare in Canada" (master's thesis, University of Toronto, 1940), p. 275.
[54]Current Events by "G," *Queen's Quarterly*, VII (July 1899), pp. 78–79.
[55]Toronto *Saturday Night* (weekly), Sept. 9, 1899, edit.: the writer continued, "I think it is Canada's desire to see the Transvaal licked into proper shape."
[56]Cf. Hutton Papers, p. 974, Hutton to Chamberlain, "Confidential," July 28, 1899.

14. Anti-Americanism and Imperial Unity

WHILE QUESTIONS of defence and aid to Britain preoccupied only a handful of Canadians, anti-Americanism intensified on the suspension of the Joint High Commission. Other types of public reaction were secondary. Doubts as to Britain's support, for example, and ranklings at her past neglect of Canadian interests tended to be muted[1] or swallowed up in affirmations of imperial unity. J. H. Bell, a Liberal from Prince Edward Island, in moving the address in answer to the speech from the throne in March 1899 proclaimed: "We are proud of Canada and of being Canadians—we shall never cease to be that—but our sentiments are rapidly taking a wider range and a loftier flight. We are prouder still of being citizens of an Empire—the freest, the strongest, and the greatest upon which the sun shines to-day."[2] Canada's independent action was also praised. Henri Bourassa was proud that the "whole political direction of the negotiations" was in Canadian hands,[3] Denison, that Canada had the courage to break off negotiations[4] and Laurier, that Canada no longer had to depend on the United States market alone.[5]

The tacit anti-Americanism implied in the foregoing statements was unimportant compared to its explicit manifestations in the abusive press campaign against the United States and Tupper's call for retaliation.[6] Although a month later in Parliament Tupper denied advocating "retaliation," his manner was retaliatory. He boasted that the United States, "however powerful, must be brought to recognize the fact that they are dealing with a country as great and as powerful as they." Canada had a

---

[1]See *Globe*, Feb. 22, 1899, remarks of G. W. Ross.

[2]*Debates*, March 20, 1899, p. 20; see also important and flamboyant speech of George E. Foster on "Canada and the Empire," in Toronto (*Globe*, Feb. 25, 1899).

[3]*Debates*, March 29, 1899, p. 629.

[4]*Globe*, Feb. 22, 1899; the *Globe* also reported the satisfaction of Toronto business men that not a single right had been sacrificed.

[5]*Debates*, March 21, 1899, p. 102.

[6]Campbell, p. 138, and " 'RETALIATE' HIS MOTTO," heading in *Globe*, Feb. 23, 1899.

claim on Britain; "we had Great Britain to look to, which is bound by every principle of justice and right to Canada, and Canada is in a position to demand that Great Britain shall put that question in a position in which it must be solved."[7] In denouncing Tupper's "role of a mischievous demagogue," Sir Richard Cartwright rejoined that Canada should act not "in the temper of angry school boys" but in that of "dignity and calmness."[8] He disclosed, however, that the United States Senate requirement of two-thirds majority prevented successful negotiations. To the taunt of an intention to make concessions he retorted that "the Canadian commissioners . . . made no concession whatever."[9] The New York *Commercial Advertiser* interpreted this as meaning that the United States commissioners would have had to concede everything but for "their unfortunate un-British form of government" and it sardonically concluded its editorial:

This seems to discover the hopelessness of negotiations with Canada for the present, a thing that will be regretted as sincerely in England as in the United States. It is pretty hard for Americans to be patient with these crass provincials, with their Brummagem titles and pinchbeck patriotism, their two-penny nationality and their Gargantuan diplomacy, their intrusion of their noisy and noisome home politics into grave business between real nations and all the monstrous impudence and assumption they build on their family connection with a great friendly power; but it is for us to reflect that Great Britain suffers more from this than we. The impertinent footman or saucy child is a greater trial to the family than to neighbors. As for the questions in dispute, they are no great matter to us, though we should like to close an open sore. But we shall neither surrender to Canada nor quarrel with Great Britain.[10]

I

Until the end of July anti-Americanism expressed itself primarily in the problems of Ontario lumber, alien labour, British Columbia mining, and the Alaska boundary.

In appointing John Charlton to the Joint High Commission Laurier had assumed that his well-known advocacy of low tariffs would facilitate an agreement with the United States. Instead his conduct on the Commission and subsequent actions alarmed advocates of high tariffs in both

[7]*Debates*, March 20, 1899, p. 60.
[8]*Ibid.*, March 22, 1899, pp. 167, 170.
[9]*Ibid.*, p. 166.
[10]March 25, 1899, Laurier Papers, pp. 225256–57; J. A. McKenna of the Department of the Interior described to Sifton this editorial of a "strong McKinley paper" as "pretty rough" (*ibid.*, p. 225255, "Personal," March 27, 1899); for some other examples of journalistic anti-Canadianism in the United States, see *Public Opinion*, XXVI (June 8, 1899), p. 711.

countries and his public attacks on the Ontario log export embargo law embarrassed the Canadian and Ontario governments. The timing and the purpose of the following incidents look like a carefully planned campaign, probably under Charlton's inspiration, to force suspension of that law. Towards the end of April 1899 a rumour from Washington declaring Congress's intention to retaliate alarmed Laurier. This rumour formed an effective preparation for attacks on the law in the May 1899 issues of the *Canadian Magazine* and the *North American Review*. The first was by John Charlton, the second by an anonymous "Canadian Liberal" who was almost certainly also Charlton.[11] The former was a devastating attack on the premises of Ontario attitudes. According to Charlton the Ontario "Jingo" regarded the log export law as a tool to pry open the American market. But the law simply undermined those American lumbermen who wanted to liberalize trade relations and, according to Nelson Dingley, diverted $10,000,000 of investment from Canada. It was absurd to suppose that "six million people" could "bring seventy-seven million people to their knees." The article in the *Canadian Magazine* produced an adverse reaction to Canada in the United States and anger in Ontario.[12] Finally the New York *Tribune* of May 4, 1899, published an interview with Charlton himself going over the same ground.

Towards the end of May Michigan lumber interests requested permission to test the constitutionality of the act in the courts. The Ontario Government refused but allowed a "suit at law." Had the former procedure been permitted, Premier Hardy replied to Laurier's remonstrance, the Tories would have charged that a deliberate conspiracy between the Government and Michigan lumber interests existed to declare the law unconstitutional—a "charge" that "would not sound well." Hardy now launched into an attack on Charlton's writings. Lumbermen looked upon them as a betrayal of Ontario lumber interests and as "intolerable . . . I cannot put this point too strongly to you," especially in view of his "personal interests known to everybody" conflicting "with our law."[13] Laurier commented: "What you say about

---

[11]The Commission's Work—Counter Influences," *Can. Mag.*, XIII, pp. 13–17, and a Canadian Liberal, "Work of the Joint High Commission," *North Amer. Rev.*, CLXVIII, pp. 615–24. The basic similarity of the two articles is shown in ideas, tone, purpose, and date of publication. The latter article also betrays information on negotiations not generally known.

[12]C.O. 42/871, p. 518, Reginald Tower (British chargé during Pauncefote's absence in Europe) to Salisbury, May 6, 1899.

[13]Laurier Papers, pp. 33681–83, "Private," May 17, 1899, and *ibid.*, p. 33679, "Confidential," May 17, 1899. Charlton even tried to induce the British Government to declare the Ontario law unconstitutional (Conf. 7309, pp. 8–13).

Charlton is only too true."[14] After much grumbling Michigan lumbermen followed the procedure allowed by Hardy. On appeal, which eventually reached the Judicial Committee of the Privy Council, they lost. Ontario thus succeeded in forcing Michigan lumber interests to transfer their operations to Georgian Bay to manufacture saw logs before exportation.[15]

A second source of anti-Americanism was the alien labour question. This question had not had an important place in the Joint High Commission negotiations, but both countries had agreed unofficially not to enforce their alien labour laws in respect of each other's nationals. Laurier had from the first been reluctant to enforce the Canadian law, partly because of his belief that Americans would one day constitute valuable Canadian immigrants. "I differ from you," he wrote to Colonel Denison,

on the Alien Labour Law. I look upon those laws, our own as well as the American, as most objectionable. It is quite certain that in a very few years a change will take place, & the current of emigration will be then reversed. It will then flow not from north to south as it has done for the last 50 years, but from south to north. On the whole it must be the very best class of emigration equal to what comes from the British Isles, & Scandinavia, in fact largely composed of those elements. Why should we put an obstacle to that class of emigrants, and apart from that consideration, what have we to gain from the existence of laws which by their injurious application, are a constant source of irritation between two friendly nations?[16]

Public complaint in Canada centred on the strict enforcement of the United States law by the immigration inspector at Buffalo, New York, but not apparently at other ports of entry. Successful Canadian travellers or agents, for example, had been deported.[17] Canadian labour was irritated by the importation of strike-breakers from the United States; this occured in a garment strike at Hamilton,[18] and Laurier's Toronto

[14]Laurier Papers, pp. 33684–85, "Private and Confidential," May 16, 1899.

[15]The courts decided that Americans were not the owners of forests but holders of licences annually renewable under such terms as the licensing authority saw fit (J. E. Defebaugh, *History of the Lumber Industry of America* (Chicago, 1906–7), I, pp. 458–59). On the lumber question for 1899 see Laurier Papers, pp. 33600–37100, *passim*.

[16]Denison Papers, pp. 3551–53, "Private," Aug. 4, 1898; this attitude partly explains the cumbersomeness of enforcement procedure (Laurier Papers, p. 25074, Mills to Laurier, "Confidential," July 15, 1898) and the appointment at Toronto of an enforcement officer reputedly unsympathetic to labour (*ibid.*, pp. 23356–57, D. J. O'Donoghue to Laurier, May 16, 1898).

[17]For grievances, see Laurier Papers, pp. 27941, 28515–16 (complaint of the Salada Tea Co.), and 28545; *Debates*, Laurier, May 30, 1899, pp. 3800–1; and Conf. 7135, pp. 105–8.

[18]*Debates*, May 30, 1899, pp. 3879–80; cf. *ibid.*, Aug. 10, 1899, p. 10126.

labour informant and father of Canada's trade union movement, D. J. O'Donoghue, advocated enforcement to prevent a similar occurrence in a Grand Trunk Railway trackmen's strike in May and June 1899.[19] The pressure for enforcement became so great that Laurier complained to Senator Fairbanks of the strict enforcement of the United States law at Buffalo, and requested permission to reveal the unofficial agreement made during the Joint High Commission negotiations and to invoke the law in cases of strike-breaking. Fairbanks agreed to the latter request only.[20] Meanwhile an unsigned memorandum had come from the Immigration Department at Buffalo explaining that, in the preceding three years, of the thousands of Canadians applying at Buffalo, only 74 were refused entry and 6 were deported.[21] Continued complaints from Canadian labour, however, forced an increase in the enforcement appropriation from $3,000 to $5,000 per annum.

The province of British Columbia also engaged in anti-Americanism by refusing to establish a mining record office at Atlin and passing legislation requiring all miners to take out provincial licences and become British subjects. In February 1899 Joseph Martin, Attorney General of the province, explained to Laurier that the legislation was the consequence of the "very bad behaviour of the Americans" in failing to remove bonding restrictions at Dyea and Skagway in the trade with the Yukon promised during the previous year.[22] One effect of British Columbia retaliation was a petition by the United States miners at Atlin to the President to restore their "rights and privileges."[23] The official United States reaction to British Columbia's policy was mild, possibly because so many of the provisions of the British Columbia law were copied from United States laws. Hay, having urged Laurier to suspend the British Columbia law, even invited the British authorities to recommend an amendment[24]—which failed to pass—to section 13 of the Alaska Government Bill (30 Stat. 409, 415), which ostensibly had permitted reciprocal mining rights since May 1898. Under this section the Secretary of the Interior issued a regulation that made the privilege

[19]Laurier Papers, pp. 34015–16, "Private," May 30, 1899.

[20]*Ibid.*, pp. 33946–54, and p. 215064, telegram, May 27, 1899.

[21]*Ibid.*, pp. 34628–44, unsigned, dated at Buffalo, June 16, 1899; *inter alia* the memorandum said that the Alien Labor Law was to prevent paupers, convicts, or contract labour entering the United States. Ontario municipal officers sent lunatics and paupers to Buffalo, Cleveland, and Detroit "in order to save the expense of keeping them at home" (*ibid.*, p. 34631). The inspector helped Canadian doctors who wrote to him to arrest people escaping bad debts (*ibid.*, p. 34642).

[22]*Ibid.*, pp. 30325–26, "Private and Confidential," Feb. 7, 1899.

[23]Conf. 7340, pp. 7–9, dated Feb. 10, 1899, inc. in Hay to Pauncefote, April 3, 1899, inc. in Pauncefote to Salisbury, April 7, 1899.

[24]C.O. 42/871, p. 48, Pauncefote to Salisbury, paraphrase telegram, March 7, 1899; the Colonial Office consulted Canada.

a "sham," as the Under-Secretary of the Colonial Office minuted.[25] Although in the Yukon territory, which came under federal and not provincial jurisdiction, Canada gave Americans the same leasing privileges as Canadians enjoyed, Canadians were denied the right to purchase a mining claim, which Americans enjoyed in Alaska, because in the Yukon Canadian law denied the right of purchase.[26] While Laurier disapproved of the British Columbia legislation, he had no intention of disallowing it until the United States consented to arbitration on the Alaska boundary.[27] Eventually the Judicial Committee declared the act unconstitutional because naturalization and immigration were federal and not provincial matters.[28]

II

The chief source of anti-Americanism in 1899 was Canada's failure to reach her Alaska boundary objectives. After the suspension of the Joint High Commission these were rigidly pursued. Canada's strategy was to obtain an arbitration tribunal modelled after the Venezuela Arbitration Treaty; her chief tactic was to negotiate matters *pari passu* and exchange Canadian for United States demands.[29]

Chamberlain at first espoused Canadian objectives and tactics, but Pauncefote's and the Foreign Office's knowledge of the impossibility of the Canadian tactics undermined his assistance.[30] His position was difficult; imperial unity implied British support of Canada in return for Canada's expected military aid to Britain, but support of Canada should not be at the price of alienation of the United States whose benevolent neutrality Britain needed in war. On the basis of treaty right, and argued by an able lawyer like Lord Herschell, Canada's case could be presented with conviction, but with Herschell gone,[31] the adamant demands of

[25]*Ibid.*, p. 424, E. Wingfield, May 17, 1899; for the regulation, see *ibid.*, pp. 433–35, interpretation of E. A. Hitchcock, Sec. of the Interior (Advanced Sheets of Consular Reports, April 29, 1899, no. 413); see also *ibid.*, pp. 437–38, C.O. to F.O., draft, "Confidential," May 22, 1899.

[26]For Laurier's summary, see *Debates*, March 21, 1899, p. 108.

[27]Conf. 7340, pp. 19–20, Minto to Pauncefote, April 25, 1899, inc. in Tower to Salisbury, "Confidential," April 28, 1899.

[28]*Union Colliery Company, Ltd.* v. *Bryden and the Attorney-General of British Columbia*, judgment delivered July 28, 1899 (C.O. 42/872, p. 391, C.O. to F.O., draft, "Immediate and Confidential," Sept. 18, 1899).

[29]For example, Clayton-Bulwer Treaty rights for the Alaska boundary concessions.

[30]C.O. 42/871, 369–70, C.O. to F.O., draft, "Confidential," May 13, 1899.

[31]The death of Lord Herschell, wrote Laurier to Charlton, was "certainly a great calamity. He was a strong and able man, and at this juncture his death is doubly so." Laurier Papers, p. 30940, March 6, 1899.

Canadian sentiment hamstrung the case and alienated the United States. Fortunately for Canada London was the buffer between Ottawa and Washington.

In contrast to the barren inflexibility of Canadian diplomacy, United States diplomacy was astutely flexible and strong, applying pressure whenever necessary to secure its ends. In the months between March and May the State Department conducted three diplomatic probing operations to explore Canada's intentions, each one resulting in Canada's demand for arbitration on the unacceptable terms of the Venezuela precedent. The United States therefore concentrated its strength on securing a temporary boundary at the key points to the Yukon, knowing that time, possession, and power would eventually make themselves felt.

The first probe in March 1898 concerned President McKinley's hints through the President of the Canadian Pacific Railway on the desirability of Canada's reconstituting the Joint High Commission.[32] Laurier objected; he thought the United States should make the first move, and later he made an arbitral board a condition of reconstitution.[33] The second concerned the making of a temporary agreement on the Dalton Trail or Chilkat Pass. The chief issue here concerned the possession of the gold-bearing area of Porcupine Creek. This lay within Canada's claim to the west of the junction of the Klehini and Chilkat rivers,[34] but it had been invaded by United States miners who were "refugees from the Atlin."[35] They swarmed in to pre-empt the area by staking claims, building a hotel, and laying out a town.[36] If the area were found to belong to Canada American miners would lose their claims by coming under British Columbia mining law; hence, rumours of Canadian police encroachments in unspecified areas caused the Americans understandable alarm. Though all three powers were anxious to keep the peace, Canada kept denying encroachments, Britain counselled Canada to keep sufficient military force available for emergency,[37] and the United States on May 5, 1899, ordered the dispatch of a company of troops under an "officer of discretion" to establish a military post at Pyramid Harbor. The Colonial Office at once protested and the order was

---

[32]Laurier Papers, pp. 30924, 31088–89, 31598, 31599, 31811, correspondence between Sir William Van Horne and Laurier.

[33]C.O. 42/868, p. 568, Minto to Chamberlain, "Secret," May 5, 1899.

[34]See above, pp. 96–97.

[35]Campbell's phrase, p. 139.

[36]C.O. 42/869, p. 3, minute of John Anderson, July 5, 1899.

[37]See indication of Chamberlain's alarmist views on this situation in Minto's notes, May 23, 1899, Minto Papers, vol. 14, p. 33.

revoked.[38] In July Senator Fairbanks confirmed the Canadian denial and the Governor of Alaska was rebuked for sending out alarmist reports.

The third exploratory probe of the United States concerned the offer to arbitrate the whole boundary by an odd-numbered arbitration tribunal of seven, with Dyea and Skagway guaranteed to the United States regardless of the arbitrator's decision. Chamberlain in a "very secret" cable warned Canada that owing to her failure to protest against the "settled occupation" of Dyea and Skagway, the terms were the "utmost that can be got."[39] But the Canadian Government made its acceptance of this proposal conditional on Canada's obtaining Pyramid Harbor, justifying the claim on the ground that "Acts of occupation and possession in those remote regions could and did take place without any knowledge of them reaching Canada, and it is therefore impossible to invoke the failure of the Dominion in protest."[40] This reply destroyed the possibility of an odd-numbered arbitral tribunal and hardened United States policy towards Canada, for Hay thought Canada wanted nothing settled.[41] The "new proposition . . . ," Choate reported to Salisbury, "was wholly unacceptable"; Pyramid Harbor was not the equivalent of settled districts.[42] Although Chamberlain defended the Canadian contention as "some kind of equivalent,"[43] he argued sharply with Canada: Canada could not plead ignorance of occupancy of remote regions for she had not protested on learning of the United States action. Furthermore, according to the United States ambassador, she lacked "vested interests" in Pyramid Harbor. Chamberlain, therefore, made a new proposal that if arbitrators found places occupied by the United States belonging to Canada, the United States should agree to money

[38]C.O. 42/871, p. 360, F.O. Conf. Print, Tower to Salisbury, cable, "Confidential," May 5, 1899; Anderson minuted on May 8, 1899, with Colonial Office concurrence, the necessity of making a *"pro forma* protest. . . . We have already damaged our case by not protesting when Dyea & Skagway were founded, and though it is rather late, we must not let this pass without notice." *Ibid.*, pp. 358–59.

[39]Laurier Papers, pp. 215055–56, to Minto, paraphrase cable, rec'd. May 12, 1899.

[40]Conf. 7340, p. 24, Minto to Chamberlain, cable rec'd. May 14, 1899, inc. in C.O. to F.O., "Confidential," May 16, 1899.

[41]Hay to J. H. Choate, U.S. Ambassador to Great Britain, "Private and Confidential," May 22, 1899, Tansill, p. 194, and cf. Hay to Henry Adams, May 18, 1899: "I have worked on this miserable Alaska question for six months" and, though Salisbury and Pauncefote had agreed, Canada would not (*Letters of John Hay and Extracts from Diary* (Washington, 1908, privately printed), III, p. 152).

[42]Conf. 7340, p. 29, Salisbury to Tower, May 20, 1899.

[43]*Ibid.*, pp. 36–37, C.O. to F.O., "Confidential," May 29, 1899; cf. *ibid.*, pp. 55–56.

compensation.[44] Canada protested that "any further concession" would make "reference to arbitrators a mere formality."[45]

III

Until mid-July Americans thought Canada politically divided on a boundary settlement. They saw Tupper early in June demanding that Laurier defend Canada against accusations of obstructionism.[46] Laurier had to put much pressure on Chamberlain before he acceded to publication of the second-last protocol of the Joint High Commission, which described in detail the differences between the governments on the question.[47] On the other hand, a careful analysis of the June debate on the Yukon railway would have shown the Conservatives in effect taking a position favourable to the United States.[48] In response to an Opposition inquiry on this matter Laurier stated that the Government had refused to permit construction of another railway to the Yukon because it would "build up an American city Pyramid Harbour" which would "weigh enormously" against Canada's boundary claims. Canada's Parliament had acted "with questionable wisdom," he lamented, in granting a charter to the British-Yukon Railway in 1897. But if Canada should fail to obtain the Lynn Canal by arbitration, the Government planned a railway from Observatory Inlet, which was "indisputably Canadian."[49] The Opposition objected to Government policy; it favoured monopoly and shutting up the country. Foster also complained that the Government's course showed lack of "strong faith . . . in the possibility, nay, the probability" of the territory belonging to Canada.[50] Alexander McNeill objected that the fact of people founding a town in knowingly disputed territory would not affect the conditions of arbitration. But

[44]*Ibid.*, p. 37, Chamberlain to Minto, draft, "Secret," inc. in C.O. to F.O., May 29, 1899; see also Minto Papers, vol. 14, p. 16, "Private," May 8, 1899.

[45]Laurier Papers, pp. 215073–74, Minto to Chamberlain, cable, June 3, 1899; and Campbell, p. 144, n. 24. Anderson also noted that the United States had good reason to be satisfied with things as they were, and the revision of the Clayton-Bulwer Treaty could not be postponed "to gain concessions for Canada in Alaska—which but for their own supineness they wd not have required" (C.O. 42/868, p. 599, May 15, 1899).

[46]Laurier Papers, pp. 34218–19, S.A. Wetmore, Boston *Herald*, to Laurier, June 5, 1899; and see *ibid.*, pp. 32866, 34140, and Conf. 7340, p. 30.

[47]*Debates*, June 5, 1899, pp. 4259–64; and see Minto Papers, vol. 7, p. 28, Laurier to Minto, June 1, 1899, and C.O. 42/868, p. 656, C.O. 42/871, pp. 698, 700–1. These efforts did not improve Canada's press in the United States or Great Britain (*Debates*, July 22, 1899, p. 8155).

[48]See *Debates*, June 9, 1899, pp. 4740–69.

[49]*Ibid.*, pp. 4742–44.　　　　　[50]*Ibid.*, p. 4747.

Sifton easily demonstrated that the existence of two towns had already done so.[51]

Throughout July anti-Americanism in Canada sharpened; accompanying it and excited by it were manifestations of loyalty to imperial unity, one of which found expression in a debate on disallowance of anti-Japanese British Columbia legislation.[52] Japanese protests against their offensive provisions and British pressure prevailed on Canada to disallow two of twenty-one acts.[53] The Government did so reluctantly, Laurier explained, but had concluded that

as British subjects . . . every other consideration should give way before that reason of Imperial necessity. It will not do for us as British subjects only to sing "God Save the Queen" and to boast of our British connection at banquets and at demonstrations and celebrations. We must also be prepared to make some sacrifices because our obligations may claim sacrifices. I suppose . . . I utter the sentiment of every hon. gentleman on this occasion . . . that we should be prepared and be ready for every sacrifice which our Imperial connection may demand at our hands. If we take the glory and the advantages we must also take the duties; we must be ready for them and abide by them.[54]

Laurier was reflecting and encouraging the prevailing mood, for his statement evoked lengthy cheering.[55] But more frequently apprehension of Canada's neighbour was expressed. When Tupper on July 10 supported the withdrawal of the "absolutely useless" Yukon Field Force, which Hutton had recommended, Laurier upheld its dispatch to and maintenance in the Yukon because of possible danger from the United States.

If I were to follow my own inclination at this moment—I do not think it is my deliberate or last judgment on the subject—I think it is a wise policy to have a military force in that distant country. We know as a matter of fact that to-day the Americans are sending a military force to Skagway, that they intend to send one to Pyramid Harbour, and that they have one in Alaska. If the Americans find that to be a wise course, I appeal to the hon. gentleman's better judgment whether it is unwise and unpatriotic for us to have a military force in the Yukon? I am not prepared to express that opinion.[56]

[51]*Ibid.*, pp. 4763–65.

[52]For a list see *Can. Sess. Pap.* (no. 110), 1899, p. 3; Chinese protests appear to have been ignored.

[53]*Ibid.*, pp. 29–32; cf. C.O. 42/868, p. 270, comment of John Anderson on draft of Chamberlain to Minto, April 19, 1899, that it was important "in view of our position with regard to the Australian Colonies to press for the repeal of the diallce [*sic*] of these measures."

[54]*Debates*, July 7, 1899, p. 6849.

[55]*Globe*, July 8, 1899.

[56]*Debates*, July 10, 1899, p. 7012; the phrase "absolutely useless" is *ibid.*, p. 7006.

By July 22 Tupper's reaction to United States press accusations that he was the stumbling block to successful boundary negotiations brought him to support the Government's Alaska policy wholeheartedly. "At this critical moment," he thundered forth, "no more monstrous . . . more insulting proposition" could have been made by the United States than to retain Dyea and Skagway regardless of the arbitrator's decision. He also warned against Britain in its dealings with the United States. Since 1868 Tupper had "been struck very forcibly with the unwillingness on the part of Her Majesty's Government to allow any circumstances whatever to even threaten a collision with the United States." The Canadian Government had only done its duty in resisting English pressure, and so long as the United States persisted in its "utterly indefensible attitude," Canada should charter a railway to Canadian territory and, while respecting existing rights, should copy the British Columbia mining law and exclude from Yukon mining all but British subjects.[57]

In reply Laurier declared Tupper's statement the best justification of the previous year's Yukon railway policy. The Government intended to maintain its present policy which seemed "impregnable" and rested on "a sense of fairness." But the lack of clarity in the treaty of 1825 meant that there were only three ways of settling the problem: "by compromise" in which he had little hope, "by arbitration," or "by war."[58] In the meantime he could only counsel "patience" until the "painful conclusion" was reached that hope of arbitration was lacking, though he had not yet reached such a conclusion. In the meantime, although supporting the British Columbia law, and becoming evasive on Tupper's reminder of provincial confiscation, he pointed to the dangers of excluding American miners from the Yukon.[59]

The reference to "war" created an international sensation. Its use was probably not intended to force the United States to yield, as the Chairman of the Senate Committee on Foreign Relations charged,[60] but to give Canadian public opinion that impression and answer Chamberlain's demand for troops in a South African demonstration.[61] Laurier was riding a tiger; he could not further yield to the demands of public

[57]*Ibid.*, July 22, 1899, pp. 8156, 8158–59, 8163; the whole speech is *ibid.*, pp. 8152–65.
[58]*Ibid.*, pp. 8165–66; cf. strikingly similar statement in Tansill, p. 192, Hay to McKinley, May 13, 1899.
[59]*Debates*, July 22, 1899, pp. 8166–71.
[60]Tansill, p. 200, Sen. Cushman K. Davis to John Hay, July 31, 1899, and reply August 4, 1899, in Tyler Dennett, *John Hay: From Poetry to Politics* (New York, 1933), pp. 235–36.
[61]See below, pp. 220–21.

sentiment without catastrophe to his Government and the country. The only escape lay in a different focus for public attention.

IV

Against this inflammatory background negotiations for a *modus vivendi* now began in earnest. Hay, angered at rejection of an odd-numbered arbitration tribunal and complaints of police encroachments, cabled to Choate that a *modus vivendi* was "imperatively required."[62] To impress on Salisbury the urgency of Hay's demand Choate let him see Hay's cable and even suggested that they settle the line between them "at once." Salisbury demurred; Canada would not agree.[63]

By this time Canada and the United States had agreed on one point of the boundary—the junction of the Klehini and Chilkat rivers—but they differed on the direction of the boundary west of the junction. The United States suggested a line vaguely in a westerly direction to the spot where the Dalton Trail crossed the Klehini River.[64] In reply Canada proposed, on grounds of accord with the Treaty of 1825, a line running in a southwesterly direction to include Porcupine Creek.[65] Hay would not hear of such a line that left American miners, many of them from Atlin, in Canada.[66] At first Canada tried to deny the presence of Americans within the Canadian claim, but was convinced by one of its own sessional papers.[67] Moved by continued rumours of agitation, Hay sent a virtual ultimatum against further concessions, through Choate softened its tone on presentation to Salisbury.[68] Irritated in turn, Canada now demanded that the United States draw the exact line it wanted on the map. To force Canada to accept the line on the Klehini River, Hay now proposed a line admitting to the British chargé its probable

[62]Tansill, p. 195, May 27, 1899; cf. C.O. 42/871, p. 603, minute of H. B. Cox, June 1, 1899: "I think that the US in view of a possible failure of agreement want to establish a modus vivendi suitable to them & once they have got it they will not care what happens."

[63]Conf. 7340, p. 42, Salisbury to Tower, June 2, 1899.

[64]C.O. 42/871, pp. 693–94, Choate to Salisbury, June 10, 1899, inc. in F.O. to C.O., "Immediate and Confidential," June 13, 1899.

[65]Conf. 7340, p. 47, Minto to Chamberlain, cable, rec'd. June 4, 1899; cf. note on C.O. 42/871, p. 314, "Copy has been circulated to Cabinet."

[66]Conf. 7340, p. 52, Tower to Salisbury, cable, June 27, 1899, and *ibid.*, pp. 58–59, Choate to Salisbury, June 28, 1899.

[67]*Ibid.*, pp. 63–64, Minto to Chamberlain, cable, July 4, 1899, inc. in C.O. to F.O., "Confidential," July 7, 1899, and *ibid.*, p. 64, Chamberlain to Minto, cable, July 6, 1899; the sessional paper cited was no. 15, pp. 103–4.

[68]Hay to Choate, July 6, 1899, Tansill, p. 196, and Conf. 7340, p. 64, Choate to Salisbury, July 8, 1899.

unacceptability, in a general northwesterly direction from the Klehini-Chilkat junction.[69] Salisbury objected to the seeking of "rights only just created in what seems obviously debatable territory" as compared to the maintenance of existing rights. Chamberlain exploded that this proposed line was "wholly inadmissible" and would "provoke an outburst of feeling" endangering the "present friendly relations" with Canada. It was useless to proceed further.[70] Fortunately for the success of the temporary negotiations, Salisbury transmitted the threat to break off negotiations in a toned-down version. Expressing himself as "greatly distressed" at the prospect, Hay drew a line along the Klehini River but deflected it in a southwesterly direction to include the Porcupine Creek area.[71]

Thus in early August the temporary boundary had been practically decided upon, but Canada continued to haggle over details for nearly three months more.

V

Meanwhile negotiations for a permanent boundary also dragged on. Early in June Chamberlain asked his staff for a careful analysis of Canada's contentions, because "feeling is rising in the U.S. & the idea is fostered that Canada is unreasonable. I do not think this is true but I should be very glad to promote an amicable arrangement."[72] Anderson wrote in a long minute that the basic problem was Canada's desire for free transit into the interior and the United States determination to maintain its privileges. But both countries were "treating the matter as a game of poker." On the letter of the treaty Canada had a good case, but all maps until 1898 were drawn according to the United States claim. The inference of the unprotested settlement of Dyea and Skagway,

---

[69]Conf. 7340, p. 75, Tower to Salisbury, cable, July 24, 1899 and C.O. 42/872, p. 299, F.O. Conf. Print, Tower to Hay, July 29, 1899, inc. in Tower to Salisbury, July 29, 1899.

[70]C.O. 42/872, p. 172, F.O. Conf. Print, Salisbury to Choate, July 24, 1899, inc. in F.O. to C.O., "Secret," July 29, 1899, and Conf. 7340, p. 76, C.O. to F.O., "Confidential," July 26, 1899.

[71]Conf. 7340, p. 93, Hay to Tower, "Private," Aug. 3, 1899, inc. in Tower to Salisbury, "Very Confidential," Aug. 7, 1899; see also *ibid.*, pp. 85–86, inc. in Tower to Salisbury, July 28, 1899, extract of New York *Tribune*, July 27, 1899: "If it [the United States] can afford . . . to grant important privileges at Lynn Canal . . . it does so as a voluntary concession, and without . . . waiving the rights of sovereignty on the whole coast. . . . The United States is in possession, and believes itself to be rightfully so. Certainly it is not to be ousted by any ill-advised talk of war by Ottawa politicians."

[72]C.O. 42/871, p. 623, minute of June 7, 1899.

the establishment of a Canadian customs post outside the American claim, and especially of the attempt to build an "all-Canadian" route was United States possession of the Lynn Canal. United States canneries, missions, mines, and an official though temporary observatory flourished without protest. "Our whole case . . . looks so much like an afterthought, and the impression in the U.S. that it is so is not without justification." But if Canada won the arbitration the United States would claim the Lynn Canal by equities and occupation. Canada might have something to say for itself; if so it should send an explanation and experts to Britain so that the "nominal principals" should be furnished with the arguments.[73] Chamberlain therefore besought the visit of a Canadian official and pointedly requested an explanation of Canada's claim to the upper waters of the Lynn Canal in order to "dispute United States' claim founded on occupation and settlement and tacit acquiescence in their interpretation of the Treaty of 1825." Canada replied that it could send no one to Britain, and in a "sort of preface to the memorial," itself to be later sent to Britain, recalled that about 1873 Canada had negotiated for a joint survey in the neighbourhood of the Lynn Canal, which owing to lack of funds fell through. Anderson minuted that in fact this referred to the marking of boundaries on the rivers, including the Chilkat. In other words, Canada had then admitted the American interpretation of the treaty.[74]

Britain's interest in a settlement is seen in the approval of the British cabinet[75] of a scheme for a perpetual lease by Canada of Pyramid Harbor. The "Chinde" proposal, so called because it resembled the British lease from Portugal on the Chinde River at the mouth of the Zambesi in Portuguese East Africa,[76] provided for the lease of a half a square mile of territory that might contain all necessary appurtenances for landing, sorting, and shipping goods, and was to be connected with the interior by a railway not to "be interfered with by the United States."[77] Under the Chinde proposal, as Davies later wrote to Laurier,

[73]C.O. 42/868, pp. 709–13, June 9, 1899.

[74]C.O. 42/868, p. 810, Minto to Chamberlain, paraphrase telegram, June 22, 1899; p. 819, Minto to Chamberlain, "Secret," June 22, 1899; p. 815, Anderson's minute, July 6, 1899. The quoted phrase is from Laurier Papers, p. 34841, Minto to Laurier, June 23 (*sic*), 1899.

[75]C.O. 42/872, p. 43, Salisbury to Tower, "Confidential," July 12, 1899.

[76]For the lease with Portugal, dated May 7, 1892, see C.O. 42/872, pp. 114–15, inc. in F.O. to C.O., "Confidential," July 21, 1899.

[77]Choate to Hay, July 19, 1899, Tansill, p. 197; the McKinley cabinet approved because as Hay wrote to Sen. C. K. Davis, a lease implied "unquestioned possession" (Aug. 4, 1899, Dennett, *John Hay*, p. 236); Davis doubted whether the Senate would approve (Hay to Choate, Aug. 18, 1899, *ibid.*, p. 237).

Pyramid Harbor would remain a " 'bonding place.' "[78] Canada, however, wanted jurisdiction in order to share in the carrying trade. To this Chamberlain rejoined that there would be no "Canadian jurisdiction." In his frankest reproof, agreed to by the Colonial and Foreign offices and initialed by Salisbury, he warned, "We desire to impress upon your Ministers that whatever arguments may be based on letter of Treaty of 1825, careful examination of United States case for possession of shores of Canal based on continuous uninterrupted jurisdiction since the date of Treaty, and admissions of Hudson [*sic*] Bay Company, Imperial and Dominion Governments, shews that it is unassailable. Delay in settlement highly prejudicial to Canadian interests." He added that the suggestion was made "after discussion with Mr. Tarte"[79] with whom he had had an interview on July 11, 1899. Chamberlain had taken advantage of a suggestion by Tarte that a neutral area at Pyramid Harbor might be acceptable to Canada, to inquire if Canada would agree to a leased area. Tarte replied that he thought so.[80] Several times in the interview Chamberlain repeated—once bitterly—that Canada had sent no delegate to Britain. To mollify Chamberlain the Canadian cabinet now agreed to send a delegate, though Sir Louis Davies did not arrive until nearly two months later. The Colonial Office had surmised that Canada's refusal to send a delegate was because of the weakness of her case.[81] Though this surmise contained some truth, Laurier had originally intended to go but was delayed by the session, and finally gave up the idea in order to conduct a political campaign in Ontario.[82]

In the meantime the Foreign Office had engaged as best it could in negotiations for a permanent boundary. On July 1 Salisbury had proposed to Choate a settlement on the basis of Venezuela arbitration because of the essential similarity of the Venezuela and Alaska boundary questions.[83] United States authorities were embarrassed at British insistence on such a tribunal, "After we had put forth our entire force and compelled—there is no other word for it—England to accept arbitration

---

[78]Laurier Papers, p. 225393, L. H. Davies to Laurier, *"Private and Confidential,"* Oct. 12, 1899.

[79]To Minto, July 21, 1899, Campbell, p. 146.

[80]Laurier Papers, p. 35327, Tarte to Laurier, "Confidentielle," July 11, 1899; Chamberlain also informed Tarte that "Notre opinion" was that the Canadian case was weak and that Cartwright and other colleagues agreed (*ibid.*, pp. 35326–27). Note Laurier's anxiety at cable version of this report: "no—leave matter altogether to us here" (*ibid.*, p. 35278, cable, July 12, 1899).

[81]C.O. 42/869, p. 121, Minto to Chamberlain, paraphrase telegram rec'd. July 25, 1899, and C.O. 42/872, p. 40, minute of Anderson, July 14, 1899.

[82]Laurier papers, p. 35769, to Tarte, July 31, 1899.

[83]*A.B.T.*, IV, pp. 128–29.

in the Venezuela matter," Hay wrote to Whitelaw Reid.[84] But the United States would not hazard territory claimed by occupation, sovereignty, and tacit admission by Canada. On August 2 Choate denied the similarity of the two boundary questions and proposed instead a "comparison of views,"[85] which Choate began on August 9. The Alaska boundary dispute and American settlement in the area had only recently been questioned whereas the Venezuela dispute and the British settlement had been in controversy for more than half a century. Britain had not objected to American claims on early maps; indeed, the Hudson's Bay Company's lease from Russia, inherited by the United States, confirmed United States ownership. Furthermore in the disputed area the United States and her citizens had exercised rights of sovereignty, which should not be jeopardized by arbitration. The United States case, in other words, rested "essentially upon the historical facts of occupancy and possession. . . ."[86] Britain postponed her reply until after the arrival of the Canadian experts in late September.

VI

The compulsive power of Canadian jingoism in 1899 was stimulated primarily by, and expressed through, anti-Americanism; and anti-Americanism in turn was largely responsible for enthusiasm for imperial unity. Thus Canada's interests in the Pacific cable and the passage of the July 31 resolution in support of the British in South Africa were largely sentimental examples of the latter phenomenon.

As a result of authorization by the Ottawa Conference of 1894[87] Canada took the lead in expediting an examination of the feasibility and the costs of a Pacific cable. When Chamberlain became Colonial Secretary the project began making headway in Britain; he appointed a Pacific Cable Committee to take evidence, discuss its practicability, and make recommendations. On January 5, 1897, the committee reported; it approved the scheme, made technical recommendations, and proposed government financing, ownership, and operation.[88] Until Britain made a specific proposal of support, colonial agitation for the cable was based on

[84]July 27, 1899, William Roscoe Thayer, *The Life and Letters of John Hay* (Boston and New York, 1915), II, p. 207.

[85]*Can. Sess. Pap.* (no. 46A), 1904, p. 5, Salisbury to Tower, Aug. 2, 1899.

[86]*A.B.T.*, IV, pp. 129–32, Choate to Salisbury; quotation, p. 132.

[87]See above, p. 10.

[88]*Parl. Pap.*, 1899, LIX (C. 9247, pp. 1–205), pp. 347–556; for the report only without the evidence, see *Can. Sess. Pap.* (no. 51), 1899, pp. 36–45; for support in Britain of the scheme see *Parl. Pap.*, 1900, LV (Cd. 46, pp. 13–16), pp. 421–24.

the assumption that Britain favoured the committee's report. Britain was not committed, and in reality official indifference masked powerful opposition by exponents of free enterprise, though Chamberlain himself was not averse to state participation. Until August 1898 the scheme stagnated. Chamberlain explained at the Colonial Conference of 1897 that he awaited proposals from Canada and Australasia; the Laurier Government was virtually indifferent;[89] and the Eastern Extension Cable Company and the British Treasury were strongly opposed. In 1897–98 the initiative rested with the Australasian colonies—the areas concerned materially with breaking a cable monopoly[90] and strategically with allaying apprehension because of seizures in China in 1897–98 and the interruptions of the Eastern Extension lines passing through shallow waters. But the cable trust, predicted to lose one-quarter of its European-Australasian revenue to a Pacific cable, and its ideological allies in the Government would not surrender its monopoly without a long fight.

For example, in March 1898, at the same time as the premiers of the eastern Australian colonies had agreed in conference to pay one-third of the costs of a Pacific cable, the Treasury was holding a conference in London among Australian agents-general and a Colonial Office official to discuss the merits of an "All-British" cable proposal of the Eastern Extension Company around Cape of Good Hope to Australia. The Treasury referred the company's proposal for the opinion of the premiers, who replied that they preferred the Pacific cable. It replied in turn that the British Government did not intend to assist in any Pacific cable scheme, an announcement "at a singularly curious time and in a singularly suspicious manner," commented a Colonial Office official.[91] Chamberlain minuted that the "Treasury seems to be indulging in some rather sharp practice,"[92] and although he succeeded in constraining the Treasury to alter its stand from "Her Majesty's Government" are not prepared "to take any part in . . . laying a Cable . . ." to the Treasury are not prepared "to advise Her Majesty's Government . . ." the damage was done. The Treasury had given the impression that the British Government was opposed although it had made no decision in the matter.[93] To correct the impression Chamberlain pressed for publication

[89]Laurier Papers, p. 8168, A. G. Jones, Canadian delegate, to Laurier, cable, Nov. 5, 1896, and *Debates*, May 26, 1898, pp. 6197–99.

[90]*Can. Sess. Pap.* (no. 51), 1899, p. 31; Chamberlain's "policy" on the Pacific cable was to "prevent a monopoly" (C.O. 42/862, p. 428, minute, Jan. 2, 1899).

[91]C.O. 42/860, pp. 582–83, minute of W. H. Mercer, March 25, 1898.

[92]*Ibid.*, p. 607, May 31, 1898.

[93]*Ibid.*, p. 584; Chamberlain minuted that if the Treasury Committee carried out its threat not to allow the Pacific scheme to be discussed, he would order the Colonial Office representatives to "protest & withdraw" (*ibid.*, March 26, 1898).

of the report of the Pacific Cable Committee, though he did not succeed until April 1899. Meanwhile the Director of Military Intelligence reported against the scheme, *inter alia* because of the vulnerability "of the connecting line across Canada."[94]

In August 1898 the scheme began moving again when New Zealand joined with Australian colonies, which together now offered to pay four-ninths of the cost provided Canada and Britain paid five-ninths.[95] Now Canada advanced the negotiations. What appeared immediately decisive was not the noisy and exaggerated influence of Sir Sandford Fleming[96] or the British Empire League, but the influence of William Mullock, fresh from his penny postage triumph and anxious to strengthen the waning fortunes of the Ontario Liberal party. In November in a series of letters to Laurier, Mulock warned of the costliness of delay. If the United States constructed a cable to Australia first, Australia would lose interest in Canadian trade, a possibility not "favorable to the development of Canadian national spirit nor to Canadian trade"; Cartwright's objection that there would be little revenue from the project was an insufficient argument. Laurier acknowledged the "great importance of forestalling the United States on this question." To Mulock's later insistence that Canada had to take the initiative, Laurier replied that after he looked over Mulock's proposal it would be pushed through the cabinet.[97] This last letter possibly implied the transfer of the Pacific cable question from Cartwright's Department of Trade and Commerce to Mulock's Post Office, for Mulock guided the question through the House of Commons. Accordingly on December 22, 1898, when the prospects of the Joint High Commission were already beginning to dim, a quasi-official authorization was cabled to the High Commissioner to inform the Colonial Office that Canada would agree to pay five-eighteenths of the cost.[98] This decision spurred Chamberlain to overcome Treasury opposition.[99]

Canada was made restless by a four-month delay and in April it applied pressure to Britain by announcing the date of the introduction

[94]C.O. 42/865, pp. 267–68, to W.O., July 18, 1898, inc. in W.O. to C.O., "Confidential," July 27, 1898.
[95]*Can. Sess. Pap.* (no. 51), 1899, p. 19, Premier, N.S.W., to Acting Agent-General, cable, Aug. 29, 1898, inc. in Agent-General to High Com. for Can., Aug. 29, 1898.
[96]Cf. C.O. 42/866, p. 520, minute of W. H. Mercer, Dec. 24, 1898, and *ibid.*, p. 525, of John Anderson.
[97]Laurier Papers, pp. 27970–74, "Private," Nov. 10, 1898; p. 27975, Nov. 14, 1898; p. 27976, "Confidential," Nov. 19, 1898; p. 27978, Nov. 24, 1898.
[98]*Can. Sess. Pap.* (no. 51), 1899, p. 61.
[99]C.O. 42/860, p. 330, minute, Dec. 26, 1898.

of a parliamentary resolution approving the scheme. Chamberlain at once cabled postponement,[100] for he had at last obtained grudging Treasury (and cabinet) approval of the payment of five-eighteenths, not of the construction, maintenance, and working costs—the recommendation of the Pacific Cable Committee—but of any deficit on operating costs of a Pacific cable up to a maximum of £20,000 per annum for twenty years, which the Chancellor of the Exchequer characterized as an "extremely liberal maximum." Nor was Britain to take an "active part in laying or working the line," but the Treasury was to supervise the colonies in doing so and treat the proposed organization as a private enterprise.[101]

This offer produced an outcry from the Canadian High Commissioner and the Australasian agents-general. ". . . . Swotted by the Imperial fist," in Chamberlain's phrase,[102] they protested that the Pacific Cable Committee had called for joint ownership and control by Britain and the colonies and not subservience to the Treasury. They affirmed that the "dominating principle" had been that the "scheme 'cannot fail to promote Imperial unity'. . . ."[103] Anderson also minuted that the Treasury proposal would increase costs of raising money by 17 per cent.[104] The outcry spread to Canada, where the province of British Columbia, moved probably more by resentment of the United States expressed through imperial unity than by the prospects of increased Pacific trade, offered to contribute an extra ninth of the cable cost to realize the orginal scheme. Laurier communicated this offer to the Canadian and British press, as justification for adherence to the original proposal.[105] Anderson defended the British offer as generous to Australia and Canada, and especially Australia and the United States, for they would benefit by cable costs lower than those between Australia and Britain,

---

[100]C.O. 42/874, p. 141, Chamberlain to Minto, paraphrase, April 21, 1899.

[101]C.O. 42/873, pp. 126–30, Hicks-Beach to Chamberlain, March 30, 1899, and memorandum of Chancellor of the Exchequer; and see *ibid.*, pp. 123–25 for minutes. See C.O. 42/860, pp. 332–38, for Chamberlain's memorandum, dated Dec. 22, 1898, inc. in Chamberlain to Hicks-Beach, "Confidential," Feb. 18, 1899. For the British Government's offer see *Parl. Pap.*, 1899, LIX (C. 9283, p. 4), p. 560, C.O. to Agents-General and High Com., April 28, 1899.

[102]C.O. 42/870, p. 129, minute May 11, 1899; cf. *ibid.*, minute of Selborne that the Treasury "certainly selected the most ungracious way possible for doing a gracious thing."

[103]*Parl. Pap.*, 1900, LV (Cd. 46, p. 3), p. 409, High Com. and Agents-General to C.O., May 9, 1899; the whole letter is in *ibid.*, pp. 408–12 (2–4).

[104]C.O. 42/870, p. 127, May 10, 1899.

[105]*Can. Sess. Pap.* (no. 51B), 1899, pp. 1–3, F. Carter-Cotton, British Columbia Min. of Finance, to Laurier, telegram May 5, 1899, letter, May 6, 1899, and reply, May 13, 1899; see also Laurier Papers, pp. 31622–23.

but he supposed that "Colonial gratitude is only a lively sense of favours to come."[106] Yet Canada stood to gain less proportionately than Britain: from 1895 to 1897 Canada's average annual trade with Australasia was only £190,000, while Britain's was £53,168,642, and letters carried were 90,000 and six to seven million respectively.[107]

In spite of protests from the cable trust[108] the Chancellor of the Exchequer yielded early in June; he agreed to use British credit when he realized that the "main factor in the situation" was the "idea of co-operation between the Mother Country and the Colonies."[109] In July the colonial representatives conferred with the Colonial Secretary and the Chancellor of the Exchequer to thrash out the details of raising money, keeping the line all-British, and allocating board members.[110] Great Britain was to have three representatives, Canada two, the Australian colonies two, and New Zealand one. On July 25, 1899, the Canadian House of Commons approved the resolution moved by Mulock for the Pacific cable. Of the nine participants in the debate only John Charlton offered opposition, preferring that the money be spent on "Continental development,"[111] though twice asserting that he did not oppose the cable *per se*. Retorts to Charlton concentrated on sentimental justifications of the cable's value to imperial unity rather than on estimates of its potential material value. A year later, when the Eastern Extension Company had succeeded in weaning Victoria and New South Wales from the agreement by lower rates and hence requiring a greater Canadian contribution, Mulock admitted Tupper's contention that the cable chiefly concerned Australia: "When I took up this subject, I was of the opinion and had difficulty in discerning the Canadian interests in it. . . . I came to the conclusion that we were common partners in the

---

[106]C.O. 42/868, p. 579, May 11, 1899; indeed Chamberlain had recent cause to complain of Canada's refusal to grant sufficient support by subsidy for a steamship line between Canada and the British West Indies: "If the Canadian Gov^t do not meet us in such a matter how can they expect assistance for Pacific Cable & Fast Service?" (*Ibid.*, p. 317, minute, April 2, 1899.)

[107]*Can. Sess. Pap.* (no. 51), 1899, pp. 63–64, Sandford Fleming to R. W. Scott, May 15, 1899.

[108]See *Parl. Pap.*, 1900, LV (Cd. 46, pp. 6–9, 26–29), pp. 414, and reply pp. 434–37; see also C.O. 42/871, p. 555, clipping of London *Times*, June 30, 1899, and pp. 549–52, for minutes.

[109]C.O. 42/870, p. 139, L. A. Guillemard (sec. to Hicks-Beach) to Lord Ampthill (sec. to Chamberlain), June 2, 1899.

[110]*Parl. Pap.*, 1900, LV (Cd. 46, pp. 24–25), pp. 432–33; cf. C.O. 42/873, p. 205, minute of Chamberlain, June 30, 1899: "I desire to go cordially into this undertaking & make it a success. I recognize that it is a new & exceptional proceeding & if we do not take care it may in its results prejudice co-operation between the Mother Country & the Colonies in the future."

[111]*Debates*, p. 8367; the whole debate is *ibid.*, pp. 8348–82.

scheme . . . that so concerns the Empire that, whether Canada is more or less concerned in it, if we are to take an interest in what concerns the Empire, we should give this scheme our unqualified allegiance."[112]

The prospect of insignificant material gain[113] and the absence of questions of national pride demonstrate something of the political power of imperial unity in Canada during 1899. In the light of Canadian-American relations and the dependence of Canada's existence on British support, the negotiations over the Pacific cable provided Canada with an opportunity to display not unflattering dependence on Britain but proud support of imperial unity. A more spectacular opportunity was provided by moral approval of Britain's position in South Africa.

VII

In July 1899 the House of Commons was twice confronted with the South African question: the offer of Colonel Hughes to lead troops and a resolution in support of the Uitlanders.

The first was provoked by the July 13 news of an official Queensland offer of 250 troops.[114] Hughes again pressed the Government to enrol a force and "fulfil our part as the senior colony," though he himself also renewed his May proposal. In reply Laurier deprecated the need for soldiers, hoped for peace, sympathized with "our fellow-countrymen in Africa," and trusted that the Transvaal would recognize British suzerainty and afford equal "justice . . . to all classes." Tupper likewise hoped for peace, but believed that avoidance of war would come from "outspoken" press support of Britain and Boer knowledge that prospective colonial action would "strengthen the arms of the mother country."[115]

The first step to obtain a resolution was taken at the end of April

[112]Cited in Henri Bourassa, *Great Britain and Canada* (Montreal, 1902), p. xcv; Bourassa termed Canada's position in the scheme as that of a "sentimental paying partner."

[113]Laurier Papers, p. 3045, Sen. L. G. Power to Laurier, "Confidential," May 11, 1899; Canadian opponents of the cable claimed it was primarily a C.P.R. scheme (*Weekly Sun*, July 5, 1899, edit., "ALL-CANADIAN LINES"). Although the C.P.R. stood to gain because of the lease of its land lines, its chief trans-Pacific interest was not Australasia but Japan and the Far East, where its steamships called.

[114]Other Australian offers were made but little attention was paid to them in Canada.

[115]*Debates*, pp. 7328–29, July 13, 1899; see also *Mail and Empire*, July 17, 1899.

1899, in an appeal to the British Empire League in Toronto from the South African League Congress of Kimberley. Probably owing to disdain for a Rhodes interest, the League rejected the request on the ground that it lacked the necessary knowledge but that it was appealing to the headquarters of the British Empire League in London as being "better informed."[116] Nor were the advocates who came to Ottawa at the same time any more successful with Laurier or Minto; Laurier trusted Britain in the matter and Minto discouraged such a resolution as inopportune.[117]

Three months later another attempt was made, this time by J. Davis-Allen, a South African imperialist *par excellence* and a founder of the Imperial South African Association, who arrived in Canada in mid-July. He explained publicly that a resolution in support of the Uitlanders would contribute to a peaceful solution of the South African question.[118] Evidently commanding powerful support in Canada he obtained the use of a Senate committee room to address senators and members of Parliament on the subject.[119] He also founded a parliamentary branch of the Imperial South African Association which, aside from its function of corralling assistance for a resolution, remained moribund.[120]

After this success Davis-Allen visited Denison in Toronto with a letter from Alexander McNeill, M.P., which urged "a very strongly worded resolution" at a meeting of the British Empire League.[121] The league balked and no meeting was held; it was jealous of an intruding organization poaching on its field and probably also wished to keep itself dissociated from a Rhodes organization. Although Davis-Allen failed to

---

[116]Denison to C. Freeman Murray, April 26, 1899, from correspondence read at the June meeting of the British Empire League, cited in *Globe*, Oct. 5, 1899.

[117]Minto Papers, vol. 7, p. 98, Laurier to Minto, May 2, 1899, and Laurier Papers, p. 33237, Minto to Laurier, May 2, 1899; see also Denison Papers, pp. 3737–38, 3747.

[118]Montreal *Star*, July 11 and 12, 1899; for an Australian resolution see J. Castell Hopkins and Murat Halstead, *South Africa and the Boer-British War* (Toronto, 1900), I, pp. 251–52 (volume II seems never to have been published). For Davis-Allen's career, see "A pioneer of Empire," by G. W. P., *MacMillans Magazine*, LXXXIII (March 1901), pp. 386–89, and Denison Papers, Scrapbook, *The Outlook*, Jan. 12, 1901, p. 95.

[119]Montreal *Star*, July 22, 1899; the Speaker of the House, Sir J. D. Edgar, had objected to the use of the Railway Common Room for this purpose (Laurier Papers, pp. 35485–86, to Laurier, "Private," July 14, 1899).

[120]For a list of the Canadian Committee, see Henri Bourassa, *Great Britain and Canada*, p. cxxxiv.

[121]Denison Papers, pp. 3801–3, McNeill to Denison, July 24, 1899, and pp. 3804–7, "Private," July 25, 1899; see also *ibid.*, pp. 3808–13, 3819–31, on this issue.

obtain help from the British Empire League he did convert Denison to supporting Britain's position in South Africa.

Davis-Allen's efforts were ultimately directed to persuading Laurier. He first tried to induce Tupper to move a resolution, but failed because Tupper declared against making the matter a party issue, and counselled a visit to Laurier and conveyance of Tupper's support.[122] Davis-Allen appears to have visited Laurier at least twice and sent him marked blue books on South African problems, a pamphlet, "Handy Notes on South Africa," and other South African material.[123] Apparently as a result of these visits he cabled to England Laurier's willingness to introduce a resolution supporting British supremacy in South Africa provided Chamberlain intimated he wished him to do so. Chamberlain, informed of Laurier's interest by the President of the Imperial South African Association, passed the information on to Lord Strathcona, who immediately cabled Chamberlain's welcome to Laurier.[124] More than a week later Laurier, delayed by sessional business, irately rejoined that "Mr. Allan [sic] had no authority from me to wire as he did,"[125] although Laurier admitted that such a resolution was being considered. Aware of Laurier's difficulties Chamberlain wrote to Strathcona that a resolution would strengthen the British Government, and Canadian opinion under a non-British leader would likely impress Boer leaders and might even restrain American sympathy for the Boers.[126]

What probably also made Laurier angry was the simultaneous Chamberlain inquiry on possible Canadian participation in a South African military demonstration. Chamberlain first called Minto's attention to the fact that the "technical grounds of [the] quarrel are, in themselves, & taken separately, of small account but what is really at stake is the influence of Great Britain and the question whether the British in South Africa are to be dominated by the Dutch." An ultimatum would only be accepted if accompanied by "a great demonstration of material force." If a demonstration were planned, Chamberlain inquired, would a Canadian force spontaneously wish to take part? If so, "it would be welcomed by the authorities," for it would show the unity of the Empire and might maintain peace. Was such an offer probable? It must not,

---

122*Debates*, Feb. 5, 1900, p. 23.
123Laurier Papers, pp. 35580–81, J. Davis-Allen to Laurier, July 17, 1899.
124July 15, 1899, Beckles Willson, *The Life of Lord Strathcona and Mount Royal* (London, 1915), p. 514.
125July 24, 1899, *ibid.* (Boston ed., 1915), II, p. 332. This part of the sentence is omitted from the London ed., p. 514; cf. also Minto Papers, vol. 35, p. 28, Lord Lorne to Minto, Aug. 8, 1899.
126July 27, 1899, Willson, *Life of Lord Strathcona and Mount Royal*, p. 515.

however, be the "result of external pressure or suggestion."[127] In an enthusiastic letter to Laurier on July 19 Minto invited the acceptance of the proposal; it would be proof of imperial solidarity and would strengthen the Empire.[128] He also cabled his assurance of its acceptance by the Canadian people, but advised of the lukewarmness of the Premier, who objected to the expense. "Matters might be accelerated if you cd. give me some hint as to possible assistance from H.M.G.,"[129] a request which the War Office had anticipated on the previous day in regard to the Australian colonies and which the Colonial Office asked be made applicable to Canada.[130] Minto added that this information would only be used in answer to inquiries and "I wd carefully avoid appearance of bringing pressure to bear. Tho' doubtful of the approval of my Govt. I have consulted General [Hutton] as to the nature of the force"; this would probably be a mixed force of 1200.[131] Laurier in effect opposed the Chamberlain inquiry by suggesting to Minto that Canadian troops might be needed in "connection with Alaska," and by making a reference to "war" in Parliament.[132]

Meanwhile further pressure began to build up in the form of intimations from Lord Strathcona, identical cables from at least two parts of South Africa,[133] and newspaper hints of the British Government's wishes.[134] When Tupper showed Laurier one of the latter in a Montreal *Star* dispatch,[135] Laurier agreed to move a resolution and requested

[127]Minto Papers, vol. 14, pp. 40–42, "Secret," July 3, 1899; Minto showed this letter to Laurier on July 17, who took note of the following: ". . . if a really spontaneous request were made from any Canadian force to serve with H.M.'s troops on such an expedition, it would be welcomed by the authorities and all necessary arrangements would be made to accept and carry it out" (notation *ibid.*, by Minto).

[128]O. D. Skelton, *Life and Letters of Sir Wilfrid Laurier* (Toronto, 1921), II, pp. 91–2.

[129]C.O. 42/869, p. 114, Minto to Chamberlain, paraphrase cable, "Secret and Confl.," July 20, 1899.

[130]*Ibid.*, p. 116, C.O. to W.O., draft, "Secret & Immediate," July 22, 1899.

[131]*Ibid.*, p. 114, Minto to Chamberlain, paraphrase telegram, "Secret and Confl.," July 20, 1899; for further details on the force see below, pp. 229–30.

[132]Minto thought this and other strong opinions were "very far-fetched" (Minto Papers, letter book no. 1, p. 134, to Chamberlain, "Private," July 25, 1899).

[133]P.C. 2050, dormants (a "dormant" is a submission to the cabinet which is not acted upon), Uitlander Council, Johannesburg, cable, July 25, 1899, and letter confirming cable from Chairman, Wm. S. Hosken, Aug. 5, 1899; and cable, lacking signature, from Newcastle, Natal, dated July 26, 1899, in Laurier Papers, p. 35936.

[134]Under heading "WANT OUR AID," George Wyndham, Under-Sec. of War, was reported as saying that "proposals were being submitted for Canada's consideration" (*Globe*, July 22, 1899).

[135]Cited in *Debates*, pp. 23–4, speech of Sir Charles Tupper, Feb. 5, 1900.

Tupper, who was about to leave for Britain, to provide a letter of assistance in lieu of seconding the resolution. The letter for Britain, doubtless
went beyond Laurier's wishes, for it stated that "we are bound to give
all the aid in our power to Her Majesty's Government in the present
crisis."[136]

In introducing the resolution Laurier justified Canada's interest in
South African affairs by recognizing that the British Empire's growth
and its "degree of consolidation" made indifference to the fate of any
part impossible. In effect Laurier was affirming that Canada had an
interest in the maintenance of British imperial power. Laurier's chief
justification, however, was an appeal to the conscience of mankind. The
Transvaal ought to grant equal rights to both races as in Cape Colony
and Canada. Canada should also "extend to our fellow-countrymen in
South Africa the right hand of good fellowship." These justifications
formed the basis of a resolution in three parts: the first regretted that
British subjects lacked political rights in the Transvaal "of which Her
Majesty is suzerain"; the second deplored the resulting "intolerable
oppression" and "dangerous excitement"; and the third resolved that
Canada, having harmonized "estrangements" through equality, sympathized with the British Government's efforts to obtain justice and recognition of "equal rights and liberties."[137] Seconding the motion, the acting
leader of the Opposition, George E. Foster, emphasized the value of
imperial solidarity and the racial heritage. Although British subjects in
the Transvaal were "Outlanders," so far as Canada was concerned they
were "Inlanders."

As children with a troubled and strenuous infancy . . . we have being [*sic*]
guided through them by the strong loving hand of a great mother power . . .
we have been given the freest opportunity to indulge our tendencies and our
sympathies; and yet under that lenient and generous sway, every one of
those colonies have come, in the time of their lusty strength, back to the old
motherland to say: We love thee still, we are children of the brood, with
thee we have been and with thee we will ever be.[138]

Of the other two speakers, Conservatives from Ontario, the ardent
imperialist Alexander McNeill commented on the absence of any offer
of "material" help. "It is because everybody knows that material assistance is here, in Canada, at any moment, if it be required." In 1896 the
House had been willing "to render material assistance" but now they

[136]Read by Laurier, *ibid.*, July 31, 1899, p. 8995.
[137]*Ibid.*, July 31, 1899, p. 8994; see app. C. Laurier's whole speech is *ibid.*, pp.
8992–95. This motion is referred to by many contemporaries indiscriminately as
the resolution or resolutions. The text will use the singular only.
[138]*Ibid.*, pp. 8995–96.

knew it was unnecessary to sustain "a one-hundred ton hammer to crack a hazel nut."[139] The short debate ended with a unanimous vote and the singing of "God Save the Queen." On the same day in the Senate a flippant note could be heard in the speech of the octogenarian James R. (later Sir James) Gowan, a leading Conservative. He observed that if the Prime Minister had to appeal "to the people of Upper Canada . . . He has but to say 'Boys I want a thousand or so of you to go to the Transvaal and assist our fellow subjects there to discuss this matter with the Boers. It is a wild country and if you have a gun in your hand it will do no harm.' (Cheers)."[140]

Although a rumbling of racialism had also appeared in the Senate debates,[141] this constituted no threat to the Government's power. But the arguments of Henri Bourassa might well do so. In selecting Monday morning, July 31, 1899, during Bourassa's weekend absence, to move the resolution, Laurier must have known of Bourassa's opposition. On his return Bourassa informed Laurier that the resolution was Chamberlain's scheme "to drag Canada" into "active participation in Imperial wars," and warned that if Laurier should "give way" he (Bourassa) would make a public protest.[142] When Laurier tried to reassure him that the resolution was unimportant and its passage at Davis-Allen's request was to impress the Transvaal Government, Bourassa was sceptical. Kruger would not care and Chamberlain would use it to force Canada's hand. Laurier now confided to Bourassa that at London, in 1897, Laurier had replied "no" to Chamberlain's inquiry whether Canada would send troops to Africa. Bourassa, still unconvinced, replied that even if Laurier repeated the story publicly, Chamberlain would deny it, and recall Laurier's speech: "Let the fire be lit on the hills."[143]

Enclosing a copy of the resolution to Minto, Laurier commented on the Governor General's preference for "material assistance. . . . The present case does not seem to be one, in which England, if there is war, ought to ask us, or even to expect us to take a part, nor do I believe that it would add to the strength of the Imperial sentiment, to assert at this juncture that the colonies should assume the burdens of military expen-

[139]*Ibid.*, pp. 8996–98.

[140]Senate *Debates*, Aug. 1, 1899, p. 1011, c. 2.

[141]*Ibid.*, July 31, 1899, p. 995, c. 2, Sen. A. C. P. Landry. On the following day he was silent. Was pressure put on him to remain silent?

[142]*Debates*, March 13, 1900, p. 1823. When Canadian troops were sent to South Africa, he resigned and was returned by acclamation; see also Minto's memorandum of conversation with Laurier, Nov. 1, 1899, Minto Papers, vol. 1, p. 33.

[143]Robert Rumilly, *Henri Bourassa: la vie publique d'un grand canadien* (Montreal, 1953), p. 47, and see *Debates*, Feb. 5, 1900, p. 44.

ditures, except—which God forbid—in the case of pressing danger."[144] Minto rejoined indignantly that Britain was not asking for assistance, but only that it would welcome a spontaneous offer. This sounds like a quibble. But a widespread Canadian belief existed, which some members of the cabinet shared, that Britain did not want colonial military aid; it had rejected offers in 1885, 1894, and 1896. Consequently, in view of the probable split in the country if an offer were made, the cabinet concealed Britain's willingness to accept a Canadian offer in 1899. Furthermore the two men differed in the implicit purposes of the quasi-national status of Canada. In effect Laurier said to Minto: "Britain should not request troops of Canada for to do so is to treat her not as a nation but as a colony." To this Minto in effect replied: "This is why Britain is not making a request. If Canada makes a spontaneous offer, she will act as a nation." Laurier assumed the national right of Canada to be isolationist; Minto, to collaborate with Britain. Whatever Minto's disappointment, Chamberlain thanked Strathcona for his part, believing that "the action of the Dominion marks a distinct stage in the history of Imperial relations."[145]

In the following year when opposition to participation had arisen, Davis-Allen was singled out as one of the malevolent imperialist devils responsible for participation. But in 1899 no one with any political astuteness could have been deceived by him: the fact of his being an agent of Cecil Rhodes was not unknown,[146] and he stated frankly that his aim was to secure a resolution from Canada. Davis-Allen's real importance lay in evoking opinion on the issue and acting as a go-between for Tupper and Laurier. Tupper's offer to second Laurier in a resolution could scarcely have been interpreted otherwise than as a threat that the Opposition would move a resolution if the Government failed to do so.[147]

But what is most striking about the passage of the July 31 resolution, in the words of the ablest contemporary historian, was the "approving

[144]In the Minto Papers this letter was headed by Lord Minto, "possible offer of troops for S. Africa," July 30, 1899 (presumably July 31), vol. 7, p. 100.

[145]Willson, *Life of Lord Strathcona and Mount Royal*, p. 515; Chamberlain's official reply will be found in *Debates*, March 1, 1901, pp. 701–2; eager South African organizations and individuals also acknowledged the resolution: Laurier Papers, pp. 36364–66, 36442, 37357–60, and *Globe*, Sept. 13 and 16, 1899.

[146]Goldwin Smith warned Laurier of Davis-Allen, and received a "shuffling reply"; Goldwin Smith to Frederic Harrison, Feb. 5, 1909, Arnold Haultain, coll., *Goldwin Smith's Correspondence* (Toronto, 1913), pp. 509–10.

[147]Goldwin Smith to J. X. Merriman, Sept. 12, 1899, *ibid.*, pp. 328–29. Davis-Allen's visit as a "fellow countryman" also testified to Canada's importance within the Empire.

indifference,"[148] even though most people assumed it might mean the dispatch of Canadian troops. Only four members participated in the House of Commons debate and newspaper references are scanty. The Toronto *Mail and Empire* wrote: "We have certain responsibilities as citizens of the British Empire. . . . For our own sakes we must be prepared . . . with any material assistance."[149] The *Westminster*, a Presbyterian Church magazine, commented on the resolution: "We are part of the Empire, and the Empire as a whole is concerned; therefore we are concerned."[150] Under these circumstances, the handful of English-speaking opponents to the resolution were not likely to be able to withstand a movement for participation once Canadian sentiment was fully aroused.[151]

[148]W. Sanford Evans, *The Canadian Contingents and Canadian Imperialism* (Toronto, 1901), p. 12.

[149]Aug. 14, 1899; see also Aug. 1, 1899; the Montreal *Gazette* agreed with this view, Aug. 1, 1899; see also Vancouver *Daily World*, Aug. 11, 1899.

[150]Aug. 5, 1899, cited in Edward A. Christie, "The Presbyterian Church in Canada and Its Official Attitude towards Public Affairs and Social Problems 1875–1925" (master's thesis, University of Toronto, 1955), p. 114.

[151]The principal opponents were Goldwin Smith and Principal Grant, who reversed his stand before the outbreak of war.

15. Hutton, Hughes, and Participation

AFTER THE PASSAGE of the July 31 resolution the South African situation caused little stir among the Canadian public until early October. But in military circles it was a different story. Hughes in particular continued his agitation for a volunteer Canadian force, even to the extent of an appeal to the public. The resulting quarrel between himself and Hutton and the rumours of official Canadian participation in South Africa roused public interest again in Canada's role in the impending war.

I

Until August 1899 Hutton and Hughes seem to have remained on friendly terms with one another. In response to Hutton's request for criticism of the militia in November 1898 Hughes had written a critical, but illuminating, letter to Hutton, especially on conditions in the rural corps.[1] In the initial plan for a brigade of all arms to serve in South Africa Hutton had planned to make Hughes lieutenant-colonel of one of the infantry battalions.[2]

Hughes evidently learned of the existence but not the details of Hutton's plan. Assuming that he was not to be one of its officers he made an offer to enrol and lead a regiment or brigade of Canadians for service with the Imperial Army in accordance with his proposal of the previous May. Hughes made the offer through three channels to avoid pigeon-holing—the fate of previous offers—the first officially through regular militia channels; the second, as a "Canadian" citizen direct to the Minister of Militia; and the third, as a "British subject" direct to the Colonial Secretary.[3]

[1]Hutton Papers, pp. 1102–18, Hughes to Lieut.-Col. C. E. Montizambert, D.O.C. Mil. Dist. No. 3 & 4, Nov. 29, 1898; see C.O. 42/874, pp. 633–35, for official and personal letters dated July 24, 1899.

[2]See below pp. 229–30.

[3]*Can. Sess. Pap.* (no. 77), 1900, pp. 7–8, Hughes to Montizambert, Sept. 2, 1899. (Much of the original material is in A.G. 69122.)

The first was coolly acknowledged; if necessity arose it would be considered with other offers.[4] The second received the Minister's cordial support, but a virtual snub from Hutton to whom Borden referred the offer for an opinion. Nevertheless a minute of council recommended its transmittal to the War Office.[5] As this was an imperial matter Minto officially consulted Hutton on the propriety of Hughes's setting himself up as a kind of representative of the militia and the suitability of his service with British officers.[6] Hutton commented that such representation was a "pure piece of presumption" and that a Canadian force under Hughes, who lacked sufficient military knowledge and experience, would risk being ignored.[7] On returning the minute to Laurier Minto deprecated Hughes's offer as implying Government support; for, when the time came for the Government to consider material aid, it would wish to select officers itself. Hughes's setting himself up as the representative of the militia in effect also discriminated against the rest of the force.[8]

The third approach was cordially acknowledged by the Colonial Secretary. In transmitting the acknowledgement to Hughes, Minto instructed Hutton also to convey Minto's rebuke because of direct correspondence with the Colonial Secretary. Hutton added that the irregularity should be explained.[9] After justifying his offer because of precedent and citizenship in the British Empire,[10] Hughes denied acting contrary to military custom and questioned Hutton's authority to forbid private volunteering to the British Government, and especially the authority "Which permits the General Officer Commanding to receive and transmit any commands from His Excellency, without its being an Order in Council, and then only by order of the Minister of Militia."[11] This letter not only "strained" military discipline, it "*caused the* EXPLOSIONS."[12] In reply Hutton characterized Hughes's letter as a "highly improper and

---

[4]*Ibid.*, July 24, p. 5.

[5]P.C. 1798, July 28, 1899, dormants.

[6]Minto Papers, letter book no. 1, pp. 149–50, "Private," Aug. 10, 1899.

[7]*Ibid.*, vol. 15, p. 78, Hutton to Minto, Aug. 11, 1899.

[8]Laurier Papers, pp. 36477–82, "Private," Aug. 14, 1899.

[9]*Can. Sess. Pap.* (no. 77), 1900, pp. 16–17, C.S.O. to D.O.C. Mil. Dist. No. 3 & 4, Aug. 24, 1899.

[10]Aug. 24, 1899, quoted in speech of Sam Hughes, *Debates*, Feb. 25, 1901, pp. 390–91.

[11]*Can. Sess. Pap.* (no. 77), 1900, p. 9, Hughes to Montizambert, Sept. 2, 1899; note also Hughes's hope that "steps might be taken by the home authorities—of course with the consent and approval, but outside of the Canadian Government —to enrol . . . a corps here" (*ibid.*, pp. 7–8).

[12]Note in Sam Hughes's handwriting beside this letter in *Can. Sess. Pap.* (no. 92), 1903, p. 7, on the copy in Private Papers of Sir Sam Hughes, in the possession of Mr. Justice S. H. S. Hughes, Toronto, Ontario.

insubordinate communication. . . ." To Hughes's plea that he "acted in his capacity as a citizen," Hutton replied that Hughes

offered his military services in his military capacity, to raise a regiment. It cannot be, therefore, considered that his application was made as a citizen, but as an officer of the Canadian Militia, serving under the command of the General Officer Commanding.

It is not within any officer's power to disassociate himself from his duties and responsibilities as an officer holding her Majesty's commission, and to plead as an excuse for disregard of regulations and orders that he is a citizen and, therefore, not amenable to discipline.

Unless a "complete apology" was made, Hutton threatened to submit the correspondence to the Minister of Militia for reference to the Governor General.[13] Although Hughes could legally volunteer to the Colonial Secretary and the Minister of Militia, the acceptance of a volunteer offer was a practical military matter, which a general of Hutton's ability was in a position to judge.

However valid the military grounds for refusal, the form of the refusal was incompatible with Hughes's view of constitutional practice. Minto's and Hutton's official communications did not go counter to the practice of responsible government, for in external military matters Canada was still a colony, and the two men could thus act on their own discretion in an external military affair. Politically, however, Canada by 1899 was ceasing to be a colony. The theory of imperial unity then current regarded Canada as part of one imperial whole, and the military distinction between "imperial" and "colonial" was becoming difficult to maintain. Indeed, to view Canada as a colony was contrary to Hutton's own theory and practice which saw Canada as a political entity co-operating for an imperial purpose but retaining its own national identity. Above all it was contrary to the ideological view of responsible government which held that some Canadian official must be responsible for any actions of a British official in Canada. Hughes's complaint of a colonial military practice helped transform it into a national practice.

Hughes's concern about the constitutionality of his application to Chamberlain, however, receded before his anxiety to obtain a position of command. In mid-August, Hughes wrote a letter—a classic in child-ish recrimination—protesting to Hutton about rumoured appointments of Permanent Force officers to command in the proposed contingent, officers, he argued, who were failures and not representative Canadians. On the other hand he boasted of his own prowess as an athlete, business

13*Can. Sess. Pap.* (no. 77), 1900, p. 11, C.S.O. to D.O.C. Mil. Dist. No. 3 & 4; "Confidential," Oct. 9, 1899.

man, citizen, and soldier. He also lectured Hutton on his own short-comings and castigated Britain for her faults.[14] In reply to this effusion Hutton pointed out Hughes's lack of judgment and self-effacement, and denied rumours of appointments.[15] This letter goaded Hughes into fury. He turned his heaviest sarcasm on lack of self-effacement; it was not to be found in the "Horse Guards" nor the "War Office." But what particularly rankled were contemptuous references to the fighting qualities of Canadians which Hutton apparently made directly to Hughes: Canadians "might as well try to fly to the moon as to take the field alongside British regulars, short of three years training, and not even then, unless led by Imperial officers." Hughes gibed: "Why? could not I retreat or surrender quickly enough to the Boers?" Accompanying this sarcasm came a prescient observation: ". . . . the old plugs of Boer farmers *walloped* the British though the odds were often against them. In the coming Boer trouble a similar result will be found to arise if ordinary British tactics be employed." No longer hoping for a command he concluded that he would use every legitimate means to obtain one.[16]

II

Meanwhile at Minto's request Hutton had planned a contingent because, as we have seen, of the Chamberlain inquiry. Hutton supplied him with a rough draft of its proposed organization and officers, and "sub rosâ" began making arrangements. In accordance with War Office establishments, it was to be a brigade of all arms—mounted rifles, field battery, and infantry. The force, "the minimum consistent" with Canada's dignity, would consist of 1200 officers and men.[17] Within a few days Hutton raised the question with Borden, whom Hutton later described to Minto as enthusiastic.[18] By September 1899 the plans had been worked out in detail. At that time Hutton, evidently moved by the rapid approach of war, began pressing Minto and Borden to offer a

[14]*Ibid.*, pp. 18–23, Aug. 18, 1899.
[15]*Ibid.*, p. 23, Aug. 26, 1899.
[16]*Ibid.*, Aug. 28, 1899, pp. 23–26; quotation on p. 26; the reference to the moon will be found in *Debates*, Feb. 25, 1901, p. 381.
[17]Minto Papers, vol. 15, pp. 100–4, "Private," July 17, 1899, and appendixes; the men were to be paid $1.00 per day and enlisted for six months; total estimated cost—£150,000 (later estimate, $300,000). To raise and embody the force would require 14 days. The phrase "sub rosâ" is in Hutton to Wolseley, Aug. 1, 1899, Hutton Papers, p. 15.
[18]Minto Papers, vol. 18, part II, p. 38, "Private and Confidential," Jan. 31, 1900. This letter is a summary of Hutton's career written before his enforced recall.

contingent without delay—otherwise it would be too late.[19] He also notified Lieutenant-Colonel Oscar C. Pelletier of his intention of making him officer commanding one of the infantry battalions if the Government offered troops.[20] Borden pressed Laurier on the need for speed and informed him that "The General had been working out (privately) a scheme which would involve an expenditure of about $300,000 for 1200 men & 300 horses—The transport if borne by this country w'd cost about as much more i.e. there & back." Laurier replied, deprecating "the scheme of sending an armed force to Africa. . . . We have too much to do in this country to go into Military expenditure."[21]

On September 4, 1899, Hutton wrote to Chamberlain and Wolseley that the Minister of Militia had informed him that a Government offer of a brigade of 1200 men was "practically certain." Hutton also personally proposed volunteering to lead the Canadian force and suggested that in South Africa he should command a combined Canadian and Australian force, emphasizing his own experience, the difficulty of commanding colonial troops, and the importance of such a combined force.[22] Such a scheme would mark the goal of Hutton's endeavours. Minto, however, dampened his enthusiasm; the Government did not then favour sending troops and he would not recommend Hutton's departure because of the harm to the militia,[23] an opinion in which Chamberlain and the War Office concurred.

Two weeks later Minto was still pessimistic regarding participation because he clearly understood the official Canadian point of view.[24] Hutton, on the contrary, was so certain of participation that to avoid the accusation of responsibility for awakening Canadian opinion he made a month-long inspection tour of the West. Just before he left Ottawa, however, the cabinet was twice annoyed with Hutton. First, having obtained Borden's assent, Hutton telegraphed disapproval of the Toronto 48th Highlanders' proposed visit to New York to honour "Admiral

[19]*Ibid.*, vol. 15, p. 109, and vol. 17, p. 16.

[20]"Private and Confidential"; Pelletier, *Mémoires, souvenirs de famille et récits* (Québec, 1940), p. 307; Robert Rumilly, *Histoire de la Province de Québec* (Montreal, n.d.), IX, p. 116.

[21]Laurier Papers, pp. 37194–95, Borden to Laurier, "Private," Sept. 4, 1899, and reply, p. 37197, Sept. 5, 1899.

[22]Hutton Papers, p. 981, to Chamberlain, "Private," Sept. 4, 1899; to Wolseley, *ibid.*, p. 16. He also wrote to Sir Evelyn Wood and Sir Redvers Buller to much the same effect, *ibid.*, pp. 67, 79–80, respectively. Hutton also informed Borden of his desire to volunteer.

[23]Minto Papers, letter book no. 1, pp. 174–75, Minto to Hutton, "Private," Sept. 5, 1899. He later told Hutton that as a matter of justice a Canadian should command.

[24]John Buchan, *Lord Minto: A Memoir* (London, 1924), p. 136, footnote.

Dewey's victories over Spain a power friendly to the British Empire."
Minto shared the regret of R. W. Scott, the acting Premier, that Hutton
had given a political reason for disapproval.[25] In the second place, Scott,
who was not noted for his tact, frigidly inquired of Hutton whether a
few volunteers could be got for South Africa. Knowing that since July
the cabinet had swung against participation partly because of Scott's
own influence, Hutton quickly replied, " 'not a few, but 5,000 without
any difficulty.' " Angrily repudiating this estimate Scott questioned
Hutton's knowledge of Canadian opinion, whereupon Hutton reiterated
to Scott, what he had already told other ministers, that if war came
"Public Opinion would be so expressed as to force any Gov' into sending Troops." Hutton later believed that this incident, which looked like a
threat but was intended as a warning, was the source of the cabinet's
belief that he had offered troops behind its back.[26]

III

Meanwhile Hughes was not to be put off. After Minto and Hutton
had pooh-poohed his scheme, an action which appeared to smack of
professional and Little-England disdain of the colonial militiaman, he
badgered Laurier for permission to make an offer. The upshot was that
Laurier finally rebuffed Hughes,[27] who quoted Hutton to the effect that
Canadians "would not go, were not wanted, and if they went, they would
be a 'menace.' "[28] Moved by this rebuff, and by announcements of war
preparations in England, Hughes sent a letter dated September 18 to
the leading newspapers of Canada with an appeal to those wishing to
enrol men and serve with him on active service. The object of the

[25]Quotation in Hutton Papers, p. 1528, Hutton to Borden, "Private," Sept. 25,
1899; see also *Globe*, Sept. 26, 1899; Minto Papers, vol. 17, p. 21, "Memo re
M. Gen. Hutton's letter, of Sept. 25, 1899," and comment, Sept. 26, 1899, and
pp. 17–18, Hutton to Minto, Sept. 25, 1899; Laurier Papers, pp. 37605–7, Scott to
Laurier, Sept. 25 (?), 1899, and p. 37563, Goldwin Smith to Laurier, Sept. 24,
1899.

[26]Hutton Papers, pp. 1746–47, "My Command in Canada: A Narrative." Sen.
L. G. Power wrote to Laurier concerning R. W. Scott as President of the Senate:
"Scott is too old to go on the bench, and owing to his age and to be frank about
the matter, want of tact, would not be very successful" (Laurier Papers, p. 4665,
"Confidential," June 25, 1896).

[27]Laurier was annoyed. "He objected to any precipitate action, and told me
I was rather presumptuous; that I did not represent anyone except the people of
my constituency, and he was not very sure that I represented them" (*Debates*,
Jan. 30, 1917, p. 256).

[28]Laurier Papers, p. 140224, memorandum "Re friction between Colonel
Hughes and General Hutton, culminating in 1900," and copy of Sam Hughes to
Lord Roberts, Nov. 17, 1908.

appeal, the letter stated, was to "upbuild the British Empire and render justice to one's fellow-countrymen"; the main issue in South Africa was taxation without representation, the "principle advanced in defence of the American war of independence"—a strange precedent to cite in view of the prevailing attitude to the United States in 1899. Newspapers gave the letter a prominent position.[29] By October 3 applications covering about 1200 names had been received.[30]

Hutton telegraphed Hughes to desist, owing to the violation of section 98 of the Army Act, which forbade unlawful enlistment.[31] A statement to this effect also appeared in the press. Hughes denied intending to act out of harmony with the Government or violating the law and derided the author of the published statement as a "weak, vain man."[32] He returned a curt refusal to Hutton's official telegram and confirming letter. Hutton now tried to ridicule him into submission by a jocular reference in the press to Hughes's violation of section 98. Ridicule evidently rankled deeply with Hughes and provoked the most childishly bitter letter complaining of Hutton's slander and demanding its repudiation.[33]

Hughes had not technically violated section 98 of the Army Act; he had not enlisted soldiers for the regular army, he had not even technically asked for names, but had asked those interested in serving with him to send their records and the number and quality of men who would serve under them in case a contingent should be "officially accepted." He later argued that he was acting in his capacity as a private citizen, and therefore did not come under the Army Act.[34] But he certainly violated its spirit, and the distrust he inspired in Hutton is understandable.

Although Hughes's offer was by far the most important, many others were received by the Militia Department.[35] But War Office policy seemed one of confusion: on the one hand, Hutton, presumably one of its agents, and Borden were reported as eagerly sending volunteer offers

[29]For the letter itself see *Debates*, Feb. 25, 1901, pp. 403–4.

[30]*Globe*, Oct. 3, 1899; according to a personal recollection of Maj.-Gen. Garnet Hughes, Sam Hughes's son, 23,000 were finally received; see also MS autobiography, p. 54 (Private Papers of Sir Sam Hughes).

[31]*Can. Sess. Pap.* (no. 77), 1900, p. 17, C.S.O. to D.O.C. Mil. Dist. No. 3 & 4, Sept. 25, 1899; see also Hutton Papers, pp. 251–52, "Strictly Confidential," Sept. 24, 1899, "Interview Dr Borden & Gen. Hutton."

[32]*Globe*, Sept. 30 and 25, 1899.

[33]*Can. Sess. Pap.* (no. 77), 1900, pp. 26–27, "Personal," Oct. 10, 1899.

[34]For Lieut.-Col. Henry Smith's legal comment on Hutton's action, see *Debates*, Feb. 25, 1901, pp. 399–403, 406–7.

[35]For a list of 11 offers, see W. Sanford Evans, *The Canadian Contingents and Canadian Imperialism* (Toronto, 1901), pp. 41–42.

to the War Office; on the other, the War Office on September 30 was reported as not accepting them. In fact Hughes's offer was the only one officially considered by the cabinet for transmittal.

IV

Acceptance of individual volunteer offers would have enabled Canada to avoid making an official offer. Avoidance of an official offer would have prevented the realization of a militarily united Empire, which to imperialists in Britain meant strength against the world and to those in Canada strength against the United States. Accordingly a group of Ontario officers summoned a special meeting at the Toronto Military Institute to press upon the Government the advisability of preparing a contingent. The presence of Sir Oliver Mowat, Liberal Lieutenant-Governor of Ontario as chairman of the meeting,[36] Colonel Denison, and other local military figures mark this meeting of September 30, 1899. Denison proclaimed that the South African question concerned the whole Empire. Canada standing alone would need a much larger force than it possessed; was it right for Canada to continue depending on Britain without rendering assistance? What kind of treatment would Canada have received in the Bering Sea or Alaska questions "if we had not had behind us the power of the empire?" Therefore Canada should prepare to send one contingent, make ready another, and be able to relieve the garrisons at Halifax and Esquimalt. "We have been children long enough, let us show the empire that we have grown to manhood." He then moved a resolution calling upon the Canadian Government to offer a contingent. The meeting was also reminded of Canadian boasts during the Diamond Jubilee and of the need to make them good. Legal difficulties were brushed aside; one speaker asserted that the oath to the Queen required service everywhere, for the "Dominion Government was only a secondary party." A second resolution voiced public support for official assumption of full costs of the contingent, including maintenance and pay in South Africa.[37] Copies of the resolutions were sent to local members of Parliament and to all battalion commanders for reference

[36]On Sept. 5, 1899, Mowat wrote to Hutton: "May I express the pleasure I feel at the seemingly universal appreciation on the part of the Canadian public of your efficient, zealous and successful administration of the Military Department of our Canadian affairs" (Hutton Papers, p. 574).

[37]*Globe*, Oct. 2, 1899, and Col. George T. Denison, *The Struggle for Imperial Unity: Recollections and Experiences* (London, 1909), pp. 261–62; Denison also sent reports of this meeting to Chamberlain and Lansdowne (Denison Papers, pp. 3848–49 and 3850).

to their members. This meeting showed that colonial and imperial motives were entwined with the more important national motives, and its resolutions revealed Hutton's influence. Hutton had steadily imbued the soldiery and the public with confidence in Canada and with expectations of sharing in an imperial war. In contrast to the Toronto Military Institute, the Montreal Military Institute made no recommendation, arguing that " 'it could do no good to volunteer or force the Government's hand in the matter.' "[38]

Coinciding with these resolutions, accurate reports appeared on the military plan that would be carried out if the Government should offer troops. The most detailed report was in an editorial of the *Canadian Military Gazette*, shorter versions of which appeared simultaneously in leading newspapers. In addition to an outline of the plan the editorial, in obvious reference to Hughes, declared it "a criminal act of folly" to appoint an inexperienced amateur militia officer. Accordingly the Government was considering appointing to the command Colonel Ivor Herbert, the former General Officer Commanding.[39] Not much is known of the origin of the editorial.[40] Internal evidence suggests its purpose was to discredit Hughes's scheme, to focus on the Government the resentment of Canadian officers aroused by the implied insult that no Canadian was capable of commanding a Canadian contingent, and to break the official silence of the Government.[41] An important but unpublicized consequence of the editorial was the vehement complaint of Willison to Sifton at the *Globe*'s failure to receive news as early as other papers; "would it not be far better that the pretense of close relations between the *Globe* and the Government should cease . . . ?"[42] Sifton telegraphed that the rumour was "foundationless," deplored the attempt to commit the Government, and declared the matter not determined but under consideration. In an elaborating letter Sifton put the agitation down to a few Tory officers lacking promotion and promised that the Govern-

[38]Quoted by Vanguard, *Mail and Empire*, Oct. 7, 1899.

[39]*Can. Mil. Gaz.* Oct. 3, 1899; *Globe*, Oct. 3, 1899. The last paragraph of the *Gazette* version, which was not given to the press, was an even more direct attack upon Hughes. See app. D.

[40]*La Patrie* accused General Hutton of inspiring "this insulting" editorial (see below, p. 254, n. 7). No question exists that it reflected Hutton's ideas, but he was too shrewd and too confident of the awakening of public opinion to become involved in any plot. The late Fred Williams (historical feature writer of the *Mail and Empire*) informed the writer in 1936 that Capt. (later Col.) E. J. Chambers, who together with Williams himself was then in the employ of the Montreal *Star*, wrote the editorial. But cf. Hutton Papers, p. 772.

[41]For the doubtless intended indignation, see *Mail and Empire*, Oct. 4, 1899, and *Globe*, Oct. 3, 1899.

[42]Sifton Correspondence, p. 55781, "Private," Oct. 3, 1899.

ment would give the *Globe* every possible advantage.[43] The fulfilment of this promise a week later was an important influence forcing the Government to send troops.

The decisive immediate consequence of the editorial was to break the Government's silence, for Laurier at once gave the *Globe* a statement flatly contradicting the editorial. Under the Militia Act, Laurier argued, the Government could do nothing unless it was "for Canada's defence"; and nothing in South Africa menaced Canada. Nor could money for a contingent be spent without parliamentary consent. If Britain's interests were menaced the Government's attitude would be clear, but there were limitations at present. Hence no contingent had been offered, and the War Office had rejected individual offers. The editorial was exclusively an invention, he concluded.[44]

Laurier's statement influenced later Canadian practice in two ways: it became a precedent for the calling of Parliament on the outbreak of war, and for the belief that Canadian participation in war should be "for Canada's defence." Apparently Laurier used the phrase officially at this juncture for the first time; where he derived it is unknown.[45] It first appeared legally in the Militia Act of 1904 (s. 70), which stated that Canada's military action must be "for the defence thereof." In March 1899 Laurier had interpreted section 79 of the Militia Act of 1886 as meaning that Britain could send Canadian troops anywhere in the world, but the use of the phrase "for Canada's defence" was evidently intended to revert to something like the Macdonald interpretation which forbade movement of the militia outside continental North America.[46]

What magnified the impact of Laurier's statement was its contrast with a Montreal *Star* report, published the same day, that Britain would accept, if it had not already accepted, a Canadian offer of troops.[47] The public now knew from that report that Britain would be glad to accept troops, an acceptance whose truth the Canadian Government could no longer ignore or deny, because of the arrival of the official dispatch on which the report was based and which will be analysed below. Laurier's statement exasperated English-Canadian opinion, for it excluded

[43]Willison Collection, pp. 27413–14, Oct. 4, 1899, and pp. 27416–18, "Confidential," Oct. 4, 1899.

[44]See app. E.

[45]Possibly the idea arose from pacifist rights accorded immigrant Doukhobors in 1898–99, against which the French Canadian, L. A. Chauvin (Conservative, Terrebonne), protested (*Debates*, March 27, 1899, p. 504).

[46]See above, p. 190.

[47]See app. F; for discussion of cable on which this report was based see below, pp. 252–53.

military co-operation from the policy of general imperial co-operation. Yet only two weeks earlier at Strathroy in western Ontario, Laurier had given expression to the policy of co-operation so ardently pursued since 1897: "The career of the British Empire is such as to make it encumbent upon every man, wherever he may be within that empire, to strengthen our bonds and the close alliance which we have with the motherland. . . . The motherland is simply wonderful in many respects. It is not more wonderful however politically than it is commercially."[48] Ontario's anti-American pro–imperial unity mood, which we have seen steadily mounting in intensity, had to be catered to.[49] By trying to arrest the military implications of this spirit, Laurier's statement had simply intensified its force. But Laurier saw in participation in South Africa not a united Empire but a divided Canada. In a letter to the editor of the *Globe* he expressed his concern at the "effort . . . systematically planned & carried by some military men, to force us to send a contingent to South Africa." While prepared to ask Parliament "in a real emergency, for millions in money, & thousands of men" he did not think it wise to take part "in all the secondary wars in which England is always engaged." Present action would only gratify a "jingo spirit" which "at present" should be discouraged.[50]

[48]*Globe*, Sept. 20, 1899.

[49]Note that to a considerable degree the Ontario outlook was reflected in Manitoba: see Laurier Papers, p. 37304, A J. Magurn (editor of the *Man. Free Press*) to Laurier, "Confidential," Sept. 10, 1899: "You ask about the political situation in Manitoba. This province is the 'Middle West' and in general sentiment does not differ materially from Ontario, whose people have colonized it." The younger and more active, however, were less conservative.

[50]Willison Correspondence, pp. 17906–8, to Willison, "Private," Oct. 5, 1899; cf. Hutton Papers, p. 1745, "My Command in Canada: A Narrative."

16. The Campaign for Participation

IN RECOMMENDING to the editor of the *Globe* that the "jingo spirit" be discouraged, Laurier apparently did not realize that his rigid stand on boundary negotiations exemplified that same spirit; nor that that spirit in relation to the United States was one of the most important underlying forces bringing about participation. But before participation occurred open manifestations of anti-Americanism had vanished, though the temporary boundary negotiations came to a dreary close and the permanent ones to an impasse, after Canada entered the war.

I

On September 6, 1899, Hay thought the *modus vivendi* at last settled,[1] but Canada still had objections to put forward. Anderson, with Davies, who by September 25 had arrived in Britain, made changes so as to grant United States miners freedom of access along the boundary waters of the Klehini River to Porcupine Creek, protect Canada's revenue rights, and emphasize the "temporary" nature of the agreement.[2] In spite of United States pressure to hasten the signing,[3] Britain mailed— not cabled—the Anderson-Davies changes to Washington. However described, the *modus vivendi* of October 20, 1899,[4] represented a victory for United States power over Canada's and Britain's weakness. This defeat, however, was masked in Canada by enthusiasm for participation in the South African War.

Meanwhile permanent boundary negotiations came to a standstill. To Choate's note of August 9 that, in effect, the Canadian case had been

[1]*Foreign Relations*, 1899, pp. 325–26, Hay to Tower.
[2]C.O. 42/872, p. 424, Davies to Anderson, Sept. 25, 1899.
[3]Cf. Conf. 7340, pp. 108–9, Alvey A. Adee, Acting Sec. of State, to Tower, Sept. 19, 1899, inc. in Tower to Salisbury, Sept. 21, 1899.
[4]*Foreign Relations*, 1899, pp. 328–31, agreement and maps; agreement only in Tansill, pp. 208–9, n. 66, and *British and Foreign State Papers*, XCI, pp. 116–18.

manufactured, Salisbury on October 14 made two replies: (1) the whole boundary was in dispute and (2) Britain had claimed the Lynn Canal area in 1888, whereas the United States had not made its claim until the meeting of the Joint High Commission; recent American settlers had thus occupied contested territory; nor was the exercise of authority in the disputed area admitted by the United States until "very recently." The immediate question, however, was whether the boundary should "be referred to arbitration" as had the Venezuela dispute, which did not differ essentially from the Alaska boundary dispute.[5]

Anderson made a last proposal for an arbitration formula. It was based on the Venezuela arbitration with the added provision that areas with settled governments before March 1898 should remain in present hands and that the losing party in the arbitration should receive compensation possibly—Pyramid Harbor, probably money. Davies objected that it was practically certain that Dyea and Skagway would go to the United States without Canada receiving a practical equivalent.[6]

Chamberlain, after learning of Laurier's rejection of this proposal, saw Davies on October 12. Though agreeing with the Canadian boundary contentions he emphasized that Washington rejected them and therefore the Imperial Government would place in an official dispatch reasons why Canada should accept the last proposal. He explained that the United States would never surrender Dyea and Skagway but that the arbitrator might award Pyramid Harbor to Canada. Davies retorted that there was no guarantee, and that without the reciprocal concession of Pyramid Harbor, it would not be a "matter of the present Government's existence, but of the existence of any government. . . ."[7]

When Davies received the draft of the dispatch he wrote that it was "such a knock down blow to us" that he found it virtually impossible to improve,[8] though he did make observations that softened its tenor. The draft introduced little that was new, but Davies' comments disclose some of the Canadian Government's fears. He protested against the overemphasis on Canada's acquiescence in the building of Dyea and Skag-

[5]*A.B.T.*, IV, pp. 132–38, "Confidential," Salisbury to Tower, Oct. 14, 1899; quotations, pp. 138, 137; note Conf. 7340, pp. 109–14, C.O. to F.O., "Confidential," Sept. 30, 1899, on which the Salisbury dispatch was based.

[6]Laurier Papers, p. 215105, Davies to Laurier, cable, Oct. 2, 1899; Anderson argued that the proposal would enable Canada to build a town alongside Skagway, but Davies countered that there would not be enough room (*ibid.*). It is inconceivable that Americans would have permitted such a scheme.

[7]*Ibid.*, pp. 225389–93, Davies to Laurier, "Private and Confidential," Oct. 12, 1899; *inter alia* Chamberlain requested Davies to read the draft dispatch over to make suggestions.

[8]C.O. 42/874, p. 346, Davies to Anderson, "Private," Oct. 19, 1899.

way, and against the statement that "transfer could not be peaceably effected," in the unlikely contingency that they were awarded to Canada. The United States (Government?) would not break the agreement but its citizens "on the spot . . . wd resist, and it is practically certain they wd." The draft also warned Canada of the dangers of an unsettled boundary and closed on a more conciliatory note of recognition of the Government's responsibility for Canadian interests and a promise to continue trying to make an agreement acceptable to Canada.[9]

Doubtless the severity of the draft was primarily due to Canada's all-or-nothing attitude[10] and the strength of the United States case. It must also have been due to Davies' admission that the United States would inevitably receive Dyea and Skagway by arbitration,[11] and to his virtual admission that if at the next election his Government were "returned to power, [it] would probably bow to the inevitable."[12] By the time of the "Very Confidential" dispatch of November 1, 1899,[13] Chamberlain had obtained the military assistance of Canadians and no longer needed to "indulge our tendencies and . . . sympathies," in Foster's phrase,[14] in virtually meaningless diplomatic negotiations[15] which denied the realities of history and power.

II

Only a handful of Canadians were to know of Britain's stiffening attitude, and until the Laurier statement of October, English Canada maintained its defiant posture against the United States. In August the Toronto *Mail and Empire*, for example, acclaimed in a two-column heading a London *Times* analysis of the boundary dispute.[16] The Halifax *Chronicle* cited with approval the Hamilton *Times* objection to Canada's surrendering important claims in advance.[17] Laurier marched at the head of this sentiment. In August he was reported as refusing to

[9]*Ibid.*, pp. 347–56, Chamberlain to Minto, draft "Very Confidential," Oct. 19, 1899, with pencil notations by Davies and one by Anderson.
[10]*Ibid.*, p. 338, comment of Anderson, Oct. 4, 1899.
[11]*Ibid.*, p. 340, minute of Anderson to Chamberlain, Oct. 4, 1899.
[12]*Ibid.*, p. 345, Anderson to Sir R. Herbert, Oct. 19, 1899.
[13]*Ibid.*, pp. 358–68, Chamberlain to Minto, draft, "Very Confidential," Nov. 1, 1899; contains a note written by Chamberlain: "Not intended to be published & in no case to be published except at the request of Canada" (*ibid.*, p. 346); for an explanation see *ibid.*, pp. 345–46.
[14]*Debates*, July 31, p. 8996; see above, p. 222.
[15]See John A. Garraty, *Henry Cabot Lodge* (New York, 1953), chap. xiv, "Settling the Alaskan Boundary," where the writer shows how power and interest, not legal argument, decided the issue.
[16]Aug. 14, 1899.
[17]Sept. 1, 1899; cf. comment in *Can. Mag.*, XIII (Oct. 1899), p. 575.

attend a Chicago ceremony—which he did in fact attend—because of harsh United States press comments and "misrepresentations" about himself. He only denied the truth of the report after three days when a Conservative member protested that "we were not at war with the United States."[18] In late September he reaffirmed that if improvement in relations with the United States was "to be paid by the sacrifice of Canadian honor" he would not pay it, for the aim of his Government was "Canada first, Canada last and Canada always. (Loud Cheers.)"[19] In October he observed before the President of the United States, the Vice-President of Mexico, Ignatio Mariscal, and other public figures at the Chicago ceremony that though good, the relations of Canada and the United States were "not as good, as brotherly, as satisfactory as they ought to be."[20]

These anti-American attitudes, their vehement expression in Parliament, and Laurier's remarks—especially concerning "war"—were noticed in the United States. In October the New York *Journal* published a cartoon depicting Laurier and Tupper as midgets shouting "War! War!" while (Brother) Jonathan and John (Bull) laughed together, saying: "It takes two to make a quarrel." A cartoon in the New York *Herald* showed John Bull with a British lion beside him watching Canada, depicted as a young girl, pulling feathers from the tail of the American eagle. Uncle Sam, sitting behind the eagle, observed to John Bull: "If the small person is not restrained the eagle may lose his temper."[21] With such intense antagonism prevailing, Laurier's statement, by shutting the constitutional door to participation in an imperial war and breaking the spell of imperial unity, disclosed to English Canadians the possibility of abandonment to the United States. In the shock of this realization, attacks on the United States gave place to attacks on the Government and on French Canadians, and to efforts to force the dispatch of troops, that is, bring about imperial military unity. This agitation provided a welcome escape from a frightening tension against the United States. During the South African War the Alaska boundary question quickly ceased to be a national issue.[22] Yet it was the underly-

[18]*Debates*, Aug. 7, 1899, pp. 9695–96; Aug. 8, 1899, pp. 9839–43; Aug. 11, 1899, p. 10220; see also Laurier Papers, pp. 36425 and 36458–61.

[19]*Globe*, Sept. 20, 1899; this speech at Strathroy was probably the one evoking Hay's comment to Henry White as "most injudicious" ("Most Confidential," Sept. 24, 1899, Tansill, p. 207).

[20]*Globe*, Oct. 10, 1899.

[21]Cartoons reproduced in W. Sanford Evans, "Current Events Abroad," *Can. Mag.*, XIII (Oct. 1899), pp. 574–75.

[22]Cf. the *Debates* for 1900 and 1901 in which Canadian-American problems on the Alaska boundary and the Yukon practically disappear.

ing issue that brought Canada into the South African War. As Hutton wrote to Minto on October 6:

> I have been watching public opinion and I feel certain that the Cabinet will be obliged to send out, or at least offer a Contingent for service in South Africa. If they do not do so, all confidence in the practical value of Canadian loyalty will receive such a shock that even Canadian securities will be affected.
>
> Considering that the Laurier Gov[t] are expecting the Imperial Gov[t] to force the Alaskan Boundary Question upon the U.S. Gov[t], & that Sir Wilfrid himself refered [*sic*] to arbitration or war (which latter can only mean armed intervention by the Imp. Gov[t]) I do not understand how they can hold aloof from giving material support to the Imperial Gov[t] in the present Crisis.[23]

III

Opposition attempts to force participation threatened to damage the Government. As early as September 27, Tupper at the Halifax Exhibition had called for enlistment of a regiment of 1000 or 1200 men and promised Opposition support. But the Conservative party as such was of far less importance in arousing public sentiment than the party press, especially the Montreal *Star*. The *Star* in 1899 was one of the most extreme[24] and financially successful journals in Canada, and a follower of the practices of its yellow contemporaries in Britain and the United States. Its philanthropic owner, the energetic Hugh Graham (later Lord Atholstan, 1848–1938), provided financial aid to the defeated Conservative party and encouraged imperial unity: in the Venezuela crisis, he had offered to raise troops, in 1897 he collected $71,000 for Indian famine relief, and in 1899 he secretly provided insurance for the first 1,000 volunteers for South Africa.

The *Star*'s encouragement of J. Davis-Allen suggests a close relationship between certain types of Canadian and British imperialists. The same is suggested by the employment as its London correspondent of Percy (later Sir Percy) Hurd; in 1898 he became editor of the new imperialistic weekly, the *Outlook*, whose chief supporter was George Wyndham, Parliamentary Under-Secretary of War and close associate of the Rhodes interests. Hurd's dispatches provided a convenient channel to retail information to Canada. In July 1899 Tupper had used the information of one such *Star* dispatch, as we have seen. The October 3

---

[23]Minto Papers, vol. 15, p. 35.
[24]Cf. Henri Bourassa: "Whoever thought of reading the Montreal *Star* for an idea or a principle? Just as well to study Chinese with a German grammar and a French dictionary." (*Debates*, March 13, 1900, p. 1807.)

news report of the British Government's acceptance of an offer of troops was, according to Minto, of decisive importance in forcing the Government's hand.[25]

The campaign of the *Star* before participation was unique in Canadian journalistic history. In its editorials during that time nationalism, imperial unity, and loyalty were recurring themes. An editorial of September 29, 1899, contended that postponement of action "would be humiliating to our national pride," because Britain was fighting "for justice, civilization and the extension of British liberty." On October 3 the *Star* warned that, should British prestige collapse, Canada would never gain its rights in the Bering Sea or on the Alaska boundary; not only was it "Canada's duty" to help demonstrate "imperial unity and imperial strength," it was to her interest. "The chief obstruction" to sending troops was a "miserable constitutional subterfuge," a position "humiliating and disgracing Canada in the eyes of the whole world."[26] Canada, the *Star* taunted on October 7, "must not be ranked as a colony of full dress parade cowards."[27] This theme of cowardice and disloyalty appeared in editorials, news stories, patriotic verse, interviews, requoted editorials, and the like. The opinions of prominent Montrealers were printed in a column headed "For Motherland!" Most of the interviews asserted that troops should be dispatched to South Africa, not because of need, but in gratitude and to show a "genuine national Canadian spirit."[28] On October 7 the paper proposed a scheme of volunteer sharpshooters. It quoted extracts from "Canada's Loyal Press"; on October 6, for example, the outcry of the Brockville *Times*: "The beggarly idea of sponging upon the Motherland is repugnant to every Canadian worthy of the name."

By October 7 the theme of racial hatred was also appearing. The paper began by saying that most French Canadians were loyal, and that the blame should fall on their leaders. Israel Tarte, the Tory renegade, was selected as a prime target of invective, and Laurier was denounced for his failure to represent the real sentiments of French Canada: J. G. H. Bergeron and R. Préfontaine were commended as members of Parliament who favoured participation.[29] If only English and French Canadians would fight side by side, the *Star* contended, a bond of sympathy

[25]Minto Papers, letter book no. 1, p. 195, Minto to Hutton, Oct. 9, 1899.
[26]Oct. 4; cf. a more moderate statement of the same idea in Montreal *Gazette*, Oct. 6, 1899.
[27]Cf. headline on p. 12: "UNITED CANADA AT GREAT BRITAIN'S COMMAND."
[28]Robert Bickerdike, member of Quebec Legislative Assembly (Oct. 5).
[29]Oct. 13, "The Cowards in Council."

would be created.[30] Critical readers must have wondered whether an English Canadian's duty was to conquer the Boers or the French Canadians. In the week before Canada entered the war a cruder Toronto newspaper was virtually saying as much.

The *Star* could have laboured under few illusions about the real sentiments of French Canadians, especially from the result of its most influential device: the dispatch to municipal officials, commanding officers, and other important citizens throughout Canada of some 6,000 telegrams, urging Canadians to fight.[31] The following telegram sent to the Mayor of Sorel, Quebec, was presumably typical: "Montreal, October 9th, 1899. To the Mayor of Sorel, we are asked if Mayors & others feel it a good thing to do to send a Canadian Contingent to the Transvaal immediately; thousands are responding in the affirmative; do you approve of it? Kindly answer quickly at the Star's expenses [*sic*] B. A. MacNab, ed. Star. Montreal."[32] Of the thousands of replies that the *Star* said poured into its office, the overwhelming majority from English Canada favoured a contingent; apparently an even greater proportion from French Canada were opposed.[33]

In general the published telegrams argued that Canada's practices should follow her professions: Canada should neither neglect her duty nor act as a coward;[34] since Britain had supplied protection in the past, Canada should offer assistance now, and "assume some of the responsibilities of Empireship";[35] the resolutions passed by Parliament seemed inconsistent "without practical steps being taken";[36] "Britain's extremity is Canada's opportunity";[37] "Pack them off at once."[38]

A few telegrams against participation from English-speaking areas were printed in the hope of public repudiation. The city council of

---

[30]Oct. 9; but see huge insulting half-page cartoon, Oct. 7.

[31]Minto Papers, vol. 20, pp. 31–49; according to the late Fred Williams, then employed by the *Star*, the telegrams were sent to every clergyman, reeve, and mayor, as well as to other prominent persons in Canada.

[32]Laurier Papers, p. 38009, inc. in C.O. Paradis, Mayor of Sorel, to Laurier, Oct. 13, 1899.

[33]Minto Papers, vol. 20, pp. 45–49; only a few French-Canadian replies, practically all opposed, appeared in the *Star*.

[34]*Ibid.*, p. 41, Lieut.-Col. Wm. Oxley, O.C. 93rd Batt., Oxford, N.S., Oct. 10, 1899: "We don't court war, but a nation of poltroons is more calamitous than war."

[35]*Ibid.*, p. 41, W. McSween of Leamington, Ont., Oct. 7, 1899.

[36]*Ibid.*, p. 39, A. C. Bertram, Mayor of North Sydney, N.S., Oct. 8, 1899.

[37]*Ibid.*, p. 36, T. H. Williamson, Mayor of Grenville, Ont., Oct. 11, 1899.

[38]*Ibid.*, p. 37, George Brasher, Tillsonburg, Ont., Oct. 7, 1899; this telegram was not published in the edition examined.

Saint John, New Brunswick, whose Mayor had opposed the dispatch of troops, passed a resolution approving Canadian support of the English people, because "the loyalty of St. John was considered to be at stake. . . ."[39] Similarly at a special meeting the Mayor of Moncton, New Brunswick, was censured.[40] To heighten the effect of the published replies, they appeared under such headings as "HALIFAX'S HEART IS RIGHT," "BROCKVILLE SPEAKS FOR ENGLAND," and "PARRSBORO, N.S., DOESN'T SKULK."[41]

The complaints at these telegrams, attempts of the Liberal press to discount their importance, and observers' opinions[42] concerning their importance suggests that the telegrams were politically influential: they registered English-Canadian sentiment, forced recipients in composing replies to make up their minds on the question of dispatching troops, and transformed a powerful sentiment into a political force.

With the failure of the telegrams immediately to move the Government, the *Star* grew more sensational. On October 9 its headline blazed forth, "CANADA STANDS FOR THE FLAG—THE HEATHER IS ON FIRE!" By October 11, the date of the expiry of Kruger's ultimatum, the campaign of the *Star* reached a crescendo. The top corner of one page (see Fig. 2) contained a large Canadian ensign on which was written "CANADA TO THE EMPIRE." The headline, "OUR COUNTRY MUST BE KEPT BRITISH," was followed by a quarter page of rather incoherent thrusts.

Having outdone itself in this effort, the *Star* in the next two days provided an anticlimax: "Shame on Canada!" it chided, "THE BOERS BLOW BRITISHERS TO PIECES!" and "THE OTTAWA GOVERNMENT STILL DALLIES."

IV

In 1899 nothing could have been better calculated to pit English and French Canada against one another than accusations of disloyalty. Loyalty had a threefold meaning for English Canadians in the nineties: the traditional and individual loyalty to the Queen and to British institutions which, except in time of crisis, was usually taken for granted;

[39]*Globe*, Oct. 10, 1899.

[40]*Star*, Oct. 18, 1899; Henri Bourassa informed the writer in 1935 that a Montreal *Star* reporter had told him that many of the telegrams were twisted. That may well be for small unimportant towns, but unlikely for large ones; cf. J. A. Hacking, Mayor of Listowel, Ont., in a letter to *Globe*, Oct. 26, 1899.

[41]*Star*, Oct. 7, 1899.

[42]It was the opinion of Fred Williams—and his associates on the Montreal *Star* staff—and many of the informed contemporaries of the event, whom the writer spoke to in the 1930's, that the telegrams were influential.

LAST EDITION.

The Montreal Daily Star.

VOL. XXXI N. 239.   MONTREAL, WEDNESDAY, OCTOBER 11, 1899.

DAILY STAR   51,221
Last Week's Average
WEEKLY STAR   106,551
Last Week's Issue
Average Circulation   157,772

PRICE ONE CENT

OUR COUNTRY MUST BE KEPT BRITISH.

All Canada Rises In Its Might and Forces the Hands of the Government by United Protest of Press and People.

While Tarte is Declaiming Against the Kind of British Connection the People Want, and Colonel Laurier is Holiday Making in Chicago, the Cabinet Takes Fright at the Patriotic Attitude of the Conservative Leader—The Warnings of Commanding Officers and the Murmurings of an Insulted Nation—A Half Hearted and Much Belated Patriotism—The Cabinet Acknowledges Its Humiliation.

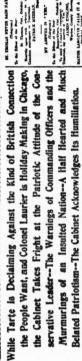

CRAWLING TO COVER

Globe Announcement of October 9th.

Globe Announcement of To-day.

loyalty to Canada as a fact and as an idea; and, because Canada lacked the economic, political, or military strength to stand alone and needed Britain's support, loyalty to the Empire in the sense of pursuit of common policies for Canada and Great Britain. The previous two years had seen the well nigh unanimous approval of imperial unity: French Canada had acquiesced in imperial preference, penny postage, and the like; when it failed to second the dispatch of troops on behalf of imperial unity, the cry of disloyalty seemed not unreasonable to English Canadians.[43]

French Canadians resented accusations of disloyalty, for they were quite loyal to their own way of life, and if attacked would have defended their country's membership in the British Empire. Their real interest, or rather their real love, was for French Canada and its culture, its language, its customs, and its faith. Until October 1899 they had generally been indifferent to Canada's external relations, but they would resist the military expression of imperial unity. The form of their opposition to participation was conditioned by the nature of the racial onslaught and by the character of Israel Tarte. Tarte was Minister of Public Works in the Laurier cabinet and owner of *La Patrie*, the most influential, and in many ways typical, of French-Canadian newspapers. Writing in 1905 André Siegfried sensed that French Canada still bore the burden of the defeat of 1759,[44] which Tarte seemed to reflect. In character he resembled Sam Hughes in his extremism, contradictions, moods, and excitability, and these were all apparent in his newspaper. In the Boer War crisis, *La Patrie* asked, why should French Canadians fight the Boers who were struggling "for their independence, language, and peculiar customs?"[45] *La Patrie* reminded its readers that the English soldiers had been "beaten by the Boers in 1881 and that Kruger was well prepared to face eventualities."[46] On the other hand, Tarte, interviewed in Europe in September, stated that if the French Canadians in the Cana-

[43]Cf. N. Clarke Wallace, an extreme Conservative Ontario Orangeman: those opposing dispatch of troops "say they are loyal to Canada. Nonsense. They cannot be loyal to Canada and disloyal to the other portions of the empire. We are one and indivisible with the empire, and disloyalty to one part of the empire is disloyalty to all." (*Debates*, Feb. 16, 1900, p. 542.)

[44]André Siegfried, *The Race Question in Canada* (London, 1907), p. 247; see also Pope Papers, Correspondence 1896–1898/N-Q, docket 36P, Joseph Pope to R. W. Scott, "Private," Oct. 1, 1899: ". . . some of the French Canadians are extremely sensitive, and are always imagining slights where none are intended."

[45]Minto Papers, vol. 20, p. 22, in the words of the summary provided by Tupper.

[46]Sept. 16, 1899. There was some expression of racial sentiment in September against Anglo-Saxon attitudes to the Dreyfus trial.

dian Northwest were refused the vote like the Uitlanders they would fight.[47]

Neither Tarte nor his newspaper remained silent as the *Star* attacks continued. *La Patrie* and other French-Canadian newspapers warmly welcomed Laurier's statement in the *Globe*. Using, but somewhat misconstruing, Tupper's arguments, which concerned the manner in which troops should be offered, Tarte argued that Canada had enough to do in building up the country.[48] "The Real Enemies of the Empire,"[49] wrote *La Patrie*, were the Tories with their accusations of disloyalty against Laurier. *La Patrie* also denounced French Canadians, like Bergeron and Préfontaine, who consented to the dispatch of troops. On October 13, it suggested that the *Star*'s campaign was "against M. Laurier," to restore Tupper to power, and to "make Mr. Hugh Graham a knight."[50]

Perhaps the most vehement opposition came from Odilon Desmarais, Montreal member of Parliament, who at a public meeting in Montreal on October 12, 1899, in the presence of F. G. Marchand, Premier of Quebec, and other important French-Canadian politicians, denounced the Conservative newspapers. They wanted the Laurier Government to send troops to make money from the sons of French Canadians dispatched "to fight with Zulus and Barbarians." But the "first loyalty" of French Canadians was to their "country . . . families . . . children." Transvaal affairs were none of their business, and participation was being raised to placate "soldiers burning with Jingoism."[51]

V

The Liberal English-speaking newspapers denounced the extremism of their Conservative counterparts, but the denunciations frequently concealed their own approval of the dispatch of troops. The Halifax *Chronicle*, for example, maintained that the *Star*'s dispatches were "evidently largely fiction based on a substratum of truth," but colonial troops in South Africa would demonstrate the solidarity of Empire and please the majority of Canadians, though the Government could not exceed its powers.[52] Furthermore, headings of news stories often

[47]*Globe*, Sept. 13, 1899, Montreal *Star* cable.
[48]*La Patrie*, Oct. 11, 1899, speech at the Montreal Reform Club.
[49]Oct. 10, 1899, title of editorial.
[50]Edit., "La Crise hystérique du 'Star'."   [51]*Star*, Oct. 12, 1899.
[52]Oct. 6, 1899, edit., "Canada and the Transvaal"; also Oct. 11, 1899, edit., "The Jingo Patriots," which assumed that if troops were needed they would be forthcoming.

contradicted their contents. The heading might be enthusiastic for participation but the contents might denounce the *Star's* sensationalism or explain the Government's inability to act.[53] The *Manitoba Free Press* displayed prominently the British news report of October 3 under the heading "The Solidarity of The Empire." It assumed that if war broke out troops "should be organized and equipped at Canada's expense and . . . led by a Canadian officer." But a Canadian force was not a matter of need: "The idea is born of the Imperial spirit now so plainly manifested on every hand" and if Canada and Australia made offers the Imperial Government would likely accept them.[54] The announcement of October 11 that the Government intended to offer troops produced gratification, but no surprise in view of the July 31 resolution.[55]

But Nova Scotia and Manitoba sentiment was of far less importance than Ontario's and especially Toronto's. Hence the position of the *Globe*, the chief English-speaking Government organ, was crucial. Would the *Globe* be able to marshal Ontario sentiment behind the Premier's do-nothing policy of October 3 or not? Already, as we have seen, the tide was moving towards participation. On October 7 the *Mail and Empire* demanded "A Contingent at Once" to demonstrate Canadian membership in the Empire and assist oppressed "fellow-subjects" in the Transvaal. With the publication in the *Mail and Empire* of some of the Montreal *Star's* telegrams the latter's frenzied influence penetrated to Toronto. The former's belligerence now assumed overtones of racialism. The head of the Canadian Red Cross Society and prominent Conservative, Dr. G. Sterling Ryerson, actually wrote to the editor: "It is time, sir, to wake up in this country to the fact that we may have questions to settle which may not be set at rest by the ballot."[56]

At a more offensive level the same evolution of racial rancour may be detected in the Toronto *Evening News*. This paper, apparently appealing to lower middle class readers, had long made periodic attacks on French Canadians because it believed they were working to create a separate state.[57] In October the *News*, hitherto carrying only a small amount of South African news, contended that Canada should do its duty. When the Montreal *La Presse* opposed French-Canadian participation on October 5 the offensiveness of its editorial to English Cana-

[53]Halifax *Chronicle*, Oct. 9, 1899; see *ibid.*, Oct. 6, 1899, front-page heading, "Colonial Troops for Transvaal," to the *Star's* London cable of Oct. 3, 1899.
[54]Oct. 9, 1899, edit., "Canada and the Transvaal."
[55]*Ibid.*, Oct. 12, 1899, edit., "The Ottawa Government's Action."
[56]Oct. 12, 1899.
[57]Sept. 20, 1899.

dians caused it to explain that the opinion had been mistakenly printed as an editorial rather than as a letter. The *News* suggested that this opinion represented the real attitude of French Canadians; why did not a French-Canadian regiment show its professed loyalty by volunteering?[58] On October 10 a heading blustered on the front page: "The French Canadians oppose a Contingent."[59] On October 12 a front page editorial warned that *La Patrie's* words were those of an "enemy." Ontarians were convinced of the necessity of "depriving" French Canadians of "special privileges," and if it could not be done "through the ballot boxes . . . other means" would be found. The *Globe's* opposition to the campaign of the *News*, a contemporary it usually ignored, suggests something of the power of racial antagonism. May not its power also have been strengthened by association with imperial unity, itself temporarily strengthened and transformed in the process from a class to a mass movement?

Amidst such intense feeling the Toronto *Globe* could no longer remain aloof. It denounced the *Mail and Empire* for raising the race issue and *La Presse*, for the same offence and for ridiculing the idea of a contingent. Denying that French Canadians opposed a contingent, it argued that Roman Catholics had freedom in Canada, but they lacked such rights in the Transvaal. It did not think a French Canadian preferred "Dreyfus justice to British justice. . . ."[60]

Willison wrote years later that to avoid embarrassing the Government the *Globe* did not advocate the dispatch of troops before the Government's decision. Its stand on the race question is one indication that it was not so "detached and indefinite" as thought.[61] Furthermore to answer Opposition charges of Government disloyalty, the *Globe* said the Government would loyally send troops when needed. On October 7 it took a position like that of *La Patrie*—Parliament ought to be consulted. Though condemning the *Star's* methods it made the English-Canadian press assumption: "We know . . . Canada will not fail in any duty that may be expected of her."[62] Although attacking the *Star's* extremism, on the South African question the *Globe* upheld British contentions wholeheartedly. Its news columns featured with appropriate headings the latest Rhodes-coloured dispatches. It reported the British

[58]Margaret A. Banks, "Toronto Opinion of French Canada during the Laurier Regime, 1896–1911" (master's thesis, University of Toronto, 1950), pp. 35–36.
[59]See also Oct. 11, 1899, edit., "The French rule Canada."
[60]*Globe*, Oct. 11, 1899.
[61]Sir John Willison, *Reminiscences Political and Personal* (Toronto, 1919), pp. 303–5.
[62]*Globe*, Oct. 9 and Oct. 10, 1899.

Empire League's resolution and published letters desiring Canada to offer troops.

The decisive *Globe* influence came from its Ottawa news correspondent, Roden Kingsmill. On October 5 he at first branded the British report of October 3 as "totally untrue," but this denial appeared in an unimportant place in the *Globe*. On the next day he qualified the denial, but added that if "necessity for official action arises" the Government would "doubtless be sustained by public opinion." On the following day, October 7, he tried to create the impression of Canadian-British harmony, and stated that plans were ready to aid Britain. On October 11 came the decisive news story, printed by no other newspaper at that hour, with an inch-high front-page headline: "WAR INEVITABLE—THE CANADIAN CONTINGENT PREPARING." This news story detailed the nature of the proposed contingent and recited the main terms of the Chamberlain dispatch. On the next day Borden publicly confirmed the *Globe*'s " 'exclusive news . . .' " and announced that the Imperial Government had been informed "weeks ago" of Canada's readiness.[63]

The *Globe*'s exclusive news story seemed partly the answer of some ministers to the editor's complaint of failure to receive important news, for Borden would scarcely have acted without Sifton's, probably Mulock's and other cabinet ministers' consent. The dispatch was evidently intended, too, as reassurance for the Government's English-Canadian supporters and constituted an answer to Tarte and *La Patrie*, whose Ottawa correspondent denied on October 12 that any formal decision had been made. Although the *Globe*'s views did not externally contradict those of *La Patrie*, the tone, the implications, and the headline all suggested the Government would send troops. The Conservative press was of course delighted to see the split and tried to wedge the papers completely apart. Both the Montreal *Star* and the Toronto *Mail and Empire* reprinted the conflicting Liberal views side by side.

VI

Newspaper sentiment does not necessarily constitute public sentiment, but in October 1899 the press revealed the opposition of French Canada to dispatching troops and the enthusiasm of English Canada

[63]Borden had already informed the *Globe*'s editor of his intention to make a public statement, but added: "Of course the question of policy is one with which I have nothing to do except in so far as I am a member of the Cabinet" ("Private," Oct. 10, 1899, Willison Correspondence, p. 2209; see also Hutton Papers, p. 203, Lieut.-Col. H. Foster to Hutton, Oct. 9, 1899). The October 11 news report in the *Globe* was incorrect in a few minor details.

for action; and the *Globe*, by revealing headquarters plans, excited the military hopes of English Canadians.[64] When Britain declared war on October 11, 1899, English-Canadian enthusiasm was not to be denied. Large crowds gathered in Toronto the next day to watch the Queen's Own Rifles drill. In contrast to conditions in 1885, when dismissal threatened some employees who left to take part in the North-West Rebellion, many employers encouraged enlistment in 1899. The Ancient Order of Foresters promised to look after the benefits of its enlisted members. The Ontario Mutual Life Assurance Company of Waterloo permitted its policy holders to serve without their policies lapsing.[65] On October 13, the Canadian Club of Toronto sang the national anthem, cheered the Queen, and passed a resolution that "a Canadian Contingent should be sent to South Africa in the present crisis."[66] The South African War was now in progress and the pressure for Government participation was becoming irresistible.

[64]In 1936, the late T. Stewart Lyon of Toronto, a city editor of the *Globe* in 1899, stated to the writer that the *Globe's* influence was decisive in forcing the Government's hand; and the late W. D. Gregory, K.C., an editorial writer of Goldwin Smith's *Weekly Sun* in 1899, offered the same opinion.

[65]*Globe*, Oct. 12 and Oct. 13, 1899, respectively.

[66]*Ibid.*, Oct. 14, 1899; it also reported an outburst of patriotism among members of the Corn Exchange in Montreal when "Rule Britannia" was sung to them (Oct. 13, 1899). Under the heading "APOLOGY" a Halifax whiskey vender advertised that "owing to the excitement over the Exhibition, Yacht Races [Shamrock Cup] and Transvaal war" he had run out of Royal Scotch Whiskey (*Chronicle*, Oct. 12, 1899).

17. The Offer of an Official Contingent

WHATEVER Canada's imperial or national aspirations, Canada was still a colony, so far as important military and foreign relations were concerned, and the mother country could determine the decisive conditions of acceptance of troops for South Africa. The Colonial Secretary laid down the conditions in a circular cable of October 3, 1899, which, as has been shown, was reported—that is, leaked—to Canada. The cable and the report stirred bitter controversies, for the cable seemed to be the acceptance either, in Bourassa's words, of "offers . . . never . . . made,"[1] or of an offer made, possibly by Hutton, behind the Government's back.

I

The cable itself was an edited version of a War Office letter to the Colonial Office accepting the apparently unacknowledged individual and government offers received from the self-governing colonies. It specified that four companies from Canada and two from each of the other colonies would be welcome. These companies, it later transpired, were to be attached to British units. Gone was Hutton's scheme of a mixed force of all arms and an Australian force proposed by general officers meeting at Melbourne in September.[2] The distrust of colonial fighting ability and of the participation of national units which this decision revealed was the direct result of the advice of Sir Redvers Buller, the South African Commander-in-Chief.[3]

The precision of the War Office letter contrasted with the equivocation of Chamberlain's cable. Chamberlain's real interest was not military but political—to confront the world with a united empire—and his

[1]*Debates*, March 13, 1900, p. 1810, and R. W. Scott in Senate *Debates*, Feb. 9, 1900, p. 98.

[2]C. D. Allin, *Colonial Participation in Imperial Wars—Australasia*, Bulletin no. 52 (Queen's University, 1926), p. 10.

[3]Cd. 1791, qq. 21138–43, evidence of Lord Lansdowne; see also Cd. 1790, q. 8850.

purpose in rephrasing the War Office letter was to compel official colonial participation.[4] The letter spoke of thanking the governments or individuals concerned; the cable expressed "high appreciation of signal exhibition of patriotic spirit of people of Canada shown by offers to serve in South Africa." The War Office letter spoke of an understanding that "1200 men are anxious to volunteer"; the cable referred to the "force offered." Indeed, the cable wavered in meaning among being a request for troops, an intimation of the acceptability of an offer, and the acceptance of a "force offered." It set out the "following information" in order "to assist organization of force offered into units suitable for military requirements": the number of men per unit, "infantry most, cavalry least, serviceable . . ."—a phrase later causing much controversy—the nature of the armament, the local provision of equipment, and the number of officers. The "Secretary of . . . War . . . would gladly accept four units," which would leave by the end of October. On arrival in South Africa the Imperial Government would bear further costs. "Inform accordingly all who have offered to raise volunteers," the dispatch concluded.

The cable thus also left confused the question whether it was (apparently) accepting an official offer or a volunteer offer, such as from Hughes, the acceptance of which Minto twice deprecated to Laurier. In 1885 Minto had seen how the confusion of a volunteer with an official offer could be used to evade making an official offer. In his view a Canadian offer must be not only official but also efficient. Laurier opposed an official unit sailing from Canada and pressed for Hughes's volunteer offer through the Minister, which seemed acceptable under the terms of the Chamberlain cable. If it were acceptable Parliament would have been called upon to pay for the equipment and transportation of such a force, thus giving the force a quasi-official status but allowing the Laurier Government to deny, for the benefit of French Canada, that Canada was officially participating. But Chamberlain did not "intend to accept any offer from volunteers. We do not want the men and the whole point of the offer would be lost unless it were endorsed by the Government of the Colony and applied to an organized body of the Colonial forces. . . ."[5]

---

[4]*Can. Sess. Pap.* (no. 20a), 1900, pp. 43–44, W.O. to C.O., Oct. 2, 1899. The circular cable is *ibid.*, (no. 20), 1900, pp. 16–17; see app. G. Davis-Allen also confidentially cabled Denison his "best reasons" for saying that a "dominion government offer" of 500 infantry would be accepted: "urgent please support" (Denison Papers, p. 3847, Oct. 4, 1899).

[5]J. L. Garvin, *The Life of Joseph Chamberlain* (London, 1934), III, pp. 531–32, to Minto, Oct. 6, 1899.

On receipt of the cable, the cabinet expressed itself as "extremely annoyed" at the evidence of "irresponsible offers" of which it knew nothing.[6] Having made no offer itself it was determined to find out who had. It suspected Hutton and even Minto. *La Patrie* had already attacked Hutton as responsible for the disclosures in the *Canadian Military Gazette.*[7] Acting Premier Scott requested Minto to inquire of Hutton whether he had communicated to the press. Hutton of course denied it. Apparently under pressure from the cabinet, Scott now asked Minto to inquire if Hutton had sent any offers to Britain or advised that he could secure volunteers. Minto refused to make such an inquiry because that would seem to imply unfitness on Hutton's part.[8] Scott also earnestly pleaded with Minto not to send a telegram to Chamberlain on the public's desire to make an offer—a plea Minto deemed wise to accept.[9]

All Hutton had done was to advise Chamberlain and War Office leaders of the existence of a plan for a mixed force of 1200, concerning which Borden and Laurier had been informed, and of his own offer to lead such a force, which he hoped would be combined with an Australian force under his leadership. He had also conveyed Borden's views on the virtual certainty of an offer from Canada.[10] For Hutton to have made a secret offer would have been contrary to his own view that any Canadian force should be national. The cabinet now irately inquired of Chamberlain as to the purported communication from Canada he had replied to,[11] though Borden announced on October 11 that Imperial authorities had long been informed of Canada's readiness to supply troops. Chamberlain answered mildly that the cable referred to the offer of Sam Hughes, one from British Columbia, and those reported in the

[6]Minto Papers, letter book no. 1, p. 204, Minto to Chamberlain, Oct. 14, 1899.
[7]Oct. 6, 1899, cited by J. G. H. Bergeron, *Debates*, Feb. 20, 1900, pp. 711–12.
[8]Minto Papers, vol. 15, p. 114, Minto to Hutton, cypher telegram, Oct. 9, 1899, and p. 116, cypher reply; *ibid.*, vol. 9, part II, p. 15, Scott to Minto, "Private," Oct. 10, 1899, and reply, letter book no. 1, p. 200, Oct. 11, 1899; see also *ibid.*, pp. 203–8, Minto to Chamberlain, Oct. 14, 1899, in which he declared his intention of being present at a cabinet meeting (p. 205).
[9]*Ibid.*, letter book no. 1, p. 205, Minto to Chamberlain, Oct. 14, 1899.
[10]See above, p. 230. Note that Laurier and the cabinet were apparently also prepared to use Hughes's charges against Minto and Hutton on the alleged unconstitutionality of their officially corresponding with one another. For one of Hughes's letters against Hutton, Hughes sought Laurier's advice (Laurier Papers, pp. 37833–34, "Private," Oct. 4, 1899, and reply p. 37836, Oct. 5, 1899); see also *Can. Sess. Pap.* (no. 77), 1900, p. 12, memo of Borden's priv. sec. to Dept. Min. of Mil., Oct. 11, 1899.
[11]Laurier Papers, p. 215113, Minto to Chamberlain, Oct. 12, 1899.

press. The "statement issued to press here referred exclusively to Australasia offers."[12]

By this time the Government's annoyance was focused not so much on the alleged acceptance of offers as on the publication of their acceptance—"the clandestine attempt . . . made to force our hands," as Laurier wrote to Minto.[13] Minto justified the leak by maintaining that the Canadian Government ought to have informed its people of British willingness to accept Canadian offers. Considered in themselves the cable and the leak of its contents put Chamberlain in relation to Canada in the poorest light during this period. But the Canadian Government in the name of imperial unity had several times forced the hand of the British Government—in imperial preference, penny postage, and the Pacific cable, for example—and it could be argued that Chamberlain was merely making the same kind of appeal to his "fellow-countrymen" in Canada to assist in the creation of imperial military unity as Canada had made in Britain in the creation of imperial economic unity. On balance Canada had obtained—or rather extracted—more favours from Britain than vice versa. Dependence on Britain soon overcame Canada's petulance; Laurier expressed himself as satisfied with Chamberlain's explanation of the October 3 cable and urged Minto to explain to Chamberlain that his actions were due not to "want of Imperial sentiment," but to doubts "as to the policy on this occasion."[14]

II

Three days after making his statement to the *Globe*—on October 6— Laurier, accompanied by L. O. David, prominent Montreal journalist, Raymond Préfontaine, M.P. and Mayor of Montreal, John Willison, and others, left for the Chicago ceremony already referred to.[15] During

[12]G 21, no. 233, vol. III, Chamberlain to Minto, paraphrase cypher cable, Oct. 13, 1899.

[13]Minto Papers, vol. 7, p. 102, Oct. 12, 1899. See also C.O. 42/869, p. 389, Minto to Chamberlain, decypher of cable, "Secret and Confidential," postscript, rec'd. Oct. 13, 1899; on the next day Anderson minuted to Chamberlain that "we must endeavour to do what we can to avoid anything likely to cause embarrassment to the Govts. of the colonies"; Chamberlain noted that things were satisfactorily settled (*ibid.*, p. 393).

[14]G 21, no. 233, vol. III, Minto to Chamberlain, paraphrase cypher cable, Oct. 13, 1899, and Minto Papers, letter book no. 1, p. 207, Minto to Chamberlain, Oct. 14, 1899.

[15]Sir John Willison, *Reminiscences Political and Personal* (Toronto, 1919), pp. 303–4, and O. D. Skelton, *Life and Letters of Sir Wilfrid Laurier* (Toronto, 1921), II, p. 95; cf. *Globe*, Oct. 12, 1899, edit., "The Premier in Chicago."

the journey there were discussions on Canada's imperial duties and the consequences of not sending troops. Believing that the Boers would yield, Laurier hoped that war could be avoided, but that if it came its pettiness would obviate Canadian aid. The South African War, however, was not to be petty. Nor could his pacifist beliefs or fears that participation would split the country prevail against Willison's warning that he would either send troops or retire from office. But he tried to cling to the belief that Britain's participation did not necessarily involve Canada.[16] The few hours stop-off at Toronto on his return must have convinced him of the truth of Willison's warning.

Laurier came back to a divided country and cabinet: newspapers were engaged in a bitter racial and constitutional dispute. In Vancouver David Mills had approved of Chamberlain's position and Borden had confirmed the accuracy of the *Globe*'s report on contingent plans, public statements of which Tarte complained. On October 11 Strathcona sent Laurier a reminder from London reciting the terms of the Boer ultimatum and a *Times* editorial upon British gratification at colonial offers, which *inter alia* emphasized the value of official rather than individual offers.[17] Davies, busy advising the Colonial Office on the Alaska boundary question, cabled the next day a sense of disappointment at Canada's failure to make an offer, and transmitted Chamberlain's reaction, that Britain could deal with South Africa "without Colonial assistance" but "from sentimental standpoint" would value a Canadian offer.[18]

On arrival in Ottawa, Laurier wrote to Minto that his views were unchanged; he doubted "the advisability of introducing the principle of military expenditure." But he was "rather disposed" to agree that any Canadian force "should not be on the puny scale proposed, but . . . more in consonance with the importance of Canada."[19] Minto took advantage of this suggestion to discuss enthusiastically the technical possibilities of a contingent of all arms.[20] On the following day, October 13, the

[16]Cf. Willison Collection, pp. 7506–8, David to Willison, Dec. 20, 1899.

[17]Laurier Papers, pp. 215111–12, cable, and P.C. Despatches, 1641K.

[18]Laurier Papers, p. 225387; in a "Private & Confidential" letter of the same date to Laurier, Davies also recorded that Chamberlain thought he understood the reasons that " 'prompted Canada not to make a similar offer.' " Davies informed him that if Britain were in great difficulty Canada would give aid with "no stinted hand"; but Canadians believed that in the present circumstances Britain could deal with the problem herself. (*Ibid.*, pp. 255386–88.)

[19]Minto Papers, vol. 7, p. 102, Oct. 12, 1899.

[20]Laurier Papers, pp. 37966–69, Minto to Laurier, Oct. 12, 1899.

Governor General reminded the Prime Minister of the unfortunate impression in England if troops were not sent: Canada was relying considerably on the British public in the Alaska question and she would have to do likewise in "any foreign complication." Once again Minto denied that any request was being made, though the press was stating that idea, but that any offer made would receive a hearty welcome.[21]

Laurier was angry at an external situation forcing him to make a decision dangerous both to his party and the unity of the country. French-Canadian leaders were bitterly opposed.[22] Of the three parties in the cabinet, the Quebec party, which must have included Scott, was opposed to offering a contingent; a second was willing to accept Chamberlain's proposals of October 3; and a third from Ontario insisted "on a Canadian contingent, preserving its individuality . . . & paid by Canada." The bitter struggle took place between Tarte of the first party, who threatened to resign, and Mulock of the third, who, it seems certain, stalked angrily out of the council chamber and had to be sent for.[23]

Realizing that the dispatch of a contingent was inevitable, Tarte, authorized by Laurier, summoned to Ottawa leading French Canadians, among whom were R. Lemieux, Lomer Gouin, and Henri Bourassa. At the meeting, on October 12 or 13, Laurier outlined the difficulties of the situation and the necessity for compromise, and promised a no-precedent guarantee. Only Bourassa protested. He warned that, if the policy proposed were followed, he would resign his seat or vote against the ministry.[24] A few days after the official decision of October 13, Bourassa did resign in protest, but was re-elected by acclamation.

[21]*Ibid.*, pp. 38006–7, Oct. 13, 1899. Minto had written privately to Chamberlain: ". . . I think it would be a mistake for me to push him" (Sept. 23, 1899, Minto Papers, letter book no. 1, p. 182).

[22]Probably R. Préfontaine's public support of a contingent was more of a help to Laurier's Ontario position than to his Quebec position (*Globe*, Oct. 13, 1899).

[23]The late Brig.-Gen. Charles F. Winter of Ottawa told the writer in 1946 that this incident became well known in Ottawa. Henri Bourassa confirmed it. For quotation see Minto Papers, letter book no. 1, p. 206, Minto to Chamberlain, Oct. 14, 1899; cf. *ibid.*, p. 248. In a recent speech Mulock had said: "It should be ever the aspirations of the people of Canada to develop the country in political union with the mother land" (*Globe*, Sept. 25, 1899); see also C.O. 42/869, p. 389, Minto to Chamberlain, decypher telegram, "Secret and Confidential," postscript, rec'd. Oct. 13, 1899: "Discussion in cabinet extremely heated."

[24]Robert Rumilly, *Henri Bourassa: la vie publique d'un grand Canadien* (Montréal, 1953), pp. 53–54; Henry Borden, ed., *Robert Laird Borden: His Memoirs* (New York, 1938), I, pp. 62–64; and C.O. 42/869, p. 590, memorandum of Lord Minto, Nov. 16, 1899.

III

On what basis could the three parties in the cabinet stay united and defend its policy? On the day before the decision, a proposed minute summarized Chamberlain's conditions, which the Government contemplated accepting; it also stated that the Government had considered dispatching and maintaining a force in South Africa under the commanding general, but had not done so because of the Colonial Secretary's conditions and because the "large departure" from past policy would require "consideration of Parliament" and "reconsideration of the present relations" between the colonies and the Empire.[25] This explanation of the failure by English Canada to attain its aim evidently did not satisfy the French Canadian members of the cabinet. Thus the official minute, which the Cabinet agreed to on October 13, 1899, after reciting Chamberlain's terms, stated:

> The Prime Minister, in view of the well known desire of a great many Canadians who are ready to take service under such conditions, is of opinion that the moderate expenditure which would thus be involved for the equipment and transportation of such volunteers may readily be undertaken by the Government of Canada without summoning Parliament, especially as such an expenditure under such circumstances cannot be regarded as a departure from the well known principles of constitutional government and colonial practice, nor construed as a precedent for future action.[26]

This "no-precedent" clause literally referred not to the precedent of sending troops, but to that of sending troops without parliamentary consent. The Ontario party, probably, and Laurier insisted that not 500 but 1,000 troops be sent to South Africa, more in keeping with Canada's military expectations. As a whole the minute was not a national offer of assistance, but a colonial acceptance of duty.

Accompanying the minute was a statement, said to have been written by W. S. Fielding, explaining the Government's delay. It commented on the inaccurate press speculation, emphasized the necessity of waiting for a full council meeting to make an important decision, and denied that co-operation with Britain for imperial interests had ever been in doubt. The important question was, was Parliamentary consent required? This was unnecessary because the limitations of the Imperial

[25]Laurier Papers, pp. 37994–96, Oct. 12, 1899.
[26]*Can. Sess. Pap.* (no. 20), 1900, p. 37; see app. H. See also C.O. 42/869, pp. 450–51, Minto to Chamberlain, "Secret," Oct. 20, 1899: there was an attempt "to minimize the official appearance of Canada's offer, and to give it as far as possible the character of a volunteer expedition with a small amount of Government assistance."

Government minimized the cost. Meanwhile the Imperial authorities had been communicated with, and had "agreed to receive into the army in Africa a contingent. . . ."[27]

In answer to English Canadians the Government argued that it acted in harmony with Colonial Office conditions; to French Canadians, that in effect it did its duty. An English-Canadian editor had suggested that Laurier take a "strong, high note" to prevent the Tories from heading the patriotic feeling.[28] Laurier replied objecting to a "young country like Canada, launching into military expenditure," for Canada had done much for imperial defence in constructing railways, and advocated that "our friends" firmly declare that Canada was acting in accordance with the "demand made by the War Office." There was "no reason to play soldiering" or to "countenance . . . Jingo bellowing."[29] In a letter to Denison he explained that Britain's plan was for a "small contingent from all the colonies, enough to show that the heart of the colonies was with the mother country, but not enough to lay a burden which some of them might little be able to bear."[30] To the editor of the French-Canadian *Le Soleil* of Quebec City, Laurier suggested the following defence of Government policy. During the summer months thousands of English Canadians had wanted to enrol in the English army; others, largely from Ontario, requested Government payment of the full costs of equipment, transportation, and maintenance in the field. The Government, however, agreed to provide for the equipment and transportation of 1000 men because Canada, owing to commercial developments during the past two years, desired to be of service to England. It was also hoped that trade would increase because of those "policies" and "this gesture."[31]

For purposes of participation the cabinet's minute suggested that

[27]The statement continued with technical discussions on the nature of a contingent and a protest against the British Government's decision to employ no colonial officer of rank higher than a major (*Globe, Mail and Empire*, Montreal *Star*, Oct. 14, 1899; the versions of the three papers differ slightly).

[28]Laurier Papers, p. 38011, John Cameron, London *Advertiser*, Oct. 13, 1899; Cameron emphasized that "patriotic feeling overrides *everything*—prosperity, temperance, everything."

[29]*Ibid.*, pp. 38013–15, Laurier to Cameron, "Private," Oct. 14, 1899; cf. Willison Correspondence, pp. 17910–13, Laurier to Willison, "Private," Oct. 14, 1899.

[30]Denison Papers, pp. 3852–53, "Private & Confidential," Oct. 14, 1899.

[31]Lucien Pacaud, sel. and ed., *Sir Wilfrid Laurier Letters to my Father and Mother* (Toronto, 1935), pp. 112–13, to Ernest Pacaud, Oct. 14, 1899; for Laurier's answers to a French-Canadian priest, L. Tremblay, curé of St Félicien, Rimouski, see Laurier Papers, pp. 37912, 38097–101, 38460; for a valuable account of the French-Canadian position see *La Patrie*, Oct. 14, 1899, cited in *Globe*, Oct. 16, 1899.

Canada in effect was still a colony which had to obey Britain. On earlier occasions political expediency similarly dictated donning the cloak of colonialism. The spirit of colonial acquiescence, which might in an earlier day otherwise have been common ground for English and French Canadians, now met opposition. The Government's cool minute misrepresented the zeal of English Canada and was scarcely evidence of imperial solidarity. Its policy ran counter to the typical enthusiasm of the *Globe* which greeted the announcement of a contingent with a headline "Soldiers of the Queen!"[32] Nor did French Canada like its colonial assumptions. The minute implied that the Colonial Secretary might accept volunteer units again. To guard against that possibility and what was termed acceptance of a request, Tarte insisted on the "no-precedent" clause. The clause also implied that, if Canada had been a nation, it could have rejected Chamberlain's request. In effect French Canada argued for the national right to stay out of war and English Canada, freely to enter.

IV

Participation saved the Government and the country from one quarter only to expose it from another. Canadian sentiment and destructive United States wrath were diverted from Alaska to South Africa by participation and the *modus vivendi* of October 20, 1899. Many English Canadians could now vent their anti-American frustrations on the Government and on French Canada as a threat to the fulfilment of imperial military unity, which now seemed the condition of the country's existence. Whether Laurier saw the demand for participation as insurance for Britain's protection against the United States is doubtful. But he did see the accompanying racial attack as a threat to the existence of his Government and to Canada's unity. The assault on French-Canadian loyalty awakened French Canada from a self-preoccupied isolationism and produced a vehement protest against imperial military unity, the ostensible reason for English Canada's desire to participate. The question of whether to enter or to stay out of war produced a national contradiction that was barely reconciled in the colonial form of the token military force sent to South Africa. Yet Laurier did save his Government and the unity of the country.

[32]Oct. 14, 1899.

18. Conclusion

THE MILITARY CLIMAX to imperial unity and the consequent racial quarrel have made the era of imperial unity an object of aversion to Canadians. The interpretation of the era fostered by Goldwin Smith,[1] Henri Bourassa,[2] and their followers has long been the accepted interpretation. It holds that imperial unity or rather imperialism and its British agents were largely responsible for Canada's entanglement in a war of no concern to the Dominion. Such an interpretation exculpates Canadians from responsibility for support of imperial unity and enables them to misconceive its origin and nature and repress the decisive place Canadian-American relations played in pushing Canada into Britain's arms.

The practice of imperial unity dates at least from the time of Confederation. Whatever its name it represented a tacit Anglo-Canadian alliance to prevent Canada's being swallowed up by the United States. It was the condition of Canada's freedom and potential nationhood during the country's dejected and difficult childhood in the last decades of the nineteenth century. Emotionally the Dominion had been virtually cast adrift by an indifferent motherland, forced to construct expensive public works and to harmonize the country's disunited groups—particularly English and French Canadians. Weighed down by these difficulties and by depression and frustration of national hopes, many Canadians compensated by adopting their neighbour's ideals and standards, masochistically using them to disdain their own great achievements.

However much Canadians in the late nineties might wish to like Americans, the shock of the Venezuela incident, the indifference to Canadian interests in the Dingley Tariff, and the predominance of

[1]*In the Court of History: An Apology for Canadians who were opposed to the South African War* (Toronto, 1902).

[2]*Debates*, March 13, 1900, pp. 1793–1837, speech, and Henri Bourassa, *Great Britain and Canada* (Montreal, 1902).

Americans in the Yukon gold rush forced Canada to turn from the United States to Britain. Imperial unity, having hitherto been a condition of Canada's existence, now also became a national policy seeking advantages from Britain. Under its aegis, Canada gained such benefits as imperial preference, penny postage, and the Pacific cable, and especially Britain's co-operation in breaking off the negotiations of the Joint High Commission and in assuming an adamant posture in the Alaska boundary negotiations of 1899. Canada, of course, could not receive such benefits without expectations of a quid pro quo. These expectations were not met in a spirit of vulgar bargaining, for by 1899 imperial unity to Canadians was not simply a policy of national selfishness, but an emotional self-offering. Thus in the name of a compulsive imperial unity, participation in the South African war was Canada's answer to Britain's expectations. But what to Britain was fulfilment of past obligations, to English Canada was also an attempt to ensure Britain's continued support of Canada's Alaska boundary contentions.

Britain, however, had been clear sighted in its aim to create imperial solidarity. The mother country used Canada's fear of the United States to stimulate militia reform and inculcate the possibility of participation in war. But while Britain was prepared to support Canada economically and politically against the United States, it would not do so to the extent of alienating its trans-Atlantic neighbour. Britain's very existence in the twentieth century was to depend on the benevolent neutrality and friendly assistance of the United States.

The alacrity with which English Canada shifted from anti-Americanism to resentment of Canada's policy and of French-Canadian attitudes demonstrates its reluctance to oppose the United States forthrightly. This reluctance also suggests that Canada's and Britain's policy towards the United States was basically the same—friendship and avoidance of enmity, a policy usually taking precedence over their friendship for one another. This similarity of policy may explain something of the anti-British resentment among English Canadians, particularly among Liberals in the late nineties, whose imperial enthusiasm often appears to compensate for their pro-Americanism in the early nineties.

In view of the preoccupied self-concern of the United States, Canada's reactions in the period abstractly considered, were not unreasonable, but practically they were excessive and provocative in relation to the limitations on Canada's power. It was precisely these limitations that English Canada was unwilling to face, partly because Britain provided a scapegoat and a means of evasion. Although participation in the South African war loosened Canada's political and emotional bonds with

Britain, English Canada's emotional relations with the United States remained the same. It wished its country to be like, if not to belong to, the United States, and this in turn contributed greatly to an underlying resignation about Canada's destiny as a nation. Ultimately this attitude of English Canada sprang from a distrust in itself; from a refusal to accept Canada as it was—a client state whose strength was derived from membership in the British Empire, adherence to its own historical and institutional past, and acceptance of its bi-racial composition; from a-whoring, not after false gods and values, but after gods and values false to its own traditions and experience, its own limitations and destiny. Because it could always look to Britain or the United States for help, English Canada, unlike French Canada, had hitherto never had to face alone threats to its existence. This continuing possibility of dependence has prolonged English Canada's ambiguity about itself and weakened Canadian nationalism.

Bibliographical Note

THE NATURE of the original sources—printed and manuscript—from which this work was written may perhaps be best understood in relation to the main problems. For an over-all picture of the period, including its external relations, politics, constitutional relationships, and public opinion, the most valuable single source consists of the Laurier Papers. Two other collections of a similar nature are the Minto Papers and the Willison Papers. The minutes of the Canadian Privy Council and the *Canada Sessional Papers* are also essential.

Canadian-American problems concerned access to the Yukon, the Alaska boundary, Ontario lumber, Bering Sea sealing, North Atlantic fisheries, alien labour, British Columbia mining; Canadian-British problems concerned imperial preference, penny postage, Pacific cable, defence questions, and Britain's relations to Canadian-American problems. The chief source for these is Colonial Office correspondence in C.O. 42/835–875. This correspondence includes much, but not all, that appears in the Foreign Office Confidential Prints bound in Confidential 7161 and 7340 on the Alaska boundary question and Confidential 7135 and 7309 on the Joint High Commission. Much of importance will also be found in the G series. These sources should be supplemented by *Canada Sessional Papers*, Sifton Papers, Mills Papers, *Papers Relating to the Foreign Relations of the United States*, vols. 1895–99 (Washington, 1896–1901), and the *Proceedings of the Alaskan Boundary Tribunal*, III, IV (Washington, 1903–4). The monographs by C. S. Campbell, Jr., *Anglo-American Understanding, 1898–1903* (Baltimore, 1957), and C. C. Tansill, *Canadian-American Relations, 1875–1911* (New Haven, 1943), contain much original material. For the imperial conferences and the Pacific cable see *Parliamentary Papers*.

For Canadian military administration and Anglo-Canadian defence relations see: the correspondence of the Deputy Minister of Militia and Defence; the Adjutant-General's correspondence; annual reports of the Department of Militia and Defence; General Orders; *Report No. I* and *Report No. II of the Committee on Canadian Defence 1898*, "Secret" (London, 1899); memoranda of the Colonial Defence Committee; Hutton Papers; Minto Papers; *Canadian Military Gazette*. The Report on the war in South Africa (Cd. 1789–92, 1903) is useful for British military policy and influences on Canada, and a basis of comparison with Canadian conditions. For a general sketch of Canadian defence and a military bibliography, see George F. G. Stanley, *Canada's Soldiers 1604–1954* (Toronto, 1958, 2nd ed.).

On the general movement for imperial unity see Denison, Parkin, and Grant Papers. For Canadian opinion generally, see *Debates of the House of Commons*, Canada, the Toronto *Globe*, *La Patrie*, and selected representative Canadian papers. For background material on most of the subjects considered, see E. A. Benians, Sir James Butler, and C. E. Carrington, eds., *The Cambridge History of the British Empire* (Cambridge, 1959), III. Other monographs and articles on the subject will be found in the footnotes.

Appendixes

APPENDIX A

Parliamentary Resolution of Loyalty to the Queen, January 29, 1890[1]

MOST GRACIOUS MAJESTY,

We, Your Majesty's most dutiful and loyal subjects, the Commons of Canada in Parliament assembled, desire most earnestly in our own name, and on behalf of the people whom we represent, to renew the expression of our unswerving loyalty and devotion to Your Majesty's person and Government.

We have learned with feelings of entire disapproval that various public statements have been made, calling in question the loyalty of the people of Canada to the political union now happily existing between this Dominion and the British Empire, and representing it as the desire of the people of Canada to sever such connection.

We desire, therefore, to assure Your Majesty that such statements are wholly incorrect representations of the sentiments and aspirations of the people of Canada, who are among Your Majesty's most loyal subjects, devotedly attached to the political union existing between Canada and the mother country, and earnestly desire its continuance.

We feel assured that Your Majesty will not allow any such statements, emanating from any source whatever, to lessen Your Majesty's confidence in the loyalty of your Canadian subjects to Your Majesty's person and Government, and will accept our assurances of the contentment of Your Majesty's Canadian subjects with the political connection between Canada and the rest of the British Empire, and of their fixed resolve to aid in maintaining the same.

We pray that the blessings of Your Majesty's reign may, for your people's sake, be long continued.

---

[1]*Debates*, p. 124; moved by William Mulock (Liberal, Ontario) and seconded by Guillaume Amyot (Liberal, Quebec); see above, p. 32.

APPENDIX B

Parliamentary Resolution of Loyalty to the Queen and Friendliness with Americans, February 5, 1896[2]

That, in view of the threatening aspect of foreign affairs, this House desires to assure Her Majesty's Government and the people of the United Kingdom of its unalterable loyalty and devotion to the British Throne and constitution, and of its conviction that, should occasion unhappily arise, in no other part of the Empire than the Dominion of Canada would more substantial sacrifices attest the determination of Her Majesty's subjects to maintain unimpaired the integrity and inviolate the honour of Her Majesty's Empire; and this House reiterates the oft-expressed desire of the people of Canada to maintain the most friendly relations with their kinsmen of the United States.

APPENDIX C

Parliamentary Resolution of Support for Britain's Position in South Africa, July 31, 1899[3]

1. Resolved, That this House has viewed with regret the complications which have arisen in the Transvaal Republic, of which Her Majesty is suzerain, from the refusal to accord to Her Majesty's subjects now settled in that region any adequate participation in its government:
2. Resolved, That this House has learned with still greater regret that the condition of things there existing has resulted in intolerable oppression, and has produced great and dangerous excitement among several classes of Her Majesty's subjects in her South African possessions;
3. Resolved, That this House, representing a people which has largely succeeded, by the adoption of the principle of conceding equal political rights to every portion of the population, in harmonizing estrangements and in producing general content with the existing system of government, desires to express its sympathy with the efforts of Her Majesty's Imperial authorities to obtain for the subjects of Her Majesty who have taken up their abode in the Transvaal such measure of justice and political recognition as may be found necessary to secure them in the full possession of equal rights and liberties.

[2]*Ibid.*, pp. 1186–87; see above, pp. 32–33.
[3]*Ibid.*, p. 8994; see above, p. 222.

APPENDIX D

Editorial, *Canadian Military Gazette*, October 3, 1899[4]

If war should be commenced in the Transvaal—which seems most probable—the offer of a force from the Canadian militia for service will be made by the Canadian Government. In that event an eight-company battalion of infantry, composed of 29 officers and 981 non-commissioned officers and men will be raised. Such a battalion should be made up from all over Canada by allotting a certain number of officers and men in proportion to the number of militia to each district. The battalions for the Red River expedition were organized on this basis, which was found to be the most satisfactory. In addition to this battalion there will be a squadron of cavalry, composed of six officers and 154 non-commissioned officers and men and 161 horses, and a battery of field artillery, made up of six guns, five officers and 166 non-commissioned officers and men and 131 horses. The above strength is the war establishment of these units. Major-General Hutton shows his predilection for his old corps by clothing the infantry battalion in the uniform of riflemen. The horses for the cavalry will be taken largely from the North-west Mounted Police, as the most suitable, with some others from the Royal Canadian Dragoons, General Hutton will select from the police suitable horses at Regina and Calgary. The battalion of infantry will be attached to and form part of an infantry brigade. The squadron of cavalry will be attached to a cavalry regiment, and the battery of artillery to a field artillery division. It is probable that the men volunteering for this service would have to undergo a rigid medical examination, in accordance with army regulations, and be unmarried. The officers should be selected for their knowledge and fitness and possess the highest qualifications. There is little doubt but that such a battalion would be uniformed, armed, equipped and paid by the Canadian Government.

As the number of troops required in the Transvaal will be limited, it is most improbable that any large force will have an opportunity to serve.

As the battalion of infantry will form a complete unit, and may have to act independently under its own commanding officer, great care has been exercised by the department in selecting an officer to command who would inspire confidence in those under him as well as in the Canadian public. The Government think it would be a criminal act of folly to appoint an amateur militia officer without army experience to command a battalion on service in the field, especially against such an enemy as the Boers. In this connection it is said that the command has been offered to Colonel Ivor Herbert, C.B., A.A.G., Home District, London, England, formerly in command of our militia. Col. Herbert in command would inspire confidence, and the battalion could depend on being handled by a highly-trained professional soldier who has seen service in Africa. If he accepts it will add great prestige to the Canadian force, as no other army officer has had the same practical experience with them as Col. Herbert. Arrangements for organizing such a force

[4]Quoted in *Globe*, Oct. 3, 1899; see above, pp. 234–35.

have been completed and the officers selected, so that when the order to concentrate is given no confusion or loss of time will ensue. The force will be concentrated at a station in Canada for a month, as it would take that length of time at least to fit it out. It is probable that it would embark on a ship and sail direct for South Africa, the additional equipment being forwarded from England to meet the men at Cape Town or Natal.

[A concluding paragraph of this editorial, which was in effect an even more direct attack on the scheme of Colonel Hughes, did not appear in the newspaper versions.]

APPENDIX E

Laurier's Statement in Reply, October 4, 1899[5]

There exists a great deal of misconception in the country regarding the powers of the Government in the present case. As I understand the militia act, and I may say that I have given it some study of late, our volunteers are enrolled to be used in the defence of the Dominion. They are Canadian troops, to be used to fight for Canada's defence. Perhaps the most widespread misapprehension is that they cannot be sent out of Canada. To my mind it is clear that cases might arise when they might be sent to a foreign land to fight. To postulate a case:—Suppose that Spain should declare war upon Great Britain. Spain has, or had, a navy, and that navy might be being got ready to assail Canada as part of the empire. Sometimes the best method of defending one's self is to attack, and in that case Canadian soldiers might certainly be sent to Spain, and it is quite certain that they legally might be so despatched to the Iberian Peninsula. The case of the South African Republic is not analogous. There is no menace to Canada, and, although we may be willing to contribute troops, I do not see how we can do so. Then, again, how could we do so without Parliament's granting us the money? We simply could not do anything. In other words, we should have to summon Parliament. The Government of Canada is restricted in its powers. It is responsible to Parliament, and it can do very little without the permission of Parliament. There is no doubt as to the attitude of the Government on all questions that mean menace to British interests, but in this present case our limitations are very clearly defined. And so it is that we have not offered a Canadian contingent to the home authorities. The Militia Department duly transmitted individual offers to the Imperial Government, and the reply from the War Office, as published in Saturday's Globe, shows their attitude on the question. As to Canada's furnishing a contingent, the Government has not discussed the question, for the reasons which I have stated—reasons which, I think, must easily be understood by everyone who understands the constitutional law on the question. The statement in The Military Gazette, published this morning, is a pure invention. Far from possessing any foundation in fact, it is wholly imaginative.

[5]*Ibid.*, Oct. 4, 1899; see above, pp. 235–36.

APPENDIX F

Montreal *Star* Cable Report of Chamberlain's Circular Cable of October 3, 1899[6]

I learn that the British Government is to-night cabling to the Canadian Government that it gladly accepts Canada's loyal offer of troops for South Africa. Acceptances have already been cabled to Queensland and New Zealand. Ministers feel that such an opportunity of giving England's enemies a magnificent object lesson in the solidarity of her empire cannot be neglected.

I understand that Canada's proposal has not taken the shape of a formal Government offer, but was outlined in a private despatch from Sir Wilfrid Laurier to Mr. Chamberlain, with a view to learning whether Canada's co-operation would be acceptable in defence of the cause of equal rights and of British supremacy in South Africa, and in what form co-operation would be most serviceable.

After full consultation with Sir Redvers Buller, the Minister is now sending to Ottawa a cordial and grateful acknowledgement, intimating that they will welcome from Canada a military unit to be transported by Canada to Cape Town for immediate service. Similar units will be received from the Australasian colonies. The British Government does not desire any large number of troops, such as a thousand, but only enough to add a fighting unit from each colony to the present united empire in the field.

APPENDIX G

Chamberlain's Circular Cable, October 3, 1899[7]

Secretary of State for War and Commander-in-Chief desire to express high appreciation of signal exhibition of patriotic spirit of people of Canada shown by offers to serve in South Africa, and to furnish following information to assist organization of force offered into units suitable for military requirements. Firstly, units should consist of about 125 men; secondly, may be infantry, mounted infantry, or cavalry; in view of numbers already available infantry most, cavalry least, serviceable; thirdly, all should be armed with .303 rifles or carbines, which can be supplied by Imperial Government if necessary; fourthly, all must provide own equipment, and mounted troops own horses; fifthly, not more than one captain and three subalterns each unit. Whole force may be commanded by officer not higher than major. In considering numbers which can be employed, Secretary of State for War

[6]*Ibid.*, Oct. 4, 1899; see above, p. 235. The heading in the *Globe* to this news story read as follows: "WILL BE WELCOME / Home Government Said to be Cabling to Ottawa—Believed the Canadian Contingent Will be Small / Sir Wilfrid Laurier's informal Despatch."

[7]*Can. Sess. Pap.* (no. 20), 1900, pp. 16–17; see above, pp. 252–54.

guided by nature of offers, by desire that each Colony should be fairly represented, and limits necessary if force is to be fully utilized by available staff as integral portion of Imperial forces; would gladly accept four units. Conditions as follows: Troops to be disembarked at port of landing South Africa fully equipped at cost of Colonial Government or volunteers. From date of disembarkation Imperial Government will provide pay at Imperial rates, supplies, and ammunition, and will defray expenses of transport back to Canada, and pay wound pensions and compassionate allowances at Imperial rates. Troops to embark not later than October 31, proceeding direct to Cape Town for orders. Inform accordingly all who have offered to raise volunteers.

APPENDIX H

Minute of Council Officially Offering Troops, October 14, 1899[8]

The Committee of the Privy Council have had under consideration a despatch dated October 3, 1899, from the Right Honourable Mr Chamberlain.

The Right Honourable Sir Wilfrid Laurier, to whom the said despatch was referred, observes that the Colonial Secretary, in answer to the offers which have been sent to him from different parts of Canada expressing the willingness and anxiety of Canadians to serve Her Majesty's Government in the war which for a long time has been threatening with the Transvaal Republic and which, unfortunately, has actually commenced, enunciates the conditions under which such offers may be accepted by the Imperial authorities. Those conditions may be practically summed up in the statement that a certain number of volunteers by units of 125 men, with a few officers, will be accepted to serve in the British Army now operating in South Africa, the moment they reach the coast, provided the expenses of their equipment and transportation to South Africa, are defrayed either by themselves or by the Colonial Government.

The Prime Minister, in view of the well known desire of a great many Canadians who are ready to take service under such conditions, is of opinion that the moderate expenditure which would thus be involved for the equipment and transportation of such volunteers may readily be undertaken by the Government of Canada without summoning Parliament, especially as such an expenditure under such circumstances cannot be regarded as a departure from the well known principles of constitutional government and colonial practice, nor construed as a precedent for future action.

Already, under similar conditions, New Zealand has sent two companies, Queensland is about to send 250 men, and West Australia and Tasmania are sending 125 men each.

The Prime Minister, therefore, recommends that out of the stores now available in the Militia Department, the Government undertake to equip a certain number of volunteers, not to exceed 1,000 men, and to provide for their transportation from this country to South Africa, and that the Minister of Militia make all necessary arangements to the above effect.

[8]*Ibid.*, p. 37; see above, pp. 258–60.

Index